CLYMER®

YAMAHA

YFS200 BLASTER • 1988-2002

The world's finest publisher of mechanical how-to manuals

PRIMEDIA
Business Directories & Books

P.O. Box 12901, Overland Park, Kansas 66282-2901

Copyright ©2002 PRIMEDIA Business Magazines & Media Inc.

FIRST EDITION
First Printing June, 1998

SECOND EDITION
First Printing January, 2000
Second Printing December, 2000

THIRD EDITION
First Printing November, 2001

FOURTH EDITION
Updated by James Grooms to include 2002 models
First Printing September, 2002

Printed in U.S.A.

CLYMER and colophon are registered trademarks of PRIMEDIA Business Magazines & Media Inc.

ISBN: 0-89287-840-1

Library of Congress: 2002111253

TECHNICAL PHOTOGRAPHY: Ron Wright. Special thanks to Clawson Motorsports in Fresno, California, for their assistance with this book.

TECHNICAL ILLUSTRATIONS: Steve Amos.

WIRING DIAGRAMS: Robert Caldwell and Bob Meyer.

COVER: Mark Clifford Photography, Los Angeles, California. Yamaha Blaster courtesy of Dick Allen's Yamaha-Honda-Sea-Doo, Newhall, California.

PRODUCTION: Veronica Bollin.

TOOLS AND EQUIPMENT: K & L Supply Co. at www.klsupply.com.

CONTENTS

QUICK REFERENCE DATA

ATV INFORMATION

MODEL:_____ YEAR:_____

VIN NUMBER:_____

ENGINE SERIAL NUMBER:_____

CARBURETOR SERIAL NUMBER OR I.D. MARK:_____

TIRE INFLATION PRESSURE

	Front kPa (psi)	Rear kPa (psi)
Operating pressure	30 (4.3)	25 (3.6)
Minimum tire pressure	27 (3.8)	22 (3.1)
Maximum tire pressure	33 (4.7)	28 (4.0)

RECOMMENDED LUBRICANTS AND FUEL

Engine oil	Yamalube 2 or an air cooled 2-stroke engine oil
Transmission oil	Yamalube 4 or a comparable 10W30 motor oil
Air filter	Foam air filter oil
Drive chain[1]	Non-tacky O-ring chain lubricant or SAE 30-50 weight engine motor oil
Steering and suspension lubricant	Multipurpose grease
Fuel	Premium unleaded fuel
Control cables	Cable lube[2]

[1] Use kerosene to clean O-ring drive chain.
[2] Do not use drive chain lubricant to lubricate control cables.

OIL TANK

	Liters	U.S. qt.	Imp. qt.
Total amount	1.3	1.4	1.1

TRANSMISSION OIL CAPACITY

	Milliliters	U.S. qt.	Imp. qt.
Oil change	650	0.69	0.57
After engine overhaul	700	0.74	0.62

FUEL TANK CAPACITY

	U.S. gal.	Liters	Imp. gal.
Full	2.38	9.0	1.98
Reserve	0.53	2.0	0.44

TUNE-UP SPECIFICATIONS

Ignition timing	16° @ 3,000 rpm (not adjustable)
Spark plug	
Canada and South Africa	BP8ES
All other	B8ES
Spark plug gap	0.7-0.8 mm (0.028-0.032 in.)
Engine idle speed	1,450-1,550 rpm
Initial pilot air screw setting	1-1/2 turns out

DRIVE CHAIN FREE PLAY MEASUREMENT

	mm	in.
Free play	30-40	1.18-1.57

MAINTENANCE TORQUE SPECIFICATIONS

	N•m	in.-lb.	ft.-lb.
Autolube pump cover	7	61.2	–
Carburetor switch	10	86.4	–
Chain adjuster locknuts	16	–	12
Chain guide roller bolts	9	–	–
Clutch adjuster locknut	7	61.2	–
Cylinder head	27	–	20
Intake manifold	8	–	–
Oil level check bolt	18	–	13
Rear axle housing nuts	50	–	36
Shift pedal	14	–	10
Spark plug	25	–	18
Tie-rod locknuts	30	–	22
Transmission drain plug	20	–	14
Wheel lugnuts	45	–	33

REPLACEMENT BULBS

Type	Bulb wattage × quantity
Headlight	12V, 45W/45W × 1
Taillight	12V, 3.4W × 1
Tail/brake light	12V, 21W × 1
Oil level indicator light	12V, 3.4W × 1

CHAPTER ONE

GENERAL INFORMATION

This manual covers the 1988-2002 Yamaha Blaster ATV models.

Troubleshooting, tune-up, maintenance and repair are not difficult, if you know what tools and equipment to use and what to do. Step-by-step instructions guide you through jobs ranging from simple maintenance to complete engine and suspension overhaul.

This manual can be used by anyone from a first time do-it-yourselfer to a professional mechanic. Detailed drawings and clear photographs give you all the information you need to do the work right.

Some of the procedures in this manual require the use of special tools. The resourceful mechanic can, in many cases, think of acceptable substitutes for special tools—there is always another way. This can be as simple as using a few pieces of threaded rod, washers and nuts to remove or install a bearing. If you find that a tool can be designed and safely used, but will require some type of machine work, you may want to search out a local community college or high school that has a machine shop curriculum. Some shop teachers welcome this type of outside work for advanced students.

Table 1 lists model coverage with engine serial numbers.

Table 2 lists general vehicle dimensions.

Table 3 lists weight specifications.

Table 4 lists conversion tables.

Table 5 lists general torque specifications.

Table 6 lists technical abbreviations.

Table 7 lists metric tap drill sizes.

Table 8 lists decimal and metric equivalents.

Tables 1-8 are at the end of the chapter.

MANUAL ORGANIZATION

This chapter provides general information and discusses equipment and tools useful both for preventive maintenance and troubleshooting.

Chapter Two provides methods and suggestions for quick and accurate diagnosis and repair of problems. Troubleshooting procedures discuss typical symptoms and logical methods to pinpoint the trouble.

Chapter Three explains all periodic lubrication and routine maintenance necessary to keep your Yamaha operating well. Chapter Three also includes recommended tune-up procedures, eliminating the need to constantly consult other chapters on the various assemblies.

Subsequent chapters describe specific systems such as the engine top end, engine bottom end, clutch, transmission, fuel, exhaust, electrical, oil pump, suspension, drive train, steering, brakes and body panels. Each chapter provides disassembly, repair, and assembly procedures in simple step-by-step form. If a repair is impractical for a home mechanic, it is so indicated. It is usually faster and less expensive to take such repairs to a Yamaha dealership or competent repair shop. Specifications concerning a particular system are included at the end of the appropriate chapter.

NOTES, CAUTIONS AND WARNINGS

The terms NOTE, CAUTION and WARNING have specific meanings in this manual. A NOTE provides additional information to make a step or procedure easier or clearer. Disregarding a NOTE could cause inconvenience, but would not cause damage or personal injury.

A CAUTION emphasizes an area where equipment damage could occur. Disregarding a CAUTION could cause permanent mechanical damage; however, personal injury is unlikely.

A WARNING emphasizes an area where personal injury or even death could result from negligence. Mechanical damage may also occur. WARNINGS *are to be taken seriously.*

SAFETY FIRST

Professional mechanics can work for years and never sustain a serious injury. If you observe a few rules of common sense and safety, you can enjoy many safe hours servicing your own machine. If you ignore these rules you can hurt yourself or damage the equipment.

1. *Never* use gasoline or any type of low flash point solvent to clean parts.

2. *Never* smoke or use a torch in the vicinity of flammable liquids, such as cleaning solvent, in an open container.

3. If welding or brazing is required on the machine, remove the fuel tank, carburetor, and rear shock to a safe distance, at least 50 ft. (15 m) away.

4. Use the proper sized wrenches to avoid damage to fasteners and injury to yourself.

5. When loosening a tight or stuck nut, be guided by what would happen if the wrench slips.

6. When replacing a fastener, make sure to use one with the same measurements and strength as the old one. Incorrect or mismatched fasteners can result in damage to the vehicle and possible personal injury. Beware of fastener kits that are filled with cheap and

poorly made nuts, bolts, washers and cotter pins. Refer to *Fasteners* in this chapter for additional information.

7. Keep all hand and power tools in good condition. Wipe greasy and oily tools after using them. They

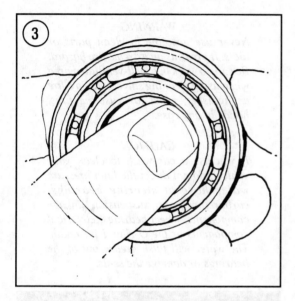

are difficult to hold and can cause injury. Replace or repair worn or damaged tools.

8. Keep your work area clean and uncluttered.

9. Wear safety goggles (**Figure 1**) during all operations involving drilling, grinding, the use of a cold chisel or *anytime* you feel unsure about the safety of your eyes. Wear safety goggles when cleaning parts with solvent and compressed air.

10. Keep an approved fire extinguisher (**Figure 2**) nearby. Be sure it is rated for gasoline (Class B) and electrical (Class C) fires.

11. When drying bearings or other rotating parts with compressed air, never allow the air jet to rotate the bearing or part. The air jet is capable of rotating them at speeds far in excess of those for which they were designed. The bearing or rotating part is very likely to disintegrate and cause serious injury and damage. To prevent bearing damage when using compressed air, hold the inner bearing race by hand (**Figure 3**).

SERVICE HINTS

Most of the service procedures covered are straightforward and can be performed by anyone reasonably handy with tools. It is suggested, however, that you consider your own capabilities carefully before attempting any operation involving major disassembly of the engine.

Take your time and do the job right. Do not forget that a newly rebuilt engine must be broken in the same way as a new one. Keep the engine speed within the limits given in your Yamaha's owner's manual when you get back out in the dirt.

1. FRONT, as used in this manual, refers to the front of the vehicle; the front of any component is the end closest to the front of the vehicle. The *left-* and *right-hand* sides refer to the position of the parts as viewed by a rider sitting on the seat facing forward. For example, the throttle control is on the right-hand side. These rules are simple, but confusion can cause a major inconvenience during service. See **Figure 4**.

2. Whenever servicing the engine or clutch, or when removing a suspension component, secure the vehicle in a safe manner with the parking brake applied.

3. Tag all similar internal parts for location and mark all mating parts for position. Record number and thickness of any shims as they are removed. Identify small parts such as bolts by placing them in

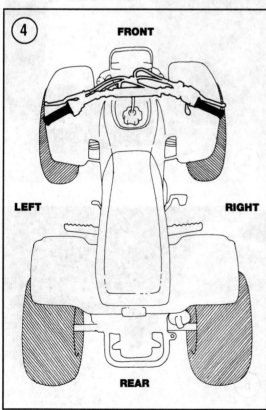

FRONT

LEFT RIGHT

REAR

plastic sandwich bags. Seal and label them with masking tape. See **Figure 5**.

4. Tag disconnected wires and connectors with masking tape and a marking pen. Again, do not rely on memory alone.

5. Protect finished surfaces from physical damage or corrosion. Keep gasoline and brake fluid off painted surfaces.

6. Use penetrating oil on frozen or tight bolts, then strike the bolt head a few times with a hammer and punch (use a screwdriver on screws). Avoid the use of heat where possible, as it can warp, melt or affect the temper of parts. Heat also ruins finishes, especially paint and plastics.

7. No parts (other than bushings, bearing and crankshaft) in the procedures given in this manual require unusual force during disassembly or assembly. If a part is difficult to remove or install, find out why before proceeding.

8. Cover all openings after removing parts or components to prevent dirt, small tools or other contamination from falling in.

9. Read each procedure *completely* while looking at the actual parts before starting a job. Make sure you *thoroughly* understand what is to be done and then carefully follow the procedure, step by step.

10. Recommendations are occasionally made to refer service or maintenance to a Yamaha dealership or a specialist in a particular field. In these cases, the work will be done more quickly and economically than if you performed the job yourself.

11. In procedural steps, the term *replace* means to discard a defective part and replace it with a new or exchange unit. *Overhaul* means to remove, disassemble, inspect, measure, repair or replace defective parts, reassemble and install major systems or parts.

12. Some operations require the use of a hydraulic press. It is wiser to have these operations performed by a shop equipped for such work, rather than to try to do the job yourself with makeshift equipment that may damage your machine.

13. Repairs go much faster and easier if your machine is clean before you begin work. There are many special cleaners on the market, like Bel-Ray Degreaser, for washing the engine and related parts. Follow the manufacturer's directions on the container for the best results. Clean all oily or greasy parts with cleaning solvent as you remove them.

CAUTION
Before using a degreaser or other chemical to clean your Yamaha, remove the O-ring drive chain. These and other chemicals may cause the O-rings in the chain to swell, permanently damaging the chain.

WARNING
Never *use gasoline to clean parts or tools. It presents an extreme fire hazard. Be sure to work in a well-ventilated area when using cleaning solvent. Keep a fire extinguisher, rated for gasoline fires, handy in any case.*

CAUTION
If you use a car wash to clean your vehicle, do not direct the high pressure water hose at steering bearings, carburetor hoses, suspension linkage components, wheel bearings, electrical components or the O-ring drive chain. The water will flush grease out of the bearings or damage the seals.

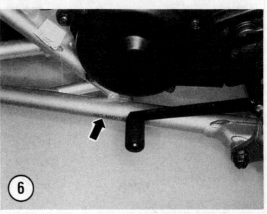

14. Much of the labor charge for repairs made at a dealership is for the time involved during the removal, disassembly, assembly, and reinstallation of other parts in order to reach the defective part. It is frequently possible to perform the preliminary operations yourself and then take the defective unit to the dealership for repair at considerable savings.

15. If special tools are required, make arrangements to get them before you start. It is frustrating and time-consuming to get partly into a job and then be unable to complete it.

16. Make diagrams (or take a Polaroid picture) wherever similar-appearing parts are found. You may think you can remember where everything came from—but mistakes are costly. There is also the possibility that you may be sidetracked and not return to work for days or even weeks—in which the time carefully laid out parts may become disturbed.

17. When assembling parts, be sure all shims and washers are installed exactly as they came out.

18. Whenever a rotating part butts against a stationary part, look for a shim or washer. Use new gaskets if there is any doubt about the condition of the old ones. A thin coat of oil on non-pressure type gaskets may help them seal more effectively.

19. Heavy grease can be used to hold small parts in place if they tend to fall out during assembly. However, keep grease and oil away from electrical and brake components.

SERIAL NUMBERS

Yamaha all-terrain vehicles are identified by frame and engine numbers. When you order parts, always order by frame and engine numbers.

The vehicle identification number (VIN) is stamped on the lower left side frame tube (**Figure 6**). Use these numbers to identify and register your Yamaha with your state licensing authority.

The engine number is stamped on a raised pad on the left crankcase (**Figure 7**). The first 3 numbers identify the model. The remaining numbers are the unit's production number.

Write the numbers down and carry them with you. Compare new parts to old before purchasing them. If they are not alike, have the parts manager explain the difference to you. **Table 1** lists engine and frame serial numbers for the models covered in this manual.

TORQUE SPECIFICATIONS

The proper tightening procedure and the correct torque is very important when installing many of the fasteners on the ATV. Cylinder head warpage, leakage, premature bearing failure and suspension failure can result from improperly tightened fasteners (overtightened or undertightened). Use an accurate torque wrench along with the torque specifications in this manual to ensure properly tightened fasteners.

Torque specifications throughout this manual are given in Newton-meters (N•m), foot-pounds (ft.-lb.) and inch-pounds (in.-lb.).

Existing torque wrenches calibrated in meter kilograms can be used by performing a simple conversion. All you have to do is move the decimal point one place to the right; for example, 3.5 mkg equals 35 N•m. This conversion is accurate enough for mechanical work even though the exact mathematical conversion is 3.5 mkg = 34.3 N•m.

Refer to **Table 5** for standard torque specifications for various size screws, bolts and nuts that are not listed in the respective chapters.

FASTENERS

Fasteners (screws, bolts, nuts, studs, pins and clips) are used to secure various pieces of the engine, frame and suspension together. Proper selection and installation of fasteners are important to ensure that the vehicle operates satisfactorily and safely.

Threaded Fasteners

Most of the components on the Yamaha ATV are mounted or held together by threaded fasteners such as screws, bolts, cap screws, nuts and studs. Most fasteners are tightened by turning them clockwise (right-hand threads). Some fasteners, however, must be turned counterclockwise (left-hand threads) to tighten. Fasteners with left-hand threads are generally used in locations where the normal rotation of a component would tend to loosen a fastener with right-hand threads.

Two dimensions are needed to match threaded fasteners: the number of threads in a given distance and the outside diameter of the threads. Two standards are currently used in the United States to specify the dimensions of threaded fasteners, the U.S. standard system and the metric system (**Figure 8**). Pay particular attention when working with unidentified fasteners; mismatching thread types can damage threads.

> *NOTE*
> *Threaded fasteners must be hand-tightened during initial assembly to be sure mismatched fasteners are not being used and cross-threading is not occurring. If fasteners are hard to turn, determine the cause before tightening.*

Metric screws and bolts are classified by length (L, **Figure 9**), diameter (D) and distance between thread crests (T). A typical bolt might be identified by the numbers 8-1.25 × 130, which indicates that the bolt has a diameter of 8 mm, the distance between threads crests is 1.25 mm and bolt length is 130 mm.

The strength of metric screws and bolts is indicated by numbers located on top of the screw or bolt as shown in **Figure 9**. The higher the number the stronger the screw or bolt. Unnumbered screws and bolts are the weakest.

> *CAUTION*
> ***Do not*** *install screws or bolts with a lower strength grade classification than installed originally by the manufacturer. Doing so may cause vehicle failure and possible injury.*

Critical torque specifications are listed in a table at the end of the appropriate chapter. If not, use the torque specifications listed in **Table 5**. The torque

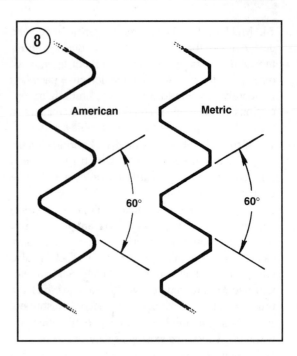

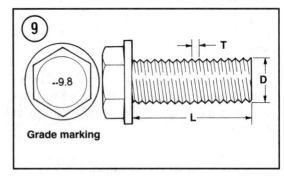

Grade marking

Common nut   Self-locking nut

Wing nut

specifications listed in the manual are for clean, dry threads (unless specified differently in text).

Screws and bolts are manufactured with a variety of head shapes to fit specific design requirements. Your Yamaha is equipped with the common hex, Phillips and Allen head types.

The most common nut used is the hex nut (**Figure 10**). The hex nut is often used with a lockwasher. Self-locking nuts have a nylon insert that prevents loosening; no lockwasher is required. Wing nuts, designed for fast removal by hand, are used for convenience in noncritical locations. Nuts are sized using the same system as crews and bolts. On hex-type nuts, the distance between 2 opposing flats indicates the proper wrench size to use.

Self-locking screws, bolts and nuts may use a locking mechanism that uses an interference fit between mating threads. Manufacturer's achieve interference in various ways: by distorting threads, coating treads with dry adhesive or nylon, distorting the top of an all-metal nut or using a nylon insert in the center or at the top of a nut. Self-locking fasteners offer greater holding strength and better vibration resistance than standard fasteners. For greatest safety, install new self-locking fasteners during reassembly.

Washers

There are 2 basic types of washers, flat washers and lockwashers. Flat washers are simple discs with a hole to fit a screw or bolt. Manufacturer's design lockwashers to prevent a fastener from working loose due to vibration, expansion and contraction. Install lockwashers between a bolt head or nut and a flat washer. **Figure 11** shows several types of washers. Washers are also used in the following functions:

   a. As spacers.
   b. To prevent galling or damage of the equipment by the fastener.
   c. To help distribute fastener load during torquing.
   d. As fluid seals (copper or laminated washers).

> *NOTE*
> *The same care must be given to the selection and purchase of washers as that given to bolts, nuts and other fasteners. Beware of washers made of thin and weak, or inappropriate material.*

Cotter Pins

In certain applications, a fastener must be secured so it cannot possibly loosen. For this purpose, a cotter pin (**Figure 12**) and slotted or castellated nut is often used. To use a cotter pin, first make sure the pin fits snugly, but not too tight. Then, align a slot in the fastener with the hole in the bolt or axle. Insert the cotter pin through the nut and bolt or axle and

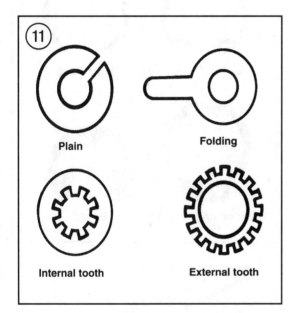

Plain   Folding

Internal tooth   External tooth

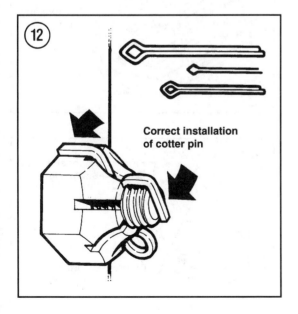

Correct installation of cotter pin

bend the ends over to secure the cotter pin tightly. If the holes do not align, tighten the nut just enough to obtain the proper alignment. Unless specifically instructed to do so, never loosen the fastener to align the slot and hole. Because the cotter pin is weakened after installation and removal, never reuse a cotter pin. Cotter pins are available in several styles, lengths and diameters. Measure cotter pin length from the bottom of its head to the tip if its longest prong.

Circlips/Snap rings

Circlips can be internal or external design (**Figure 13**). Circlips retain items on shafts (external type) or within tubes (internal type). In some applications, circlips of varying thickness are used to control the end play of assembled parts. These are often called selective circlips. You must replace circlips during reassembly and installation, as removal weakens and deforms them. Two other types of clips used on your Yamaha are the plain snap ring and E-ring (**Figure 13**).

Two basic styles of circlips are available: machined and stamped circlips. Machined circlips (**Figure 14**) can be installed in either direction (shaft or housing) because both faces are machined, thus creating 2 sharp edges. Stamped circlips (**Figure 15**) are manufactured with one sharp edge and one rounded edge. When installing stamped circlips in a thrust situation, the sharp edge must face away from the part producing the thrust. When installing circlips, observe the following:

 a. Remove and install circlips with circlip pliers. See *Circlip Pliers* in this chapter.

 b. Compress or expand circlips only enough to install them.

 c. After installing a circlip, make sure it seats in its groove completely.

 d. Remove E-clips with a flat blade screwdriver—pry between the shaft and E-clip. To install an E-clip, center it over its shaft groove, then tap into place.

Transmission circlips become worn with use. For this reason, always use new circlips when reassembling a transmission shaft.

LUBRICANTS

Periodic lubrication helps ensure long life for any type of equipment. The *type* of lubricant used is just as important as the lubrication service itself, although in an emergency the wrong type of lubricant is better than none at all. The following paragraphs

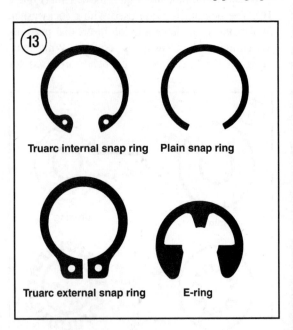

Truarc internal snap ring   Plain snap ring

Truarc external snap ring   E-ring

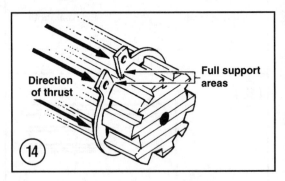

Direction of thrust

Full support areas

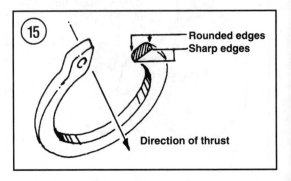

Rounded edges
Sharp edges

Direction of thrust

describe the types of lubricants most often used on ATV and motorcycle equipment. Be sure to follow the manufacturer's recommendations for lubricant types.

Generally, all liquid lubricants are called oil. They may be mineral-based (including petroleum bases), natural-based (vegetable and animal bases), synthetic-based or emulsions (mixtures). Grease is an oil to which a thickening base has been added so the end product is semi-solid. Grease is often classified by the type of thickener added; lithium soap is commonly used.

Engine Oil

The Yamaha Blaster is equipped with an oil pump. Premixing of the fuel is not required unless the oil pump is removed from the engine. Yamaha recommends the use of the following 2-stroke engine oil:

    a. Yamalube 2-cycle oil (**Figure 16**).

    b. Any good-quality 2-stroke engine oil designed for use in air-cooled engines.

Transmission Oil

Yamaha recommends the use of the following 4-cycle engine oils that meets API service classification SE or SF.

    a. Yamalube 4 (**Figure 17**).

    b. SAE 10W-30 engine oil.

Another type of oil to consider is a good-quality 2-cycle motorcycle transmission oil. These oils have the same lubricating qualities as an API SE or SF oil but have additional shear additives that prevent oil break down and foaming from transmission operation. For example, the Bel-Ray Gear Saver SAE 80 transmission oil shown in **Figure 18** replaces SAE 30, SAE 10W-30 and SAE 10W-40 motor oils.

Grease

Grease is graded by the National Lubricating Grease Institute (NLGI). Grease is graded by number according to the consistency of the grease; these range from No. 000 to No. 6, with No. 6 being the most solid. A typical multipurpose grease is NLGI No. 2. For specific applications, equipment manufacturer's may require grease with an additive such as molybdenum disulfide (MOS2) (**Figure 19**).

Antiseize Lubricant

An antiseize lubricant (**Figure 20**) may be specified in some assembly applications. The antiseize lubricant prevents the formation of corrosion that may lock parts together.

SEALANT, ADHESIVE AND CLEANERS

Sealants

Many mating surfaces of an engine require a gasket or seal between them to prevent fluids and gases from passing through the joint. At times, the gasket or seal is installed as is. However, some times a sealer is applied to enhance the sealing capability of the gasket or seal. Note, however, that a sealing compound may be added to the gasket or seal during manufacturing and adding a sealant may cause premature failure of the gasket or seal. Yamaha O.E.M. gaskets do not normally require a sealer.

> *NOTE*
> *If a new gasket leaks, check the 2 mating surfaces for warpage, old gasket residue or cracks. Also make sure the new gasket was properly installed and if the assembly was torqued correctly.*

RTV Sealants

One of the most common sealants is RTV (room temperature vulcanizing) sealant (**Figure 21**). This sealant hardens (cures) at room temperature over a period of several hours, which allows sufficient time to reposition parts if necessary without damaging the gaskets. RTV sealant is designed for different uses, including high temperatures. If in doubt as to the correct type to use, ask a vendor or read the manufacturer's literature.

Adhesives

A variety of adhesives and cements are available (**Figure 22**) and their use is dependent on the type of materials to be sealed, and to some extent, the personal preference of the mechanic. Automotive parts stores offer adhesives and cements in a wide selection. Some points to consider when selecting adhesives or cements: the type of material being sealed (metal, rubber, plastic); the type of fluid contacting the seal (gasoline, oil, water); whether the seal is permanent or must be broken periodically, in which case a pliable sealant might be desirable. Unless you are experienced in the selection of cements and adhesives, follow the recommendation if the text specifies a particular sealant.

Threadlocking Compound

A threadlocking compound (**Figure 23**) is a fluid applied to fastener threads. After tightening the fas-

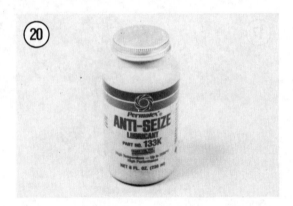

tener, the fluid dries to a solid filler between the mating threads, thereby locking the threads in position and preventing loosening due to vibration.

Threadlocking compound is available in different strengths, so follow the manufacturer's recommendations when using their particular compound. Two manufacturer's of threadlocking compound are ThreeBond of America and the Loctite Corporation.

Before applying a threadlocking compound, clean the contacting threads with an aerosol electrical contact cleaner. Use only as much compound as necessary, usually 1 or 2 drops depending on the size of the fastener.

Cleaners and Solvents

Cleaners and solvents are helpful in removing oil, grease and other residue when maintaining and overhauling your motorcycle. Before purchasing cleaners and solvents, consider how they will be used and disposed of, particularly if they are not water soluble. Local ordinances may require special proce-

dures for the disposal of certain cleaners and solvents.

WARNING
Some cleaners and solvents are harmful and may be flammable. Follow any safety precautions noted on the container or in the manufacturer's literature. Use petroleum-resistant gloves to protect hands and arms from the harmful effect of cleaners and solvents.

Figure 24 shows a variety of cleaners and solvents. Cleaners designed for ignition contact cleaning are excellent for removing light oil from a part without leaving a residue. Some degreasers will wash off with water. Ease the removal of stubborn gaskets with a gasket remover.

One of the more powerful cleaning solutions is carburetor cleaner. It is designed to dissolve the varnish that may build up in carburetor jets and orifices. Good carburetor cleaner is usually expensive and requires special disposal. Carefully read directions before purchase; do not immerse nonmetallic parts in carburetor cleaner.

Gasket Remover

Stubborn gaskets can present a problem during engine service as they can take a long time to remove. Consequently, there is the added problem of secondary damage occurring to the gasket mating surfaces from the incorrect use of gasket scraping tools. To remove stubborn gaskets, use a spray gasket remover. Spray gasket remover can be purchased through automotive parts houses. Follow the manufacturer's directions for use.

EXPENDABLE SUPPLIES

Certain expendable supplies are required during maintenance and repair work. These include grease, oil, gasket cement, wiping rags and cleaning solvent. Ask your dealership for the special locking compounds, silicone lubricants and other products which make vehicle maintenance simpler and easier. Cleaning solvent or kerosene is available at some service stations, paint or hardware stores.

BASIC HAND TOOLS

Many of the procedures in this manual can be carried out with simple hand tools and test equipment familiar to the average home mechanic. Keep your tools clean and in a tool box. Keep them organized with related tools stored together. After using a tool, wipe off dirt and grease with a clean cloth and return the tool to its correct place.

Top quality tools are essential; they are also more economical in the long run. If you are now starting to build your tool collection, avoid the advertised specials featured at some parts houses, discount stores and chain drug stores. These are usually a poor grade tool that can be sold cheaply and that is exactly what they are—*cheap*. They are usually made of inferior material, and are thick, heavy and clumsy. Their rough finish makes them difficult to clean and they usually do not last very long. If it is ever your misfortune to use such tools, you will probably find out that the wrenches do not fit the heads of bolts and nuts correctly and damage the fastener.

Quality tools are made of alloy steel and are heat treated for greater strength. They are lighter and better balanced than cheap ones. Their surface is smooth, making them a pleasure to work with and easy to clean. The initial cost of good quality tools may be more but they are less expensive in the long run. Do not try to buy everything in all sizes in the beginning; purchase a little at a time until you have the necessary tools.

Screwdrivers

The screwdriver is a very basic tool, but if used improperly it will do more damage than good. The slot on a screw has a definite dimension and shape. A screwdriver must be selected to conform with that shape.

Two basic types of screwdrivers are required; common (flat-blade) screwdrivers (**Figure 25**) and Phillips screwdrivers (**Figure 26**).

Screwdrivers are available in sets which often include an assortment of common and Phillips blades. If you buy them individually, buy at least the following:

    a. Common screwdriver—5/16 × 6 in. blade.

    b. Common screwdriver—3/8 × 12 in. blade.

    c. Phillips screwdriver—size 2 tip, 6 in. blade.

    d. Phillips screwdriver—size 3 tip, 6 and 10 in. blade.

Use screwdrivers only for driving screws. Never use a screwdriver for prying or chiseling metal. Do

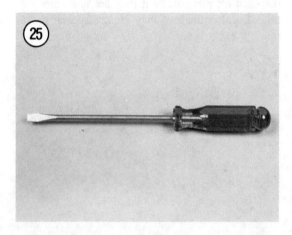

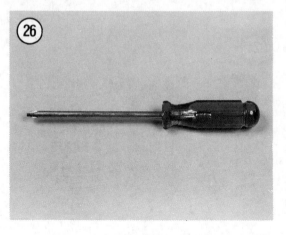

not try to remove a Phillips or Allen head screw with a common screwdriver (unless the screw has a combination head that will accept either type); you can damage the head so that even the proper tool will be unable to remove it.

Keep screwdrivers in the proper condition and they will last longer and perform better. Always keep the tip of a common screwdriver in good condition.

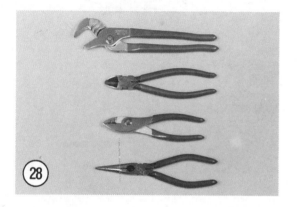

Figure 27 shows how to grind the tip to the proper shape if it becomes damaged. Note the symmetrical sides of the tip.

Pliers

Pliers come in a wide range of types and sizes. Pliers are useful for cutting, bending and crimping. Do not use them to cut hardened objects or to turn bolts or nuts. **Figure 28** shows several pliers useful for ATV and motorcycle repair.

Each type of pliers has a specialized function. Slip-joint pliers are general purpose pliers and are used mainly for holding things and for bending.

Needlenose pliers are used to hold or bend small objects. Groove-joint pliers can be adjusted to hold various sizes of objects; the jaws remain parallel to grip around objects such as pipe or tubing. There are many more types of pliers. The ones described here are most suitable for vehicle repairs.

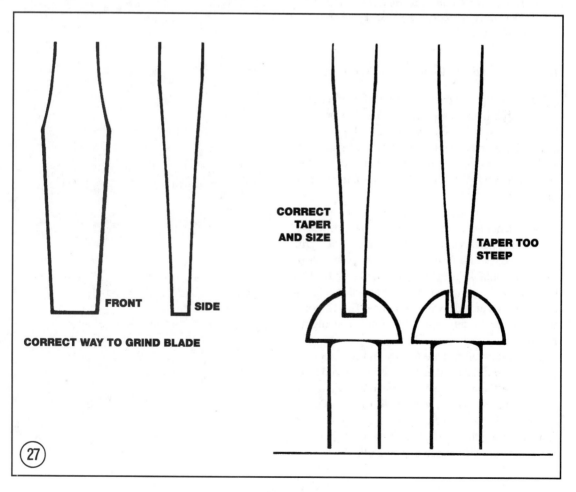

CORRECT TAPER AND SIZE

TAPER TOO STEEP

FRONT   SIDE

CORRECT WAY TO GRIND BLADE

Locking Pliers

Locking pliers (**Figure 29**) are used to hold objects very tightly like a vise. However, avoid using them unless absolutely necessary since their sharp jaws will permanently scar any objects which are held. Locking pliers are available in many types for more specific tasks.

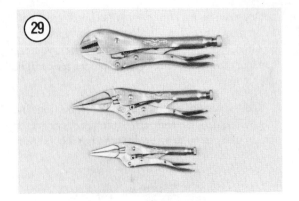

Circlip Pliers

Circlip pliers (**Figure 30**) are special in that they are only used to remove and install circlips from shafts or within engine or suspension housings. When purchasing circlip pliers, there are 2 kinds to distinguish from. External pliers (spreading) are used to remove circlips that fit on the outside of a shaft. Internal pliers (squeezing) are used to remove circlips which fit inside a gear or housing.

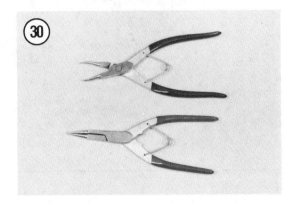

> *WARNING*
> *Because circlips can sometimes slip and fly off when removing and installing them, always wear safety glasses when servicing them.*

Box-, Open-end and Combination Wrenches

Box-end, open-end and combination wrenches ~~e available in sets or separately in a variety of sizes. On open- and box-end wrenches, the number stamped near the end refers to the distance between 2 parallel flats on the hex head bolt or nut. On combination wrenches, the number is stamped near the center.

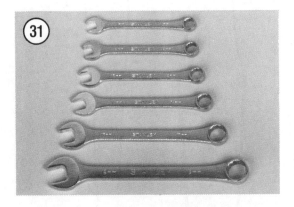

Box-end wrenches require clear overhead access to the fastener but can work well in situations where the fastener head is close to another part. They grip on all 6 edges of a fastener for a very secure grip. They are available in either 6-point or 12-point. The 6-point gives superior holding power and durability but requires a greater swinging radius. The 12-point works better in situations with limited swinging radius.

Open-end wrenches are speedy and work best in areas with limited overhead access. Their wide flat jaws make them unstable for situations where the bolt or nut is sunken in a well or close to the edge of a casting. These wrenches grip only 2 flats of a fastener so if either the fastener head or the wrench jaws are worn, the wrench may slip off.

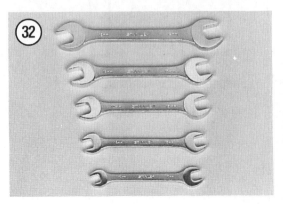

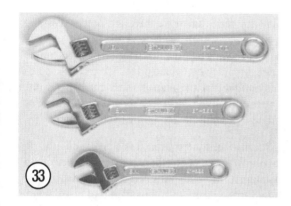

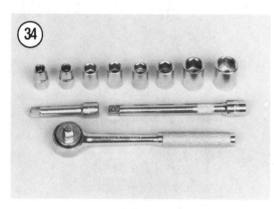

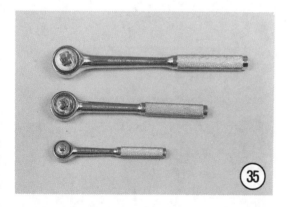

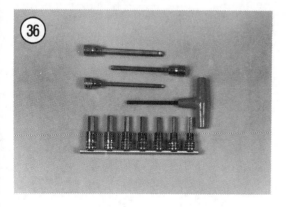

Combination wrenches (**Figure 31**) have open-end on one side and box-end on the other with both ends being the same size. These wrenches are favored by professionals because of their versatility. **Figure 32** shows a set of open-end wrenches.

Adjustable Wrenches

An adjustable wrench (sometimes called crescent wrench) can be adjusted to fit nearly any nut or bolt head which has clear access around its entire perimeter. Adjustable wrenches (**Figure 33**) are best used as a backup wrench to keep a large nut or bolt from turning while the other end is being loosened or tightened with a proper wrench.

Adjustable wrenches have only 2 gripping surfaces which make them more subject to slipping off the fastener and damaging the part and possibly injuring your hand. The fact that one jaw is adjustable only aggravates this shortcoming.

These wrenches are directional; the solid jaw must be the one transmitting the force. If you use the adjustable jaw to transmit the force, it can loosen and possibly slip off.

Socket Wrenches

This type is undoubtedly the fastest, safest and most convenient to use. Sockets which attach to a ratchet handle (**Figure 34**) are available with 6-point or 12-point openings and 1/4, 3/8, 1/2 and 3/4 in. drives. The drive size indicates the size of the square hole which mates with the ratchet handle (**Figure 35**).

Allen Wrenches

Allen wrenches are available in sets or separately in a variety of sizes. These sets come in U.S. standard and metric size, so be sure to buy a metric set. Allen bolts are sometimes called socket-head bolts. Sometimes the bolts are difficult to reach and it is suggested that a variety of Allen wrenches be purchased (such as socket driven, T-handle and extension type) as shown in **Figure 36**.

Impact Driver

This tool might have been designed with the ATV and motorcycle rider in mind. This tool makes removal of fasteners easy and eliminates damage to bolts and screw slots. Impact drivers and interchangeable bits (**Figure 37**) are available at most large hardware, motorcycle or auto parts stores. Sockets can also be used with a hand impact driver. However, make sure that the socket is designed for use with an impact driver or air tool. Do not use regular hand sockets, as they may shatter during use.

Hammers

It is important to select the correct type of hammer (**Figure 38**) during disassembly and reassembly. A hammer with a rubber or plastic face, or the soft-face type filled with lead shot is often necessary during engine disassembly. *Never* use a metal-face hammer on engine or suspension parts. Ball-peen or machinist's hammers are required when striking another tool, such as a punch or cold chisel. If it is necessary to strike hard against a steel part without damaging it, use a brass or lead hammer. When using a hammer, always observe the following precautions:

   a. *Always* wear suitable eye protection when using a hammer.
   b. Inspect the hammer for a damaged or broken handle. Repair or replace the hammer as required. *Do not use* a hammer with a cracked handle.
   c. Strike the object or tool squarely. Never use the side of the hammer or handle to strike an object.
   d. Always wipe oil or grease from the hammer handle prior to using it.
   e. Always use the correct hammer for the job.

Torque Wrench

A torque wrench is used with a socket, torque adapter or similar extension to measure how tightly a nut, bolt or other fastener is installed. They come in a wide price range and with either 1/4, 3/8 or 1/2 in. square drive. The drive size indicates the size of the square drive which mates with the socket, torque adapter or extension. Popular types are the deflecting beam (A, **Figure 39**), the dial indicator and the audible click (B, **Figure 39**) torque wrenches. As

with any series of tools, there are advantages and disadvantages with each type of torque wrench. When choosing a torque wrench, consider its torque range, accuracy rating and price. The torque specifications listed at the end of most chapters in this manual will give you an idea regarding the range of torque wrench needed to service your Yamaha.

Because the torque wrench is a precision tool, do not throw it in with other tools and expect it to maintain its accuracy. Always store a torque wrench in its carrying case or in a padded tool box drawer.

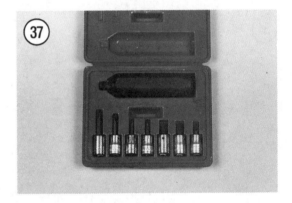

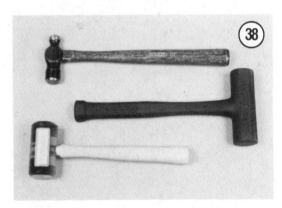

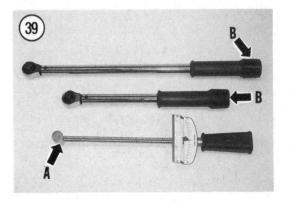

All torque wrenches require periodic calibration. To find out more about this, read the information provided with the torque wrench or write to its manufacturer.

Torque Wrench Adapters

Torque adapters and extensions allow you to extend or reduce the reach of your torque wrench. For example, the torque adapter wrench shown in **Figure 40** can be used to extend the length of the torque wrench to tighten fasteners that cannot normally be reached with a torque wrench and socket. Because a torque adapter lengthens or shortens the torque wrench (**Figure 40**), the torque reading on the torque wrench will not be the same amount of torque that is applied to the fastener. Before using a torque adapter, it is necessary to recalculate the listed torque specification to compensate for the effect of the added torque adapter length.

To recalculate a torque reading when using a torque adapter, it is first necessary to know the lever length of the torque wrench, the length of the adapter from the center of square drive to the center of the nut or bolt, and the actual amount of torque desired at the nut or bolt (**Figure 41**). The formula can be expressed as:

$$TW = \frac{TA \times L}{L + A}$$

TW is the torque setting or dial reading to set on the torque wrench.

TA is the actual torque setting. This is the torque specification listed in the service manual and will be the actual amount of torque applied to the fastener.

A is the length of the adapter from the centerline of the square drive (at the torque wrench) to the centerline of the nut or bolt. If the torque adapter extends straight from the end of the torque wrench (**Figure 42**), the centerline of the torque adapter and torque wrench are the same. However, if the center lines of the torque adapter and torque wrench do not align, the distance must be measured as shown in **Figure 42**. Also note in **Figure 42** that when the torque adapter is set at a right-angle to the torque wrench, no calculation is needed (the lever length of the torque wrench did not change).

L is the lever length of your torque wrench. This specification is usually listed in the instruction manual that came with your torque wrench, or you can determine its length by measuring the distance from the center of the square drive on the torque wrench to the center of the torque wrench handle (**Figure 41**).

Example:

What should the torque wrench preset reading or dial reading be if:

TA = 20 ft.-lb.

A = 3 in.

L = 14 in.

$$TW = \frac{20 \times 14}{14 + 3} = \frac{280}{17} = 16.5 \text{ ft.-lb.}$$

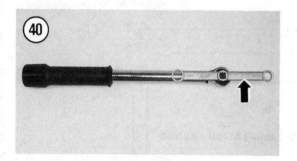

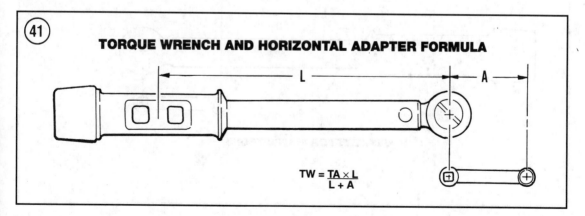

TORQUE WRENCH AND HORIZONTAL ADAPTER FORMULA

$$TW = \frac{TA \times L}{L + A}$$

In this example, the recalculated torque value of 16.5 ft.-lb. would be the amount of torque to set on the torque wrench. When using a dial or beam-type torque wrench, torque is applied until the pointer aligns with the 16.5 ft.-lb. dial reading. When using a click type torque wrench, the micrometer dial would be preset to 16.5 ft.-lb. In all cases, even though the torque wrench dial or preset reading is 16.5 ft.-lb., the fastener would actually be tightened to 20 ft.-lb.

PRECISION MEASURING TOOLS

Measurement is an important part of vehicle and engine service. When performing many of the service procedures in this manual, you will be required to make a number of measurements. These include basic checks such as engine compression and spark plug gap. As you become more involved with engine work, measurements will be required to determine the size and condition of the piston and cylinder

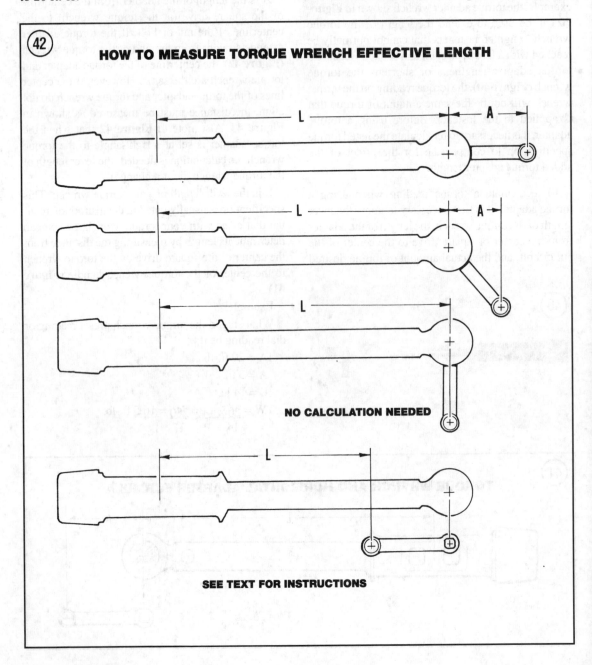

(42)

HOW TO MEASURE TORQUE WRENCH EFFECTIVE LENGTH

NO CALCULATION NEEDED

SEE TEXT FOR INSTRUCTIONS

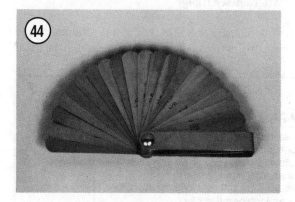

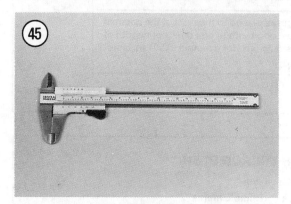

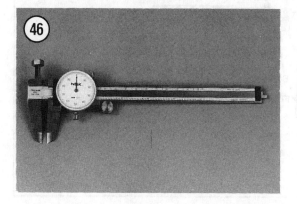

bore, crankshaft runout and so on. When making these measurements, the degree of accuracy will dictate which tool is required.

Precision measuring tools are expensive. If this is your first experience at engine or suspension service, it may be worthwhile to have the checks made at a Yamaha dealership or machine shop. However, as your skills and enthusiasm for doing your own service work increase, you may want to begin purchasing some of these specialized tools. The following is a description of the measuring tools required to perform the service procedures described in this manual.

Feeler Gauge

Feeler gauges come in assorted sets and types. The feeler gauge is made of either a piece of a flat or round hardened steel of a specified thickness. Wire gauges (**Figure 43**) are used to measure spark plug gap. Flat gauges (**Figure 44**) are used for most other measurements.

Vernier Caliper

This tool (**Figure 45**) is used to take inside, outside and depth measurements. Although this tool is not as precise as a micrometer, it allows reasonably accurate measurements, typically to within 0.025 mm (0.001 in.). Common uses of a vernier caliper are measuring the length of clutch springs, the thickness of clutch plates, shims and thrust washers, brake pad thickness or the depth of a bearing bore. The jaws of the caliper must be clean and free of burrs at all times in order to obtain an accurate measurement. There are several types of vernier calipers available. The standard vernier caliper (**Figure 45**) has a highly accurate graduated scale on the handle in which the measurements must be calculated. The dial indicator caliper (**Figure 46**) is equipped with a small dial and needle that indicates the measurement reading, and the digital electronic type with a LCD display that shows the measurement on the small display screen. Some vernier calipers must be calibrated prior to making a measurement. Refer to the manufacturer's instructions for this procedure.

Outside Micrometers

An outside micrometer is a precision tool used to accurately measure parts using the decimal divisions of the inch or meter (**Figure 47**). While there are many types and styles of micrometers, this section describes steps on how to use the outside micrometer. The outside micrometer is the most common type of micrometer used when servicing ATVs and motorcycles. It is useful in accurately measuring the outside diameter, length and thickness of parts. These parts include the piston, piston pin, crankshaft, piston rings and various shims. The outside micrometer is also used to measure the dimension taken by a small hole gauge or a telescoping gauge

described later in this section. After the small hole gauge or telescoping gauge has been carefully expanded to a limit within the bore of the component being measured, carefully remove the gauge and measure the distance across its arms with the micrometer.

Other types of micrometers include the depth micrometer and screw thread micrometer. **Figure 48** illustrates the various parts of an outside micrometer with its part names and markings identified.

Micrometer Range

A micrometer's size indicates the minimum and maximum size of part that it can measure. The usual

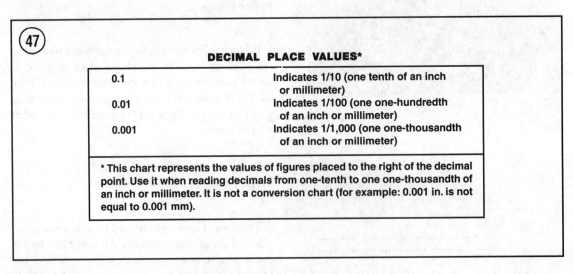

47

DECIMAL PLACE VALUES*

0.1	Indicates 1/10 (one tenth of an inch or millimeter)
0.01	Indicates 1/100 (one one-hundredth of an inch or millimeter)
0.001	Indicates 1/1,000 (one one-thousandth of an inch or millimeter)

* This chart represents the values of figures placed to the right of the decimal point. Use it when reading decimals from one-tenth to one one-thousandth of an inch or millimeter. It is not a conversion chart (for example: 0.001 in. is not equal to 0.001 mm).

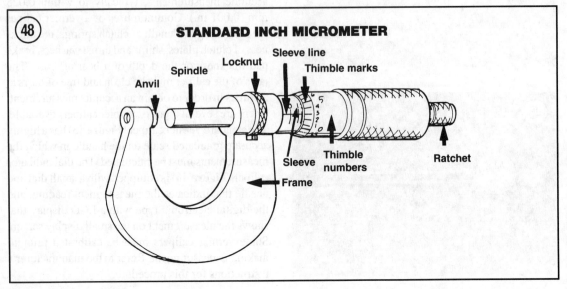

48

STANDARD INCH MICROMETER

Anvil
Spindle
Locknut
Sleeve line
Thimble marks
Sleeve
Thimble numbers
Ratchet
Frame

sizes are: 0-1 in. (0-25 mm), 1-2 in. (25-50 mm), 2-3 in. (50-75 mm) and 3-4 in. (75-100 mm). These micrometers use fixed anvils.

Some micrometers use the same frame with interchangeable anvils of different lengths. This allows you to install the correct length anvil for a particular job. For example, a 0-4 in. interchangeable micrometer is equipped with 4 different length anvils. Although purchasing 1 or 2 interchangeable micrometers to cover a range from 0-4 in. or 0-6 in. is less expensive, its large frame size makes it less convenient to use.

How to Read a Micrometer

When reading a micrometer, numbers are taken from different scales and then added together. The following sections describe how to read the standard inch micrometer, the vernier inch micrometer, the standard metric micrometer and the metric vernier micrometer.

Standard inch micrometer

The standard inch type micrometer is accurate to one-thousandth of an inch (0.001 in.). The heart of the micrometer is its spindle screw with 40 threads per inch. Every turn of the thimble will move the spindle 1/40 of an inch or 0.025 in. (to change 1/40 of an inch to a decimal: divided by 40 equals 0.025 in.).

Before you learn how to read a micrometer, study the markings and part names in **Figure 48**. Then take your micrometer and turn the thimble until its zero mark aligns with the zero mark on the sleeve line. Now turn the thimble counterclock-

wise and align the next thimble mark with the sleeve line. The micrometer now reads 0.001 in. (one one-thousandth) of an inch. Thus, each thimble mark is equal to 0.001 in. Every fifth thimble mark is numbered to help with reading: 0, 5, 10, 15 and 20.

Reset the micrometer so the thimble and sleeve line zero marks align. Then turn the thimble counterclockwise one complete revolution and align the thimble zero mark with the first line in the sleeve line. The micrometer now reads 0.025 in. (twenty-five thousandths) of an inch. Thus, each sleeve line represents 0.025 in.

Now turn the thimble counterclockwise while counting the sleeve line marks. Every fourth mark on the sleeve line is marked with a number ranging from 1 through 9. Manufacturer's usually mark the last mark on the sleeve line with a 0. This indicates that you have reached the end of the micrometer's measuring range. Each sleeve number represents 0.100 in. For example, the number 1 represents 0.100 in. The number 9 represents 0.900 in.

When reading a standard micrometer, take the following 3 measurements described and add them together. Take the first 2 readings from the sleeve and the last reading from the thimble. The sum of the 3 readings gives you the measurement in thousandths of an inch.

To read a micrometer, perform the following steps while referring to the example in **Figure 49**.

1. Read the sleeve line to find the largest number visible—each sleeve number mark equals 0.100 in.

2. Count the number of sleeve marks visible between the numbered sleeve mark and the thimble edge—each sleeve mark equals 0.025 in. If there is no visible sleeve mark, continue with Step 3.

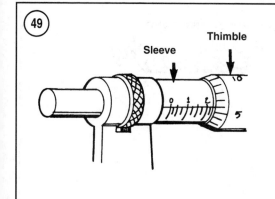

(49)

Sleeve	Thimble
1. Largest number visible on the sleeve line	0.200 in.
2. Number on sleeve marks visible between the numbered sleeve mark and the thimble edge	0.025 in.
3. Thimble mark that aligns with sleeve line	0.006 in.
Total reading	0.231 in.

3. Read the thimble mark that lines up with the sleeve line—each thimble mark equals 0.001 in.

NOTE
If a thimble mark does not align exactly with the sleeve line but falls between 2 lines, estimate the decimal amount between the lines. For a more accurate reading, you must use a vernier inch micrometer.

4. Add the micrometer readings in Steps 1-3 to obtain the actual measurement.

Vernier inch micrometers

A vernier micrometer can accurately measure in ten-thousandths of an inch (0.0001 in.) increments. While it has the same markings as a standard micrometer, a vernier scale scribed on the sleeve (**Figure 50**) makes it unique. The vernier scale consists of eleven equally spaced lines marked 0-10 or 1-9 with a 0 on each end. These lines run parallel on the top of the sleeve where each line is equal to 0.0001 in. Thus, the vernier scale divides a thousandth of an inch (0.001 in.) into ten-thousandths of an inch (0.0001 in.).

To read a vernier inch micrometer, perform the following steps while referring to the example in **Figure 51**.

1. Read the micrometer in the same way as the standard micrometer. This is your initial reading.
2. If a thimble mark aligns exactly with the sleeve line, reading the vernier scale is not necessary. If a thimble mark does not align exactly with the sleeve line, read the vernier scale in Step 3.
3. Read the vernier scale to find which vernier mark aligns with one thimble mark. The number of that vernier mark is the number of ten-thousandths of an inch to add to the initial reading taken in Step 1.

Metric micrometers

The metric micrometer is very similar to the standard inch type. The differences are the graduations on the thimble and sleeve as shown in **Figure 52**.

The standard metric micrometer is accurate of measuring to one one-hundredth of a millimeter (0.01 mm). On the metric micrometer, the spindle screw is ground with a thread pitch of 1/2 millimeter (0.5 mm). Thus, every turn of the thimble will move the spindle 0.5 mm.

The sleeve line is graduated in millimeters and half millimeters. The marks on the upper side of the sleeve line are equal to 1.00 mm. Every fifth mark above the sleeve line is marked with a number. The actual numbers depend on the size of the micrometer. For example, on a 0-25 mm micrometer, the sleeve marks are numbered 0, 5, 10, 15, 20 and 25. On a 25-50 mm micrometer, the sleeve marks are numbered 25, 30, 35, 40, 45 and 50. This numbering sequence continues with larger size metric micrometers (50-75 and 75-100). Each mark on the lower side of the sleeve line is equal to 0.5 mm.

The thimble scale is divided into 50 graduations where one graduation is equal to 0.01 mm. Every fifth thimble graduation is numbered to help with

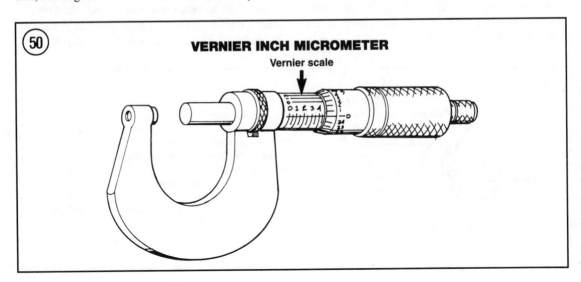

⑤⓪   **VERNIER INCH MICROMETER**
Vernier scale

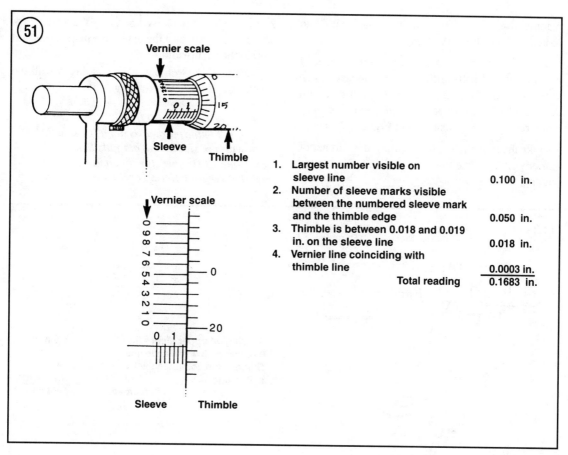

1. Largest number visible on
   sleeve line   0.100 in.
2. Number of sleeve marks visible
   between the numbered sleeve mark
   and the thimble edge   0.050 in.
3. Thimble is between 0.018 and 0.019
   in. on the sleeve line   0.018 in.
4. Vernier line coinciding with
   thimble line   0.0003 in.
                          Total reading   0.1683 in.

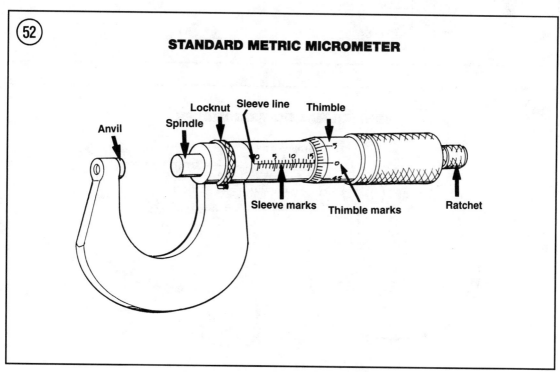

STANDARD METRIC MICROMETER

reading from 0-45. The thimble edge is used to indicate which sleeve markings to read.

To read a metric micrometer, add the number of millimeters and half-millimeters on the sleeve line to the number of one one-hundredth millimeters on the thimble. To do so, perform the following steps while referring to the example in **Figure 53**.

1. Take the first reading by counting the number of marks visible on the upper sleeve line. Record the reading.

2. Look below the sleeve line to see if a lower mark is visible directly past the upper line mark. If so, add 0.50 to the first reading.

3. Now read the thimble mark that aligns with the sleeve line. Record this reading.

NOTE
If a thimble mark does not align exactly with the sleeve line but falls between 2 lines, estimate the decimal amount between the lines. For a more accurate

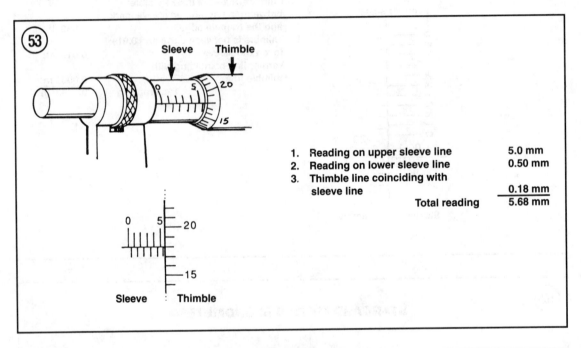

1.	Reading on upper sleeve line	5.0 mm
2.	Reading on lower sleeve line	0.50 mm
3.	Thimble line coinciding with sleeve line	0.18 mm
	Total reading	5.68 mm

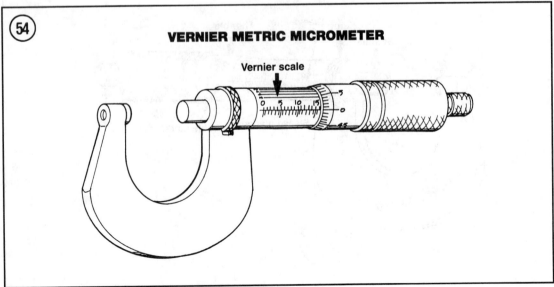

VERNIER METRIC MICROMETER

reading, you must use a metric vernier micrometer.

4. Add the micrometer readings in Steps 1-3 to obtain the actual measurement.

Metric vernier micrometers

A metric vernier micrometer can accurately measure to 2 thousandths of a millimeter (0.002 mm). While it has the same markings as a standard metric micrometer, a vernier scale scribed on the sleeve (**Figure 54**) makes it unique. The vernier scale consists of 5 equally spaced lines marked 0, 2, 4, 6 and 8. These lines run parallel on the top of the sleeve where each line is equal to 0.002 mm.

To read a metric vernier micrometer, perform the following steps while referring to the example in **Figure 55**.

1. Read the micrometer in the same way as the metric standard micrometer. This is the initial reading.
2. If a thimble mark aligns exactly with the sleeve line, reading the vernier scale is not necessary. If a thimble mark does not align exactly with the sleeve line, read the vernier scale in Step 3.
3. Read the vernier scale to find which vernier mark aligns with one thimble mark. The number of

that vernier mark is the number of thousandths of a millimeter to add to the initial reading taken in Step 1.

Micrometer Accuracy Check

You must check a micrometer frequently for accuracy. The following steps show you how to do this.

1. Make sure the anvil and spindle faces (**Figure 49**) are clean and dry.
2. To check a 0-1 in. (0-25 mm) micrometer, perform the following:
   a. Turn the thimble until the spindle contacts the anvil. If the micrometer has a ratchet stop, use it to ensure that the proper amount of pressure is applied against the contact surfaces.
   b. Read the micrometer. If the adjustment is correct, the 0 mark on the thimble will align exactly with the 0 mark on the sleeve line. If the 0 marks do not align, the micrometer is out of adjustment
   c. To adjust the micrometer, follow its manufacturer's instructions provided with the micrometer.
3. To check the accuracy of micrometers above the 1 in. (25 mm) size, perform the following:

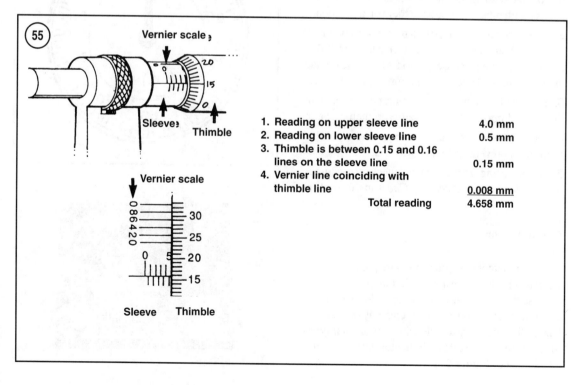

55

Vernier scale

Sleeve

Thimble

Vernier scale

Sleeve   Thimble

1. Reading on upper sleeve line	4.0 mm
2. Reading on lower sleeve line	0.5 mm
3. Thimble is between 0.15 and 0.16 lines on the sleeve line	0.15 mm
4. Vernier line coinciding with thimble line	0.008 mm
Total reading	4.658 mm

a. Manufacturer's usually supply a standard gauge with these micrometers. A standard is a steel block, disc or rod that is ground to an exact size to check the accuracy of the micrometer. For example, a 1-2 in. micrometer is equipped with a 1 in. standard gauge. A 25-50 mm micrometer is equipped with a 25 mm standard gauge.

b. Place the standard gauge between the micrometer's spindle and anvil and measure its diameter or length. Read the micrometer. If the adjustment is correct, the 0 mark on the thimble will align exactly with the 0 mark on the sleeve line. If the 0 marks do not align, the micrometer is out of adjustment.

c. To adjust the micrometer, follow its manufacturer's instructions given with the micrometer.

Proper Care of the Micrometer

Because the micrometer is a precision instrument, you must use it correctly and with great care. When using and storing a micrometer, note the following.

1. Store a micrometer in its box or in a protected place where dust, oil and other debris cannot come in contact with it. Do not store micrometers in a drawer with other tools or hang them on a tool board.

2. When storing a 0-1 in. (0-25 mm) micrometer, the spindle and anvil must not contact each other. If they do, the contact may cause rust to form on the contact ends or spindle damage from temperature changes.

3. Do not clean a micrometer with compressed air. Dirt forced into the tool can cause premature wear.

4. Occasionally lubricate the micrometer with a light oil to prevent rust and corrosion.

5. Before using a micrometer, check its accuracy. Refer to *Micrometer Accuracy Check* in this section.

Dial Indicator

Dial indicators (**Figure 56**) are precision tools used to check dimension variations on machined parts such as transmission shafts and axles, and to check crankshaft and axle shaft end play or gear lash. Dial indicators are available with various dial types; for ATV service, select an indicator with a continuous dial face (**Figure 57**).

Cylinder Bore Gauge

The cylinder bore gauge is a very specialized precision tool. The gauge set shown in **Figure 58** is comprised of a dial indicator, handle and a number of length adapters to adapt the gauge to different bore sizes. The bore gauge can be used to make cylinder bore measurements such as bore size, taper and

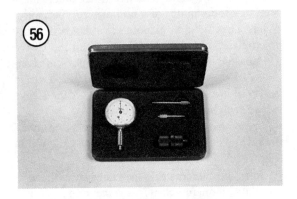

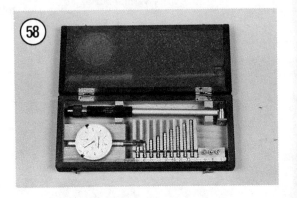

out-of-round. In some cases, an outside micrometer must be used to calibrate the bore gauge to a specific bore size.

Select the correct length adapter (A, **Figure 59**) for the size of the bore to be measured. Zero the bore gauge according to its manufacturer's instructions, insert the bore gauge into the cylinder, then carefully move it around in the bore to make sure it is centered and that the gauge foot (B, **Figure 59**) is sitting correctly on the bore surface. This is necessary to obtain a correct reading. Refer to the manufacturer's instructions for reading the actual measurement.

Screw Pitch Gauge

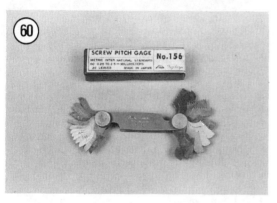

A screw pitch gauge (**Figure 60**) determines the thread pitch of bolts, screws and studs. The gauge is made up of a number of thin plates. Each plate has a thread shape cut on one edge to match one thread pitch. When using a screw pitch gauge to determine a thread pitch size, try to fit different blade sizes onto the bolt thread until both threads match (**Figure 61**).

Magnetic Stand

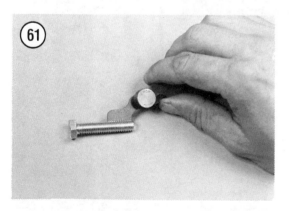

A magnetic stand (**Figure 62**) holds a dial indicator securely when checking the runout of a round object or when checking the end play of a shaft.

V-Blocks

V-blocks (**Figure 63**) are precision ground blocks used to hold a round object when checking its runout or condition. V-blocks can be used when checking the runout of such items as the clutch pushrod, transmission shafts and rear axle.

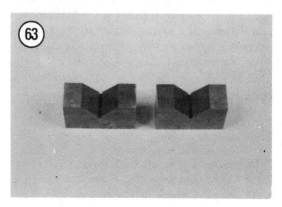

TEST EQUIPMENT

Spark Tester

A quick way to check the ignition system is to connect a spark tester (**Figure 64**) to the end of the spark plug wire and operate the engine's kickstarter. A visible spark should jump the gap on the tester. A variety of spark testers are available from engine and aftermarket manufacturers.

Compression Gauge

An engine with low compression cannot be properly tuned and will not develop full power. A compression gauge (**Figure 65**) measures engine compression. The one shown has a flexible stem with an extension that can allow you to hold it while kicking the engine over. Open the throttle all the way when checking engine compression. See Chapter Three.

Cylinder Leakage Tester

A cylinder leakage tester (**Figure 66**) is used to check for air leaks in a 2-stroke engine. This test should be made when troubleshooting the engine, after installing the reed valve assembly or after reassembling the engine's top end. Air leaks through the engine seals and/or gaskets can cause engine seizure, carburetor problems and power loss. This test is fully described in Chapter Two.

Strobe Timing Light

This instrument is used to check ignition timing. By flashing a light at the precise instant the spark plug fires, the position of the timing mark can be seen. The flashing light makes a moving mark appear to stand still opposite a stationary mark.

Suitable lights range from inexpensive neon bulb types (**Figure 67**) to powerful xenon strobe lights. A light with an inductive pickup is recommended to eliminate any possible damage to ignition wiring.

Multimeter or VOM

This instrument (**Figure 68**) is invaluable for electrical system troubleshooting. See *Electrical Troubleshooting* in Chapter Two for its use.

SPECIAL TOOLS

A few special tools may be required for major service. These are described in the appropriate chapters and are available either from a Yamaha dealership or other manufacturer's as indicated.

This section describes special tools unique to this type of vehicle's service and repair.

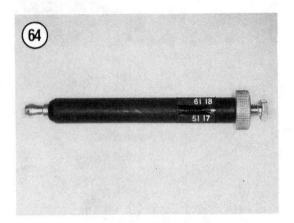

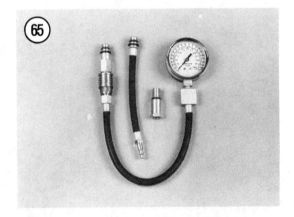

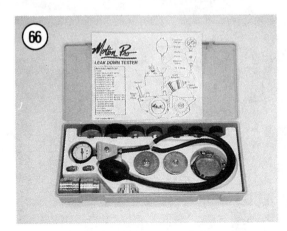

Flywheel Puller

A flywheel puller (**Figure 69**) is required when it is necessary to remove the flywheel from the end of the crankshaft. There is no satisfactory substitute for this tool. Because the flywheel is a taper fit on the crankshaft, makeshift removal often results in crankshaft and flywheel damage. Do not attempt to remove the flywheel without this tool. A puller can be ordered through Yamaha and aftermarket dealerships.

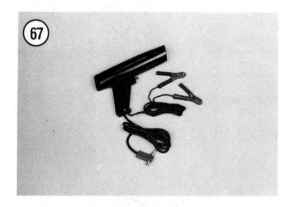

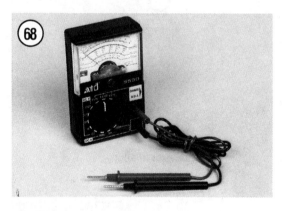

The correct puller for your Yamaha is described in Chapter Nine.

Clutch and Flywheel Holding Tools

A holder is required whenever removing and tightening the flywheel and clutch hub nuts. These tools are described in Chapter Six and Chapter Nine.

Engine Crankcase Tools

A number of special tools are required for crankcase disassembly and reassembly. These are described in Chapter Five.

Rear Axle Nut Wrench

A rear axle nut wrench is required to loosen and tighten the rear axle locknuts. This tool is described in Chapter Twelve.

MECHANIC'S TIPS

Removing Frozen Nuts and Screws

If a fastener rusts and cannot be removed, several methods may be used to loosen it. First, apply penetrating oil such as Liquid Wrench or WD-40 (available at hardware or auto supply stores). Apply it liberally and let it penetrate for 10-15 minutes. Rap the fastener several times with a small hammer; do not hit it hard enough to cause damage. Reapply the penetrating oil if necessary.

For frozen screws, apply penetrating oil as described, then insert a screwdriver in the slot and rap the top of the screwdriver with a hammer. This loosens the rust so the screw can be removed in the normal way. If the screw head is too damaged to use this method, try to grip the fastener head with locking pliers and twist the screw out.

Avoid applying heat unless specifically instructed, as it may melt, warp or remove the temper from parts.

Removing Broken Screws or Bolts

If the head breaks off a screw or bolt, several methods are available for removing the remaining portion.

If a large portion of the remainder projects out, try gripping it with locking pliers. If the projecting portion is too small, file it to fit a wrench or cut a slot in it to fit a screwdriver. See **Figure 70**.

If the head breaks off flush, use a screw extractor. To do this, centerpunch the exact center of the remaining portion of the screw or bolt. Drill a small hole in the screw and tap the extractor into the hole. Back the screw out with a wrench on the extractor. See **Figure 71**.

Remedying Stripped Threads

Occasionally, threads are stripped through carelessness or impact damage. Often the threads can be

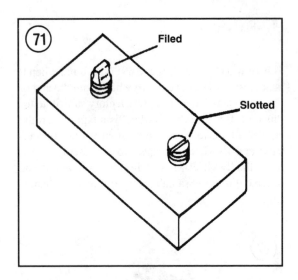

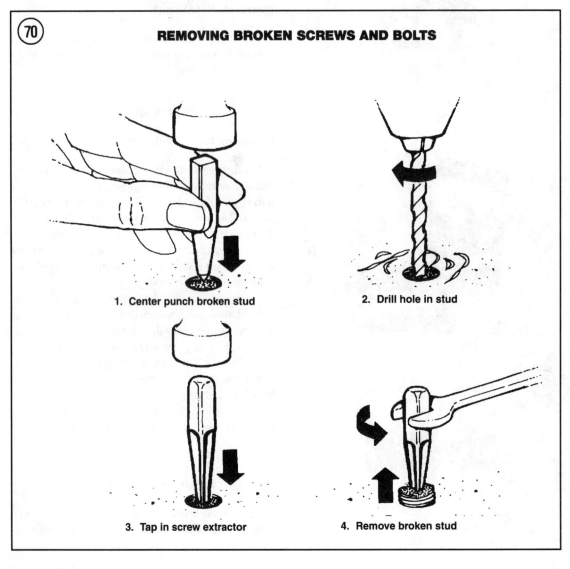

REMOVING BROKEN SCREWS AND BOLTS

1. Center punch broken stud

2. Drill hole in stud

3. Tap in screw extractor

4. Remove broken stud

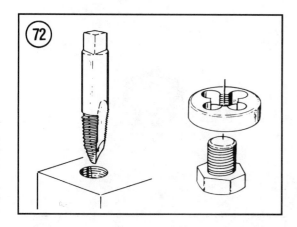

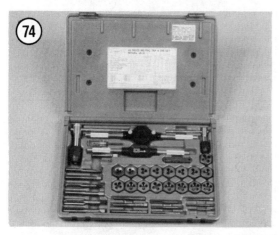

repaired by running a tap (for internal threads on nuts) or die (for external threads on bolts) through the threads. See **Figure 72**. To clean or repair spark plug threads, use a spark plug tap (**Figure 73**).

NOTE
Taps and dies can be purchased individually or in a set as shown in ***Figure 74***.

If an internal thread is damaged, it may be necessary to install a thread insert. See **Figure 75**, typical. Follow the manufacturer's instructions when using their product.

If it is necessary to drill and tap a hole, refer to **Table 7** for metric tap drill sizes.

Removing Broken or Damaged Studs

1. Measure the height of the installed stud so that the new stud can be installed correctly.

2A. If some threads of a stud are damaged, but some remain, remove the old stud as follows. If there are no usable threads, remove the stud as described in Step 2B.

   a. Thread 2 nuts onto the damaged stud (**Figure 76**), then tighten the nuts against each other so they are locked.

   b. Turn the bottom nut (**Figure 77**) and unscrew the stud.

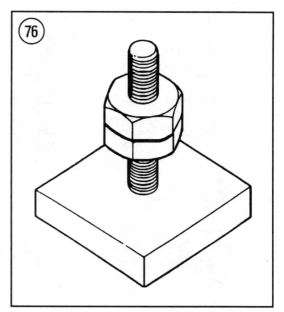

2B. If the threads on the stud are damaged, remove the stud with a stud remover or, if possible, with a pair of locking pliers.

3. Clean the threads with solvent or contact cleaner and allow to dry thoroughly.

4. Install 2 nuts on the top half of the new stud as in Step 2A. Make sure they are locked securely.

5. Apply a high-strength threadlocking compound to the bottom threads on the new stud.

6. Turn the top nut and thread the new stud in. Install the stud to its correct height position (Step 1) or tighten it to its correct torque specification (see appropriate chapter).

7. Remove the nuts and repeat for each stud as required.

BALL BEARING REPLACEMENT

Ball bearings (**Figure 78**) are used throughout the engine and chassis to reduce power loss, excessive heat and noise resulting from friction. Because ball bearings are precision-made parts, they must be maintained by proper lubrication and maintenance. If a bearing is damaged, replace it immediately. However, when installing a new bearing, you must take care to prevent damage to the new bearing. While bearing replacement is covered in individual chapters where applicable, use the following as a guideline.

NOTE
Unless otherwise specified, install bearings with their manufacturer's mark or number facing outward.

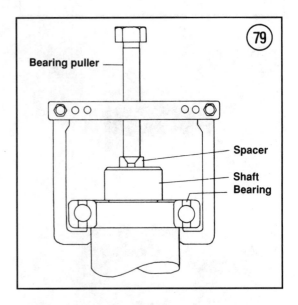

Bearing puller

Spacer

Shaft

Bearing

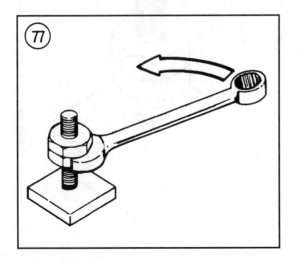

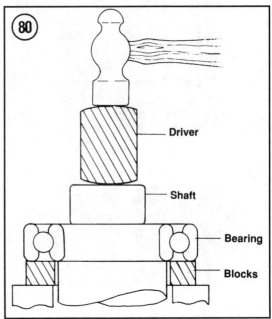

Driver

Shaft

Bearing

Blocks

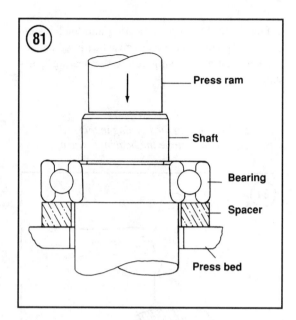

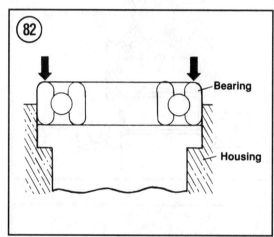

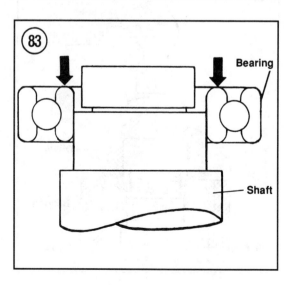

Bearing Removal

While bearings are normally removed only if damaged, there may be times when it is necessary to remove a bearing that is in good condition. However, improper bearing removal will damage the bearing and maybe the shaft or case half. Observe the following when removing bearings.

1. When using a puller to remove a bearing on a shaft, you must take care so that shaft damage does not occur. Always place a spacer (**Figure 79**) between the end of the shaft and the puller screw. In addition, place the puller arms next to the inner bearing race.

2. When using a hammer to remove a bearing from a shaft, do not strike the hammer directly against the shaft. Instead, support the bearing with wooden blocks (**Figure 80**) and use a brass or aluminum driver between the hammer and shaft.

> *WARNING*
> *Failure to use proper precautions will probably result in damaged parts and may cause personal injury.*

3. The ideal method of bearing removal is with a hydraulic press. However, certain procedures must be followed or damage may occur to the bearing, shaft or case half. Observe the following when using a press:

    a. Always support the inner and outer bearing races with a suitable size wooden or aluminum spacer (**Figure 81**). If only the outer race is supported, the balls and/or the inner race will be damaged.

    b. Make sure the press ram (**Figure 81**) aligns with the center of the shaft. If the ram is not centered, it may damage the bearing and/or shaft.

    c. The moment the shaft is free of the bearing, it will drop to the floor. Secure or hold the shaft to prevent it from falling.

Bearing Installation

Refer to the following when installing bearings.

1. When installing a bearing in a housing, apply pressure to the *outer* bearing race (**Figure 82**). When installing a bearing on a shaft, apply pressure to the *inner* bearing race (**Figure 83**).

2. When installing a bearing as described in Step 1, some type of driver is required. Never strike the bearing directly with a hammer or the bearing will be damaged. When installing a bearing, a bearing driver with an outside diameter that matches the bearing race is required to prevent bearing damage. **Figure 84** shows the correct way to use a bearing driver and hammer when installing a bearing over a shaft.

3. Step 1 describes how to install a bearing in a case half or over a shaft. However, when installing a bearing or over a shaft and into a housing at the same time, a snug fit is required for both outer and inner bearing races. In this situation, a spacer must be installed underneath the driver tool so that pressure is applied evenly across *both* races (**Figure 85**). If the outer race is not supported as shown in **Figure 85**, the balls will push against the outer bearing race and damage it.

Shrink Fit

1. *Installing a bearing over a shaft*—If a tight fit is required, the bearing inside diameter will be smaller than the shaft. In this case, simply driving the bearing on the shaft may cause bearing damage. Instead, heat the bearing before installation.

    a. Secure the shaft so it is ready for bearing installation.

    b. Clean the bearing surface on the shaft of all residue. Remove burrs with a file or sandpaper.

    c. Fill a suitable pot or beaker with clean mineral oil. Place a thermometer (rated higher than 120° C [248° F]) in the oil. Support the thermometer so it does not rest on the bottom or side of the pot.

    d. Secure the bearing with a piece of heavy wire bent to hold it in the pot. Hang the bearing in the pot so that it does not touch the bottom or sides of the pot.

    e. Turn the heat on and monitor the thermometer. When the oil temperature rises to approximately 120° C (248° F), remove the bearing from the pot and quickly install it. If necessary, place a driver on the inner bearing race (**Figure 83**) and tap the bearing into place. As the bearing chills, it will tighten on the shaft so you must work quickly when installing it. Make sure the bearing is installed all the way.

2. *Installing a bearing in a housing*—Bearings are generally installed in a housing with a slight in-terference fit. Driving the bearing into the housing may damage the housing or cause bearing damage. Instead, heat the housing before the bearing is installed.

CAUTION
Before heating the housing in this procedure to remove the bearings, wash

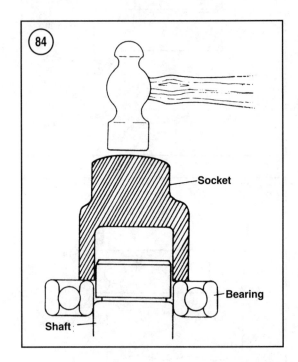

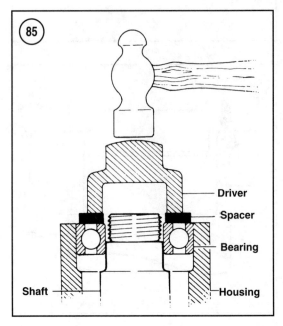

the housing thoroughly with detergent and water. Rinse and rewash the housing as required to remove all traces of oil and other chemical deposits.

a. Heat the housing to approximately 100° C (212° F) in a shop oven or on a hot plate. An easy way to see if it is at the proper temperature is to place tiny drops of water on the housing; if they sizzle and evaporate immediately, the temperature is correct. Heat only one housing at a time.

CAUTION
Do not heat the housing with a torch (propane or acetylene)—never bring open flames into contact with the bearing or housing. The direct heat will destroy the case hardening of the bearing and will likely warp the housing.

b. Remove the housing from the oven or hot plate. Hold onto the housing with welding gloves—it is hot.

NOTE
A suitable size socket and extension work well for removing and installing bearings.

c. Hold the housing with the bearing side down and tap the bearing out. Repeat for all bearings in the housing.

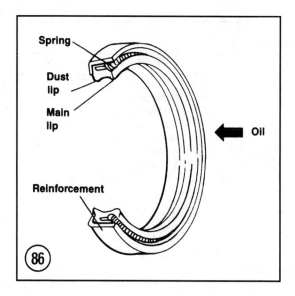

Spring

Dust lip

Main lip

Oil

Reinforcement

86

d. Before heating the housing, place the new bearings in a freezer, if possible. Chilling them will slightly reduce their overall diameter while the hot housing assembly is larger due to heat expansion. This will make installation much easier.

NOTE
Always install bearings with their manufacturer's mark or number facing outward unless the text directs otherwise.

e. While the housing is still hot, install the new bearing(s) into the housing. Install the bearings by hand, if possible. If necessary, lightly tap the bearing(s) into the housing with a driver placed on the outer bearing race. *Do not install new bearings by driving on the inner bearing race.* Install the bearing(s) until it seats completely.

SEALS

Seals (**Figure 86**) are used to prevent leakage of oil, grease or combustion gasses from between a housing and a shaft. The seal has a rubber or neoprene lip that rests against the shaft to form a seal. Depending on the application, the seal may have one or more lips, as well as a garter spring behind the lip to increase pressure on the seal lips. Using an improper procedure to remove a seal can damage the housing or shaft. Improper installation can damage the seal. Note the following:

a. Prying is generally the easiest and most effective method of removing a seal from a housing. However, always place a rag underneath the pry tool to prevent damage to the housing.

b. A low-temperature grease should be packed in the seal lips (**Figure 86**) before the seal is installed.

c. Seals should always be installed so their manufacture's numbers or marks face out unless the text directs otherwise.

d. A driver of the correct size can often be used as a seal driver. Select a driver that fits the seal's outer diameter properly and clears any protruding shafts.

e. Make sure the seal is driven squarely into the housing. Never install a seal by hitting directly against the top of the seal with a hammer.

Table 1 MODELS ENGINE SERIAL NUMBERS

Year and model	Engine serial number[1]
1988 YFS200U	2XJ-000101-on
1989 YFS200W	3JM-000101-on
1990 YFS200A	3JM-046101-on
1991 YFS200B	3JM-091101-on
1992 YFS200D	3JM-113101-on
1993 YFS200E	3JM-142101-on
1994 YFS200F	3JM-160101-on
1995 YFS200G	3JM-179101-on
1996 YFS200H	3JM-206101-on
1997 YFS200J	3JM-130101-on
1998 YFS200K	3JM-262637-on
1999 YFS200L	3JM-289187-on
2000 YFS200M	3JM-317393-on
2001 YFS200N	3JM-344326-on
2002 YFS200P	N/A

[1]Models sold in Maine and New Hampshire have different frame numbers. See a Yamaha dealer in one of these states for more information.

Table 2 GENERAL DIMENSIONS

	mm	in.
Overall length		
1988-1989	1,695	66.7
1990-on	1,735	68.3
Overall width	1,035	40.7
Overall height	1,040	40.9
Seat height	740	29.1
Minimum ground clearance	120	4.72
Wheelbase	1,100	43.3

Table 3 WEIGHT SPECIFICATIONS

	kg	lb.
Vehicle weight with oil and full tank of fuel		
1988-1989	150	331
1990-on	153	337

Table 4 CONVERSION TABLES

Multiply:	By:	To get the equivalent of:
Length		
Inches	25.4	Millimeter
Inches	2.54	Centimeter
Miles	1.609	Kilometer
Feet	0.3048	Meter
Millimeter	0.03937	Inches
Centimeter	0.3937	Inches
Kilometer	0.6214	Mile
Meter	3.281	Mile
Fluid volume		
U.S. quarts	0.9463	Liters
U.S. gallons	3.785	Liters
U.S. ounces	29.573529	Milliliters

(continued)

Table 4 CONVERSION TABLES (continued)

Multiply:	By:	To get the equivalent of:
Imperial gallons	4.54609	Liters
Imperial quarts	1.1365	Liters
Liters	0.2641721	U.S. gallons
Liters	1.0566882	U.S. quarts
Liters	33.814023	U.S. ounces
Liters	0.22	Imperial gallons
Liters	0.8799	Imperial quarts
Milliliters	0.033814	U.S. ounces
Milliliters	1.0	Cubic centimeters
Milliliters	0.001	Liters
Torque		
Foot-pounds	1.3558	Newton-meters
Foot-pounds	0.138255	Meters-kilograms
Inch-pounds	0.11299	Newton-meters
Newton-meters	0.7375622	Foot-pounds
Newton-meters	8.8507	Inch-pounds
Meters-kilograms	7.2330139	Foot-pounds
Volume		
Cubic inches	16.387064	Cubic centimeters
Cubic centimeters	0.0610237	Cubic inches
Temperature		
Fahrenheit	$(F - 32°) \times 0.556$	Centigrade
Centigrade	$(C \times 1.8) + 32$	Fahrenheit
Weight		
Ounces	28.3495	Grams
Pounds	0.4535924	Kilograms
Grams	0.035274	Ounces
Kilograms	2.2046224	Pounds
Pressure		
Pounds per square inch	0.070307	Kilograms per square centimeter
Kilograms per square centimeter	14.223343	Pounds per square inch
Kilopascals	0.1450	Pounds per square inch
Pounds per square inch	6.895	Kilopascals
Speed		
Miles per hour	1.609344	Kilometers per hour
Kilometers per hour	0.6213712	Miles per hour

Table 5 GENERAL TORQUE SPECIFICATIONS

Thread diameter	N•m	ft.-lb.
5 mm	3.4-4.9	30-43 in.-lb.
6 mm	5.9-7.8	52-69 in.-lb.
8 mm	14-19	10.0-13.5
10 mm	25-39	19-25
12 mm	44-61	33-45
14 mm	73-98	54-72
16 mm	115-155	83-115
18 mm	165-225	125-165
20 mm	225-325	165-240

Table 6 TECHNICAL ABBREVIATIONS

ABDC	After bottom dead center
ATDC	After top dead center
BBDC	Before bottom dead center
BDC	Bottom dead center
BTDC	Before top dead center
C	Celsius (Centigrade)
cc	Cubic centimeters
CDI	Capacitor discharge ignition
cu. in.	Cubic inches
F	Fahrenheit
ft.-lb.	Foot-pounds
gal.	Gallons
H/A	High altitude
hp	Horsepower
in.	Inches
kg	Kilogram
kg/cm2	Kilograms per square centimeter
kgm	Kilogram meters
km	Kilometer
L	Liter
m	Meter
MAG	Magneto
ml	Milliliter
mm	Millimeter
N•m	Newton-meters
oz.	Ounce
psi	Pounds per square inch
PTO	Power take off
pt.	Pint
qt.	Quart
rpm	Revolutions per minute

Table 7 METRIC TAP DRILL SIZES

Metric (mm)	Drill size	Decimal equivalent	Nearest fraction
3 × 0.50	No. 39	0.0995	3/32
3 × 0.60	3/32	0.0937	3/32
4 × 0.70	No. 30	0.1285	1/8
4 × 0.75	1/8	0.125	1/8
5 × 0.80	No. 19	0.166	11/64
5 × 0.90	No. 20	0.161	5/32
6 × 1.00	No. 9	0.196	13/64
7 × 1.00	16/64	0.234	15/64
8 × 1.00	J	0.277	9/32
8 × 1.25	17/64	0.265	17/64
9 × 1.00	5/16	0.3125	5/16
9 × 1.25	5/16	0.3125	5/16
10 × 1.25	11/32	0.3437	11/32
10 × 1.50	R	0.339	11/32
11 × 1.50	3/8	0.375	3/8
12 × 1.50	13/32	0.406	13/32
12 × 1.75	13/32	0.406	13/32

Table 8 DECIMAL AND METRIC EQUIVALENTS

Fractions	Decimal in.	Metric mm	Fractions	Decimal in.	Metric mm
1/64	0.015625	0.39688	33/64	0.515625	13.09687
1/32	0.03125	0.79375	17/32	0.53125	13.49375
3/64	0.046875	1.19062	35/64	0.546875	13.89062
1/16	0.0625	1.58750	9/16	0.5625	14.28750
5/64	0.078125	1.98437	37/64	0.578125	14.68437
3/32	0.09375	2.38125	19/32	0.59375	15.08125
7/64	0.109375	2.77812	39/64	0.609375	15.47812
1/8	0.125	3.1750	5/8	0.625	15.87500
9/64	0.140625	3.57187	41/64	0.640625	16.27187
5/32	0.15625	3.96875	21/32	0.65625	16.66875
11/64	0.171875	4.36562	43/64	0.671875	17.06562
3/16	0.1875	4.76250	11/16	0.6875	17.46250
13/64	0.203125	5.15937	45/64	0.703125	17.85937
7/32	0.21875	5.55625	23/32	0.71875	18.25625
15/64	0.234375	5.95312	47/64	0.734375	18.65312
1/4	0.250	6.35000	3/4	0.750	19.05000
17/64	0.265625	6.74687	49/64	0.765625	19.44687
9/32	0.28125	7.14375	25/32	0.78125	19.84375
19/64	0.296875	7.54062	51/64	0.796875	20.24062
5/16	0.3125	7.93750	13/16	0.8125	20.63750
21/64	0.328125	8.33437	53/64	0.828125	21.03437
11/32	0.34375	8.73125	27/32	0.84375	21.43125
23/64	0.359375	9.12812	55/64	0.859375	22.82812
3/8	0.375	9.52500	7/8	0.875	22.22500
25/64	0.390625	9.92187	57/64	0.890625	22.62187
13/32	0.40625	10.31875	29/32	0.90625	23.01875
27/64	0.421875	10.71562	59/64	0.921875	23.41562
7/16	0.4375	11.11250	15/16	0.9375	23.81250
29/64	0.453125	11.50937	61/64	0.953125	24.20937
15/32	0.46875	11.90625	31/32	0.96875	24.60625
31/64	0.484375	12.30312	63/64	0.984375	25.00312
1/2	0.500	12.70000	1	1.00	25.40000

1

CHAPTER TWO

TROUBLESHOOTING

Diagnosing a mechanical or electrical problem is relatively simple if you use an orderly procedure and keep a few basic principles in mind. The first step in a troubleshooting process is to define the symptoms as closely as possible and then localize the problem. Subsequent steps involve testing and analyzing those areas which could cause the symptoms. A haphazard approach may eventually solve the problem, but it can be very costly in terms of wasted time and unnecessary parts replacement.

Proper lubrication, maintenance and periodic tune-ups as described in Chapter Three will reduce the necessity for troubleshooting. However, even with the best of care, all vehicles are prone to problems which will require troubleshooting.

Never assume anything. Check all switches and electrical connections. If the engine will not start, is the engine stop switch malfunctioning? Is the engine flooded with fuel?

If the engine suddenly quits, what sound did it make? Consider this and check the easiest, most accessible problem first. If the engine sounded like it ran out of fuel, check to see if there is fuel in the tank. If there is fuel in the tank, is it reaching the carburetor? If not, the fuel tank vent hose may be plugged, preventing fuel from flowing from the fuel tank to carburetor.

If nothing obvious turns up in a quick check, look a little further. Learning to recognize and describe symptoms will make repairs easier for you or a mechanic at the shop. Describe problems accurately and fully.

Gather as many symptoms as possible to aid in diagnosis. Note whether the engine lost power gradually or all at once, what color smoke (if any) came from the exhaust and so on.

After the symptoms are defined, areas which could cause the problem can be tested and analyzed.

Guessing at the cause of a problem may provide the solution, but it usually leads to frustration, wasted time and a series of expensive, unnecessary parts replacements.

You do not need expensive equipment or complicated test gear to determine whether you should attempt the repair at home. A few simple checks could save a large repair bill and lost time while your vehicle sits in a dealer's service department. On the other hand, be realistic and attempt repairs that are within your abilities and shop experience. Service departments tend to charge heavily for putting together an engine that someone else has disassembled or damaged. Some will not take on such a job, so use common sense and do not get in over your head.

OPERATING REQUIREMENTS

An engine needs 3 basics to run properly: correct fuel/air mixture, sufficient compression and a spark at the right time (**Figure 1**). The engine can not run if one basic requirement is missing. Two-stroke en-

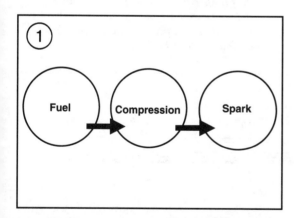

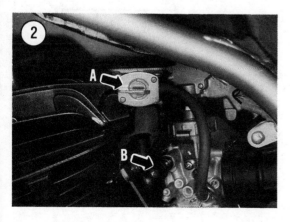

gine operation is described in Chapter Four under *Engine Operating Principles*.

If the vehicle has been sitting for any length of time and refuses to start, check and clean the spark plug. If the plug tip is clean, inspect the fuel delivery system. This includes the fuel tank, fuel shutoff valve, in-line fuel filter (if used) and fuel line. Gasoline deposits may have gummed up the carburetor's fuel inlet needle, jets and small air passages. Gasoline tends to lose its potency after standing for long periods. Condensation may also contaminate it with water. Drain the old gasoline and try starting with a fresh mixture.

STARTING THE ENGINE

If your engine refuses to start, frustration can cause you to forget basic starting principles and procedures. The following outline will guide you through basic starting procedures. In all cases, make sure that there is an adequate supply of gasoline in the fuel tank and that the oil tank is full of oil.

> *NOTE*
> *In the following sections, the choke is considered CLOSED when its knob is pushed all the way into the carburetor. The choke is considered OPEN when its knob is pulled all the way out of the carburetor.*

Starting a Cold Engine

> *WARNING*
> *Before starting the engine in freezing weather, make sure the throttle cable and carburetor throttle valve (slide) moves freely. Operating the vehicle with a sluggish or tight throttle cable can cause you to lose control.*

1. Shift the transmission into NEUTRAL.
2. Turn the fuel valve (A, **Figure 2**) ON.
3. Turn the main switch to ON.
4. Turn the engine stop switch to RUN.
5. Pull the choke knob (B, **Figure 2**) out to the detent position that matches the ambient temperature range shown in **Figure 3**.
6. With the throttle completely CLOSED, crank the engine.

7. When the engine starts, position the choke lever as follows:

    a. If the choke knob is pulled all the way out, push it into its second position to warm the engine.

    b. If the choke knob is originally set at its second position, leave it at this position to warm the engine.

    c. Work the throttle slightly to keep the engine running.

8. Idle the engine until the throttle responds cleanly and the choke can be closed.

Starting a Warm or Hot Engine

1. Shift the transmission into NEUTRAL.

2. Turn the fuel valve (A, **Figure 2**) ON.

3. Turn the main switch to ON.

4. Turn the engine stop switch to RUN.

5. Make sure the choke is closed. The choke knob (B, **Figure 2**) should be pushed all the way in. See **Figure 3**.

6. Open the throttle slightly and crank the engine.

Starting a Flooded Engine

If the engine is hard to start and there is a strong gasoline smell, the engine may be flooded. If so, close the choke and open the throttle all the way, then kick the engine over until it starts. Depending on how badly the engine is flooded, it will generally start after a few kicks. If the engine is flooded badly, you may have to remove and dry off the spark plug, or install a new one before the engine will run. When the engine first starts to run, it will cough and run slowly, and then when the excess fuel is burned, the engine will accelerate quickly to a high speed. Release the throttle lever at this point and work it slowly to make sure the engine is running cleanly. Because of the overly rich condition, the engine will smoke badly when it first starts to run. Thus you should always start a flooded engine outside and with its silencer pointing away from all objects. Do not start a flooded engine in your garage or workshop.

NOTE
If the engine refuses to start, check the carburetor overflow hose attached to the fitting at the bottom of the float bowl. If fuel is running out of the hose, the float valve is stuck open, allowing the carburetor to overfill.

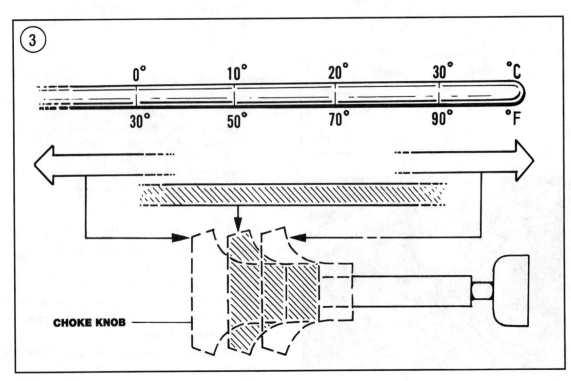

STARTING DIFFICULTIES

If the engine turns over but is difficult to start, or will not start at all, it does not help to wear out your leg on the kick starter. Check for obvious problems even before getting out your tools. Go down the following list step by step. Do each one while remembering the 3 engine operating requirements described under *Operating Requirements* earlier in this chapter.

1. Make sure the choke (B, **Figure 2**) is in the correct position. Pull the choke knob OUT for a cold engine and push it IN for a warm or hot engine (**Figure 3**).

2. Make sure there is fuel in the tank. Remove the filler cap and rock the vehicle from side-to-side. Listen for fuel sloshing around. Make sure the fuel is in good condition. If in doubt, drain the fuel and fill with a fresh tankful. Check for a clogged fuel tank vent tube (**Figure 4**). Remove the tube from the filler cap, wipe off one end and blow through it. Remove the filler cap and check its air vent passage for any obstructions.

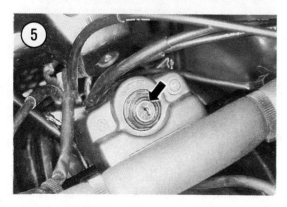

WARNING
Using an open flame to check the fuel level in the tank will cause a serious explosion.

3. Pull off the fuel line at the carburetor and insert the end of the hose into a clear container. Turn the fuel valve (A, **Figure 2**) ON and check fuel flow through the hose. If the hose is plugged, remove the hose and fuel filter (if equipped), then turn the fuel valve on again. If fuel flows, the hose or filter is clogged; clean the fuel hose or replace the clogged fuel filter. If there is no fuel flow through the valve, the valve is blocked by foreign matter, or the fuel cap vent may be plugged.

4. If you suspect that the cylinder is flooded, or there is a strong smell of gasoline, open the throttle all the way and kick the engine over several times. If the cylinder is severely flooded (fouled or wet spark plug), remove the plug and dry the base and electrode thoroughly with a soft cloth. Reinstall the plug and attempt to start the engine.

5. Check the carburetor overflow hose on the bottom of the float bowl. If fuel is running out of the hose, the float is stuck open. Turn the fuel valve OFF and tap the carburetor a few times to help break any sediment loose and allow the fuel valve to close. Check again by turning the fuel valve back on. If fuel continues to run from the overflow hose, remove and service the carburetor as described in Chapter Eight. Check the carburetor vent hoses to make sure they are clear. Check the end of each hose for contamination.

NOTE
If fuel is reaching the carburetor, the fuel system could still be the problem. The pilot jet could be clogged or the air filter could be severely restricted. A good sign of a plugged pilot jet is the choke must be opened to start a warm or hot engine. Opening the choke enrichens the fuel mixture and thus compensates for the fuel that is not passing through the plugged pilot jet.

NOTE
Before removing the carburetor, continue with Step 6 to make sure that the vehicle has an adequate spark.

6. Make sure the main switch (**Figure 5**) and the engine stop switch (**Figure 6**) are working properly.

Test the switches as described under *Switches* in Chapter Nine.

7. Make sure the spark plug wire (**Figure 7**) is on tight. Push it on and slightly rotate it to clean the electrical connection between the plug and the connector. Check also that the plug cap is installed tightly onto the secondary lead.

8. Perform a spark test as described under *Engine Fails to Start (Spark Test)* in this chapter. If there is a strong spark, perform Step 9. If there is no spark, or if the spark is very weak, test the ignition system as described in this chapter.

> *NOTE*
> *The ignition system is equipped with a throttle override system (T.O.R.S.). This system disables the ignition system if the throttle cable is stuck open or damaged. If there is no spark, check the T.O.R.S. system as described under **Ignition System Troubleshooting** in this chapter.*

9. Check cylinder compression as follows:
   a. Turn the main switch to OFF and the engine stop switch to STOP.
   b. Turn the fuel valve OFF.
   c. Remove and ground the spark plug shell against the cylinder head.
   d. Put your finger tightly over the spark plug hole.
   e. Operate the kickstarter. As the piston comes up on the compression stroke, rising pressure in the cylinder will force your finger off of the spark plug hole. This indicates that the cylinder probably has sufficient cylinder compression to start the engine.

> *NOTE*
> *Engine compression can be checked more accurately with a compression gauge as described under **Tune-up** in Chapter Three.*

> *NOTE*
> *If the cylinder compression is sufficient, the engine may be suffering from a loss of crankcase pressure. During 2-stroke operation, the air/fuel mixture is compressed twice, first in the crankcase and then in the combustion chamber. Crankcase pressure forces the air/fuel mixture to flow from the crankcase*

*chamber through the transfer ports and into the combustion chamber. Before continuing, perform the **2-Stroke Crankcase Pressure Test** described in this chapter.*

Engine Fails to Start (Spark Test)

Perform the following spark test to determine if the ignition system is operating properly.

> *CAUTION*
> *Before removing the spark plug in Step 1, clean all dirt and debris away from the plug base. Dirt that falls into the cylinder will cause rapid piston, ring and cylinder wear.*

1. Disconnect the plug wire (**Figure 7**) and remove the spark plug.

> *NOTE*
> *A spark tester is a useful tool to check the ignition system. **Figure 8** shows the Motion Pro Ignition System Tester. This*

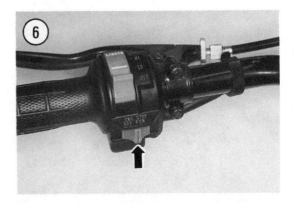

tool is inserted in the spark plug cap and its base is ground against the cylinder head. The tool's air gap is adjustable, and it allows you to see and hear the spark while testing the intensity of the spark. This tool is available through most motorcycle dealerships.

2. If using an adjustable spark tester, set its air gap to 6 mm (0.24 in.).

3. Insert the spark plug (or spark tester) into the plug cap and touch its base against the cylinder head to ground it (**Figure 8**). Position the plug so you can see the electrodes.

> ### CAUTION
> *Mount the spark plug or spark tester away from the plug hole in the cylinder head so the spark from the plug or tester cannot ignite the gasoline vapor in the cylinder.*

4. Crank the engine with the kickstarter. A fat blue spark should be evident across the spark plug electrodes or spark tester terminals.

> ### WARNING
> *Do not hold or touch the spark plug (or spark checker), wire or connector when making a spark check. A serious electrical shock may result.*

5. If the spark is good, check for one or more of the following possible malfunctions:
   a. Obstructed fuel line or fuel filter.
   b. Low compression or engine damage.
   c. Flooded engine.

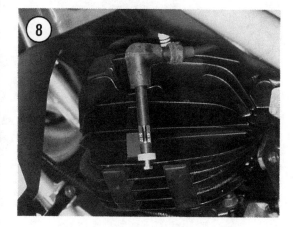

6. If the spark is weak (white or yellow in color) or if there is no spark, check for one or more of the following conditions:
   a. Fouled or wet spark plug. Repeat the spark test with a new spark plug.
   b. Loose or damaged spark plug cap connection. Hold the secondary wire and turn the spark plug cap to tighten it. Then install the spark plug into the cap and repeat the spark test.
   c. Loose or damaged high tension wiring connections (at coil and plug cap).
   d. Faulty ignition coil or faulty ignition coil ground wire connection.
   e. Faulty CDI unit or stator coil(s).
   f. Sheared flywheel key.
   g. Loose flywheel nut.

> ### NOTE
> *If the engine backfires when you are attempting to start it, the ignition timing may be incorrect. Incorrect ignition timing can be caused by a loose flywheel, loose stator plate mounting screws or a faulty ignition component.*

   h. Loose electrical connections.
   i. Dirty electrical connections.

Engine is Difficult to Start

If the vehicle has spark, compression and fuel, but it is difficult to start, check for one or more of the following possible malfunctions:
1. Incorrect air/fuel mixture:
   a. Clogged air filter element.
   b. Incorrect carburetor adjustment.
   c. Clogged pilot jet.
   d. Clogged air passage.
2. Engine flooded:
   a. Incorrect starting procedure.
   b. Incorrect fuel level (too high).
   c. Worn carburetor fuel valve and seat assembly.
   d. Fuel valve stuck open.
   e. Damaged float.
3. No fuel flow:
   a. Clogged fuel line.
   b. Clogged fuel filter (if used).
   c. Clogged fuel valve.
   d. Clogged or restricted fuel valve.
   e. Clogged fuel tank cap vent hose (**Figure 4**).
   f. Fuel valve turned off.

g. Fuel tank empty.

4. Weak spark:
   a. Fouled or wet spark plug.
   b. Loose or damaged spark plug cap connection.
   c. Loose or damaged secondary lead connection at spark plug cap or coil.
   d. Faulty ignition coil.
   e. Faulty CDI unit.
   f. Faulty stator plate coils.
   g. Sheared flywheel key.
   h. Loose flywheel nut.
   i. Loose electrical connections.
   j. Dirty electrical connections.

5. Low engine compression:
   a. Loose spark plug or missing spark plug gasket.
   b. Stuck piston ring.
   c. Excessive piston ring wear.
   d. Excessively worn piston and/or cylinder.
   e. Loose cylinder head fasteners.
   f. Cylinder head incorrectly installed and/or torqued down.
   g. Warped cylinder head.
   h. Blown head gasket.
   i. Blown base gasket.
   j. Loose cylinder base nuts.
   k. Broken or damaged reed valve(s) assembly.

Engine Will Not Turn Over

If a mechanical problem prevents the engine from being cranked, check for one or more of the following possible conditions:

NOTE
*After referring to the following list, refer to **Drive Train Noise** in this chapter for additional information.*

a. Defective kickstarter and/or gear.
b. Broken kick shaft return spring.
c. Damaged kickstarter ratchet gear.
d. Seized or damaged idler gear.
e. Seized piston.
f. Broken piston skirt (pieces of the piston are wedged between the crankshaft and crankcase). Look at the bottom of the crankcase, directly underneath the crankshaft, for cracks or other damage.
g. Seized crankshaft bearings.

h. Seized connecting rod small end bearing.
i. Seized connecting rod big end bearing.
j. Broken connecting rod.
k. Seized primary drive gear/clutch assembly.

ENGINE PERFORMANCE

This section describes conditions where the engine is running but at a reduced performance level. This will serve as a starting point from which to isolate the problem. To help isolate the problem area quickly, perform the *2-Stroke Leak Down Test* described in this chapter.

Engine Will Not Idle or the Throttle Sticks Open

NOTE
A stuck or damaged throttle cable or carburetor throttle valve will cause the T.O.R.S. system to disable the ignition system.

a. Damaged throttle cable.
b. Damaged throttle lever.
c. Incorrect throttle cable routing.
d. Dirt is trapped between the carburetor throttle valve and bore.
e. Excessively worn carburetor throttle valve and/or bore.

Engine Will Not Idle

Poor idle speed performance is usually traced to a carburetor problem. If the engine wil not idle as described in Chapter Three, check the following:

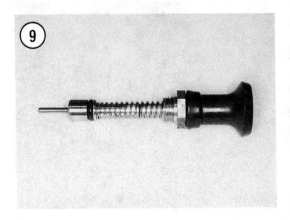

a. Stuck or damaged choke assembly (**Figure 9**).
b. Incorrect carburetor adjustment.
c. Loose or clogged pilot jet.

NOTE
If the engine starts with the choke on but misfires or dies when the choke is closed, or will idle only if the choke is on, check for a plugged pilot jet.

d. Obstructed fuel line or fuel shutoff valve.
e. Fouled or improperly gapped spark plug.
f. Leaking head gasket.
g. Loose carburetor hose clamps.

Poor Low-Speed Performance

Check for one or more of the following possible malfunctions:
1. Incorrect air/fuel mixture:
   a. Clogged air filter element.
   b. Incorrect carburetor adjustment.
   c. Clogged pilot jet.
   d. Clogged air passage.
   e. Loose or cracked air box boot.
   f. Loose carburetor hose clamps.
   g. Clogged fuel tank cap vent hose (**Figure 4**).
   h. Carburetor choke stuck open.
   i. Incorrect fuel level (too high or too low).
2. Weak spark:
   a. Fouled or wet spark plug.
   b. Incorrect spark plug heat range.
   c. Loose or damaged spark plug cap connection.
   d. Loose or damaged secondary coil wire at coil or plug cap.
   e. Faulty ignition coil.
   f. Faulty CDI unit.
   g. Faulty stator coils.
   h. Loose electrical connections.
   i. Dirty electrical connections.
   j. Incorrect ignition timing.
3. Low engine compression:
   a. Loose spark plug or missing spark plug gasket.
   b. Stuck piston ring.
   c. Excessive piston ring wear.
   d. Excessively worn piston and/or cylinder.
   e. Loose cylinder head fasteners.
   f. Cylinder head incorrectly installed and/or torqued down.
   g. Warped cylinder head.

h. Damaged cylinder head gasket.
i. Blown base gasket.
j. Loose cylinder base nuts.
4. Excessively worn, cracked or broken reed valves.
5. Dragging brakes. Refer to *Brakes* in this chapter for additional information.

Poor High-Speed Performance

Check for one or more of the following possible malfunctions:
1. Incorrect air/fuel mixture:
   a. Clogged air filter element.
   b. Clogged carburetor air vent tubes.
   c. Incorrect jet needle clip position.
   d. Incorrect main jet.
   e. Clogged main jet.
   f. Worn jet needle and/or needle jet.
   g. Clogged air jet or air passage.
   h. Loose or cracked air box boot.
   i. Loose carburetor hose clamps.
   j. Clogged fuel tank cap vent hose (**Figure 4**).
   k. Worn fuel valve and seat.
   l. Incorrect fuel level (too high or too low).
   m. Clogged fuel line.
   n. Clogged fuel filter.
   o. Clogged fuel valve.
   p. Fuel contaminated with water.
2. If the engine speed drops off or cuts out abruptly:
   a. Clogged air filter element.
   b. Restricted silencer.
   c. Clogged exhaust system.
   d. Clutch slippage.
   e. Clogged main jet.
   f. Incorrect fuel level (too high or too low).
   g. Choke valve partially stuck.
   h. Throttle valve does not open all the way.
   i. Dragging brakes.
   j. Engine overheating.
   k. Fuel contaminated with water.
3. Low engine compression:
   a. Loose spark plug or missing spark plug gasket.
   b. Stuck piston ring.
   c. Excessive piston ring wear.
   d. Excessively worn piston and/or cylinder.
   e. Loose cylinder head fasteners.
   f. Cylinder head incorrectly installed and/or torqued down.

g. Warped cylinder head.

h. Damaged cylinder head gasket.

i. Blown base gasket.

j. Loose cylinder base nuts.

k. Cracked or broken reed valves.

Engine Overheating

Check for one or more of the following possible malfunctions:.

1. Clogged, broken or missing cylinder head and cylinder cooling fins.

2. Overrunning the engine in sand.

3. Autolube oil injection pump system:

a. Air in oil hose or delivery line(s).

b. Oil tank empty.

c. Autolube injection pump, drive shaft or oil pump gear failure.

4. Other causes of engine overheating are:

a. Excessive carbon buildup in the combustion chamber.

b. Incorrect air/fuel mixture.

c. Clutch slippage.

d. Brake drag.

e. Transmission oil level too high.

Black Exhaust and Engine Runs Roughly

a. Clogged air filter element.

b. Carburetor adjustment incorrect—mixture too rich.

c. Carburetor floats damaged or incorrectly adjusted.

d. Choke not operating correctly.

e. Water or other contaminants in fuel.

f. Excessive piston-to-cylinder clearance.

Engine Loses Power

a. Incorrect carburetor adjustment.

b. Engine overheating.

c. Ignition timing incorrect.

d. Incorrectly gapped spark plug.

e. Cracked or broken reed valve.

f. Obstructed silencer.

g. Dragging brake.

Engine Lacks Acceleration

a. Incorrect carburetor adjustment.

b. Clogged fuel line.

c. Ignition timing incorrect.

d. Cracked or broken reed valve.

e. Dragging brake.

ENGINE

Engine problems are generally symptoms of something wrong in another system, such as ignition, fuel or starting.

Preignition

Preignition is the premature burning of fuel and is caused by hot spots in the combustion chamber. The fuel actually ignites before it is supposed to. Glowing deposits in the combustion chamber, inadequate cooling or an overheated spark plug can all cause preignition. This is first noticed in the form of a power loss but will eventually result in extensive damage to the internal parts of the engine because of higher combustion chamber pressure and temperatures.

Detonation

Commonly called spark knock or fuel knock, detonation is the violent explosion of fuel in the combustion chamber instead of the controlled burn that occurs during normal combustion. Severe damage can result. Use of low octane gasoline is a common cause of detonation.

Other causes are over-advanced ignition timing, lean fuel mixture at or near full throttle, inadequate engine cooling, or the excessive accumulation of deposits on the piston and combustion chamber.

Power Loss

Several factors can cause a lack of power and speed. Look for a clogged air filter or a fouled or damaged spark plug. A piston or cylinder that is galling, incorrect piston clearance or worn or sticky piston rings may be responsible. Look for loose bolts, defective gaskets or leaking machined mating surfaces on the cylinder head, cylinder or crankcase.

Also check the crankshaft seals; refer to *2-Stroke Leak Down Test* in this chapter.

Piston Seizure

This is caused by incorrect bore clearance, piston rings with an improper end gap, compression leak, incorrect engine oil, spark plug of the wrong heat range, incorrect ignition timing or the use of an incorrect fuel/oil mixture. Overheating from any cause may result in piston seizure.

Piston Slap

Piston slap is an audible slapping or rattling noise resulting from excessive piston-to-cylinder clearance. When allowed to continue, piston slap will eventually cause the piston skirt to shatter. In some cases, a shattered piston will cause some form of secondary engine damage. This type of damage can be prevented by measuring the cylinder bore and piston diameter at specified intervals (see Chapter Three), and by close visual inspection of all top end components, checking each part for scuff marks, scoring, cracks and other signs of abnormal wear. Replace parts that exceed service limits or show damage.

ENGINE NOISES

1. *Knocking or pinging during acceleration*—Caused by using a lower octane fuel than recommended. May also be caused by poor quality fuel. Pinging can also be caused by a spark plug of the wrong heat range and incorrect carburetor jetting. Refer to *Correct Spark Plug Heat Range* in Chapter Three. Check also for excessive carbon buildup in the combustion chamber or a faulty CDI unit.
2. *Slapping or rattling noises at low speed or during acceleration*—May be caused by excessive piston-cylinder wall clearance. Check also for a bent connecting rod or worn piston pin and/or piston pin holes in the piston.
3. *Knocking or rapping while decelerating*—Usually caused by excessive rod bearing clearance.
4. *Persistent knocking and vibration or other noise*—Usually caused by worn main bearings. If the main bearings are good, consider the following:
   a. Loose engine mounts.
   b. Cracked frame.
   c. Leaking cylinder head gasket.
   d. Exhaust pipe leakage at cylinder head.
   e. Stuck piston ring.
   f. Broken piston ring.
   g. Partial engine seizure.
   h. Excessive small end connecting rod bearing clearance.
   i. Excessive big end connecting rod bearing clearance.
   j. Excessive crankshaft runout.
   k. Worn or damaged primary drive gear.
5. *Rapid on-off squeal*—Compression leak around cylinder head gasket or spark plug.

2-STROKE LEAK DOWN TEST

Many owners of 2-stroke vehicles are plagued by hard starting and generally poor running for which there seems to be no cause. Carburetion and ignition may be good, and compression tests may show that all is well in the engine's upper end.

However, the engine may still be suffering from a lack of primary compression. The crankcase in a 2-stroke engine is alternately under pressure and vacuum. After the piston closes the intake port, further downward movement of the piston causes the entrapped mixture to be pressurized so that it can rush quickly into the cylinder when the intake ports are opened. Upward piston movement creates a slight vacuum in the crankcase, enabling the air/fuel mixture to be drawn in from the carburetor.

If the crankcase seals or cylinder gaskets leak, the crankcase cannot hold pressure or vacuum, and proper engine operation becomes impossible. Any other source of leakage such as a defective cylinder base gasket or porous or cracked crankcase castings will result in the same condition. See **Figure 10**.

It is possible, however, to test for and isolate primary compression leaks. The test is simple but requires the use of a leak down tester like the one shown in **Figure 11**. To perform a leak down test, all of the natural engine openings are sealed off, then a small amount of air pressure is pumped into the engine. If the engine does not hold air, there is an air leak.

The following procedure describes how to perform a leak down test on the Blaster engine.
1. Remove the exhaust pipe (Chapter Four).
2. Remove the carburetor (Chapter Eight).

NOTE
Do not remove the intake manifold and reed valve from the cylinder. The manifold must remain on the engine during this test as it can be the source of the leak.

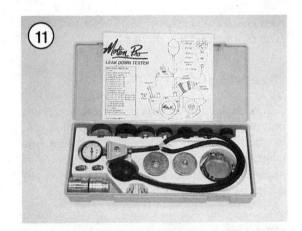

3. Remove the flywheel and stator plate (Chapter Nine) to access to the left side crankshaft seal (**Figure 12**).

4. Turn the crankshaft so the piston is at bottom dead center (BDC).

NOTE
To get an air tight seal in the exhaust port, the port must be fairly clean of all carbon residue and oil.

5. Plug the exhaust port with an expandable rubber plug (**Figure 13**). Tighten the plug securely.

6. Plug the intake manifold with a suitable adapter plug (A, **Figure 14**) and tighten the manifold's hose clamp.

7. Install the pressure gauge hose adapter (B, **Figure 14**) into the intake manifold plug fitting.

8. Squeeze the pressure gauge lever or bulb until the gauge (**Figure 15**) indicates 5-6 psi (35-41 kPa).

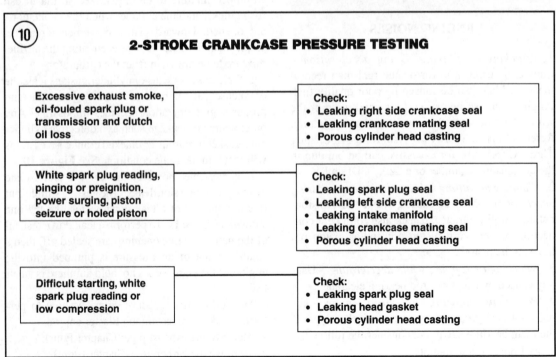

2-STROKE CRANKCASE PRESSURE TESTING

Excessive exhaust smoke, oil-fouled spark plug or transmission and clutch oil loss	Check: • Leaking right side crankcase seal • Leaking crankcase mating seal • Porous cylinder head casting
White spark plug reading, pinging or preignition, power surging, piston seizure or holed piston	Check: • Leaking spark plug seal • Leaking left side crankcase seal • Leaking intake manifold • Leaking crankcase mating seal • Porous cylinder head casting
Difficult starting, white spark plug reading or low compression	Check: • Leaking spark plug seal • Leaking head gasket • Porous cylinder head casting

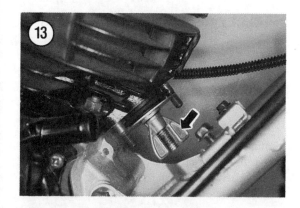

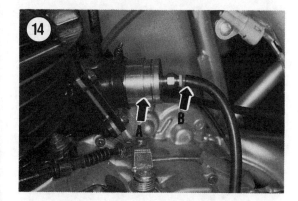

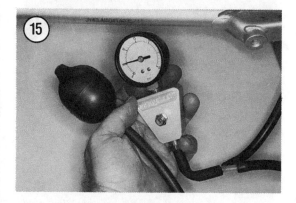

CAUTION
The engine does not require a lot of pressure during this test. Applying more than 8 psi (55 kPa), can force the crankcase seals to pop out of the crankcase.

9. Read the pressure gauge. A pressure drop of less than 1 psi (7 kPa) in 3-5 minutes indicates a properly sealed engine. A good rule of thumb is that an engine should hold 6 psi (41 kPa) for 5-6 minutes. Any immediate pressure loss or a pressure loss of 1 psi (7 kPa) in 1 minute indicates a serious sealing problem. Before condemning the engine, first make sure there are no leaks in the test equipment or sealing plugs. Check the equipment sealing points by spraying them with a soap and water solution (**Figure 16**). When all of the test equipment and its hose fittings are air tight, go over the entire engine carefully. If the pressure gauge shows a loss of pressure, spray all of the engine sealing points. When the solution bubbles up, you have found a leak at that spot. **Figure 17** shows an air leak between the cylinder and intake manifold gasket surfaces. Some possible leakage points are listed below:

   a. Left side crankcase seal (**Figure 12**).

   b. Right side crankshaft seal. To check this seal when the right crankcase cover is installed on the engine, pour some of the soap and water solution into the transmission breather tube (**Figure 18**) while the engine is pressurized. If the tube blows bubbles, the right side crankcase seal (**Figure 19**) is leaking. A leaking right side crankcase seal will allow oil to be drawn into the crankcase, causing excessive exhaust smoke and spark plug fouling. Con-

firm this seal's condition by removing the primary drive gear as described in Chapter Five, then repeat the test with the seal exposed. Spray some soap and water directly onto the seal and check for bubbles.

NOTE
Because the right side crankcase seal seals against the primary drive gear spacer, this spacer must be left in place during testing. Remove only the primary drive gear.

   c. Spark plug.
   d. Cylinder head joint.
   e. Intake manifold.
   f. Cylinder base joint.
   g. Crankcase joint.
   h. Porous crankcase, cylinder or cylinder head casting.

10. If a leak is detected, repair it or replace the damaged part. Repeat the test after reassembling the engine.

11. Remove the test equipment and reverse Steps 1 and 2 to complete engine assembly.

FUEL SYSTEM

Many riders automatically assume that the carburetor is at fault if the engine runs poorly. While fuel system problems do occur, carburetor adjustment is seldom the answer. In many cases, adjusting the carburetor only compounds the problem by making the engine run worse.

When troubleshooting the fuel system, start at the fuel tank and work through the system, reserving the carburetor as the final point. Most fuel system problems result from an empty fuel tank, a plugged fuel filter or fuel valve, or sour fuel. Fuel system troubleshooting is covered thoroughly under *Starting Difficulties* and *Engine Performance* in this chapter.

A malfunctioning carburetor choke can also cause engine starting and operating problems. Check the choke (B, **Figure 2**) by opening and closing it at the carburetor. The choke lever must move between its OFF and ON positions without binding or sticking in one position. If necessary, remove the choke (Chapter Eight) and inspect its plunger and spring (**Figure 9**) for excessive wear or damage.

ELECTRICAL TROUBLESHOOTING

This section describes the basics of electrical troubleshooting, how to use test equipment and the basic test procedures using the various pieces of test equipment.

Electrical troubleshooting can be very time-consuming and frustrating without proper knowledge and a suitable plan. Refer to the wiring diagrams at the end of the book and to the individual system diagrams included with the ignition system section

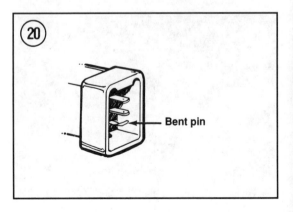
Bent pin

in this chapter. Wiring diagrams will help you determine how the circuit should work by tracing the current paths from the power source through the circuit components to ground.

As with all troubleshooting procedures, analyze typical symptoms in a systematic procedure. Never assume anything and never overlook the obvious like an electrical connector that has separated. Test the simplest and most obvious areas first.

Preliminary Checks and Precautions

Prior to starting any electrical troubleshooting procedure perform the following:

a. Disconnect each electrical connector in the suspect circuit and make sure there are no bent metal pins on the male side of the electrical connector (**Figure 20**). A bent pin will cause an open circuit.

b. Check each female end of the connector. Make sure that the metal connector on the end of each wire (**Figure 21**) is pushed all the way into the plastic connector. To check, carefully push them in with a narrow-blade screwdriver.

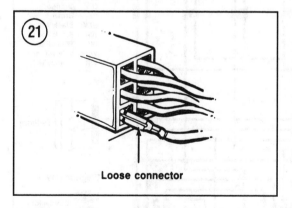

Loose connector

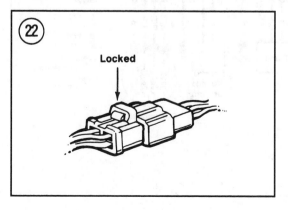

Locked

c. Check all electrical wires where they enter the individual metal connector in both the male and female plastic connector.

d. Make sure all electrical connectors within the connector are clean and free of corrosion. Clean, if necessary, and pack the connectors with dielectric grease.

e. After all is checked out, push the connectors together and make sure they are fully engaged and locked together (**Figure 22**).

f. Never pull on the electrical wires when disconnecting an electrical connector—pull only on the connector plastic housing.

Using a Test Lamp or Voltmeter

To check for battery voltage in a circuit, attach 1 lead to a good engine ground and the other lead to various points along the circuit. Where battery voltage is present the test lamp will light.

A voltmeter is used in the same manner as the test lamp to find out if battery voltage is present in any given circuit. The voltmeter, unlike the test lamp, will also indicate how much voltage is present at each test point. When using a voltmeter, attach the red lead (+) to the component or wire to be checked and the negative (−) lead to a good ground.

Self-powered Test Lamp and Ohmmeter

Use a self-powered test lamp as follows:

a. Touch the test leads together to make sure the light bulb goes on.

b. Select 2 points within the circuit where there should be continuity.

c. Attach 1 lead of the self-powered test lamp to each point.

d. If there is continuity, the self-powered test lamp will come on.

e. If there is no continuity, the self-powered test lamp will not light, indicating an open circuit.

An ohmmeter can be used in place of the self-powered test lamp. The ohmmeter, unlike the test light, will also indicate how much resistance is present between each test point. Low resistance means good continuity in a complete circuit. Before using an analog ohmmeter, it must first be calibrated. This is done by touching the leads together and turning the ohms calibration knob until the meter reads ZERO.

Voltage Testing

Unless otherwise specified, all voltage tests are made with the electrical connector still connected. Insert the test leads into the backside of the connector and make sure the test lead touches the electrical wire or metal connector within the connector. If the test lead only touches the wire insulation you will get a false reading.

Always check both sides of the connector as one side may be loose or corroded thus preventing current flow through the connector. This type of test can be performed with a test lamp or a voltmeter. An AC voltmeter will give the best results.

NOTE
If using a test lamp, it does not make any difference which test lead is attached to ground.

1. Attach the negative test lead (if using a voltmeter) to a good ground (bare metal). If necessary, scrape away paint from the frame or engine (retouch later with paint). Make sure the part used for ground is not insulated with a rubber gasket or rubber grommet.

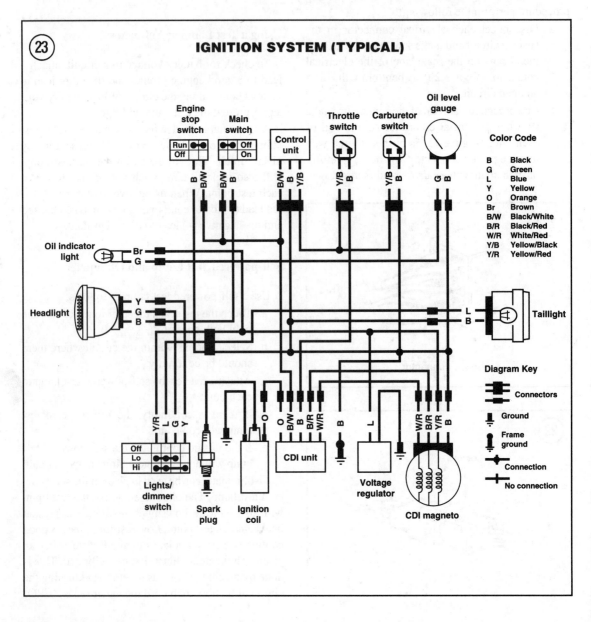

2. Attach the positive test lead (if using a voltmeter) to the point (electrical connector) you want to check.

3. Turn the ignition switch ON. If using a test lamp, the light will come on if voltage is present. If using a voltmeter, note the voltage reading. The reading should be within 1 volt of battery voltage (12 volts). If the voltage is 10 volts or less, there may be a problem in the circuit.

Continuity Test

A continuity test is used to determine the integrity of a particular circuit or component.

Insert the test leads into the backside of the connector and make sure the test lead touches the wire or metal connector within the connector. If the test lead only touches the wire insulation you will get a false reading.

Always check both sides of the connectors as 1 side may be loose or corroded thus preventing current flow through the connector. This type of test can be performed with a self-powered test lamp or an ohmmeter. An ohmmeter will give the best results. If using an ohmmeter, calibrate the meter by touching the leads together and turning the ohms calibration knob until the meter reads ZERO.

1. Attach one test lead (test lamp or ohmmeter) to 1 end of the circuit to be tested.

2. Attach the other test lead to the other end of the circuit to be tested.

3. The self-powered test lamp will come on if there is continuity. The ohmmeter will indicate either low or no resistance (means good continuity in a complete circuit) or infinite resistance (means an open circuit).

IGNITION SYSTEM

All models are equipped with a capacitor discharge ignition (CDI) system (**Figure 23**, typical). Problems with the CDI system are relatively few. However, if a problem occurs, it generally causes the ignition system to have a weak spark or no spark at all.

It is relatively easy to troubleshoot a weak or no spark condition. But, it is difficult to test an ignition system with an intermittent malfunction that only occurs when the engine is hot or under load.

Ignition System Troubleshooting

If there is no spark or if the spark is intermittent, perform the following steps in order.

NOTE
If the problem is intermittent, perform the tests with the engine cold, then hot.

1. Remove the seat (Chapter Fourteen).
2. Remove the fuel tank (Chapter Eight).
3. Disconnect the T.O.R.S. control unit (A, **Figure 24**) electrical connector. The connector has 3 wires: black/white, yellow/black and black. Start the engine and note the following:
   a. If the engine does not start, continue with Step 4.
   b. If the engine starts, go to the *Throttle Override System (T.O.R.S.) Troubleshooting* procedure in this chapter.
4. Perform the ignition spark gap test.

NOTE
*If you do not have an adjustable spark tester, perform the spark test as described under **Engine Fails to Start (Spark Test)** in this chapter.*

   a. Disconnect the plug wire.

NOTE
*A spark tester is a useful tool to check the ignition system. **Figure 8** shows the Motion Pro Ignition System Tester. This tool is inserted in the spark plug cap and its base is ground against the cylinder head. The tool's air gap is adjustable, and it allows you to see and hear the spark while testing the intensity of the spark.*

b. Set the spark tester air gap to 6 mm (0.24 in.).

c. Insert the spark tester into the plug cap and touch its base against the cylinder head to ground it (**Figure 8**). Position the tester so you can see its terminals.

CAUTION
If the spark plug is removed from the engine, mount the spark tester away from the plug hole in the cylinder head so the spark from the tester cannot ignite the gasoline vapor in the cylinder.

d. Crank the engine with the kickstarter. A fat blue spark should be evident across the spark tester terminals.

WARNING
Do not hold the spark tester or connector or a serious electrical shock may result.

e. If a dark blue spark jumps the gap, the ignition system is operating correctly. If the spark does not jump the gap, hold the spark plug cable and twist the plug cap a few times to tighten it. Then recheck the spark gap. If there is still no spark or if it jumps the gap but is yellow or white in color, continue with Step 5.

f. Remove the spark tester from the spark plug cap.

5. Unscrew the spark plug cap from the spark plug lead and hold the end of the wire 6 mm (0.24 in.) from the cylinder head. See **Figure 25**. Have an assistant crank the engine and note the spark plug wire. A crisp blue spark should be noted. If a good spark is noted, the spark plug cap is probably faulty. Test the spark plug cap resistance as described in Chapter Nine.

6. If a weak or no spark is noted in Step 5, test the following components in the sequence provided. The test procedures are described in Chapter Nine.

a. Main switch.

b. Engine stop switch.

c. Ignition coil primary and secondary winding resistance.

d. Source coil (under *Stator Coil Testing* in Chapter Nine).

e. Pickup coil (under *Stator Coil Testing* in Chapter Nine).

7. If all ignition components are in acceptable condition, carefully inspect the ignition wiring harness

for damaged wiring or loose, dirty or damaged connections (especially grounds). If the wiring harness and all connectors are in acceptable condition, the CDI unit (B, **Figure 24**) is faulty.

NOTE
The CDI unit cannot be effectively tested. But, if all other ignition components, wiring and connections are good, consider the CDI unit to be defective by a process of elimination.

Throttle Override System (T.O.R.S.) Troubleshooting

The throttle override circuit of the ignition system consists of the T.O.R.S. control unit (A, **Figure 24**), carburetor switch (**Figure 26**) and throttle lever switch (**Figure 27**). An incorrectly adjusted or faulty T.O.R.S. system will prevent the ignition system from operating.

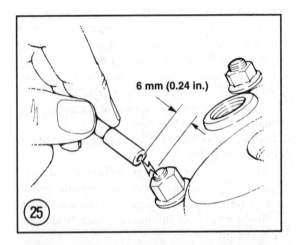

6 mm (0.24 in.)

25

26

Before troubleshooting the T.O.R.S. system, perform the *Ignition System Troubleshooting* procedure in this chapter to determine if the T.O.R.S. system is inoperative. If there is no spark with the T.O.R.S. control unit (A, **Figure 24**) connected, but normal spark with it disconnected, perform the following steps to isolate the faulty T.O.R.S. component(s).

NOTE
Before checking the throttle cable free play in Step 1, make sure the throttle cable is in good condition. A damaged or malfunctioning throttle cable can activate the T.O.R.S. system and cause it to disable the ignition system.

1. Check the throttle cable free play as described under *Throttle Cable Adjustment* in Chapter Three.

a. If the cable free play is incorrect, adjust it, then try to start the engine. If there is still no spark, continue with Step 2.

b. If the cable free play is correct, continue with Step 2.

2. Test the throttle lever switch as described under *Switches* in Chapter Nine.

a. If the throttle lever switch tests good, perform Step 3.

b. If the throttle lever switch fails to pass the tests described in Chapter Nine, the throttle lever switch is faulty. Replace the throttle lever switch and retest the ignition system.

3. Test the carburetor switch as described under *Switches* in Chapter Nine.

a. If the carburetor switch tests good, perform Step 4.

b. If the carburetor lever switch fails to pass the tests described in Chapter Nine, the carburetor switch is faulty. Replace the carburetor switch and retest the ignition system.

4. If you have not been able to locate the damaged component, check the T.O.R.S. system wiring harness and connectors. Check for damaged wires or loose, dirty or damaged connectors. If the wiring and connectors are in good condition, the T.O.R.S. control unit (A, **Figure 24**) is faulty and must be replaced.

CLUTCH

The most common clutch problems are clutch slip (clutch does not engage fully) and clutch drag (clutch does not disengage fully).

The main cause of clutch slip or drag is incorrect clutch adjustment or a rough operating clutch lever or clutch push lever (**Figure 28**) at the engine. Before removing the clutch for inspection, perform the following checks:

1. With the engine turned OFF and the transmission in NEUTRAL, pull and release the clutch lever. If the clutch lever is hard to pull or its movement is rough, check for the following:

a. Damaged clutch cable.

b. Incorrect clutch cable routing.

c. Dry clutch cable.

d. Damaged clutch lever and perch assembly at the handlebar.

e. Damaged clutch push lever (**Figure 28**) at the engine.

2. If the items in Step 1 are good, and the clutch lever moves without any excessive roughness or binding, check the clutch adjustment as described in Chapter Three. Note the following:
   a. If the clutch cannot be adjusted within the limits specified in Chapter Three, check for a stretched or damaged clutch cable.
   b. If the clutch cable is good, the friction plates may be excessively worn.
3. If you have not found the problem, refer to the *Clutch Slipping* or *Clutch Dragging* procedure that follows in this section.

Clutch Slipping

If the clutch slips, the engine accelerates faster than what the actual forward speed indicates. Because the clutch plates are spinning against each other and not engaging, an excessive amount of heat builds in the clutch. This heat causes rapid and severe clutch plate wear and warpage and clutch spring fatigue.

If the clutch slips, check for one or more of the following possible malfunctions.
1. Clutch wear or damage:
   a. Incorrect clutch adjustment.
   b. Weak or damaged clutch springs.
   c. Loose clutch springs.
   d. Worn friction plates.
   e. Warped steel plates.
   f. Incorrectly assembled clutch.
2. Clutch/Transmission oil:
   a. Low oil level.
   b. Oil additives.
   c. Low viscosity oil.

Clutch Dragging

Clutch drag occurs when the clutch does not slip enough. When in gear and releasing the clutch, the vehicle will jerk or jump forward. Once underway, shifting becomes difficult. If this condition is not repaired, transmission gear and shift fork wear and damage will occur from the grinding of the transmission gears.

If the clutch drags, check for one or more of the following possible malfunctions.
1. Clutch wear or damage:
   a. Incorrect clutch adjustment.

b. Incorrect push lever (**Figure 28**) installed position.
c. Incorrect push lever and pushrod engagement.
d. Warped steel plates.
e. Swollen friction plates.
f. Warped pressure plate.
g. Incorrect clutch spring tension.
h. Incorrectly assembled clutch.
i. Loose clutch nut.
j. Burnt primary driven gear bushing.
k. Notched clutch boss splines.
l. Notched clutch housing grooves.
m. Damaged clutch pushrod and ball assembly.
2. Clutch/transmission oil:
a. Oil level too high.
b. High viscosity oil.

TRANSMISSION

The YFS200 engine is equipped with a 6-speed constant mesh transmission. Some transmission symptoms are hard to distinguish from clutch symptoms. For example, if the gears grind during shifting, the problem may be caused by a dragging clutch. However, if the clutch drag problem is not repaired, transmission damage will eventually occur. An incorrectly adjusted or damaged external shift mechanism assembly will also cause shifting problems. Always investigate the easiest and most accessible areas first. To prevent an incorrect diagnosis, perform the following inspection procedure to troubleshoot the external shift mechanism and transmission. At the same time, refer to the troubleshooting chart in **Figure 29** for a list of common transmission symptoms and possible causes.

> *NOTE*
> *When trying to shift a constant mesh transmission, one of the transmission shafts must be turning. An easy way to do this is to have an assistant turn the rear wheels (with the drive chain installed) while you shift the gearshift lever or turn the shift drum.*

1. First ensure that the clutch is properly adjusted. Eliminate any clutch drag or slipping problem and replace any damaged or severely worn component.
2. Support the vehicle so the rear wheels are off the ground.
3. Remove the clutch as described in Chapter Six.

(29)

TRANSMISSION TROUBLESHOOTING

2

Excessive gear noise

Check:
- Worn bearings
- Worn or damaged gears
- Excessive gear backlash

Difficult shifting

Check:
- Damaged gears
- Damaged shift forks
- Damaged shift drum
- Damaged shift lever assembly
- Incorrect mainshaft and countershaft engagement
- Incorrect clutch disengagement

Gears pop out of mesh

Check:
- Worn gear or transmission shaft splines
- Shift forks worn or bent
- Worn dog holes in gears
- Insufficient shift lever spring tension
- Damaged shift lever linkage

Incorrect shift lever operation

Check:
- Bent shift lever
- Bent or damaged shift lever shaft
- Damaged shift lever linkage or gears

Incorrect shifting after engine reassembly

Check:
- Missing transmission shaft shims
- Incorrectly installed parts
- Shift forks bent during reassembly
- Incorrectly assembled crankcase assembly
- Incorrect clutch adjustment
- Incorrectly assembled shift linkage assembly

4. Have an assistant slowly turn the rear wheels while you shift the transmission with the gearshift lever. When doing so, push against the shift shaft (**Figure 30**) with your other hand to prevent it from disengaging the shift drum. Note the following:

   a. Check that the shift shaft return spring is centered around the shift fork shaft as shown in **Figure 30**.

   b. If the transmission will not shift properly, remove the gearshift lever and slide the shift shaft (**Figure 30**) out of the engine.

   c. Check the shift shaft for damage (Chapter Six).

5. If the shift shaft is in good condition, have your assistant turn the rear wheels while you turn the shift drum (A, **Figure 31**) by hand. When doing so, watch the movement and operation of the stopper lever assembly (B, **Figure 31**). When turning the shift drum, the stopper lever roller should move in and out of the shift drum detents. Each detent position represents a different gear position. The raised detent position on the shift drum is the NEUTRAL position.

NOTE
Figure 31 shows the stopper lever and shift drum with the transmission in NEUTRAL.

6. The stopper lever assembly is held under tight spring tension. When the shift drum turns and moves the stopper lever roller out of a detent, spring tension forces the stopper lever to stay in contact with the shift drum and to move into the next detent position. If this is not happening, remove the stopper lever assembly (Chapter Six) and check it for damage.

7. Check the shift drum as follows:

   a. Shift the transmission into NEUTRAL (if possible). Make a mark on the crankcase that aligns with the shift drum NEUTRAL detent position (**Figure 32**).

   b. While turning the rear wheels or the mainshaft, turn the shift drum to change gears. Each time the shift drum moves and a new detent position aligns with the mark made in substep a (**Figure 33**), the transmission should change gears.

   c. The transmission should shift into each gear. If the shift drum cannot be turned, or if it locks into a particular gear position, the transmission is damaged. A locked shift drum indicates

a damaged shift fork, a seized transmission gear or damaged shift drum.

7. To service the transmission, disassemble the engine and remove the transmission as described in Chapter Five, then service the transmission as described in Chapter Seven.

KICKSTARTER

If the kickstarter lever becomes stuck at the bottom of its stroke, or if it slips, the problem is usually

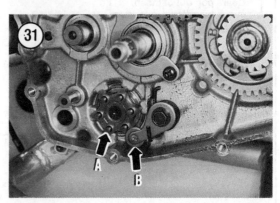

easy to find once the clutch cover is removed. On the YFS200 engine, the kickstarter assembly can be serviced with the engine mounted in the frame.

Refer to the following troubleshooting information for a list of common kickstarter symptoms and possible causes. To service the kickstarter (**Figure 34**), refer to *Kickstarter* in Chapter Six.

Kickstarter Lever or Shaft Slips

a. Excessively worn or damaged kickstarter shaft.
b. Excessively worn or damaged kick gear.
c. Excessively worn or damaged kick idle gear.
d. Weak or damaged kick clip spring.
e. Kick clip coming out of kick gear groove.
f. Damaged kick clip stopper (in crankcase).
g. Low viscosity gear oil.
h. Deteriorated gear oil.

Kickstarter Does Not Return

a. Damaged kickstarter return spring.
b. Kickstarter return spring disengaging from one or both ends.
c. Kick clip coming out of kick gear groove.
d. Damaged kickstarter return spring stopper.
e. Incorrectly assembled kickstarter assembly.

Kickstarter is Hard to Kick Over

1. Kickstarter axle:
   a. Seized kickstarter gear.
   b. Seized kickstarter idler gear.
   c. Incorrect kick clip (too tight).
2. Engine:
   a. Seized piston and cylinder.
   b. Broken piston.
   c. Damaged crankcase assembly.
   d. Damaged clutch cover.
   e. Seized or broken crankshaft.
   f. Seized crankshaft main bearings.
3. Transmission oil:
   a. Low viscosity gear oil.
   b. Deteriorated gear oil.

DRIVE TRAIN NOISE

This section deals with noises that are restricted to the drive train assembly—drive chain, clutch and transmission. While some drive train noises have little meaning, abnormal noises are a good indicator of a developing problem. The problem is recognizing the difference between a normal and abnormal noise. A new noise, no matter how minor, must be investigated.

1. *Drive chain noise*—Normal drive chain noise can be considered a low-pitched, continuous whining sound. The noise will vary, depending on the speed of the vehicle and the terrain you are riding on, as well as proper lubrication, wear (both chain and sprocket) and alignment. When checking abnormal drive chain noise, consider the following:

   a. *Inadequate lubrication*—A dry chain will produce a loud whining sound. Clean and lubricate the drive chain at regular intervals as described in Chapter Three.
   b. *Incorrect chain adjustment*—Check and adjust the drive chain as described in Chapter Three.

c. *Worn chain*—Check chain wear at regular intervals and replace it when its overall length exceeds the wear limit specified in Chapter Three.

d. *Worn or damaged sprockets*—Worn or damaged sprockets accelerate chain wear. Inspect the sprockets carefully as described in Chapter Three.

e. *Worn, damaged or missing drive chain sliders and rollers*—Chain sliders and rollers are in constant contact with the chain. Check them often for loose, damaged or missing parts. A missing chain slider or roller will increase chain slack and may allow the chain to contact the frame or swing arm.

2. *Clutch noise*—Investigate any noise that develops in the clutch. First, drain the transmission oil, checking for bits of metal or clutch plate material. If the oil looks and smells good, remove the clutch (Chapter Six) and check for the following:

a. Worn or damaged clutch outer gear teeth.

b. Excessive clutch outer axial play.

c. Excessive clutch outer-to-friction plate clearance.

d. Excessive clutch outer gear-to-primary drive gear backlash.

3. *Transmission noise*—The transmission will exhibit more normal noises than the clutch, but like the clutch, a new noise in the transmission must be investigated. Drain the transmission oil into a clean container. Wipe a small amount of oil on a finger and rub the finger and thumb together. Check for the presence of metallic particles. Inspect the drain container for water separation from the oil. Some transmission associated noises are caused by:

a. Insufficient transmission oil level.

b. Contaminated transmission oil.

c. Transmission oil viscosity too thin. An oil viscosity that is too thin will raise the transmission operating temperature.

d. Worn transmission gear(s).

e. Chipped or broken transmission gear(s).

f. Excessive gear side play.

g. Worn or damaged crankshaft-to-transmission bearing(s).

h. Worn or damaged kickstarter idle gear.

i. Kickstarter pinion gear does not disengage from the starter ratchet.

NOTE
If metallic particles are found in Step 2 or Step 3, remove and inspect the clutch, then if necessary, disassemble the engine and inspect the transmission.

HEADLIGHT TROUBLESHOOTING

The headlight and taillight are controlled by the light switch mounted on the left side handlebar. The lights can only be turned on when the engine is running. If the headlight does not come on with the engine running and the light switch turned on, perform the following inspection procedure.

1. Remove the fuel tank cover (Chapter Fourteen).

2. Remove the headlight (Chapter Nine).

3. Remove the headlight bulb (Chapter Nine) from its socket (**Figure 35**) and check it for a broken filament. Then check the bulb contacts in the socket

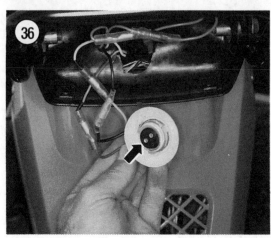

(**Figure 36**) for corrosion. Clean the contacts if necessary. If the bulb is not visibly blown, check it with an ohmmeter as follows:

    a. Switch an ohmmeter to R X 1.

    b. Touch one ohmmeter lead to the bulb housing and the other lead to one of the bulb terminals. The ohmmeter should read continuity. Repeat to check continuity at the second bulb terminal. The ohmmeter should read continuity at both terminals.

    c. Replace the bulb if blown or if it does not show continuity at both terminals.

    d. If the bulb is good, continue with Step 4.

4. Install the headlight bulb into its socket, then disconnect the 3 socket bullet connectors (**Figure 35**) and remove the socket and bulb from the headlight housing.

    a. Connect an ohmmeter between the yellow and black leads (**Figure 37**). The reading should be zero ohms.

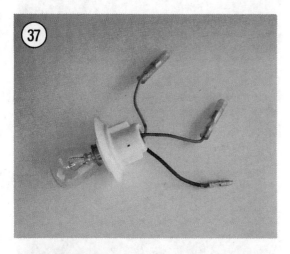

    b. Connect the ohmmeter between the green and black leads. The reading should be zero ohms.

    c. If either reading is no continuity, replace the bulb socket and repeat the test.

    d. If both readings indicate continuity continue with Step 5.

5. Test the dimmer switch as described in Chapter Nine. If the switch operates correctly, continue at Step 6.

6. Check the lighting voltage as described in Chapter Nine. If the voltage is as specified, the lighting system is operating properly. Check the wiring harness and all connectors for damage, loose or corroded connections. If the voltage is not as specified, continue at Step 7 to isolate the problem.

7. Test the lighting coil resistance as described under *Stator Coil Testing* in Chapter Nine.

    a. Replace the lighting coil if its resistance is not as specified in Chapter Nine.

    b. If the lighting coil resistance is as specified, closely inspect the wiring harness and all connections, especially grounds. If all wiring and connections are in acceptable condition, replace the voltage regulator (**Figure 38**) as described in Chapter Nine.

> *NOTE*
> *It is difficult to test the voltage regulator, effectively. However, if all other lighting system components, including the wiring harness and all connections, are in acceptable condition, consider the voltage regulator faulty by a process of elimination.*

TAILLIGHT TROUBLESHOOTING

The headlight and taillight are controlled by the light switch mounted on the left side handlebar. 2002 models are equipped with a brake light. If the brake light is inoperative check the bulb and switches. See Chapter Nine. The lights can only be turned on when the engine is running. If the headlight comes on but the taillight does not, first check the taillight for a blown bulb. If both bulbs do not light, or the taillight does not light with a new bulb, troubleshoot the taillight system as follows:

1. Remove the fuel tank cover (Chapter Fourteen).

2. Remove the taillight lens and bulb (Chapter Nine). Check the bulb for a broken filament (**Figure 39**). Then check the bulb contacts in the socket for corrosion or other contamination. If the bulb is not visibly blown, check it with an ohmmeter as follows:

    a. Switch an ohmmeter to R × 1.

    b. Touch both ohmmeter leads across the 2 bulb terminals. The ohmmeter should read continuity.

    c. Replace the bulb if blown or if it does not show continuity.

    d. If the bulb is good, continue with Step 3.

3. Install the taillight bulb into its socket, then disconnect the 2 socket terminals (**Figure 40**) from the wiring harness. Connect an ohmmeter between the blue and black taillight leads. The ohmmeter should indicate zero ohms. If high resistance or no continuity is noted, replace the bulb socket.

4. Test the dimmer switch as described in Chapter Nine. If necessary, replace the switch as described in Chapter Nine.

5. Next, check lighting coil voltage output as described in Chapter Nine. If voltage output is not as specified, continue at Step 6. If voltage output is as specified, the lighting system is operating properly. Inspect the wiring harness and all connections (especially grounds) for damage or loose or corroded connections.

6. Test the lighting coil resistance as described under *Stator Coil Testing* in Chapter Nine.

    a. Replace the lighting coil if resistance is not as specified. If the lighting coil resistance is as specified, inspect the wiring harness and all connections for damage or loose or corroded connections.

    b. If all wiring and connections are in acceptable condition, replace the voltage regulator.

NOTE
The voltage regulator cannot be effectively tested. However, if all lighting system components, including the wiring harness and all connectors, are in acceptable condition, the voltage regulator can be considered faulty by a process of elimination.

OIL LEVEL INDICATOR SYSTEM TROUBLESHOOTING

The oil level indicator (**Figure 41**) is mounted on the headlight housing. The indicator lights when the oil level in the engine oil tank is low. To troubleshoot this system, first perform the *Oil Level Indicator System Check* procedure in this section. Follow the steps in the procedure for additional troubleshooting and service information.

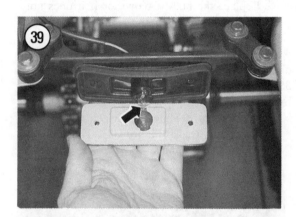

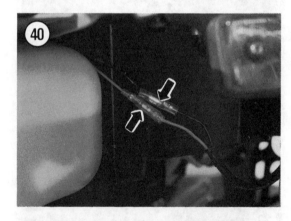

Oil Level Indicator System Check

Perform the following steps before starting the troubleshooting procedure.

1. Turn the main switch to ON and the engine stop switch to RUN.
2. Start the engine and allow it to idle.
3. Observe the oil level indicator (**Figure 41**).
   a. If the indicator does not light, perform the *Oil Level Indicator System Troubleshooting* procedure in this chapter.

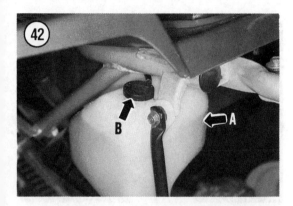

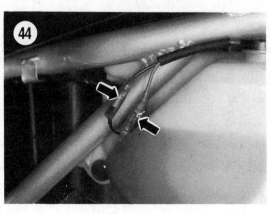

   b. If the indicator lights, go to Step 4.
4. The oil level indicator should turn off after a few seconds.
   a. If the indicator turns off, the engine oil level indicator circuit is working correctly.
   b. If the indicator does not turn off, turn off the engine and continue with Step 5.
5. Fill the engine oil tank with the correct type of 2-stroke injection oil as described in Chapter Three.
6. Repeat the test, starting with Step 2.

Oil Level Indicator System Troubleshooting

If the oil level indicator does not light after starting the engine, troubleshoot the oil level indicator electrical circuit as follows.

1. Check the oil level in the engine oil tank (A, **Figure 42**). If necessary, fill with the correct type of 2-stroke injection oil (Chapter Three).
2. Remove the fuel tank cover (Chapter Fourteen).
3. Remove the oil level indicator (Chapter Nine) and check for a blown bulb (**Figure 43**). If the bulb is not visibly blown, check it with an ohmmeter as follows:
   a. Switch an ohmmeter to the R × 1 scale.
   b. Connect the ohmmeter between the 2 bulb terminals.
   c. Replace the bulb if continuity is not indicated.
4. If the bulb is good, reinstall it into its socket. Then, disconnect the socket terminals and remove the socket and bulb (**Figure 43**) from the wiring harness.
5. Connect an ohmmeter between the brown and green bulb socket wires. The meter should indicate zero ohms. If not, replace the socket and bulb assembly.
6. If the socket and bulb are good, check lighting voltage as described in Chapter Nine. If voltage output is not as specified, continue at Step 7. If voltage output is as specified, continue at Step 8.
7. Test the lighting coil resistance as described under *Stator Coil Testing* in Chapter Nine.
   a. Replace the lighting coil if resistance is not as specified. If the lighting coil resistance is as specified, continue at Step 8.
   b. If all wiring and connections are in acceptable condition, replace the voltage regulator.
8. Disconnect the oil level gauge green and black wires (**Figure 44**) from the oil tank. Connect a

jumper wire between the green and black wires (wiring harness side). Then start the engine and allow it to idle and observe the oil level indicator (**Figure 41**).

    a. If the oil level indicator lights, the oil level gauge is faulty. Replace the gauge (B, **Figure 42**).

    b. If the oil level indicator does not light, continue at Step 8.

9. Inspect the oil level indicator system wiring harness and connections (especially grounds) for damaged wiring or loose or corroded connections. Repair as required.

AUTOLUBE OIL INJECTION PUMP

The YFS200 engine is lubricated by the Autolube oil injection pump. The Autolube oil pump (**Figure 45**) is mounted on the right crankcase cover. On this system, the pump feeds oil directly into the carburetor.

The Autolube pump is driven by the primary drive gear and meters oil to the engine with respect to engine speed. When a problem is experienced with the oil injection system, do not attempt to disassemble and repair the oil pump. The Autolube pump is a sealed unit and there are no replacement parts and overhaul gaskets available. Furthermore, the pump itself is seldom the problem as it is highly reliable and requires no maintenance.

If a problem is experienced with the engine oil system, note the following.

1. The oil pump must be bled whenever one of the following conditions have occurred:

    a. The oil tank ran empty.

    b. When any of the oil injection hoses were disconnected.

    c. The machine was turned on its side.

    d. Predelivery service.

2. The oil level indicator light (**Figure 41**) comes on when the oil level in the tank is low. Check the engine oil tank (A, **Figure 42**) to make sure it is full. If necessary, fill the tank with the correct type of 2-stroke injection oil as described in Chapter Three.

3. If there is little or no oil reaching the engine and the oil tank is full, check the oil line (A, **Figure 45**) between the oil tank and oil pump. If the line seems okay, disconnect the line at the oil pump. With the line disconnected, oil should flow freely from the line. If there is no oil flow from the line, check for a plugged or damaged line.

4. If oil flows from the oil line, check oil delivery line (B, **Figure 45**) connected between the oil pump and carburetor.

5. Repair any loose or damaged hose. Bleed the oil pump (Chapter Ten) if a hose was loose or disconnected.

6. If the problem has not been found and the oil pump has been successfully bled, perform the *Autolube Pump Output Test* in Chapter Ten.

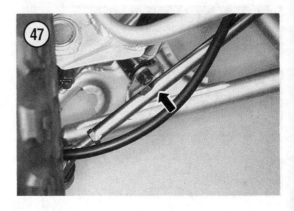

HANDLING

Poor handling can cause you to lose control of the vehicle. When experiencing handling problems, check the following items:

1. Handlebars:
   a. Loose or damaged handlebar clamps.
   b. Incorrect handlebar clamp installation.
   c. Bent or cracked handlebar.
2. Tires:
   a. Incorrect tire pressure.
   b. Uneven tire pressure (both sides).
   c. Worn or damaged tires.
3. Wheels:
   a. Loose or damaged hub bearings.
   b. Loose or bent wheel axle.
   c. Damaged wheel.
   d. Loose wheel nuts.
   e. Excessive wheel run out.
4. Steering:
   a. Incorrect toe-in adjustment.
   b. Damaged steering shaft (**Figure 46**).
   c. Damaged steering shaft bushing(s).
   d. Incorrectly installed steering shaft.

   e. Bent tie rods (**Figure 47**).
   f. Damaged steering knuckles (A, **Figure 48**).
   g. Bent upper (B, **Figure 48**) and/or lower (C, **Figure 48**) arms.
5. Swing arm:
   a. Damaged swing arm.
   b. Worn or damaged swing arm bushings and bearings.
   c. Improperly tightened swing arm pivot shaft.
   d. Damaged axle bearing housing.
6. Rear axle:
   a. Loose rear axle mounting bolts.
   b. Seized or otherwise damaged rear axle bearings (**Figure 49**).
   c. Bent rear axle.
   d. Loose or damaged rear axle bearing housing.
   e. Loose rear axle nuts.
7. Shock absorber(s):
   a. Damaged damper rod.
   b. Leaking damper housing.
   c. Sagged shock spring(s).
   d. Incorrect shock adjustment.
   e. Loose or damaged shock mount bolts.
8. Frame:
   a. Damaged frame.
   b. Cracked or broken engine mount brackets.

FRAME NOISE

Noises that can be traced to the frame or suspension is usually caused by loose, worn or damaged parts. Various noises that relate to the frame are listed below:

1. *Brake noise*—A screeching sound during braking is the most common brake noise. Some other brake associated noises can be caused by:
   a. Glazed brake shoe or pad surface.
   b. Excessively worn brake shoes or pads.
   c. Warped front brake drum(s).
   d. Warped rear brake disc.
   e. Loose rear brake disc mounting bolts.
   f. Loose or missing rear brake caliper mounting bolts.
   g. Damaged caliper.
2. *Rear shock absorber noise*—Check for the following:
   a. Loose shock absorber mounting bolts.
   b. Cracked or broken shock spring.
   c. Damaged shock absorber.

3. Some other frame associated noises are caused by:

   a. Broken frame.

   b. Broken swing arm.

   c. Loosen engine mounting bolts.

   d. Damaged steering bearing.

   e. Loose mounting bracket(s).

BRAKES

The front drum brakes (A, **Figure 50**) and rear disc brake (A, **Figure 51**) units are critical to riding performance and safety. Inspect the brakes frequently and repair or replace damaged parts immediately.

1. Ineffective front drum brakes:

   a. Incorrect front brake adjustment.

   b. Stretched or damaged front brake cable(s).

   c. Worn or damaged front brake shoes (**Figure 52**).

   d. Worn, out of round or damaged front brake drum(s).

   e. Brake shoes and drums contaminated with oil or grease.

   f. Weak or damaged brake shoe return springs.

   g. Incorrect brake cam lever position (B, **Figure 50**).

   h. Damaged brake cam lever splines.

   i. Damaged brake shoe plate.

2. Front brake drum shudder:

   a. Out of round brake drum.

   b. Unevenly worn brake shoes.

   c. Damaged brake shoes.

   d. Damaged brake shoe plate.

3. Ineffective rear mechanical disc brake:

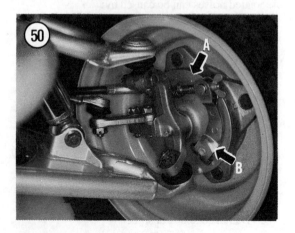

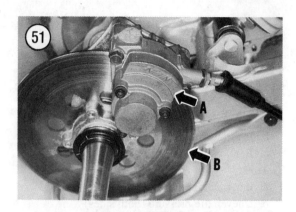

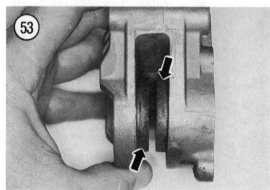

a. Incorrect parking brake adjustment.
b. Stretched or damaged rear/parking brake cable.
c. Worn or damaged brake pads (**Figure 53**).
d. Brake pads and brake disc (B, **Figure 51**) contaminated with oil or grease.
e. Damaged rear brake caliper adjuster unit (A, **Figure 54**).
f. Damaged rear brake caliper cam ratchet (B, **Figure 54**).
g. Weak or damaged ratchet spring (**Figure 55**).

2

CHAPTER THREE

LUBRICATION, MAINTENANCE AND TUNE-UP

The Yamaha ATV requires periodic maintenance to operate efficiently without breaking down. This chapter covers all of the required periodic service procedures that do not require major disassembly. Regular, careful maintenance is the best guarantee for a trouble-free, long lasting vehicle. All-terrain vehicles are high-performance vehicles that demand proper lubrication, maintenance and tune-ups to maintain a high level of performance and extend engine, suspension and chassis life. Procedures at the end of this chapter also describe steps on how to prepare your Yamaha for storage.

You can do your own lubrication, maintenance and tune-ups if you follow the correct procedures and use common sense. Always remember that damage can result from improper tuning and adjustment. In addition, where special tools or testers are called for during a particular maintenance or adjustment procedure, the tool should be used or you should refer service to a qualified Yamaha dealership or repair shop.

Tables 1-8 are at the end of this chapter.

SERVICE INTERVALS

The intervals shown in **Table 1** are recommended by Yamaha for the routine service of your vehicle. Strict adherence to these recommendations will ensure long service from your vehicle. However, if the vehicle is run in an area of high humidity the lubrication and service must be done more frequently to prevent possible rust damage. This is also true when riding through water (especially saltwater) and sand or if the vehicle is used in competition.

TUNE-UP

The number of definitions of the term tune-up is probably equal to the number of people defining it. For the purpose of this book, a tune-up is a general adjustment and maintenance to ensure peak engine and suspension performance.

Tune-up procedures are usually listed in some logical order. For example, some procedures should be done with the engine cold and others with the engine hot. You should check the cylinder head nuts when the engine is cold and adjust the carburetor and drain the transmission oil when the engine is hot. Also, because the engine needs to run as well as possible when adjusting the carburetor, always service the air filter, spark plug and throttle cables first. If you adjust the carburetor and then find that the air filter needs service, you will have to readjust the carburetor.

After completing a tune-up, record the date, the vehicle operating time interval and the type of service performed. This information will provide an accurate record of the type of service performed. This record can also be used to schedule future service procedures at the correct time.

To perform a tune-up on your Yamaha, service the following engine and chassis items, in the order given, as described in this chapter.

Engine Tune-Up Procedure

a. Tighten cylinder head nuts.
b. Clean or repack silencer.
c. Check exhaust pipe fasteners for tightness.
d. Clean and re-oil air filter.
e. Check and service spark plug.
f. Check compression.
g. Check throttle operation and cables.
h. Start engine and allow to warm to normal operating temperature.
i. Check clutch operation.
j. Adjust carburetor.
k. Change transmission oil.
l. Check all exposed engine nuts and bolts for tightness.

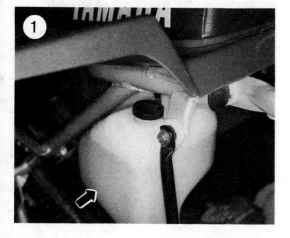

Chassis Tune-Up Procedure

a. Clean and lubricate drive chain.
b. Check drive chain tension and alignment.
c. Check brake operation and cable adjustment.
d. Check wheel rims and tires.
e. Check operation of front and rear suspension.
f. Check the lights for proper operation.
g. Check all exposed steering and suspension nuts and bolts for tightness.

Test Ride

The test ride is an important part of the tune-up or service procedure because it is here where you find out whether the vehicle is ready to ride or if it needs more work. When test riding a vehicle, always start slowly and ride in a safe place away from all vehicles and people. Concentrate on the areas that were worked on and how they can effect other systems. If the brakes were worked on, never apply full brake pressure at high speed (except emergencies). It is safer to check the brakes at slower speeds and with moderate pressure. Do not continue to ride the vehicle if the brakes or any suspension or steering component is not working correctly.

ENGINE OIL

The YFS200 2-stroke engine is lubricated by oil injected into the carburetor. This oil mixes with the incoming fuel charge and circulates through the crankcase and enters the combustion chamber where it is burned with the fuel. The 2-stroke engine components (piston, rings, cylinder, connecting rod, crankshaft and crankcase bearings) are lubricated by the oil as it passes through the crankcase and cylinder.

All Blaster 2-stroke engines are equipped with a gear driven oil injection system. The injection system automatically maintains the optimum fuel/oil ratio according to engine speed. There is no cable or shim adjustment on the oil pump. For complete oil pump service, refer to Chapter Ten.

Engine Oil Level
Check and Adjustment

The oil tank is located at the left rear of the vehicle. Check the oil level in the tank (**Figure 1**) daily, when refueling the vehicle or if the oil level indicator light (**Figure 2**) comes on while the engine is running.

1. Park the vehicle on a level surface and visually check the oil level in the tank (**Figure 1**). To add oil, continue with Step 2.

> *CAUTION*
> *If the oil tank is empty, or a new oil tank installed, fill it as described in this procedure and bleed the oil pump before starting the engine, otherwise, air drawn or trapped in the delivery line will prevent oil from reaching the engine. This will cause engine damage at start-up. Refer to Chapter Ten for steps on bleeding the oil pump.*

2. Remove the seat (Chapter Fourteen).

3. Wipe off the area around the oil tank cap so no dirt can fall into the tank.

4. Remove the oil tank cap (**Figure 3**) from the oil tank.

> *NOTE*
> *The mesh screen (**Figure 4**) installed in the top of the oil tank filters the oil before it enters the tank. When adding oil in Step 5, pour it into the tank slowly so it does not spill out. If the screen is missing from the oil tank, use a funnel with a filter screen when adding oil. This step is critical as any dirt or sand that enters the tank can pass through and block the oil line or damage the oil pump, preventing oil from reaching the engine.*

5. Add the recommended type of 2-stroke engine oil listed in **Table 2**. **Table 3** lists oil tank capacity.

6. Push the oil fill cap (**Figure 3**) firmly into the tank.

7. Install the seat (Chapter Fourteen).

TRANSMISSION OIL

The transmission oil lubricates all of the components that operate behind the right crankcase cover and within the transmission portion of the crankcase. The transmission oil does not lubricate the 2-stroke engine components (piston, rings, cylinder, connecting rod, crankshaft and main bearings).

Yamaha suggests the use of a high-quality 10W-30 motor oil with an API rating of SE. The quality rating is stamped or printed on top of the can or label on plastic bottles (**Figure 5**).

Another type of oil that you should be aware of is a gear oil designed exclusively for use in 2-stroke transmissions. These oils have the same lubricating qualities as an API SE motor oil but are formulated with different load carrying agents and extreme pressure additives that prevent oil break down and foaming caused by clutch and transmission opera-

tion. For example, the Bel-Ray Gear Saver SAE 80 transmission oil shown in **Figure 6** is a light oil that corresponds to motor oil grades SAE 30, SAE 10W-30 and SAE 10W-40. There are a number of 2-stroke transmission oils available for use in the transmission. However, do not confuse this type of gear oil with a Hypoid gear oil used in motorcycle and ATV shaft drive units. Before using a gear oil, pay attention to its service designation, making sure it is specified for use in 2-stroke transmissions only.

Try to use the same brand of oil at each oil change. Yamaha cautions against the use of oil additives as they may cause clutch slippage.

Oil Level Check

Check the transmission oil level through the oil level window (**Figure 7**) mounted on the bottom left corner of the right crankcase cover.

1. Park the vehicle on level ground and set the parking brake.

2. Start the engine and let it idle approximately 2-3 minutes. Then turn the engine off and allow the oil to settle for a few minutes before checking the oil level.

3. The oil level should be between the upper and lower oil level window marks (**Figure 7**). If necessary remove the oil fill cap (**Figure 8**) mounted on the right crankcase cover and add oil to bring the level up to the upper window mark. Fill with the correct type of transmission oil listed in **Table 2**. Do not overfill.

NOTE
If there is no oil visible in the window, check the drain plug, right crankcase cover and crankcase seals for oil leaks.

Oil Change

Regular oil changes will contribute to increased crankcase bearing, transmission and clutch component longevity. The factory recommended oil change interval is listed in **Table 1**. This assumes that the vehicle is operated in moderate climates. If it is operated under dusty conditions, the oil will get dirty more quickly and should be changed more frequently than recommended.

To change the transmission oil you need the following:

a. Drain pan.

b. Funnel.

c. 12 mm wrench or socket.

d. 1 qt. (0.9 L) of oil.

NOTE
Never dispose of motor oil in the trash, on the ground, or down a storm drain. Many service stations accept used motor oil and waste haulers provide curbside used motor oil collection. Do not combine other fluids with motor oil to be recycled. To locate a recycler, contact the American Petroleum Institute (API) at www.recycleoil.org.

1. Park the vehicle on level ground and set the parking brake.

2. Start the engine and warm it up to normal operating temperature, then turn the engine off.

NOTE
Warming the engine allows the oil to heat and flow freely carrying contamination and any sludge out with it.

3. Place a clean drain pan underneath the engine and remove the drain plug and gasket (**Figure 9**).

4. Remove the oil fill cap (**Figure 8**) to help speed up the flow of oil.

5. Allow the oil to drain completely.

6. Clean and inspect the drain plug and gasket. Replace the drain plug if its hex corners are starting to round off or if the threads are damaged. Replace the gasket if it is warped, grooved or if oil is leaking from around the drain plug.

7. After all the oil has drained out, inspect the drain hole threads in the crankcase for damage. Wipe off this area with a clean rag before installing the drain plug.

8. Install the drain plug and gasket and tighten to the torque specification in **Table 4**.

9. Insert a funnel into the oil fill hole and fill the transmission with the correct type (**Table 2**) and quantity (**Table 5**) transmission oil.

NOTE
*The 650 cc oil capacity reading cast into the top of the right crankcase cover (**Figure 8**) is the amount of oil that should be added during a routine oil change. If the engine was disassembled,*

*use the after engine overhaul capacity listed in **Table 5**.*

10. Install the oil fill cap (**Figure 8**) and its O-ring and tighten securely.

11. Start the engine and allow it to idle.

12. Check the drain plug for leaks.

13. Turn the engine off and after waiting 2-3 minutes for the oil to settle, check the engine oil level (**Figure 7**). Add more oil if necessary to bring the oil level up to the upper mark on the window.

WARNING
Prolonged contact with used oil may cause skin cancer. It is advisable to wash your hands thoroughly, with soap and water as soon as possible after handling or coming in contact with any type of engine or transmission oil.

AIR FILTER

The job of an air filter is to trap dirt, grit, sand and other abrasive particles before they enter the engine. And even though the air filter is one of the cheapest parts on your ATV, it is often neglected at the expense of engine performance and wear. Never run the engine without a properly oiled and installed air filter element. Likewise, running the engine with a dry or damaged air filter element will allow unfiltered air to enter the engine. A well-oiled but dirty or clogged air filter will reduce the amount of air that enters the engine and cause a rich air/fuel mixture, resulting in poor engine starting, spark plug fouling and reduced performance. Frequent air filter inspection and cleaning service is critical part of minimiz-

ing engine wear and maintaining engine performance.

Table 1 lists intervals for cleaning the air filter. Clean the air filter more often when racing, riding in sand or in wet and muddy conditions.

Figure 10 is an exploded view of the air filter assembly.

Air Box Check Hose

A check hose (**Figure 11**) is mounted in the bottom of the air box. If the check hose is filled with dirt and water, check the air box and air filter for contamination.

Foam Element

Follow this procedure when servicing the stock foam element or one of the aftermarket foam type air filter elements.

1. Remove the seat (Chapter Fourteen).
2. Remove the screws holding the air box cover (**Figure 12**) to the air box. Lift the cover off the air box and remove it.
3. If necessary, wipe the inside of the air box to prevent any loose dust or dirt from falling into the intake part of the air box when removing the air filter in Step 4.
4. Remove the screw and washer (**Figure 13**) securing the air filter to the air box. Then lift out and remove the air filter (**Figure 13**).
5. Use a flashlight and check the air box-to-carburetor boot inside diameter (**Figure 14**) for dirt or other residue.
6. Inspect the holder guide (**Figure 14**) and plate mounted in the bottom of the fender. If it appears that the guide or plate are loose and allowing dirt to bypass the air filter, remove the rear fender (Chapter Fourteen) to inspect and service these items. Replace any cracked or damaged parts.
7. Cover the air box opening with a clean shop rag.

NOTE
To prevent air leaks and dirty air from entering the engine, make sure all connections between the carburetor, air boot and air box are sealed properly.

8. Inspect all fittings, hoses and connections from the air box to the carburetor. Check each hose clamp for tightness.

9. Carefully pull the foam element off its guide (**Figure 15**).
10. Before cleaning the air filter, check it for brittleness, separation or other damage. Replace the filter if damaged or if its condition is questionable. If the air filter is in good condition, continue with Step 11.

WARNING
Do not clean the air filter element with gasoline.

CAUTION
To prevent damage to the filter, do not wring or twist it during cleaning.

11. Soak the air filter in a container filled with kerosene or an air filter cleaner. Gently squeeze the filter to dislodge and remove the oil and dirt from the filter pores. Swish the filter around in the cleaner a few times, then remove the air filter and set aside to air-dry.
12. Fill a clean pan with warm soapy water.
13. Submerge the filter into the cleaning solution and gently work the cleaner into the filter pores. Soak and squeeze (gently) the filter to clean it.
14. Rinse the filter under warm water while gently squeezing it.
15. Repeat Steps 13 and 14 until there are no signs of dirt being rinsed from the filter.
16. After cleaning the element, inspect it again. Replace the air filter if it is torn or broken in any area. Do not run the engine with a damaged element as it may allow dirt to enter the engine.
17. Set the filter aside and allow to air-dry.
18. Clean the screw and washer (**Figure 16**) in solvent and dry thoroughly.

CAUTION
A damp filter will not trap fine dust. Make sure the filter is completely dry before oiling it.

19. Correctly oiling an air filter element is a messy job. You may want to wear a pair of disposable rubber gloves when performing this procedure. Oil the filter as follows:
   a. Place the air filter into a gallon size storage bag (**Figure 17**).
   b. Pour air filter oil onto the filter to soak it completely.

NOTE
While Yamaha recommends the use of a 10W-30 motor oil to oil the filter, it does

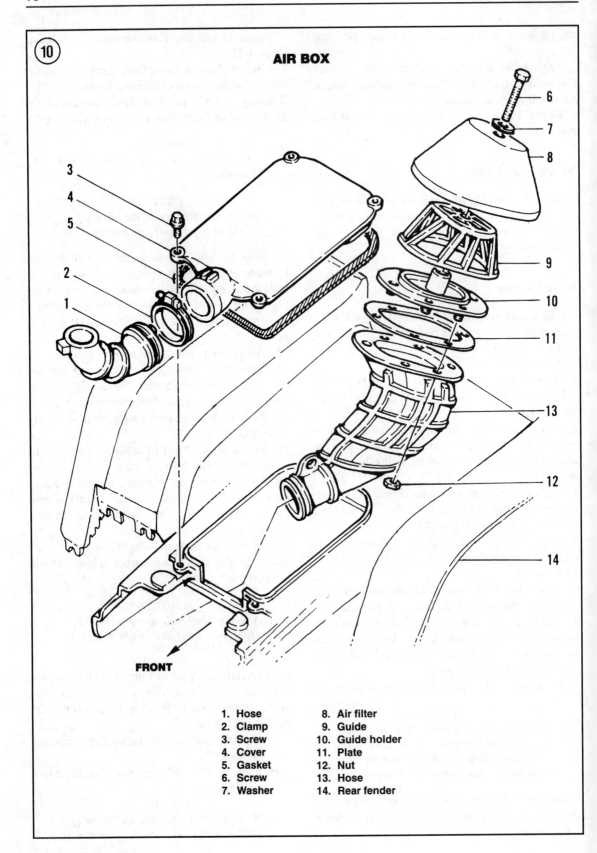

AIR BOX

FRONT

1. Hose
2. Clamp
3. Screw
4. Cover
5. Gasket
6. Screw
7. Washer
8. Air filter
9. Guide
10. Guide holder
11. Plate
12. Nut
13. Hose
14. Rear fender

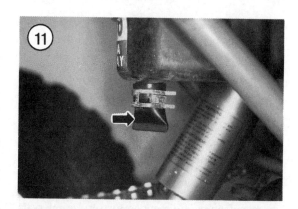

not do as good a job as a dedicated air filter oil. Motor oils are too thin to be used on air filters. When motor oil is applied to an air filter, some of the oil drains down the filter and collects in the bottom of the air box and carburetor boot. When the engine is running, this oil and some of the other oil in the filter pores is drawn into the engine, thus enrichening the air/fuel mixture and causing the engine to sputter and run poorly. The engine will eventually smooth out after this excess oil is used,

3

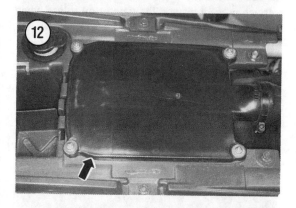

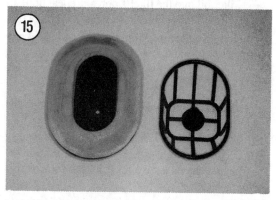

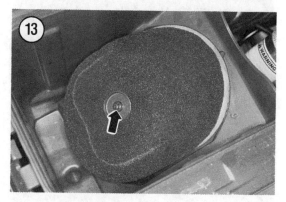

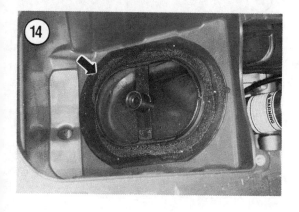

but because there is less oil on the filter, dirt is more likely to pass through the air filter and into the engine. Air filter oils are specially formulated for use in polyurethane foam air filters. A low viscosity solvent in the filter oil helps the oil to be applied easily and thoroughly into the filter pores. This solvent evaporates after application and leaves behind a tacky, viscous fluid that stays in the filter pores while allowing maximum air flow through the filter.

   c. Gently squeeze and release the filter to soak filter oil into the filter's pores. Repeat until all of the filter's pores are saturated with the oil.

   d. Remove the filter from the bag and check the pores for uneven oiling. This is indicated by light or dark areas on the filter. If necessary, soak the filter and squeeze it again.

   e. When the filter oiling is even, squeeze the filter a final time.

   f. Remove the air filter from the bag and inspect it for any excessive oil or uneven oiling. Remove any excessive oil from the filter with a paper towel.

20. Slide the air filter over its guide, making sure the guide is centered properly inside the air filter (**Figure 18**).

21. Apply a coat of waterproof wheel bearing grease to the foam sealing surface (**Figure 18**) on the bottom of the filter. This grease will help seal the air filter against the holder guide in the bottom of the air box.

22. Install the air filter into the air box as shown in **Figure 13**, making sure to seat the bottom of the filter evenly against the holder guide in the bottom of the air box.

23. Install the washer over the filter screw with its shoulder side facing up (**Figure 16**), then apply some grease to the bottom of the washer.

24. Install the screw and washer. Thread the screw into the threaded hole in the holder guide and tighten securely.

25. Run your fingers along the bottom of the air filter, making sure there are no gaps between the filter and the holder guide. If so, loosen the filter screw and reposition the air filter.

26. Check the gasket installed in the groove in the bottom side of the air box cover (**Figure 19**). Replace the gasket if missing or damaged.

27. Install the air box cover (**Figure 12**) and secure it with its mounting screws. Tighten the screws evenly and securely.

28. Install the seat (Chapter Fourteen).

29. Pour any left over filter oil back into the bottle for reuse.

Gauze Element

If a gauze type air filter element is used, refer to its manufacturer's directions for service intervals, service procedures and the type of oil to use when reoiling the filter.

SPARK PLUG

Table 6 lists the standard heat range spark plug for the models covered in this manual.

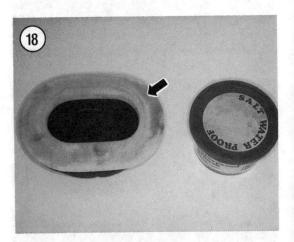

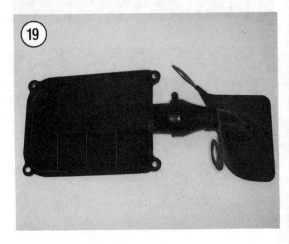

Correct Spark Plug Heat Range

Spark plugs are available in various heat ranges, hotter or colder (**Figure 20**) than the plug originally installed in the factory.

Select a spark plug of the heat range designed for the loads and conditions under which the Yamaha will be operating. Use of an incorrect heat range can cause the plug to foul, engine overheating and piston damage.

In general, use a hot plug for low speeds and low temperatures. Use a cold plug for high speeds, high engine loads and high temperatures. The plug must operate hot enough to burn off unwanted deposits, but not so hot that it overheats and causes preignition. A spark plug of the correct heat range will show a light tan color on the insulator.

The reach (length) of a spark plug is also important. A spark plug that is too short will cause excessive carbon buildup, hard starting and plug fouling (**Figure 21**).

Spark Plug Removal

1. Grasp the spark plug lead (**Figure 22**) as near the plug as possible and pull it off the plug. If it is stuck to the plug, twist it slightly to break it loose.

2. Blow any dirt and other debris away from the spark plug and spark plug hole in the cylinder.

> *CAUTION*
> *Dirt that falls through the spark plug hole will increase piston, ring and cylinder wear.*

3. Remove the spark plug with a 14 mm spark plug wrench.

> *NOTE*
> *If the plug is difficult to remove, apply penetrating oil, like WD-40 or Liquid Wrench, around the base of the plug and let it soak in about 10-20 minutes.*

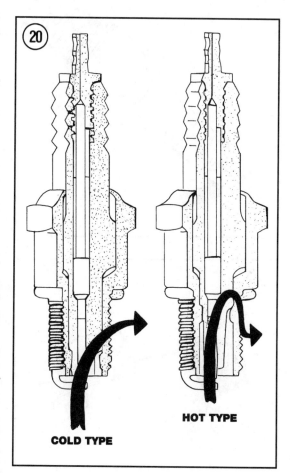

COLD TYPE HOT TYPE

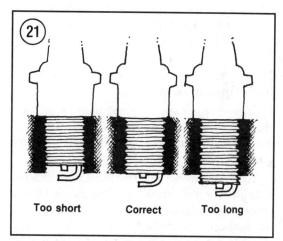

Too short   Correct   Too long

4. Inspect the plug carefully. Look for a broken center porcelain, excessively eroded electrode and excessive carbon or oil fouling.

Gapping and Installing the Plug

Gap each new spark plug to ensure a reliable, consistent spark. Gap new and used spark plugs with a spark plug gapping tool and a wire feeler gauge as described in this procedure.

1. If necessary, screw the small terminal adapter onto the end of the spark plug (**Figure 23**).

2. Refer to the spark plug gap listed in **Table 6**. Then insert a wire feeler gauge between the center and side electrode (**Figure 24**). If the gap is correct, you will feel a slight drag as you pull the wire through. If there is no drag, or the gauge will not pass through, bend the side electrode with a gapping tool (**Figure 25**) to set the proper gap.

> *NOTE*
> *Do not use a flat gauge to check the spark plug gap on a used spark plug or too large of a gap will result.*

3. Apply an anti-seize lubricant to the plug threads before installing the spark plug.

4. Screw the spark plug in by hand until it seats. Very little effort should be required. If force is necessary, the plug may be cross-threaded. Unscrew it and try again.

5. Tighten the spark plug to the torque specification in **Table 4** or use a spark plug wrench and tighten the plug an additional 1/4 to 1/2 turn after the gasket has made contact with the head. If you are installing an old, regapped plug and reusing the old gasket, only tighten an additional 1/4 turn.

> *NOTE*
> *Do not overtighten. This may crush the gasket and cause a compression leak.*

6. Install the spark plug cap (**Figure 22**) onto the spark plug. Make sure it is on tight.

> *CAUTION*
> *Make sure the spark plug wire is pulled away from the exhaust pipe.*

Reading Spark Plugs

Careful examination of the spark plug can determine valuable engine and spark plug information. This information is only valid after performing the following steps.

1. Ride the vehicle at full throttle in a suitable area.

> *NOTE*
> *You must ride the vehicle long enough to obtain an accurate reading or color on the spark plug. If the original plug was fouled, use a new plug.*

2. Push the engine stop switch to OFF before closing the throttle and simultaneously pull in the clutch or shift to neutral, then coast and brake to a stop.

3. Remove the spark plug and examine it. Compare it to **Figure 26** and note the following.

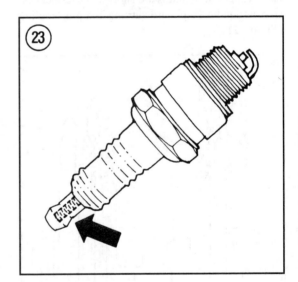

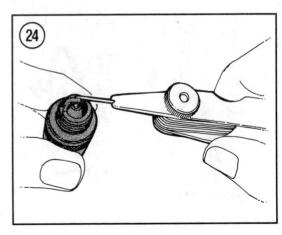

Normal condition

If the plug has a light tan- or gray-colored deposit and no abnormal gap wear or erosion, good engine, carburetion and ignition condition are indicated. The plug in use is of the proper heat range and may be serviced and returned to use.

Carbon fouled

A soft, dry, sooty deposit covering the entire firing end of the spark plug is evidence of incomplete combustion. Even though the firing end of the plug is dry, the plug's insulation decreases. The carbon accumulation forms an electrical path that short circuits the spark plug electrodes and causes a misfire. Carbon fouling is caused by one or more of the following.

    a. Excessively rich fuel mixture.
    b. Spark plug heat range too cold.
    c. Clogged air filter.
    d. Over-retarded ignition timing.
    e. Ignition component failure.
    f. Low engine compression.
    g. Prolonged idling.

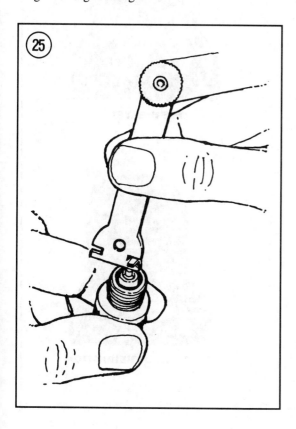

Oil fouled

The tip of an oil fouled plug has a black insulator tip, a damp oily film over the firing end and a carbon layer over the entire nose. The electrodes will not be worn. Common causes for this condition are:

    a. Incorrect carburetor jetting.
    b. Low idle speed or prolonged idling.
    c. Ignition component failure.
    d. Spark plug heat range too cold.
    e. Engine not fully broken in.

Oil fouled spark plugs may be cleaned in an emergency, but is better to replace them. It is important to correct the cause of fouling before you return the engine to service.

Gap bridging

Plugs with this condition exhibit gaps shorted out by combustion deposits between the electrodes. The engine can still run with a bridged spark plug, but it will misfire badly. If you encounter this condition, check for an improper oil type or excessive carbon in the combustion chamber or in the exhaust port. Be sure to find and correct the cause of this condition.

Overheating

Badly worn electrodes and premature gap wear are signs of overheating, along with a gray or white blistered porcelain insulator surface. The most common cause for this condition is using a spark plug of the wrong heat range (too hot). If you have not changed to a hotter spark plug and the plug is overheated, consider the following causes:

    a. Excessively lean fuel mixture.
    b. Ignition timing too advanced.
    c. Incorrect oil pump flow.
    d. Engine air leak.
    e. Improper spark plug installation (overtightening).

Worn out

Corrosive gases formed by combustion and high voltage sparks have eroded the electrodes. Spark plugs in this condition require more voltage to fire under hard acceleration. Replace with a new spark plug.

(26)

SPARK PLUG CONDITION

NORMAL

GAP BRIDGED

CARBON FOULED

OVERHEATED

OIL FOULED

SUSTAINED PREIGNITION

Preignition

If the electrodes are melted, preignition is almost certainly the cause. Check for carburetor mounting or intake manifold leaks and over-advanced ignition timing. It is also possible that a plug of the wrong heat range (too hot) is being used. Find the cause of the preignition before returning the engine into service.

CARBURETOR

This section describes service to the fuel hose, shutoff valve, intake manifold and carburetor.

Fuel Hose and Shutoff Valve Inspection

Inspect the fuel hose (A, **Figure 27**) from the fuel tank to carburetor for any leaks, a damaged hose or missing or weak hose clamps. Replace the fuel hose and hose clamps if damaged.

Inspect the fuel shutoff valve (B, **Figure 27**) for any leaks or damage. Two O-rings installed in the valve can go bad and cause the valve to leak fuel. If

there is insufficient fuel flow from the ON or RES fuel lever positions, the screen mounted at the top of each pickup tube may be restricted. To service the fuel valve, refer to *Fuel Shutoff Valve* in Chapter Eight.

> *WARNING*
> *A leaking fuel hose may cause the engine to catch fire. Do not start the engine with a leaking or damaged fuel hose or fuel shutoff valve.*

Intake Manifold Inspection

The intake manifold (A, **Figure 28**) mounts to the back of the cylinder and connects the reed valve and carburetor to the engine. A loose or damaged intake manifold will allow air to leak into the engine and cause a lean fuel mixture. To accurately check for a loose or damaged intake manifold, perform the *2-Stroke Leak Down Test* in Chapter Two.

1. Visually inspect the intake manifold for cracks, deterioration or other damage. Replace a damaged intake manifold as described under *Reed Valve* in Chapter Four.

2. Inspect the intake manifold (A, **Figure 28**) for loose mounting bolts and a loose or damaged carburetor hose clamp. Tighten the intake manifold mounting bolts in a crisscross pattern to the torque specification listed in **Table 4**.

Carburetor Choke

Check the choke by pulling out and pushing in the choke knob (B, **Figure 28**). The choke shaft should move smoothly and lock in both positions. To check the choke, perform the following.

1. Start the engine and allow to warm to its normal operating temperature.

2. When the engine has warmed completely with the choke pushed all the way in, pull the choke knob all the way out. If the engine does not stall, the choke may not be working correctly.

> *NOTE*
> *Pulling the choke knob out OPENS the choke circuit. Pushing the choke knob in CLOSES the choke circuit.*

3. To service the choke, refer to *Carburetor* in Chapter Eight. The choke can be serviced with the carburetor mounted on the engine.

Carburetor Idle Speed and Mixture Adjustment

Proper idle speed is a balance between a low enough idle to give adequate compression braking and a high enough idle to prevent engine stalling. The idle air/fuel mixture effects transition from idle to 1/8 throttle openings.

Turning the pilot air screw (C, **Figure 28**) IN enriches the fuel mixture and turning it OUT leans the mixture.

1. Make sure that the throttle cable free play is correct. Check and adjust the throttle cable as described in this chapter.

2. Turn the pilot air screw (C, **Figure 28**) in until it seats lightly, then back it out the number of turns indicated in **Table 6**.

> *CAUTION*
> *Never turn the pilot air screw in tight; otherwise, you will damage the screw or the soft aluminum seat in the carburetor.*

3. Connect a portable tachometer to the engine following its manufacturer's instructions.

4. Start the engine and allow it to warm to normal operating temperature.

5. Remove the seat.

6. Turn the throttle stop screw (**Figure 29**) to set the engine idle speed within the range listed in **Table 6**.

7. Turn the pilot air screw (C, **Figure 28**) clockwise or counterclockwise to obtain the highest idle speed as possible.

> *NOTE*
> *Do not open the pilot air screw more than 3 turns or it may vibrate out. If you cannot get the engine to idle properly, first make sure the air filter is clean. If the air filter is clean and other engine systems are operating correctly, the pilot jet size may be incorrect. Refer to Chapter Eight for information on jetting the carburetor.*

8. Finally, turn the throttle stop screw (**Figure 29**) to set the engine idle speed (**Table 6**).

9. Open and then close the throttle a few times, making sure the idle speed returns to the specified rpm.

10. Turn the engine off and remove the tachometer.

11. Install the seat.

12. Test ride the vehicle. Throttle response from idle must be rapid and without any hesitation. If there is hesitation, readjust the carburetor.

> *WARNING*
> *With the engine idling, move the handlebar from side to side. If idle speed increases during this movement, the*

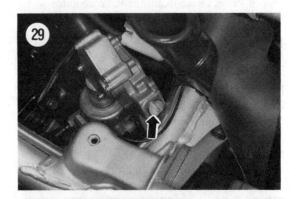

throttle cable needs adjusting or it may be incorrectly routed through the frame. Correct this problem immediately. Do not ride the vehicle in this unsafe condition.

EXHAUST SYSTEM

Inspection

Refer to Chapter Four for service and repair procedures.

1. Inspect the exhaust pipe for cracks or dents which could alter performance.

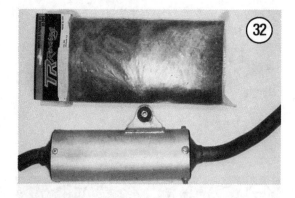

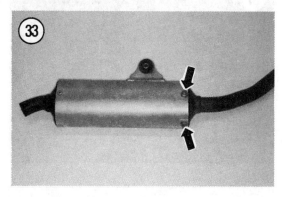

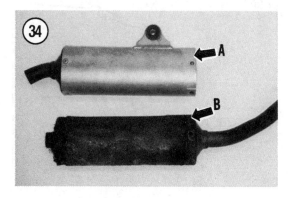

2. Check all of the exhaust pipe fasteners and mounting points for loose or damaged parts.
3. Check the exhaust pipe where it is bolted against the exhaust port on the front of the cylinder (**Figure 30**). Make sure the 2 nuts are tight and that there are no exhaust leaks. If the exhaust pipe is leaking at this point, remove the exhaust pipe (Chapter Four) and replace the gasket installed between the pipe and cylinder.
4. Decarbonize the exhaust pipe when servicing the engine top end.

Silencer Cleaning
(Stock Silencer)

1. Remove the screws holding the outlet pipe (**Figure 31**) into the end of the silencer housing. Then twist and remove the outlet pipe and gasket.
2. Decarbonize the outlet pipe with a wire wheel or scraper. Then clean in solvent and dry thoroughly.
3. Replace the gasket if torn or leaking.
4. Reverse these steps to install the outlet pipe. Tighten the screws securely.

Repacking Glass Wool
(Aftermarket Silencer)

Use the following steps as a guideline for replacing the glass wool in an aftermarket type aluminum body silencer (**Figure 32**). Use this information to supplement the instructions that came with the aftermarket silencer or exhaust pipe assembly.

1. Remove the silencer as described in Chapter Four.
2. The inner pipe is usually secured to the outer housing with screws or rivets. Remove the inner pipe assembly by following one of the following steps:
   a. Remove the screws (**Figure 33**) securing the silencer housing to the inner pipe.
   b. Drill out the rivets securing the silencer housing to the inner pipe.
3. Pull the silencer housing off of the inner pipe as shown in A, **Figure 34**.
4. Pull the glass wool packing (B, **Figure 34**) off the inner pipe and discard it.
5. Clean the inner pipe (**Figure 35**) with a wire brush.
6. Check the width of the new packing with the inner pipe and if necessary, cut the width of the glass wool to fit the inner pipe.

7. Wrap the new glass wool around the inner pipe (A, **Figure 36**) then slide the housing over the inner pipe and secure it with the mounting screws (**Figure 33**) or rivet it in place with a rivet gun.

8. Install the silencer as described in Chapter Four.

AUTOLUBE PUMP AND ENGINE OIL LINES

The autolube pump supplies oil to the engine. To prevent an engine lubrication problem, periodically inspect the engine oil lines and the pump assembly for loose, missing or damaged parts. Refer to Chapter Ten for all autolube pump and oil line inspection and service procedures.

> *CAUTION*
> *If the oil tank is empty, or a new oil tank installed, fill it as described under **Engine Oil** in this chapter, then bleed the oil pump before starting the engine; otherwise, air drawn or trapped in the delivery line will prevent oil from reaching the engine. This will cause engine damage at start-up. Refer to Chapter Ten for steps on bleeding the oil pump.*

CRANKCASE VENTILATION HOSE INSPECTION

The crankcase ventilation hose (**Figure 37**) prevents a pressure buildup in the crankcase that could force transmission oil to blow out or leak past the countershaft and shift shaft seals.

Remove the fuel tank (Chapter Eight) and inspect the ventilation hose as it is routed from the crankcase (**Figure 37**) to the front of the vehicle. Remove any contamination from the hose with compressed air or replace the hose if damaged.

ENGINE COMPRESSION CHECK

A cylinder cranking compression check is one of the quickest ways to check the internal condition of the engine. It is a good idea to check compression at each tune-up, write it down and compare it with the reading you get at the next tune-up. This will help you spot any developing problems.

1. Clean the area around the spark plug, then remove it from the cylinder head.

2. Thread or insert the tip of a compression gauge into the cylinder head spark plug hole (**Figure 38**). Make sure the gauge is seated properly. If necessary, remove the fuel tank to make room for the compression gauge.

3. Turn the main switch off and move the engine stop switch to its OFF position.

4. Hold the throttle wide open and kick the engine over until the gauge needle gives its highest reading. The YFS200 engine, should have a compression reading of 140-160 psi (965-1103 kPa). If the

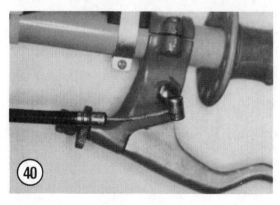

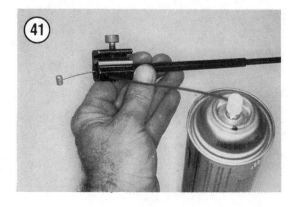

compression reading is well below 140 psi (965 kPa), the engine top end should be disassembled and the parts inspected. See Chapter Four for engine top end service.

5. If the reading is higher than normal, there may be a buildup of carbon deposits in the combustion chamber or on the piston crown.

NOTE
If the compression is low, the engine cannot be tuned to maximum performance.

6. Push the release button on the compression gauge, then remove it from the cylinder. Reinstall the spark plug and connect its spark plug cap.

IGNITION TIMING

Ignition timing is not adjustable on the YFS200 engine. The stator plate (**Figure 39**) position is fixed to the crankcase (the mounting screw holes are not slotted for adjustment).

CONTROL CABLE LUBRICATION

This section describes complete lubrication procedures for the brake, clutch, throttle cable and lever assemblies.

Clutch and Brake Lever
Pivot Bolt Lubrication

Periodically, remove the clutch and brake lever pivot bolts at the handlebar and lubricate the bolts with 10W-30 motor oil. Reinstall the pivot bolts and nuts and tighten securely. Make sure the lever pivots smoothly without binding or roughness.

Control Cable Lubrication

Clean and lubricate the clutch, throttle and brake cables at the intervals indicated in **Table 1**. In addition, check the cables (**Figure 40**) for kinks, wear, damage or fraying that could cause a cable to stick or break during use. Cables are expendable items and will not last forever under the best of conditions.

Lubricate the control cables with a cable lubricator (**Figure 41**) and a can of cable lube or a multipurpose lubricant. *Do not* use a dedicated chain lube to lubricate control cables unless it is also specified as a control cable lubricant. If the stock cables were replaced with Teflon type control cables, follow the manufacturer's instructions on cleaning and servicing these cables.

1. Disconnect both clutch cable (**Figure 42**) ends as described under *Clutch Cable Replacement* in Chapter Six.

2. Disconnect the 3 front brake cables (A, **Figure 43**) from all of their attachment points as described under *Front Brake Cable Replacement* in Chapter Thirteen.

3. Disconnect the rear brake/parking brake cable from the parking brake lever (B, **Figure 43**) and from the brake caliper (**Figure 44**) as described under *Rear/Parking Brake Cable Replacement* in Chapter Thirteen. When lubricating this cable, note the following:

   a. This cable consists of a front half and a rear half.

   b. Lubricate the front half (A, **Figure 45**), then the rear half (B, **Figure 45**) separately.

> *CAUTION*
> *Do not lubricate the brake/parking brake cable while the cable is attached to the brake caliper. The oil and dirt that is flushed from the end of the cable will contaminate the inner brake caliper components.*

4. Disconnect the throttle cable from the throttle lever (**Figure 46**) and from the carburetor (**Figure 47**) as described under *Throttle Cable Replacement* in Chapter Eight.

> *CAUTION*
> *Do not lubricate the throttle cable while the cable is attached to the carburetor assembly. The oil and dirt that is flushed from the end of the cable will contaminate the T.O.R.S. housing and carburetor switch (**Figure 47**) assembly.*

5. Attach a cable lubricator to the end of the cable following its manufacturer's instructions (**Figure 41**).

6. Insert the lubricant can nozzle into the lubricator, press the button on the can and hold down until the lubricant begins to flow out of the other end of the cable. If you cannot get the cable lube to flow

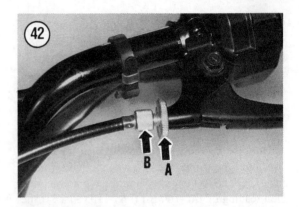

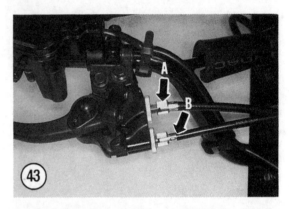

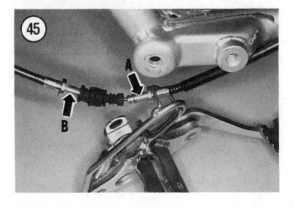

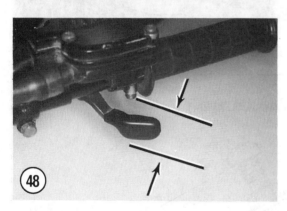

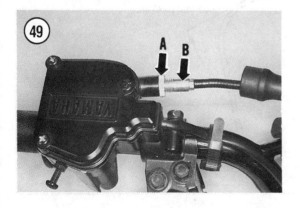

through the cable at one end, remove the lubricator and try at the opposite cable end.

NOTE
Place a shop cloth at the end of the cable to catch the oil as it runs out.

7. Disconnect the lubricator.

8. Apply a light coat of grease to the cable ends, except the rear brake/parking brake cable end (**Figure 44**) and the throttle cable end (**Figure 47**), before reconnecting them.

9. Reverse Steps 1-4 to reconnect the control cables.

10. Adjust all of the control cables as described in this chapter.

11. Check that each cable operates correctly and does not bind or move roughly.

WARNING
Do not ride the vehicle until all of the control cables are properly adjusted.

THROTTLE CABLE AND SPEED LIMITER ADJUSTMENT

Throttle Cable Adjustment

Some throttle cable play is necessary to prevent changes in the idle speed when you turn the handlebars. Yamaha specifies a throttle cable free play of 4-6 mm (3/16-7/32 in.), measured at the end of the throttle lever as shown in **Figure 48**.

In time, the throttle cable free play will become excessive from cable stretch. This will delay throttle response and effect low-speed operation. On the other hand, if there is no throttle cable free play, an excessively high idle can result.

1. Set the engine idle speed as described under *Idle Speed Adjustment* in this chapter.

2. Start the engine and allow it to idle in NEUTRAL.

3. With the engine running at idle speed, push the throttle lever to increase engine speed.

4. Measure the amount of movement (free play) required to raise the engine speed from idle. If the free play measurement (**Figure 48**) is incorrect, continue with Step 5.

5. Turn the engine off.

6. At the throttle housing, loosen the throttle cable adjuster locknut (A, **Figure 49**) and turn the adjuster

(B, **Figure 49**) in or out to achieve proper free play movement. Tighten the locknut.

7. If the correct adjustment cannot be corrected at the throttle housing adjuster, the throttle cable is excessively stretched and must be replaced. Refer to *Throttle Cable Replacement* in Chapter Eight.

8. Slide the rubber boot back over the cable adjuster.

9. Push and release the throttle lever (**Figure 48**), making sure it moves smoothly with no binding or roughness.

10. Start the engine and allow it to idle in NEU-TRAL. Turn the handlebar from side to side. If the idle increases, the throttle cable is routed incorrectly or there is not enough cable free play.

> *WARNING*
> *Do not ride the vehicle with a throttle cable or throttle lever that sticks.*

Speed Limiter Adjustment

The throttle housing is equipped with a speed limiter (A, **Figure 50**) that can be set to prevent the throttle from being opened all the way. The speed limiter can be set to limit engine speed for beginning riders or to control engine speed when breaking in a new or rebuilt engine.

Adjust the speed limiter by varying the length of the speed limiter screw (A, **Figure 50**), measured from the throttle housing to the bottom of the screw head. The standard speed limiter setting is 12 mm (0.47 in.). See **Figure 51**.

1. Check throttle cable free play as described in this chapter. If necessary, adjust throttle cable free play, then continue with Step 2.

2. Loosen the locknut (B, **Figure 50**).

3. Turn the speed limiter screw (A, **Figure 50**) in or out as required. Do not exceed the 12 mm (0.47 in.) adjustment limit (**Figure 51**). Tighten the locknut (B, **Figure 50**).

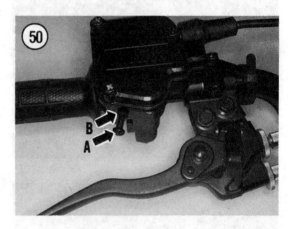

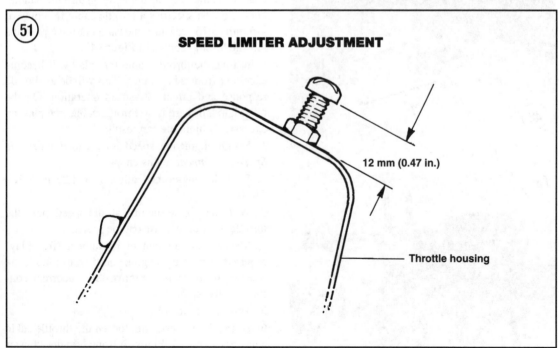

SPEED LIMITER ADJUSTMENT

12 mm (0.47 in.)

Throttle housing

WARNING
Do not operate the vehicle with the speed limiter screw removed from the housing. Do not exceed the 12 mm (0.47 in.) adjustment limit. When adjusting the speed limiter for a beginning rider, start and ride the vehicle yourself, making sure the vehicle speed is not too fast.

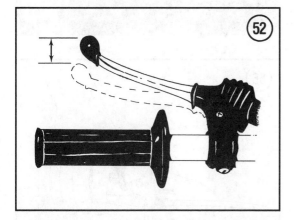

CLUTCH CABLE ADJUSTMENT

Clutch adjustment takes up slack caused by cable stretch and clutch plate wear. Insufficient free play will cause clutch slippage and rapid clutch disc wear.

Clutch Free Play Adjustment

1. Measure the clutch lever free play at the end of the clutch lever as shown in **Figure 52**. On 1988-2001 models the free play is 5.8 mm (0.20-0.31 in.). On 2002 models, the free play is 2-3 mm (0.08-0.12 in.). If the free play measurement is incorrect, continue with Step 2.
2. See **Figure 42**. At the hand lever, loosen the locknut (A) and turn the clutch cable adjuster (B) in or out to obtain the correct amount of free play. Tighten the locknut.
3. If the proper amount of free play cannot be achieved at the clutch cable adjuster, perform the *Clutch Mechanism Adjustment* procedure in this section.

Clutch Mechanism Adjustment

If you cannot obtain the correct clutch adjustment with the clutch cable adjuster, adjust the clutch mechanism (mounted on the clutch pressure plate) as follows.
1. Park the vehicle on level ground and set the parting brake.
2. Remove the right crankcase cover as described in Chapter Six.
3. At the clutch lever, loosen the locknut (A, **Figure 42**) and turn the clutch adjuster (B) in all the way to obtain as much cable slack as possible.
4. At the clutch pressure plate, hold the hold the clutch mechanism adjuster with a screwdriver and loosen its locknut (**Figure 53**).
5. Move the clutch push lever (A, **Figure 54**) toward the front of the engine until it stops and hold in this position.
6. Turn the clutch mechanism adjuster (**Figure 53**) to align the mark on the end of the clutch push lever with the raised cast mark on the crankcase (B, **Figure 54**).
7. Hold the clutch mechanism adjuster in this position and tighten the locknut (**Figure 53**).
8. Perform the *Clutch Free Play Adjustment* procedure to complete clutch adjustment.
9. If the proper amount of free play cannot be achieved after performing this adjustment proce-

dure, either the clutch cable or the friction discs are excessively worn and need replacement. Refer to Chapter Six for clutch cable and clutch plate replacement.

10. When the clutch adjustment is correct, install the right crankcase cover as described in Chapter Six.

BRAKE INSPECTION AND ADJUSTMENT

This section describes inspection and adjustment procedures for the front and rear brake assemblies.

Refer to Chapter Thirteen for complete brake lining and drum inspection and repair procedures.

Front Brake Lining Inspection

Each front brake is equipped with a wear indicator that allows the brake lining wear to be checked without brake drum removal. The wear indicator consists of an arrow (A, **Figure 55**) installed on the brake camshaft and a wear limit gauge (B, **Figure 55**) with front and rear marks cast into the brake panel. When the front brake is applied the arrow moves with the camshaft and points to the wear limit gauge.

1. Park the vehicle on a level surface.

2. Apply the front brake lever fully and check the position of the arrow (A, **Figure 55**) on each front wheel brake panel (B, **Figure 55**). The arrow should be within the front and rear marks on the wear limit gauge. If the arrow falls even with or outside the rear wear limit gauge mark (B, **Figure 55**), the brake linings are worn and require replacement. Replace both shoe pairs (left and right sides) at the same time as described in Chapter Thirteen.

> *NOTE*
> *If there is any question about the accuracy of the wear indicators, remove the brake drums and measure the brake lining thickness as described in Chapter Thirteen.*

Front Brake Lever Adjustment

Brake lever free play increases as the brake linings wear. As the free play increases, the brake lever must

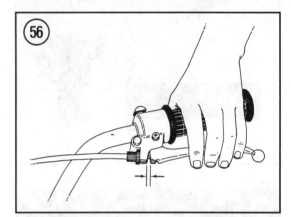

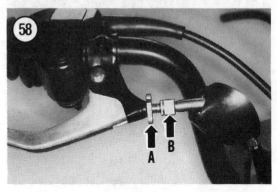

travel farther before the brake is applied. Brake adjustment compensates for brake lining wear by setting the free play to the manufacturer's standard setting. Always check brake adjustment at the intervals listed in **Table 1** or whenever brake lever travel has increased. If the brakes cannot be adjusted as described in this section, the brake linings are worn

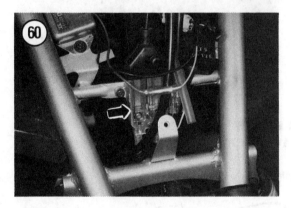

and require replacement. Front brake cable free play is necessary to prevent brake drag and to compensate for brake lining wear.

1. Perform the *Front Brake Lining Inspection* procedure as described in this section. If the brake shoes are not excessively worn, continue with Step 2.

> *WARNING*
> *Do not attempt to compensate for excessively worn brake shoes by overadjusting the front brake. At this point, braking effectiveness is reduced and brake failure may occur.*

2. Pull the front brake lever until resistance is felt and hold in this position. Then measure the distance between the brake lever perch and brake lever as shown in **Figure 56**. On 1988-2001 models the free play is 5.8 mm (0.20-0.31 in.). On 2002 models, the free play is 2-3 mm (0.08-0.12 in.). If the free play measurement is incorrect, continue with Step 3.

3. Remove the front cover (**Figure 57**) as described in Chapter Fourteen.

4A. On 1988-1989 models, loosen the brake adjuster locknut (A, **Figure 58**) and turn the adjuster (B) clockwise to obtain as much brake cable slack as possible.

4B. On 1990-2002 models, loosen the brake adjuster locknut (A, **Figure 59**) and turn the adjuster (B) clockwise to obtain as much brake cable slack as possible.

5. Visually check the position of the equalizer arm in the equalizer housing (**Figure 60**). The sides of equalizer arm must be equal as shown in A, **Figure 61**. If not, turn the brake adjusters (**Figure 62**) at the left and right brake panels until the equalizer arm is equal.

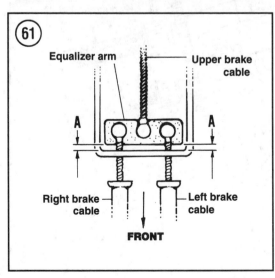

6A. On 1988-1989 models, turn the brake adjuster (B, **Figure 58**) to obtain the correct amount of free play. Tighten the locknut (A, **Figure 58**).

6B. On 1988-1989 models, turn the brake adjuster (B, **Figure 59**) to obtain the correct amount of free play. Tighten the locknut (A, **Figure 59**).

CAUTION
If the brake free play is set at less than 5 mm (0.20 in.), brake drag may result

and cause rapid brake lining and drum wear.

Rear Brake Pad Wear Check

Each rear brake pad (**Figure 63**) has a wear indicator hole machined in the friction material next to the pad's backing plate. When the friction material wears down to the wear indicator hole (**Figure 64**), the brake pad must be replaced. Replace both rear

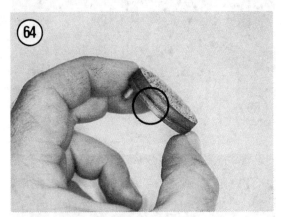

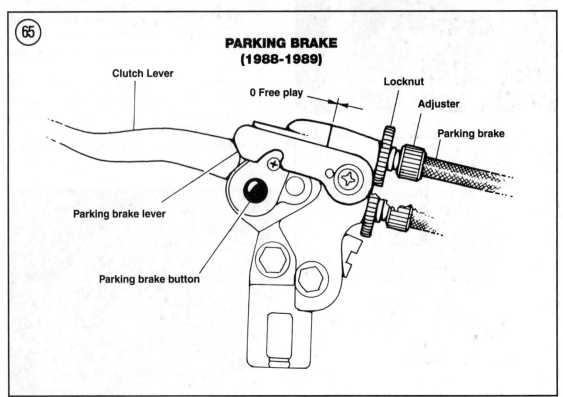

PARKING BRAKE
(1988-1989)

Clutch Lever

0 Free play

Locknut

Adjuster

Parking brake

Parking brake lever

Parking brake button

brake pads at the same time. Refer to Chapter Thirteen for rear brake pad replacement.

Parking Brake Adjustment

The parking brake acts on the rear wheels only. Adjust the parking brake when it fails to hold the vehicle securely or after replacing the rear brake pads.

On 1988-1989 models, the parking brake assembly is mounted on the left side handlebar (**Figure**

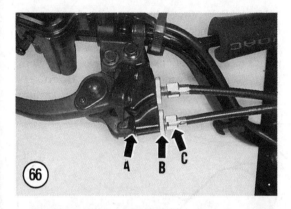

(66)

(67)

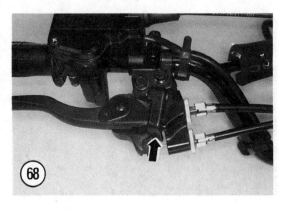

(68)

65). On 1990 and later models, the parking brake is mounted on the right side handlebar (**Figure 66**).

1. To check the parking brake adjustment, perform the following:

   a. When the parking brake is properly adjusted, there should be 0 mm free play between the edge of the clutch (1988-1989) or brake (1990-on) lever and its mounting perch as shown in **Figure 65** and A, **Figure 66**.

   b. Depress the parking brake button (**Figure 67**) and pull in the clutch (1988-1989) or brake (1990-on) lever.

   c. While holding the button down and the lever in, move the parking brake lever (**Figure 68**) over so its hooked end falls between the lever assembly and perch. Release the parking brake lever and button. The parking brake is now set.

   d. With the parking brake set and the transmission in NEUTRAL, the vehicle should not roll in either direction. If the vehicle moves with the parking brake set, or if the there is measurable free play between the edge of the lever and its mounting perch, adjust the parking brake starting with Step 2.

2. Release the parking brake by squeezing the clutch (1988-1989) or front brake (1990-on) lever.

3. Loosen the brake cable adjuster locknut (**Figure 65** or B, **Figure 66**) and turn the adjuster (**Figure 65** or C, **Figure 66**) in or out as required to set the free play at 0 mm. Tighten the locknut.

4. With the vehicle resting on a level surface, block the front wheels so the vehicle cannot roll in either direction. Then support the vehicle so the rear wheels are off the ground.

5. Turn the rear wheels to make sure there is no brake drag. If brake drag is noticed, repeat the adjustment steps again.

6. Lower the vehicle so both rear wheels are on the ground and set the parking brake.

DRIVE CHAIN

All models are equipped at the factory with an O-ring drive chain (**Figure 69**).

Service the drive chain at the intervals listed in **Table 1** or earlier if riding the vehicle in wet or sandy conditions.

Drive Chain Master Link Inspection

Make sure the master link is properly installed and secured to the drive chain. The spring clip must be installed so its closed end (**Figure 70**) is facing in the direction of chain travel. To remove and install the master link, refer to *Drive Chain Removal/Installation* in Chapter Twelve.

Chain Guide Rollers and Guide Inspection

The chain guide and rollers protect the swing arm from chain damage. Inspect these parts frequently and replace them when excessively worn or damaged.

a. To replace the swing arm roller (A, **Figure 71**) mounted on the swing arm, remove and install the swing arm as described in Chapter Twelve.

b. Tighten the upper and lower chain guide roller bolts (B, **Figure 71**) to the torque specification in **Table 4**.

c. When replacing the chain guide (**Figure 72**), make sure its channel width is wide enough for the O-ring drive chain.

Drive Chain Lubrication

Use SAE 30-50 weight motor oil to lubricate the original equipment drive chain. When lubricating an aftermarket O-ring drive chain, follow its manufacturer's recommendations on the type of chain lubricant to use. Some chain manufacturers recommended the use of a specific O-ring chain lube

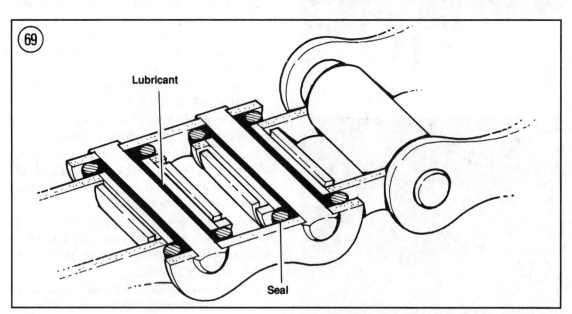

69

Lubricant

Seal

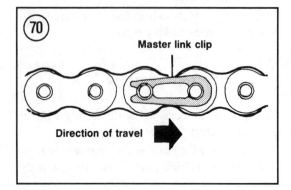

70

Master link clip

Direction of travel

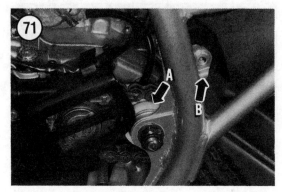

71

and others recommended the use of a light-weight aerosol type penetrating oil. Because the chemical makeup of the O-rings may differ between chain manufacturers, using the wrong type of lubricant can cause the O-rings to swell and permanently damage the chain.

> *NOTE*
> *If a tacky chain lubricant was previously used to lubricate the*

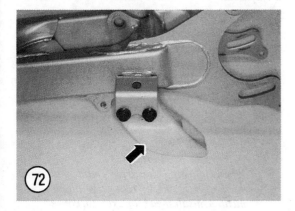

O-ring chain, the chain (and sprockets) should be cleaned in kerosene to remove all residue, dirt and grit. Clean the chain as described under **Drive Chain** *in Chapter Twelve.*

1. Ride the vehicle for 5 minutes to warm the chain. Then turn the engine off.
2. Support the vehicle with both rear wheels off the ground.
3. Shift the transmission into NEUTRAL.
4. Externally lubricate the D.I.D. drive chain with SAE 30-50 weight motor oil (**Figure 73**).

> *CAUTION*
> *Do not use a tacky chain lubricant on O-ring chains. Dirt and other abrasive materials that stick to the lubricant will cause rapid and permanent O-ring damage. An O-ring chain is prelubricated during its assembly at the factory. External oiling is only required to prevent chain rust and to keep the O-rings pliable.*

5. Wipe off all excess oil from the rear hub and axle.

Drive Chain
Cleaning

Refer to *Drive Chain* in Chapter Twelve.

Drive Chain/Sprocket
Wear Inspection

Frequently inspect the drive chain and replace if it is excessively worn or damaged.

A quick check will give you an indication of when to actually measure chain wear. At the rear sprocket, pull one of the links away from the sprocket. If the link pulls away more than 1/2 the height of a sprocket tooth, the chain is excessively worn (**Figure 74**).

To measure chain wear accurately, perform the following.

1. Support the vehicle with both rear wheels off the ground.
2. Loosen the upper and lower axle housing mounting bolts.
3. Loosen the chain adjuster locknuts.
4. Tighten the chain adjusters to move the rear axle rearward until the drive chain is tight (no slack).

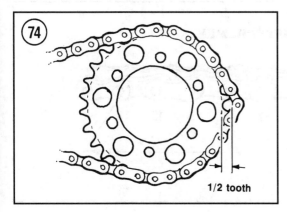

1/2 tooth

5. Lay a scale along the top chain run and measure the length of any 10 links (11 pins) in the chain. Measure from the inside of the first pin to the inside of the eleventh pin as shown in **Figure 75**. Turn the wheel and repeat the measurement with 2 different sets of links along the drive chain. If the 10 link length measurement exceeds 150.1 mm (5.915 in.), the drive chain is excessively worn and should be replaced.

6. Check the inner plate chain faces. They should be lightly polished on both sides. If they show considerable uneven wear on one side, the sprockets are not aligned. Severe wear requires chain and sprocket replacement.

7. Inspect the drive and driven sprockets for:

   a. Undercutting or sharp teeth.

   b. Broken teeth.

8. If wear is evident, replace the chain and both sprockets as a set, or the new chain will soon wear out. Replace the drive chain as described under *Drive Chain* in Chapter Twelve.

9. Adjust the drive chain as described in this chapter.

Drive Chain Adjustment

The drive chain must have adequate play so the chain is not too tight when the swing arm is horizontal. On the other hand, too much play may cause the chain to jump off the sprockets with potentially disastrous results.

When riding in mud and sand, the dirt and debris buildup that collects in the chain will make the chain tighter. Recheck chain play and readjust as required.

Check the drive chain free play and alignment before each ride. Drive chain free play is listed in **Table 7**.

1. Support the vehicle with both rear wheels off the ground.

2. Slowly turn the rear wheel and check the chain for binding and tight spots by moving the links up and down by hand. Each link must move freely against its connecting links. If a group of chain links or the entire chain is tight, remove and clean the drive chain as described in Chapter Twelve. When the chain is clean, check for swollen or damaged O-rings. Do not attempt to adjust and align a kinked drive chain.

3. Slowly turn the rear axle and check the chain tightness at several spots in the middle of the upper chain run (**Figure 76**). Because the chain wears unevenly, you will find that the chain's tightness varies. Check and adjust the chain at its *tightest* point.

4. Compare the drive chain free play with the specifications listed in **Table 7**. If necessary, adjust the drive chain as follows.

NOTE
When adjusting the drive chain, you must also maintain rear axle alignment. A misaligned rear axle can cause poor handling and pulling to one side or the other, as well as increased chain and sprocket wear. All models have wheel alignment marks on the axle housing and chain adjusters.

5. Hold the upper and lower axle housing (**Figure 77**) bolts and loosen their mounting nuts.

6. Loosen the chain adjuster locknuts (A, **Figure 78**) and turn the adjuster bolts (B, **Figure 78**) so the same mark (or point between each mark) on each adjuster aligns with the axle housing mark (C, **Figure 78**). Recheck chain free play.

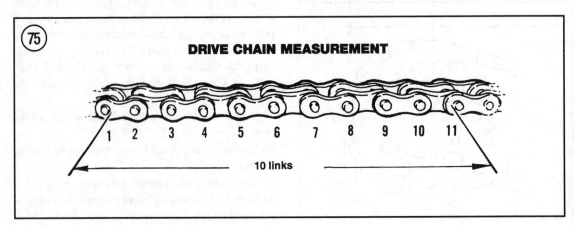

(75)

DRIVE CHAIN MEASUREMENT

1 2 3 4 5 6 7 8 9 10 11

10 links

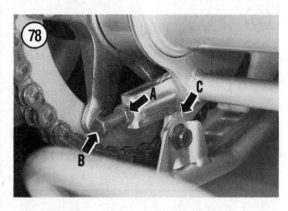

7. When chain free play is correct, check wheel alignment by sighting along the chain from the rear sprocket. It should leave the sprocket in a straight line. If it is cocked to one side or the other, adjust wheel alignment by turning one adjuster or the other. Recheck chain play.

> **NOTE**
> *If it is hard to align the drive chain with the chain adjuster marks, some part of the rear swing arm, rear axle, axle housing or chain adjusters is bent or damaged. Remove and inspect these parts as described in Chapter Twelve.*

8. Tighten the chain adjuster locknuts (A, **Figure 78**) to the torque specification in **Table 4**.

9. Tighten the upper and lower axle housing nuts to the torque specification in **Table 4**.

TIRES, WHEELS AND BEARINGS

Tire Pressure

Incorrect tire pressure can cause handling problems or tire damage. Check and adjust tire pressure and adjusted to maintain the smoothness of the tire, good traction and handling, and to get the maximum life out of the tire. When checking tire pressure, note the following:

a. Use a low-pressure tire gauge (**Figure 79**) to check the air pressure in the tires. See **Table 8** for the recommended tire pressure readings.

b. Always check and adjust tire pressure when the tires are cold.

c. When checking tire pressure, make 2 readings and use the second reading. The first reading may be incorrect due to dirt or other debris in the valve stem.

d. A tire pressure below the minimum pressure listed in **Table 8** could cause the tire(s) to dislodge from the rim, especially during hard riding.

> **NOTE**
> *The tire pressure specifications listed in **Table 8** are for the original tires. If you have installed different tires, follow the tire pressure recommendations specified by the tire manufacturer.*

WARNING
The front and rear tire pressure readings are different. Always inflate both tire sets (front and back) to the correct tire pressure listed in Table 8. Unequal tire pressure in the front or rear tires can cause poor handling and loss of control.

Tire Inspection

The tires take a lot of punishment due to the variety of terrain they are subject to. Inspect them periodically for excessive wear, cuts or abrasions. If you find a nail or other object in the tire, mark its location with a light crayon prior to removing it. This will help locate the hole for repair. Refer to Chapter Eleven for tire changing and repair information.

Measure tire wear with a ruler as shown in **Figure 80**. To obtain an accurate measurement of tire wear, measure a number of different knobs around the tire. The minimum tire tread for front and rear tires is 3.0 mm (1/8 in.).

WARNING
Do not ride your vehicle with worn out tires. Flat, worn or damaged tires can cause you to lose control of the ATV. Replace excessively worn or damaged tires immediately.

Wheel Inspection

Frequently inspect the condition of the wheel rims, especially the outer side (**Figure 81**). If the wheel has hit a tree or large rock, rim damage may be sufficient to cause an air leak or knock it out of alignment. Improper wheel alignment can cause severe vibration and result in an unsafe riding condition. Check wheel runout as described in Chapter Eleven.

Make sure the 4 wheel nuts (**Figure 81**) are securely in place on all wheels. Do not operate the vehicle if any of the wheel mounting studs are broken or missing or if any of the wheel nuts are missing or loose.

Tighten the wheel nuts to the torque specification in **Table 4**.

Front Wheel Bearings Inspection and Lubrication

At the service intervals listed in **Table 1**, remove the front hubs and inspect the wheel bearings (**Figure 82**) for lubrication and wear. The original wheel bearings are not sealed and require periodic cleaning and lubrication. Refer to *Front Brake Drum/Bearing Assembly* in Chapter Eleven for complete inspection and service procedures.

Rear Axle Bearings and Seals Inspection

Double sealed bearings are installed in the rear axle housing. Periodic lubrication of these bearings is not required. Periodically, inspect the outer seals (**Figure 83**). Worn or damaged seals should be replaced immediately as they will allow dirt, water and sand to enter the axle housing, damaging the bearing and causing rust and corrosion to build on the axle and center hub spacer. If dirt has contaminated the

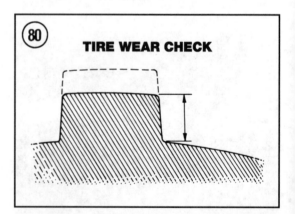
80 TIRE WEAR CHECK

81

axle housing, remove and service it as described in Chapter Eleven.

Whenever the rear axle has been removed, pack the seal lips with grease before reinstalling the axle.

STEERING AND FRONT SUSPENSION

This section describes inspection and lubrication procedures for the steering and front suspension components and toe-in adjustment.

Steering Inspection

Check the steering and front suspension at the intervals indicated in **Table 1**.
1. Park the vehicle on a level surface.
2. Visually inspect all components of the steering system. Pay close attention to the tie rods and steering shaft, especially after a hard spill or collision. If damage is apparent, the steering components must be repaired. Refer to the service procedures described in Chapter Eleven.
3. Check the tightness of the handlebar holder bolts.

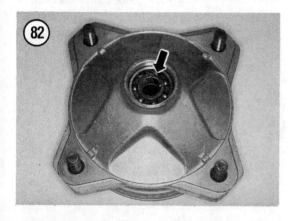

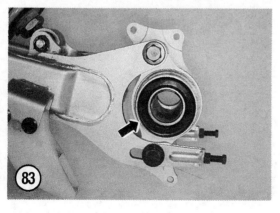

4. Make sure the front wheel nuts and axle nuts are tight.
5. Make sure the cotter pins are in place on all steering components. If any cotter pin is missing, check the nut for looseness. Torque the nut and install a new cotter pin.
6. Check steering shaft play as follows:
   a. To check steering shaft radial play, move the handlebar from side to side (without attempting to move the wheels). If radial play is excessive, the upper steering bearing blocks are probably worn and should be replaced.
   b. To check steering shaft thrust play, lift up, then push down on the handlebar. If excessive thrust play is noted, check the lower steering shaft nut for looseness. If the nut is tight, the lower steering shaft bushings are worn and should be replaced.
   c. Replace worn or damaged steering shaft parts as described in Chapter Eleven.
7. Check the steering knuckle and tie rod ball joints as follows:
   a. Turn the handlebar quickly from side to side. If there is appreciable looseness or play between the handlebar and tires, check the ball joints for excessive wear or damage.
   b. Turn the handlebar all the way to one side until it stops. Then slightly move the handlebar from side to side (without attempting to move the wheels) and check for any vertical play in the tie rod ends.
   c. If there is any vertical play, replace the tie rod ends as described in Chapter Eleven.
   d. Repeat for the other tie rod.

> *CAUTION*
> *Do not reuse cotter pins. Where removed, new cotter pins must be installed.*

Steering and Suspension Lubrication (Grease Fittings)

Lubricate the following components with a grease gun equipped with lightweight lithium soap base grease.

> *NOTE*
> *Prior to and after lubricating the following components, wipe off the grease fitting with a clean rag.*

a. Lower steering shaft bushings (**Figure 84**).

b. Upper arm pivot bolt (**Figure 85**).

c. Lower arm pivot bolts (**Figure 86**).

Upper Steering Bearing Block and Dust Seals

While not a part of the periodic maintenance schedule, the upper steering bearing block and dust seals (**Figure 87**) should be occasionally removed, cleaned and lubricated. Refer to Chapter Eleven for service procedures.

Toe-in
Check and Adjustment

Toe-in is a condition where the front of the tires are closer together than the back; see **Figure 88**. Check the toe-in alignment after servicing the steering assembly and occasionally through the riding season. Adjust toe-in by changing the length of the tie rods.

1. Inflate all 4 tires to the recommended tire pressure listed in **Table 8**.

2. Park the vehicle on level ground and set the parking brake. Then raise and support the front end so both front tires just clear the ground.

3. Turn the handlebar so it is facing straight ahead.

4. Mark the center of both front tires with a piece of chalk.

5. Using a ruler, carefully measure the distance between the center of both front tires (chalk mark) as shown in A, **Figure 88**. Write down the measurement.

6. Turn each tire exactly 180° and measure the distance between the center of both front tires at the points marked in Step 4. Write down the measurement.

7. Subtract the measurement in Step 5 from Step 6. The correct toe-in measurement is 0-10 mm (0-0.39 in.). If the toe-in is incorrect, continue with Step 8.

8. Loosen the locknuts securing each tie rod. See A, **Figure 89** and **Figure 90**.

9. Use a wrench on the flat portion (B, **Figure 89**) of the tie rods and slowly turn both tie rods the *same* amount until the tie rod measurement is correct.

NOTE
The tie rods must be turned the same number of turns. This ensures that the tie rod length will remain the same.

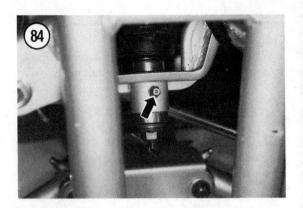

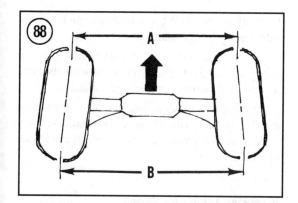

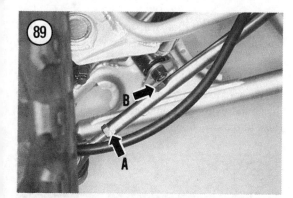

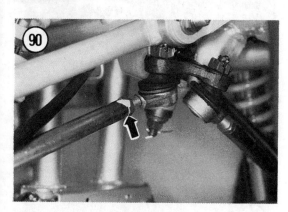

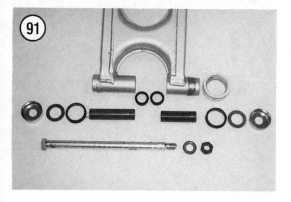

10. When the tie rod adjustment is correct, tighten the locknuts as follows:
   a. Spray the threads on each end of the tie rod with electrical contact cleaner and allow to dry.
   b. Apply a medium strength threadlocking compound onto the tie rod threads, then tighten the locknuts to the torque specification in **Table 4**.

11. Lower the vehicle so both front tires are on the ground.

12. Start the engine and ride the vehicle for a suitable distance to check handling and steering. Refer to *Tie Rods* in Chapter Eleven for tie rod inspection and its overall length specification.

> ### WARNING
> *Do not ride the vehicle at speed or for any distance until the toe-in adjustment is correct and the vehicle tracks correctly. Doing otherwise could cause you to lose control and crash.*

REAR SUSPENSION

Perform the following rear suspension inspection and lubrication procedures at the intervals listed in **Table 1**.

Swing Arm Bearing Play

Perform the *Swing Arm Bearing Inspection* under *Rear Swing Arm* in Chapter Twelve.

Swing Arm Bearing Assembly Lubrication

Lubricate the swing arm pivot shaft, collars, bushings and bearings (**Figure 91**) at the intervals specified in **Table 1**. The swing arm must be removed and partially disassembled to lubricate these parts—do not remove the needle bearings (**Figure 92**) for periodic lubrication. Refer to Chapter Twelve for service procedures.

Rear Shock Absorber Bearing and Pivot Bolt Lubrication

Lubricate the shock absorber bushings and pivot bolts (**Figure 93**) at the intervals indicated in **Table**

1. The shock absorber must be removed to lubricate these parts. Do not remove the bushings for periodic lubrication. Refer to Chapter Eleven.

FRAME

At the intervals specified in **Table 1**, inspect the frame and all of its welded joints for cracks, bent parts or other damage. Refer all frame repair to a qualified welding or metal fabrication shop.

NUTS, BOLTS AND OTHER FASTENERS

Constant vibration can loosen many of the fasteners on the vehicle. Check the tightness of all fasteners, especially those on:

    a. Engine mounting hardware.

    b. Engine crankcase covers.

    c. Handlebar.

    d. Gearshift lever.

    e. Brake pedal and lever.

    f. Exhaust system.

    g. Steering and suspension components.

LIGHTING EQUIPMENT

At the intervals specified in **Table 1**, inspect all of the lighting equipment for proper operation. Refer to Chapter Nine to replace any blown bulbs. Refer to Chapter Two for procedures on troubleshooting lighting system problems.

STORAGE

Several months of inactivity can cause serious problems and a general deterioration of the vehicle's condition. This is especially true in areas of weather extremes. During the winter months or during long periods of nonuse, it is advisable to prepare your Yamaha for storage.

Selecting a Storage Area

Most riders store their ATV in their home garage. If you do not have a home garage, facilities suitable for long-term storage are readily available for rent or lease in most areas. When selecting a building, consider the following points.

1. The storage area must be dry. Heating is not necessary, but the building should be well insulated to minimize extreme temperature variations.

2. Buildings with large window areas should be avoided, or such windows should be masked (also a good security measure) if direct sunlight can fall on the vehicle.

Preparing Vehicle for Storage

Careful preparation will minimize deterioration and make it easier to restore the vehicle to service later. Use the following procedure.

1. Wash the vehicle completely. Remove all dirt in all the hard to reach parts like the cooling fins on the head and cylinder. Completely dry all parts of the bike to remove all moisture.

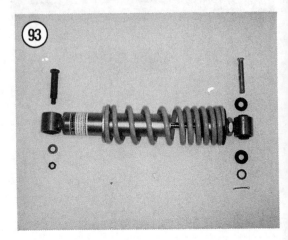

2. Run the engine for about 20-30 minutes to warm up the transmission oil. Drain the oil, regardless of the time since the last oil change. Refill with the normal quantity and type of oil.

3. Drain all gasoline from the fuel tank, fuel hose and the carburetor.

4. Clean and lubricate the drive chain and control cables, as described in this chapter. Also, refer to *Drive Chain* in Chapter Twelve.

5. Remove the spark plug and add about one teaspoon of engine oil into the cylinder. Reinstall the spark plug and turn the engine over to distribute the oil to the cylinder wall and piston.

6. Tape or tie a plastic bag over the end of the silencer to prevent the entry of moisture.

7. Check the tire pressure, and move the vehicle to the storage area. Place it securely on a stand with all 4 wheels off the ground.

8. Cover the vehicle with a blanket or heavy drop cloth. Place this cover over the ATV mainly as a dust cover. Do not use any plastic material, as it may trap moisture. Leave room for air to circulate around the vehicle.

Inspection During Storage

Try to inspect the vehicle each week while in storage. Correct any deterioration as soon as possible.

For example, if corrosion is observed, cover it with a light coat of grease or silicone spray.

Turn the engine over a couple of times, but do not start it.

Restoring Vehicle to Service

A vehicle that has been properly prepared and stored in a suitable area requires only light maintenance to restore to service.

1. Check and clean the vehicle of any spider webs and wasp nests that may have taken up residence during the vehicle's storage.

2. Before removing the vehicle from the storage area, reinflate the tires to the correct pressures. Air loss during storage may have nearly flattened the tires.

3. When the vehicle is brought to the work area, refill the fuel tank with fresh gasoline.

4. Check the engine oil tank (described in this chapter) and bleed the oil pump (Chapter Ten).

5. Install a fresh spark plug and start the engine.

6. Check the operation of the engine stop switch. Oxidation of the switch contacts during storage may make it inoperative.

7. Clean and test ride the vehicle.

Table 1 MAINTENANCE AND LUBRICATION SCHEDULE[1]

Initial 1 month or after engine or suspension break-in
  Change transmission oil
  Clean and oil air filter
  Check spark plug
  Check carburetor idle speed and starter operation
  Lubricate control cables
  Adjust clutch cable
  Inspect and adjust the front brake free play
  Lubricate drive chain
  Check drive chain tension and alignment
  Inspect tire pressure
  Inspect tires
  Inspect front hub bearings
  Inspect rear axle bearings
  Inspect steering and suspension system
  Lubricate front suspension
  Inspect rear swing arm
  Lubricate rear swing arm
  Check all external fasteners for looseness
  Check lighting equipment operation
Initial 3 months
  Clean and oil air filter
  Check spark plug
  Check carburetor fuel hose

(continued)

Table 1 MAINTENANCE AND LUBRICATION SCHEDULE[1] (continued)

Initial 3 months (continued)
  Check carburetor idle speed and starter operation
  Lubricate control cables
  Inspect and adjust the front brake free play
  Inspect tire pressure
  Inspect tires
  Inspect front hub bearings
  Inspect rear axle bearings
  Inspect steering and suspension system
  Lubricate front suspension
  Inspect rear swing arm
  Lubricate rear swing arm
  Inspect the frame
  Check all external fasteners for looseness
  Check lighting equipment operation
Every 6 months
  Change transmission oil
  Clean and oil air filter
  Check spark plug
  Check carburetor fuel hose
  Check carburetor idle speed and starter operation
  Check crankcase breather system
  Check exhaust system and clean spark arrester
  Lubricate control cables
  Adjust clutch cable
  Check front brake lining wear
  Inspect and adjust the front brake free play
  Check rear brake pad wear
  Lubricate drive chain
  Check drive chain tension and alignment
  Inspect tire pressure
  Inspect tires
  Inspect front hub bearings
  Inspect rear axle bearings
  Inspect steering and suspension system
  Lubricate front suspension
  Inspect rear swing arm
  Lubricate rear swing arm
  Inspect the frame
  Check all external fasteners for looseness
  Check lighting equipment operation

[1] Consider this maintenance schedule to be a guide to general maintenance and lubrication intervals. Harder than normal use (racing) and exposure to mud and water will require more frequent maintenance.

Table 2 RECOMMENDED LUBRICANTS AND FUEL

Engine oil	Yamalube 2 or an air cooled 2-stroke engine oil
Transmission oil	Yamalube 4 or a comparable 10W30 motor oil
Air filter	Foam air filter oil
Drive chain[1]	Non-tacky O-ring chain lubricant or SAE 30-50 weight engine motor oil
Steering and suspension lubricant	Multipurpose grease
Fuel	Premium unleaded fuel
Control cables	Cable lube[2]

[1] Use kerosene to clean O-ring drive chain.
[2] Do not use drive chain lubricant to lubricate control cables.

Table 3 OIL TANK

	Liters	U.S. qt.	Imp. qt.
Total amount	1.3	1.4	1.1

Table 4 MAINTENANCE TORQUE SPECIFICATIONS

	N•m	in.-lb.	ft.-lb.
Autolube pump cover	7	62	–
Carburetor switch	10	8	–
Chain adjuster locknuts	16	–	12
Chain guide roller bolts	9	80	–
Clutch adjuster locknut	7	–	–
Cylinder head	27	–	20
Intake manifold	8	71	–
Oil level check bolt	18	–	13
Rear axle housing nuts	50	–	36
Shift pedal	14	–	10
Spark plug	25	–	18
Tie-rod locknuts	30	–	22
Transmission drain plug	20	–	14
Wheel lugnuts	45	–	33

Table 5 TRANSMISSION OIL CAPACITY

	Milliliters	U.S. qt.	Imp. qt.
Oil change	650	0.69	0.57
After engine overhaul	700	0.74	0.62

Table 6 TUNE-UP SPECIFICATIONS

Ignition timing	16° @ 3,000 rpm (not adjustable)
Spark plug	
Canada and South Africa	BP8ES
All other	B8ES
Spark plug gap	0.7-0.8 mm (0.028-0.031 in.)
Engine idle speed	1,450-1,550 rpm
Initial pilot air screw setting	1-1/2 turns out

Table 7 DRIVE CHAIN FREE PLAY MEASUREMENT

	mm	in.
Free play	30-40	1.18-1.57

Table 8 TIRE INFLATION PRESSURE

	Front kPa (psi)	Rear kPa (psi)
Operating pressure	30 (4.3)	25 (3.6)
Minimum tire pressure	27 (3.8)	22 (3.1)
Maximum tire pressure	33 (4.7)	28 (4.0)

CHAPTER FOUR

ENGINE TOP END

This chapter covers the exhaust pipe, cylinder head, cylinder, piston, piston rings and reed valve assembly (**Figure 1**). Service to the engine lower end (crankshaft, transmission removal and installation, shift drum and shift forks) is covered in Chapter Five.

Before working on the engine, read the information listed under *Service Hints* in Chapter One. It is easier to work on a clean engine and you will do a better job.

The text often refers to left and right sides of the engine as it sits in the vehicle's frame, not as it happens to be sitting on your workbench. Left and right sides refer to the rider sitting on the seat and facing in the normal operating direction (forward).

Engine specifications are listed in **Tables 1-4** at the end of this chapter.

ENGINE PRINCIPLES

Figure 2 explains how a typical 2-stroke engine works. Understanding basic principles of engine operation will help you troubleshoot problems if the engine does not start or run properly.

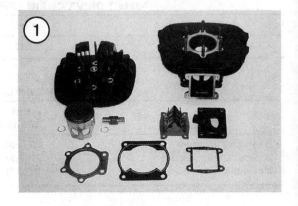

②

2-STROKE OPERATING PRINCIPLES

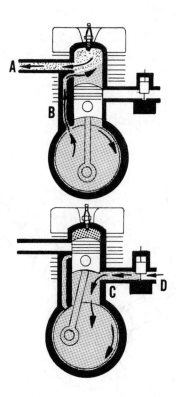
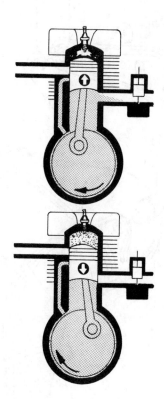

The crankshaft in this discussion is rotating in a clockwise direction.

As the piston travels downward, it uncovers the exhaust port (A) allowing the exhaust gases, which are under pressure, to leave the cylinder. A fresh fuel/air charge, which has been compressed slightly, travels from the crankcase into the cylinder through the transfer port (B). Since this charge enters under pressure, it also helps to push out the exhaust gases.

While the crankshaft continues to rotate, the piston moves upward, covering the transfer port (B) and exhaust port (A). The piston is now compressing the new fuel/air mixture and creating a low pressure area in the crankcase at the same time. As the piston continues to travel, it uncovers the intake port (C). A fresh fuel/air charge, from the carburetor (D), is drawn into the crankcase through the intake port, because of the low pressure within it.

Now, as the piston almost reaches the top of its travel, the spark plug fires, thus igniting the compressed fuel/air mixture. The piston continues to top dead center (TDC) and is pushed downward by the expanding gases.

As the piston travels down, the exhaust gases leave the cylinder and the complete cycle starts all over again.

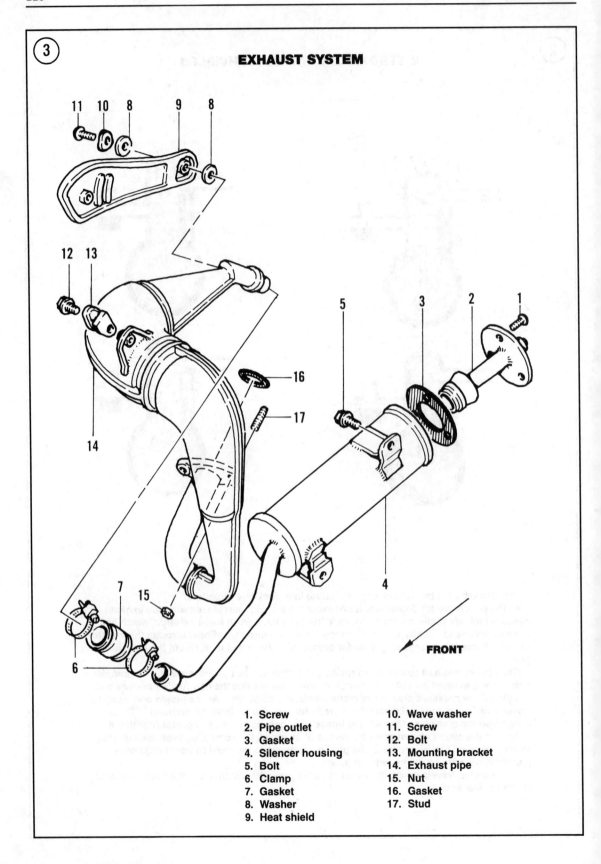

EXHAUST SYSTEM

③

1. Screw
2. Pipe outlet
3. Gasket
4. Silencer housing
5. Bolt
6. Clamp
7. Gasket
8. Washer
9. Heat shield
10. Wave washer
11. Screw
12. Bolt
13. Mounting bracket
14. Exhaust pipe
15. Nut
16. Gasket
17. Stud

FRONT

ENGINE LUBRICATION

The 2-stroke engine is lubricated by the Yamaha Autolube oil injection system. Oil is injected into the carburetor where it mixes with the air/fuel mixture and enters the engine. The oil is burned with the fuel and expelled through the exhaust. The engine top and bottom end components are lubricated by this oil, which clings to the various parts as it passes through the crankcase and cylinder. This oil is not

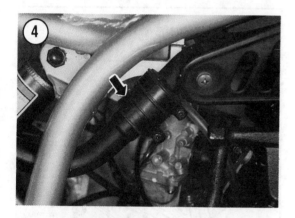

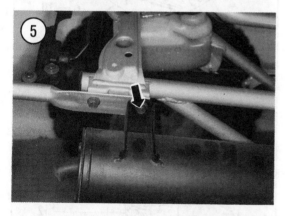

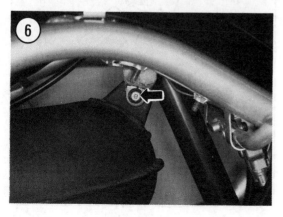

reused and the amount of oil in the oil tank will diminish as the oil is being used.

Check the oil level in the oil tank daily and whenever refueling the vehicle. Refer to Chapter Three for oil tank refilling. Refer to Chapter Ten for Autolube pump service.

CLEANLINESS

Repairs go much faster and easier if your engine is clean before you begin work. When servicing the engine top end with the engine installed in the frame, dirt trapped underneath the fuel tank and upper frame tube can fall into the cylinder or crankcase opening. To prevent this, remove the fuel tank and wrap the frame tube with a large, clean cloth.

EXHAUST SYSTEM

The exhaust system is a critical part to the overall performance and operation of your 2-stroke engine. Check the exhaust system for deep dents and fractures and repair them or replace damaged parts immediately. Check the exhaust pipe and silencer for loose or missing fasteners. Running the vehicle with a loose exhaust system will increase the likelihood of damage to the exhaust pipe and frame mounting brackets. In addition, a loosely mounted exhaust pipe will increase the vehicle's noise level. A loose exhaust pipe-to-cylinder head connection will reduce engine performance, cause excessive noise and possible piston seizure.

Refer to **Figure 3** when servicing the stock exhaust system.

Removal/Installation

1. Park the vehicle on level ground and set the parking brake.
2. Loosen the silencer joint pipe clamps (**Figure 4**), then remove the silencer mounting bolt (**Figure 5**) and silencer.
3. Loosen the exhaust pipe bracket bolt (**Figure 6**) and exhaust pipe mounting nuts (**Figure 7**).
4. Remove the bolt and nuts, then remove the exhaust pipe from the engine and frame.
5. Remove and discard the exhaust pipe gasket from the cylinder's exhaust port.

6. Check the exhaust pipe for cracks or other damage. Refer service to a professional welding shop.

7. Remove any exhaust residue from the exhaust port and exhaust pipe mating surfaces.

8. Check for loose or damaged exhaust pipe studs. Replace or tighten studs as described in Chapter One.

9. Install a new exhaust pipe gasket (**Figure 8**) into the cylinder head.

10. Install the exhaust pipe and secure it with its 2 mounting nuts (**Figure 7**) and bracket bolt. Tighten these fasteners hand-tight only. Make sure the exhaust pipe gasket is centered in the cylinder exhaust port and not pinched between the pipe and port opening.

11. Install the silencer and secure it with its rear mounting bolt (**Figure 5**).

12. Tighten the exhaust pipe fasteners in the following order:

    a. Tighten the exhaust pipe nuts (**Figure 7**) to the torque specification in **Table 4**.

    b. Tighten the exhaust pipe bracket bolt (**Figure 6**) securely.

    c. Tighten the silencer joint pipe clamps (**Figure 4**) securely.

    d. Tighten the silencer mounting bolt (**Figure 5**) to the torque specification in **Table 4**.

13. Start the engine and check for exhaust leaks.

CYLINDER HEAD

The cylinder head may be serviced with the engine mounted in the frame.

Refer to **Figure 9** when servicing the cylinder head in this section.

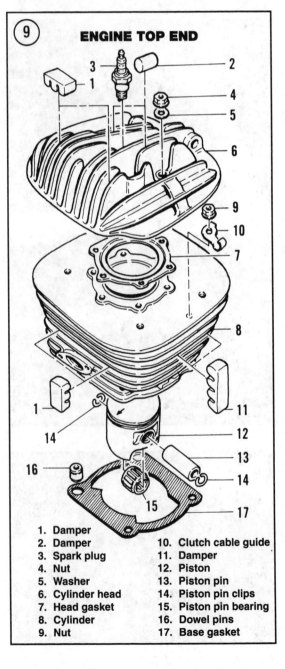

ENGINE TOP END

1. Damper
2. Damper
3. Spark plug
4. Nut
5. Washer
6. Cylinder head
7. Head gasket
8. Cylinder
9. Nut
10. Clutch cable guide
11. Damper
12. Piston
13. Piston pin
14. Piston pin clips
15. Piston pin bearing
16. Dowel pins
17. Base gasket

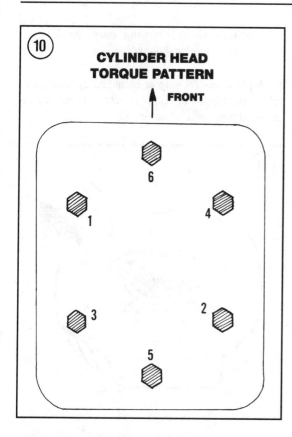

CYLINDER HEAD
TORQUE PATTERN

FRONT

6

1

4

3

2

5

Removal

CAUTION
To prevent warpage and damage to any
component, remove the cylinder head
when the engine is cold.

1. Remove the seat (Chapter Fourteen) and fuel tank
(Chapter Eight).
2. Clean the upper frame rail of all dirt and debris
that could fall into the cylinder.
3. Remove the exhaust system as described in this
chapter.
4. Perform the *2-Stroke Leak Down Test* described
in Chapter Two to check for cylinder head or other
engine leaks.
5. Disconnect the spark plug wire from the plug,
then loosen the spark plug.
6. Loosen the cylinder head nuts 1/4 turn at a time
in the pattern shown in **Figure 10**. Then remove the
nuts and washers.
7. Remove the cylinder head (**Figure 11**).
8. Remove and discard the cylinder head gasket
(**Figure 12**).
9. Turn the crankshaft and bring the piston to top
dead center (TDC). Lay a clean rag over the cylinder
to prevent dirt from falling into the cylinder.
10. Inspect the cylinder head as described in this
chapter.

Inspection

1. Wipe away any soft deposits from the cylinder
head combustion chamber (**Figure 13**). Remove
hard deposits with a wire brush mounted in a drill or
with a soft metal scraper (**Figure 14**).

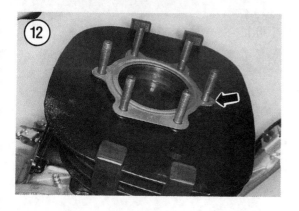

CAUTION
Do not gouge the gasket or combustion chamber surfaces when cleaning the cylinder head. Burrs created from improper cleaning may cause preignition and heat erosion.

2. Remove the spark plug and check the cylinder head threads (A, **Figure 15**) for carbon buildup or thread damage. Chase threads with a spark plug tap (B, **Figure 15**).

3. Measure the cylinder head flatness with a straightedge and feeler gauge (**Figure 16**). If the cylinder head warpage exceeds the service limit in **Table 2**, resurface the head as follows:

    a. Tape a piece of 400-600 grit wet emery sandpaper onto a piece of thick plate glass or surface plate (**Figure 17**).

    b. Slowly resurface the head by moving it in figure-eight patterns on the sandpaper.

    c. Rotate the head several times to avoid removing too much material from one side. Check progress often with the straightedge and feeler gauge.

    d. If the cylinder head warpage still exceeds the service limit, take the cylinder head to your dealership for further inspection and possible repair.

NOTE
Repair damaged threads with a spark plug tap or install a thread insert.

4. Clean, dry and inspect the cylinder head nuts and flat washers (**Figure 18**). Replace damaged cylinder head flange nuts. Replace nuts with damaged threads or rounded off hex corners. Replace washers that are warped or damaged in any way.

5. Check for loose or damaged cylinder head studs (**Figure 12**). Replace or tighten studs as described in Chapter One.

6. Wash the cylinder head in hot soapy water and rinse with clean, cold water.

7. Check the cylinder head for any cracked or missing cooling fins. Refer repair to a competent welding company.

CAUTION
Missing or damaged cylinder head cooling fins should be repaired or replaced before operating the vehicle;

otherwise overheating may result, causing engine damage.

8. Replace any missing or damaged cylinder head rubber dampers. The dampers help to reduce cylinder head noise and vibration.

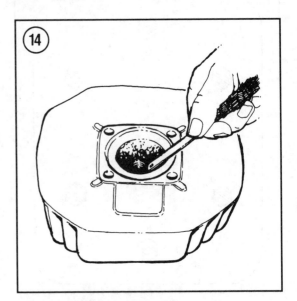

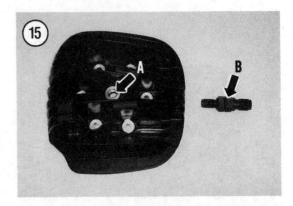

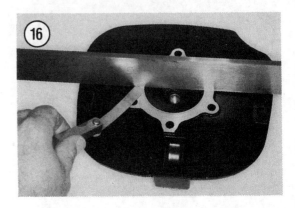

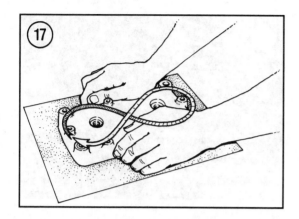

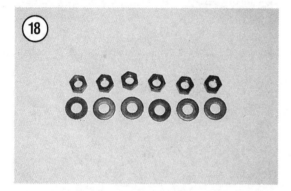

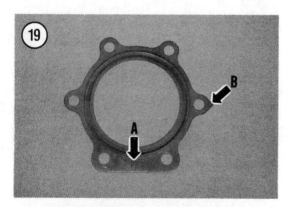

Installation

1. Clean and inspect the cylinder head as described under *Inspection* in this chapter.

2. Remove all carbon residue from the cylinder gasket surface.

3. Install a new cylinder head gasket with its UP mark facing up (A, **Figure 19**) and surface point (B, **Figure 19**) facing forward. See **Figure 12**.

4. Guide the cylinder head over the cylinder studs and seat it onto the head gasket (**Figure 11**).

5. Install the cylinder head washers and nuts (**Figure 18**) and tighten finger-tight. Then tighten the nuts in 2-3 steps in the numerical order shown in **Figure 10** to the final torque specification listed in **Table 4**.

6. Install the spark plug and tighten to the torque specification in **Table 4**. Reconnect the spark plug lead.

7. Install the exhaust system as described in this chapter.

8. Install the fuel tank (Chapter Eight) and seat (Chapter Fourteen).

9. Perform the *2-Stroke Leak Down Test* in Chapter Two to check for engine leaks.

CYLINDER

Refer to **Figure 9** when servicing the cylinder.

Removal

1. Remove the exhaust pipe as described in this chapter.

2. Remove the carburetor as described in Chapter Eight.

3. Remove the cylinder head as described in this chapter.

4. If necessary, remove the reed valve assembly as described in this chapter.

5. Loosen the cylinder base nuts (**Figure 20**) in a crisscross pattern and then remove them. Remove the clutch cable bracket (**Figure 21**) from the left rear stud.

> *CAUTION*
> *When removing the cylinder in Step 6, do not twist the cylinder so far that the piston rings could snap into the intake port. This would cause the cylinder to bind and damage the piston and rings.*

NOTE
The shop towel used in Step 6 prevents dirt, carbon or pieces of a broken piston ring from falling into the crankcase.

6. Tap the cylinder (**Figure 22**) to break it loose from the crankcase, then pull it off the crankcase studs and stop. Stuff a shop towel around the connecting rod and under the cylinder before sliding the cylinder off the piston. Then pull the cylinder straight up and off the crankcase studs. If the cylinder is stuck to the crankcase or piston, do not pry it off as scratches left between the mating surfaces could cause an air leak. To remove a stuck cylinder, note the following:

   a. Two dowel pins are installed in the crankcase on the right side of the cylinder (**Figure 9**). Rusted or damaged dowel pins will lock the cylinder in place, making it difficult to remove. To remove a stuck cylinder, spray a penetrating liquid down the cylinder studs at each of the dowel pin positions. Allow the liquid to soak in, then rap the cylinder squarely with your mallet to break the dowel pins loose from the cylinder or crankcase.

   b. A seized piston or rusted and corroded cylinder bore will also make it difficult to remove the cylinder. If the cylinder lifts off the crankcase, but is stuck to the piston, soak the piston crown and cylinder bore with a penetrating liquid. If the seizure or corrosion is severe, you may have to break the piston to separate it from the cylinder bore.

7. Remove and discard the cylinder base gasket (A, **Figure 23**).

8. Remove the 2 dowel pins (B, **Figure 23**).

9. Soak any remaining gasket material on the crankcase, then carefully scrape it off. Be careful not to gouge the gasket surfaces.

Inspection

The original cylinder block uses a cast-iron liner. It can be bored to accept oversize pistons. Yamaha offers 2 oversize pistons. Wiseco offers 5 piston sizes (standard and 4 oversizes).

A bore gauge and a 50-75 mm (2-3 in.) micrometer or an inside micrometer will be required to accurately measure the cylinder bore. If you do not have

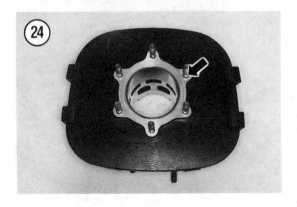

these tools, have the measurements performed at a dealership or qualified machine shop.

1. If you have not done so, remove the reed valve as described in this chapter.

2. Remove all gasket and carbon residue from the cylinder's upper (**Figure 24**) and lower (**Figure 25**) gasket surfaces.

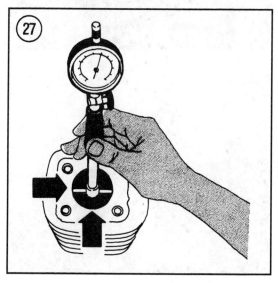

3. Tighten or replace the cylinder head and exhaust pipe studs as described under *Stud Replacement* in Chapter One.

4. Remove all carbon residue from the exhaust port (**Figure 26**) with a drill mounted wire wheel or rounded scraper. Be careful not to damage the cylinder bore or change the exhaust port chamfer.

> *NOTE*
> *A good way to protect the cylinder bore when cleaning the exhaust port is to block off the exhaust port with an old piston or with a piece of plastic or cardboard.*

5. Measure the cylinder bore with a bore gauge (**Figure 27**) or an inside micrometer at the 3 depth positions shown in **Figure 28**. Except for the bottom measurement, measure both in line with the piston pin and at 90° to the pin. Note the following:

    a. Use the largest bore measurement to determine cylinder wear.

    b. Record measurements for cylinder wear, taper and out-of-round.

    c. If the cylinder bore, taper or out-of-round measurement exceeds the wear limit in **Table**

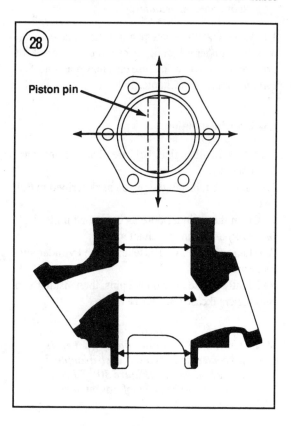

Piston pin

2, the cylinder bore must be rebored to the next oversize and fitted with a new piston.

6. To determine piston-to-cylinder clearance, refer to *Piston/Cylinder Clearance* in this chapter.

7. When installing new piston rings, hone the cylinder (**Figure 29**) to deglaze the cylinder and help the new rings to seat. If necessary, refer this service to a dealership or motorcycle repair shop.

> *CAUTION*
> *If the cylinder was bored or honed with a rigid type hone, the ports must be chamfered to prevent the rings from snagging a port.*

8. Before installing the cylinder, wash the bore in hot soapy water, then rinse with clear water. Then check the bore cleanliness by running a white cloth over the bore surface. Repeat the wash process until the white cloth comes out clean—no smudge or dark marks.

9. Dry the cylinder with compressed air, then lubricate the bore with 2-stroke oil.

> *CAUTION*
> *The cast iron bore will rust if not lubricated immediately.*

10. When installing new piston rings, a new piston or if the cylinder is bored, perform the same break-in procedure that you would use on a new machine. See *Engine Break-In* in Chapter Five.

Cylinder Installation

Make sure all engine parts are clean before starting assembly.

1. If removed, install the piston as described in this chapter.

2. Clean the cylinder bore as described under *Cylinder Inspection* in this chapter.

3. Make sure the crankcase and both cylinder surfaces are clean.

4. Lightly grease the 2 dowel pins, then install them into the crankcase (B, **Figure 23**).

> *NOTE*
> *The stock Yamaha base gasket is precoated and has a sealer strip applied to the bottom side (**Figure 30**). Silicone sealer or other types of gasket sealers are not required.*

5. Install a new base gasket (A, **Figure 23**).

6. Lubricate the piston skirt, piston ring and cylinder bore with 2-stroke engine oil.

7. Make sure the piston pin clips are seated in the piston grooves completely.

8. Make sure the piston ring end gaps are properly aligned with the piston ring locating pins (**Figure 31**).

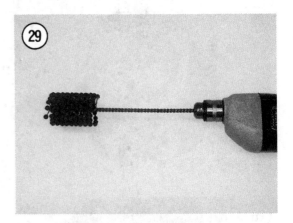

9. Compress the rings with your fingers and start the bottom edge of the cylinder over the piston. Then hold the piston and slide the cylinder down until it covers the rings. Continue to slide the cylinder down over the crankcase mounting studs, and seat it against the base gasket. Make sure the cylinder seats onto both dowel pins. See **Figure 22**.

10. Hold the cylinder in place with one hand and operate the kickstarter lever with your other hand. If the piston catches or stops in the cylinder, the piston ring(s) are not aligned with the locating pins in the piston ring groove. The piston must move up and down the cylinder bore smoothly.

NOTE
If the rings are not correctly aligned with the locating pins, remove the cylinder and check for damage.

11. Install the cylinder base nuts (**Figure 20**)and tighten finger-tight. Install the clutch cable guide on the left rear base stud (**Figure 21**).

12. Tighten the cylinder nuts as follows:

NOTE
*Because the cylinder fins extend past the cylinder nuts, the nuts cannot be tightened with a torque wrench and socket. The Motion Pro torque adapter wrench (**Figure 32**) or an equivalent extension must be attached to the torque wrench to reach these nuts. However, because the torque adapter or extension can increase the length of the torque wrench, the torque applied may be greater than the torque or dial reading on the torque wrench. When using a torque adapter and it increases the length of the torque wrench, the torque specification **must be** recalculated.*

   a. Before tightening the nuts with a torque adapter and torque wrench, refer to **Table 4** for the cylinder base nut torque specification. If necessary, recalculate the torque specification by following the instructions that came with the torque wrench or torque adapter, or use the information listed under *Torque Wrench Adapter* in Chapter One.
   b. Tighten the cylinder base nuts (**Figure 33**) in a crisscross pattern in 2 or 3 steps to the torque specification in **Table 4**.

13. Install the cylinder head as described in this chapter.

14. If removed, installed the reed valve as described in this chapter.

15. Perform the *2-Stroke Leak Down Test* in Chapter Two to ensure that the engine is air tight.

16. Install the carburetor (Chapter Eight).

17. Install the exhaust system as described in this chapter.

18. Follow the *Break-in Procedure* in this chapter if new parts were installed (piston and rings) or if the cylinder was bored.

PISTON, PISTON PIN AND PISTON RINGS

The piston is made of an aluminum alloy. The piston pin is a precision fit and is held in place by a clip at each end. A caged needle bearing is used on the small end of the connecting rod. **Figure 34** shows the piston components.

Piston and
Piston Ring Removal

1. Remove the cylinder as described in this chapter.
2. Before removing the piston, hold the rod tightly and rock the piston to detect excessive clearance between the piston, piston pin and connecting rod (**Figure 35**). Any rocking motion (do not confuse with the normal sliding motion) indicates wear on the piston pin, needle bearing, piston pin bore, or more likely, a combination of all three.
3. Wrap a clean shop cloth under the piston so the clips cannot fall into the crankcase.

> *WARNING*
> *Piston pin clips can slip and fly off during removal. Wear safety glasses to prevent eye injury.*

4. Remove the clip from each side of the piston pin bore (**Figure 36**). Hold your thumb over one edge of the clip when removing it to prevent it from springing out.
5. Use a wooden dowel or socket extension and push the piston pin (**Figure 37**) out of the piston.

> *CAUTION*
> *The piston pin is a floating type and should remove with only slight hand pressure. If the engine ran hot or seized, piston warpage may lock the piston pin in place, making it difficult to remove. If the pin is tight, do not drive it out of the piston. Doing so may damage the piston, needle bearing and connecting*

rod. To remove a tight piston pin, use the tool and procedure in Step 6.

6. If the piston pin is tight, fabricate the tool shown in **Figure 38**. Assemble the tool onto the piston and pull the piston pin out of the piston. Install a pad between the piston and piece of pipe to prevent the tool from damaging the piston.

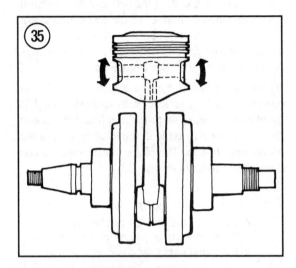

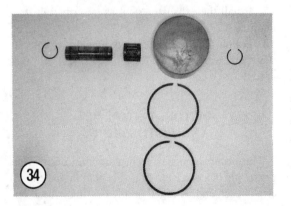

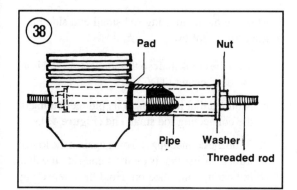

7. Lift the piston off the connecting rod.

8. Remove the needle bearing (**Figure 39**).

9. Place a piece of foam insulation tube, or shop cloth, over the end of the connecting rod to protect it.

NOTE
The 2 piston rings are the same size and type. If the piston rings are going to be reused, identify them for reassembly.

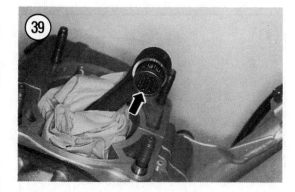

10. Spread the top piston ring ends with your fingers and slide the ring out of the ring land and up and off the piston (**Figure 40**).

11. Repeat Step 10 for the other piston ring.

Piston Pin and Needle Bearing Inspection

Yamaha does not list operating clearances for the piston pin and piston. This procedure describes basic visual and free play checks that can be made to these 2 parts. Since piston pin-to-piston clearance is small, refer inspection to a dealership if there is any questionable play.

1. Clean the piston pin and needle bearing in solvent, then in hot, soapy water. Rinse with clean, hot water then, dry thoroughly.

2. Inspect the needle bearing (A, **Figure 41**) for:

   a. Needle wear, flat spots or damage.

   b. A cracked or otherwise damaged bearing cage.

3. Check the piston pin (B, **Figure 41**) for excessive wear, scoring and cracks along the outer diameter. Replace the piston pin if necessary.

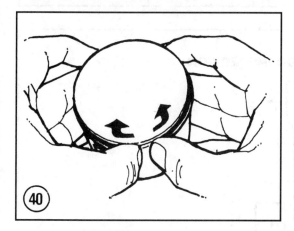

4. Lubricate the needle bearing and piston pin and install them into the connecting rod (**Figure 42**). Try to move the piston pin back and forth as shown in **Figure 42**. There must be no noticeable play in either

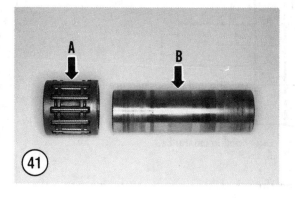

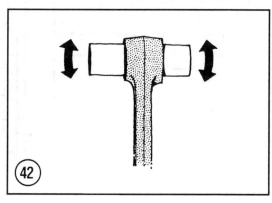

direction. If there is free play, repeat the check with a new bearing and pin. If there is still free play, replace the connecting rod.

5. Install the piston pin partway into one side of the piston as shown in **Figure 43**. Try to move the piston pin in each of the 4 positions shown in **Figure 43**. Repeat for the other side of the piston. There must be no noticeable play in either direction. If there is free play, repeat the check with a new piston pin. If there is free play with the new pin, the piston is worn and must be replaced.

Connecting Rod Inspection

The following checks can be made with the crankshaft installed in the engine and the engine installed in the frame. When checking the connecting rod in this section, compare the actual measurements to the specifications in **Table 2**. Replace the connecting rod if damaged or if any measurement is out of specification.

1. Visually inspect the connecting rod small and large ends for galling, cracks or other damage.

2. Measure the connecting rod small end side play (**Figure 44**) as follows:

    a. Turn the crankshaft so the connecting rod is at top dead center (TDC).

    b. Mount a dial indicator so its plunger contacts the connecting rod small end (**Figure 45**).

    c. Slide the connecting rod over against the lower thrust washer that is on the same side the dial indicator is installed on. Hold the connecting rod in this position.

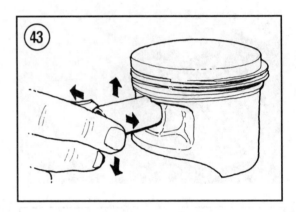

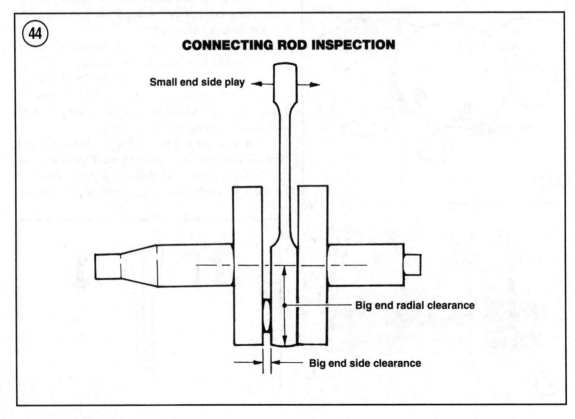

CONNECTING ROD INSPECTION

Small end side play

Big end radial clearance

Big end side clearance

d. While holding the lower part of the connecting rod, try to move the upper end by hand. Any movement is small end side play. Compare the actual reading to the small end free play clearance in **Table 2**.

3. Check connecting rod big end radial clearance (**Figure 44**) as follows:

a. Turn the crankshaft so the connecting rod is at TDC.

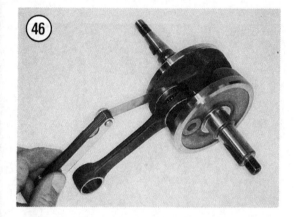

b. Move the connecting rod over against one of the lower thrust washers.

c. Hold the connecting rod in this position, then try to move it up and down as shown in **Figure 44**. If radial clearance can be felt, the lower end bearing assembly is worn.

4. Measure the connecting rod big end side clearance (**Figure 44**) with a feeler gauge and check against the specification in **Table 2**. **Figure 46** shows the clearance being measured with the crankshaft removed from the engine.

5. To replace the connecting rod and its lower end bearing, the engine must be disassembled and the crankshaft overhauled. Refer to Chapter Five for engine and crankshaft overhaul.

Piston and Ring Inspection

When measuring the piston and ring components, compare the actual measurements to the specifications in **Table 2**. Replace parts that are damaged or out of specification.

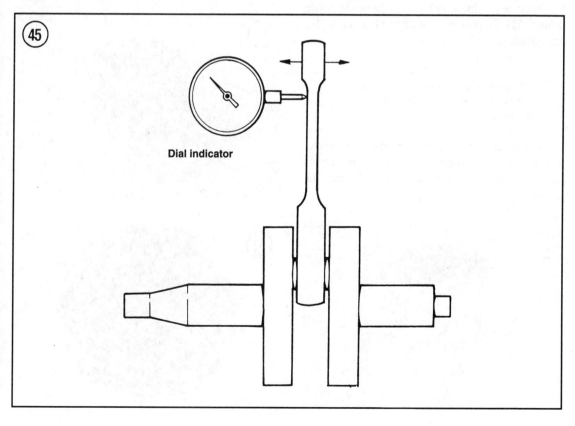

Dial indicator

1. Check the piston for cracks at the transfer cut-aways (A, **Figure 47**) and along the piston skirt (B, **Figure 47**).

2. Check the piston skirt reed valve windows (**Figure 48**) for cracks or other damage.

3. Check the piston skirt for galling and abrasion which may have resulted from piston seizure. If light galling is present, smooth the affected area with No. 400 emery paper and oil or a fine oilstone. However, if the galling is severe or if the piston is deeply scored, replace the piston.

4. Check for loose or damaged ring locating pins (**Figure 49**). Each pin must be tight with no outer cracks or other damage. Replace the piston if either pin is loose or damaged.

> *CAUTION*
> *If a piston ring locating pin falls out, the piston ring can then rotate in its groove. This will allow the ring's end gap to catch in a port and cause the type of damage shown in **Figure 50**.*

5. Check the piston pin retaining clip grooves (C, **Figure 47**) for wear or damage.

6. Check the condition and color of the piston crown (**Figure 51**). Remove normal carbon buildup with a wire wheel mounted in a drill.

> *CAUTION*
> *Do not use a wire brush to clean the piston skirt or gouge the piston when cleaning it.*

7. Remove carbon buildup from the ring groove with a broken ring (**Figure 52**). Work carefully to prevent removing any piston material from the groove.

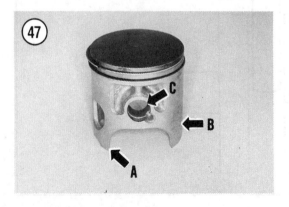

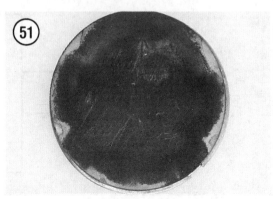

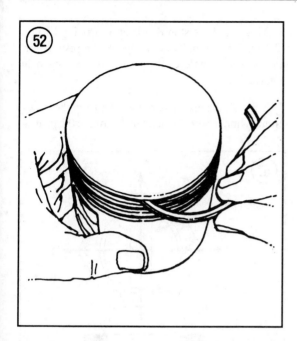

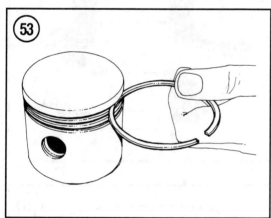

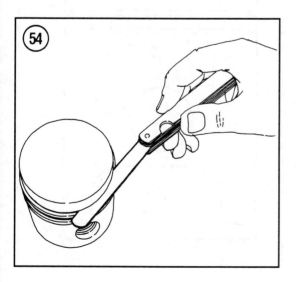

8. Inspect the ring grooves (**Figure 49**) for burrs, nicks, broken or cracked lands. Replace the piston if either ring groove is worn or damaged.

9. Roll the ring around its groove (**Figure 53**) and check for tight spots in the groove. Repair minor damage with a fine-cut file.

10. Install each ring in its groove and measure the piston ring-to-groove side clearance (**Figure 54**) with a feeler gauge. If the clearance is out of specification, the next step would be to recheck the clearance with a new piston ring. However, this is not always a practical step for the home mechanic. Instead, measure the side clearance of each groove using the second or lower ring. Because this ring normally receives less wear than the upper ring, you may be able to better approximate whether the wear is caused by the ring or piston (or both).

11. Measure the piston ring end gap as follows:

   a. Place a ring into the bottom of the cylinder and push it in to a point where cylinder wear is minimal. Then measure the ring gap with a flat feeler gauge (**Figure 55**).

   b. Replace the rings as a set if the end gap of any ring is out of specification.

12. Measure the piston diameter as described under *Piston/Cylinder Clearance* in this chapter.

Piston/Cylinder Clearance

Yamaha does not list service limit specifications for their standard and oversize piston sizes. They only list new piston sizes (**Table 2**). To determine piston wear, first measure the cylinder bore wear. If

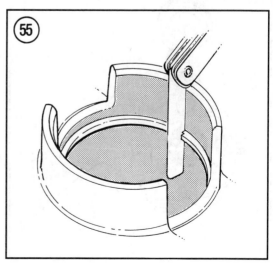

it is within specification, measure the piston diameter and subtract this dimension from the bore diameter to determine the piston-to-cylinder clearance. If the piston clearance is good, the piston diameter is also good. If the piston clearance is out of specification (and the bore wear is good), the piston is worn and must be replaced. If the piston clearance is just out of specification, and the cylinder bore wear is minimal, it may be possible to install a new piston to help take up some of the excessive piston-to-cylinder clearance. If the piston-to-cylinder clearance is excessive, and the bore wear is just within specification, it may be better to rebore the cylinder to the next oversize.

1. Measure the cylinder bore with a bore gauge (**Figure 56**) or an inside micrometer at the 3 depth positions shown in **Figure 57**. Except for the bottom measurement, measure both in line with the piston pin and at 90° to the pin. Note the following:

   a. Use the largest bore measurement to determine cylinder wear.

   b. Record measurements for cylinder wear, taper and out-of-round.

   c. If the cylinder bore, taper or out-of-round measurement exceeds the service limit in **Table 2**, the cylinder bore must be rebored to the next oversize and fitted with a new piston.

2. Measure the piston diameter at a point 10 mm (0.40 in.) from the bottom edge of the piston skirt and at a 90° angle to the piston pin as shown in **Figure 58**.

3. Subtract the piston skirt diameter from the maximum cylinder bore diameter to determine the piston-

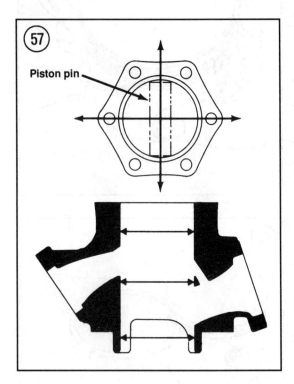

57

Piston pin

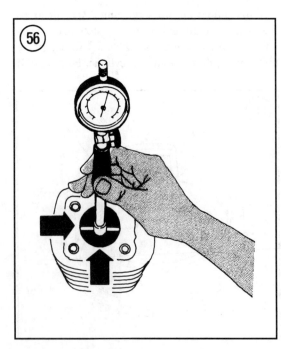

56

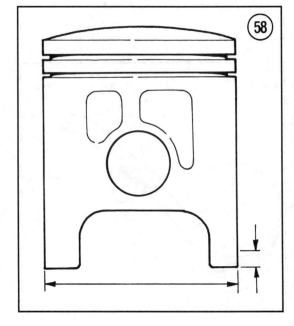

58

to-cylinder clearance. Compare this measurement with the service limit in **Table 2**. If out of specification, replace the piston or rebore the cylinder.

Piston Ring Installation

1. Check the piston ring end gap before assembling the piston and rings; refer to *Piston Inspection* in this

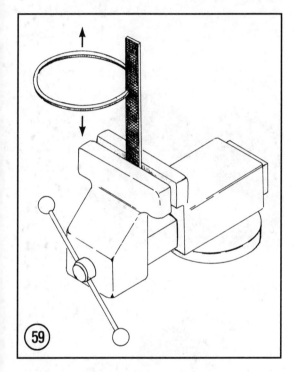

chapter. The end gap measurement must be within specification (**Table 2**). If the end gap is too narrow after boring the cylinder, remeasure the cylinder bore to make sure it is within specification. If it is, enlarge the gap by carefully filing the ring ends with a fine-cut file (**Figure 59**).

2. Wash the piston and ring in solvent and then with soapy water to remove any oil and carbon particles. Rinse the piston with clean, hot water and dry with compressed air.

3. Install the piston rings as follows:

    a. The top and bottom piston rings are identical Keystone type rings (**Figure 60**). See **Table 3** for piston ring dimensions.

    b. Install new piston rings in both piston grooves.

    c. Install used piston rings in their original mounting position. Refer to your identification marks made during removal.

    d. Install both piston rings with the manufacturer's stamped mark facing up.

    e. Install the lower piston ring by carefully spreading its ends with your thumbs and slipping it over the top of the piston (**Figure 61**). Center the ring end gap around the pin in the ring groove (**Figure 62**).

    f. Repeat to install the top piston ring.

4. Make sure each ring floats smoothly in its ring groove.

Piston Installation

Make sure all engine parts are clean before starting assembly.

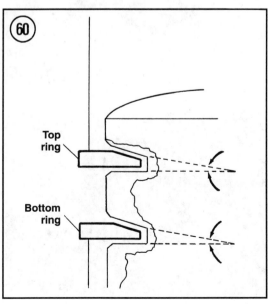

Top ring

Bottom ring

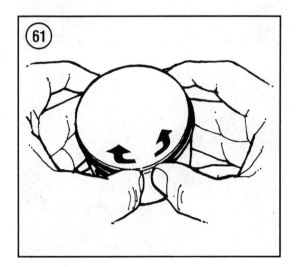

1. Lubricate the needle bearing with 2-stroke oil, then install it in the connecting rod (**Figure 63**).

2. Install the first *new* piston pin clip (**Figure 65**) into one of the piston clip grooves. Make sure the clip seats in the groove completely. Turn the clip so its open end does not align with the notch in the piston.

3. Oil the piston pin and install it partway into the piston (**Figure 66**).

4. Place the piston over the connecting rod with its arrow mark facing toward the exhaust side of the engine. Align the piston pin with the bearing, then push the pin (**Figure 67**) into the piston.

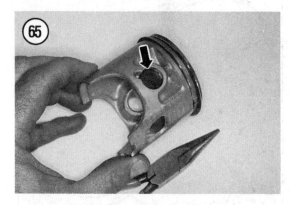

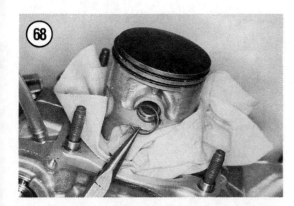

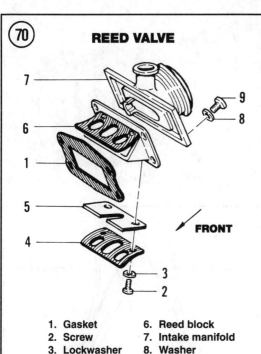

REED VALVE

FRONT

1. Gasket
2. Screw
3. Lockwasher
4. Stopper plate
5. Reed valve
6. Reed block
7. Intake manifold
8. Washer
9. Bolt

NOTE
If the arrow mark is not visible on the piston crown, install the piston with its piston ring locating pins facing toward the intake side of the engine.

CAUTION
If the piston pin will not slide in the piston smoothly, use the home-made tool described during **Piston Removal** *to install the piston pin.*

5. Wrap a clean shop cloth under the piston so the clip cannot fall into the crankcase.

WARNING
Piston pin clips can slip and fly off during installation. Wear safety glasses to prevent eye injury.

6. Install the second *new* piston pin clip (**Figure 68**) into the clip groove in the piston. Make sure the clip is seated in the groove (**Figure 69**) completely. Turn the clip so its open end does not align with the piston slot.
7. Check that both rings are seated in their grooves with their end gaps centered around the piston ring locating pins.

REED VALVE ASSEMBLY

Refer to **Figure 70** when servicing the reed valve.

NOTE
If your model is equipped with an aftermarket reed valve, refer to its manufacturer's instructions on removal, installation and inspection procedures.

Removal/Installation

1. Remove the carburetor (Chapter Eight).
2. Remove the intake manifold mounting bolts and remove the manifold (**Figure 71**).
3. Remove the reed block and gasket (**Figure 72**).
4. Inspect the reed valve assembly (**Figure 73**) as described in this chapter.
5. Remove all gasket residue from the cylinder and reed block mating surfaces.
6. Install a new gasket onto the reed block, then install the reed block (**Figure 72**) on the cylinder.
7. Install the intake manifold (**Figure 71**) and its mounting bolts. Tighten the intake manifold mount-

ing bolts in 2-3 steps in a crisscross pattern to the torque specification in **Table 4**.

8. Install the carburetor (Chapter Eight).

Inspection

When measuring the reed valve components (**Figure 73**) in this section, compare the actual measurements to the specifications in **Table 2**. Replace parts that are out of specification or show damage as described in this section.

1. Carefully examine the reed block (**Figure 74**) for wear, distortion or damage.

2. Check each reed plate for warpage, cracks or other damage. A damaged reed plate will reduce engine performance.

3. Use a flat feeler gauge and measure the clearance between the reed valve and the reed block sealing surface (**Figure 75**). Replace the reed valves if the clearance exceeds the service limit.

4. Measure the reed valve stopper distance as shown in **Figure 76**. If the reed valve stopper height measures 0.4 mm (0.016 in.) more or less than the specification in **Table 2**, replace the stopper plate.

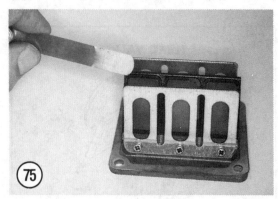

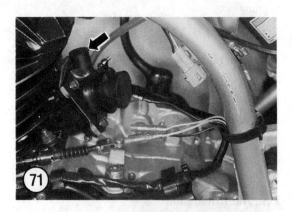

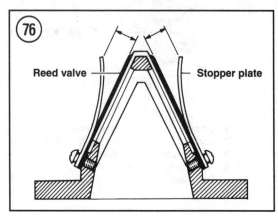

Reed valve — Stopper plate

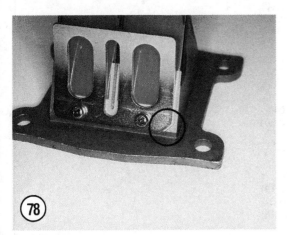

5. Inspect the intake manifold (**Figure 77**) for cracks, warpage or other damage.

Reed Valve
Replacement

1. Remove the screws securing the stopper plate to the reed block and disassemble the reed assembly (**Figure 70**).

2. Clean all parts in solvent and dry thoroughly. Remove all thread sealer from the mounting screws and the threaded holes in the reed block.

3. Check the reed valves and replace them if cracked or worn.

4. Replace damaged screws and lockwashers.

5. Reassemble the reed cage as follows:

   a. The reeds are not perfectly flat, but instead, one side will bow out slightly. Install the reed so the bowed section faces away from the reed block.

   b. The reed stops and reed valves have an alignment notch cut into one corner. Install these parts so that the notches align as shown in **Figure 78**.

   c. Apply ThreeBond TB1342 or equivalent threadlocking compound to the mounting screws prior to installation. Assemble the reed valves, stopper plate (**Figure 74**) and secure with the mounting screws. Tighten the screws securely.

Table 1 GENERAL ENGINE SPECIFICATIONS	
Engine type	Air cooled 2-stroke, reed valve induction
Displacement	195 cc (11.89 cu. in.)
Bore × stroke	66 × 57 mm (2.598 × 2.244 in.)
Compression ratio	6.6:1
Lubrication system	Yamaha Autolube (pump)

Table 2 ENGINE TOP END SERVICE SPECIFICATIONS

	New mm (in.)	Service limit mm (in.)
Cylinder head warpage limit	–	0.03 (0.0012)
Cylinder		
Bore size	66.00-66.02 (2.598-2.599)	66.1 (2.602)
Taper limit	–	0.08 (0.003)
Out of round limit	–	0.05 (0.002)
Piston		
Diameter		
Standard		
1988-2001	65.965-66.000 (2.597-2.598)	–
2002	65.940-66.000 (2.596-2.598)	
1st oversize	66.25 (2.608)	–
2nd oversize	66.50 (2.618)	–
Piston measuring point	See text	–
Piston-to-cylinder clearance	0.035-0.040 (0.0014-0.0016)	0.1 (0.004)
Piston rings		
Type	Keystone	
End gap		
1988-2001	0.20-0.35 (0.008-0.014)	–
2002	0.20-0.40 (0.008-0.016)	
Side clearance	0.03-0.05 (0.0012-0.0020)	–
Reed valve		
Thickness	0.35-0.49 (0.014-0.019)	–
Reed valve stopper height	8.3-8.7 (0.33-0.34)	–
Reed valve bend limit	–	0.5 (0.02)
Connecting rod and crankshaft		
Connecting rod small end side play	0.8-1.0 (0.031-0.039)	–
Connecting rod big end radial clearance	0.021-0.035 (0.0008-0.0014)	–
Connecting rod big end side clearance		
1988-2001	0.4-0.7 (0.016-0.028 in.)	–
2002	0.2-0.1 (0.008-0.028)	

Table 3 PISTON RING SECTIONAL DIMENSIONS

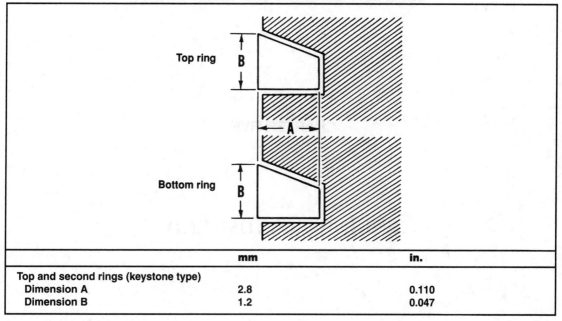

	mm	in.
Top and second rings (keystone type)		
Dimension A	2.8	0.110
Dimension B	1.2	0.047

Table 4 ENGINE TIGHTENING TORQUES

	N•m	in.-lb.	ft.-lb.
Cylinder head nuts	27	–	20
Cylinder base nuts	25	–	18
Exhaust pipe nuts	21	–	15
Intake manifold mounting bolts	8	71	–
Silencer mounting bolt	23	–	17
Spark plug	25	–	18

4

CHAPTER FIVE

ENGINE BOTTOM END

This chapter describes service procedures for the following lower end components (**Figure 1**):

a. Crankcase.

b. Crankshaft and connecting rod.

c. Balancer shaft.

d. Transmission (removal and installation).

e. Internal shift mechanism (removal and installation).

Before working on the engine, read the information listed under *Service Hints* in Chapter One.

Engine specifications are listed in **Tables 1** and **2** at the end of this chapter.

SERVICING ENGINE IN FRAME

Some of the components can be serviced while the engine is mounted in the frame (the frame is a great holding fixture—especially for breaking loose stubborn bolts and nuts):

a. Cylinder head.

b. Cylinder.

c. Piston.

d. Carburetor.

e. Reed valve.

f. Flywheel and stator plate.

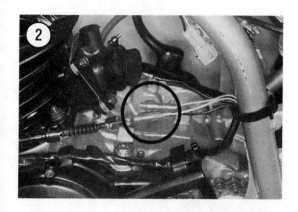

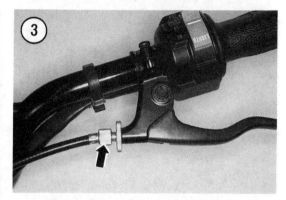

g. Clutch.

h. External shift mechanism.

i. Primary drive gear and balancer shaft gears.

j. Kickstarter.

ENGINE

Removal/Installation

1. Park the vehicle on level ground and set the parking brake.

2. Drain the transmission oil as described in Chapter Three.

3. Remove the carburetor (Chapter Eight).

4. Remove the exhaust pipe (Chapter Four).

5. Disconnect the spark plug lead from the spark plug.

6. Disconnect the CDI magneto electrical connectors (**Figure 2**).

7. Loosen the clutch cable adjuster (**Figure 3**) at the handlebar and disconnect the clutch cable from the clutch release lever at the engine (**Figure 4**).

8. Remove the shift lever pinch bolt and remove the shift lever.

9. Disconnect the crankcase breather hose from the crankcase.

10. Disconnect the oil pump hoses as follows:

   a. Remove the Autolube pump cover screws and cover (**Figure 5**).

   b. Remove the screw and hose clamp (**Figure 6**) from the clutch cover.

   c. Disconnect the oil hose (A, **Figure 7**) and the oil delivery hose (B, **Figure 7**) from the oil pump.

   d. Plug both hoses to prevent oil leakage and contamination.

11. Remove the left and right side footpeg assemblies (Chapter Fourteen).

12. Remove the drive chain (A, **Figure 8**) as follows:

    a. If you are going to disassemble the engine, remove the drive sprocket as described in this chapter.

    b. If you are not going to disassemble the engine, disconnect the drive chain as described in Chapter Twelve.

13. If you are going to disassemble the engine, remove the following engine subassemblies before removing the engine from the frame:

    a. Cylinder head (Chapter Four).

    b. Cylinder (Chapter Four).

    c. Piston (Chapter Four).

    d. Flywheel (Chapter Nine).

    e. Stator plate (Chapter Nine).

    f. Clutch (Chapter Six).

    g. Kickstarter and idler gear (Chapter Six).

    h. Primary drive gear and balancer gears (Chapter Six).

14. Remove the pivot shaft nut (B, **Figure 8**).

15. Remove the front (C, **Figure 8**) and rear (D, **Figure 8**) engine mounting nuts and bolts.

16. Slide the pivot shaft (B, **Figure 8**) out until it is free of the engine. Do not remove it completely from the other side of the swing arm.

17. Lift the engine out of the left side of the frame and remove it.

18. Slide the swing arm pivot shaft through the frame and swing arm (**Figure 9**). This will keep the swing arm in position while steadying the vehicle.

19. Clean all corrosion and rust from the engine mount bolts. Inspect these parts for cracks or other damage and replace if necessary.

20. Check the frame and engine brackets (**Figure 10**) for cracks or other damage.

21. Check the swing arm pivot bosses (**Figure 9**) for cracks or other damage.

22. Install the engine by reversing these removal steps. Note the following.

23. Lubricate the pivot shaft with grease and insert it partway through the right side of the swing arm (**Figure 11**).

24. Lubricate the engine mount bolts with grease or with a spray-type lubricant.

25. Install the engine into the frame, then secure it with the pivot shaft (B, **Figure 8**). Tighten the nut hand-tight.

26. Install the front engine mount bolt (C, **Figure 8**) from the right side. Tighten the nut hand-tight.

27. Install the lower engine mount bolt (D, **Figure 8**) from the left side. Tighten the nut hand-tight.

28. Tighten the following fasteners to the torque specifications in **Table 2**:

    a. Pivot shaft nut (B, **Figure 8**).

    b. Front engine mount bolt nut (C, **Figure 8**).

    c. Rear engine mount bolt nut (D, **Figure 8**).

29. After installing the carburetor (Chapter Eight), service the oil pump as follows:

    a. Reconnect the oil hose (A, **Figure 7**) and the oil delivery hose (B, **Figure 8**) onto the oil pump.

    b. Install the Autolube pump hose clamp and screw (**Figure 6**) at the clutch cover. Tighten the clutch cover screw to the torque specification in **Table 2**.

    c. Bleed the oil pump as described in Chapter Three.

    d. Install the Autolube pump cover (**Figure 5**) and tighten its mounting screws to the torque specification in **Table 2**.

30. Before starting the engine, check the following items as described in Chapter Three:

    a. Transmission oil level.

    b. Clutch adjustment.

    c. Throttle adjustment.

    d. Drive chain adjustment.

31. Start the engine and check for leaks.

DRIVE SPROCKET

The drive sprocket is also referred to as the engine or countershaft sprocket.

Removal

1. Park the vehicle on level ground and set the parking brake.

2. Remove the left crankcase cover screws and cover (**Figure 12**).

3. If the chain is mounted on the vehicle, loosen the rear axle housing and chain adjusters as described under *Drive Chain Adjustment* in Chapter Three.

4. Remove the sprocket holder mounting bolts (**Figure 13**), then remove the sprocket holder and drive sprocket. See **Figure 14**.

Inspection

1. Check the countershaft seal (**Figure 15**) for damage. If necessary, replace the seal as described under *Countershaft Seal Replacement* in this chapter.

2. Inspect the sprocket for cupping, excessive wear or damage. If you replace the drive sprocket, you should also replace the drive chain and driven sprocket at the same time. Refer to *Drive Chain* in Chapter Twelve for more information.

3. Inspect the sprocket, holder and mounting bolts (**Figure 14**); replace worn or damaged parts.

Installation

1. Install the drive sprocket with its numbered side facing out.

2. Install the sprocket holder over the countershaft splines, then turn it to align its mounting holes with the drive sprocket threaded holes.

3. Install the sprocket holder mounting bolts (**Figure 13**) and tighten to the torque specification in **Table 2**.

4. Install the drive chain.

5. Install the engine sprocket cover and its mounting bolts.

6. Adjust the drive chain as described in Chapter Three.

COUNTERSHAFT SEAL REPLACEMENT

The countershaft seal (**Figure 15**) is susceptible to damage from rocks, dirt and other debris thrown from the drive chain and sprocket. With care, you can replace this seal (**Figure 16**) without splitting the engine case.

1. Remove the drive sprocket as described in the previous section.

2. Clean the engine case around the countershaft seal thoroughly. Do not force any water past the seal.

3. Thread 1 or 2 small sheet metal screws into the seal and pull the seal out with a pair of pliers. Do not install the screws to deeply or you may score the countershaft bearing.

4. Wipe the seal sealing area in the crankcase with a clean rag. Check the crankcase for cracks or other damage. If the case half is damaged, disassemble the engine and repair the crankcase.

5. Pack the new seal lip with grease.

6. Slide the seal over the countershaft with its manufacturer's marks facing out, and tap it squarely into the crankcase bore with a long, hollow driver. Seat the seal so it is flush with the crankcase (**Figure 15**).

7. Install the drive sprocket as described in the previous section.

8. Recheck the transmission oil level as described in Chapter Three.

LEFT SIDE MAIN BEARING SEAL

A leaking left side main bearing seal (**Figure 17**) will allow some of the fuel mixture to escape during crankcase compression and draw air during crankcase vacuum. This causes an excessively lean air/fuel mixture, reduced power and erratic idling. A damaged seal is usually discovered during a 2-stroke leakdown test, or through visual inspection. Dirt that leaks past the flywheel cover can cause this type of seal damage.

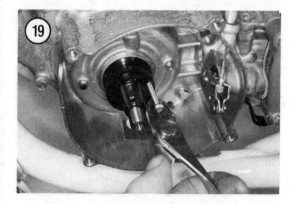

This procedure describes how to replace the seal with the engine assembled and installed in the frame. With care, you can replace this seal without having to split the engine crankcase. Before removing the oil seal, read the procedure through to familiarize yourself with the steps and tools required.

1. Remove the flywheel and stator plate (Chapter Nine).

2. Install a mechanical stop on the drill bit to prevent it from contacting the main bearing after it passes through the seal in Step 3.

3. Carefully drill a hole through the seal (**Figure 18**). This seal has a metal backing, so make sure you use a sharp drill bit. If the drill bit skips across the seal, use a punch to make a small starting indentation in the seal. When drilling the hole, hold the drill steady and perpendicular so you do not damage the crankshaft surface or crankcase bore.

> *CAUTION*
> *Do not try to pry the seal out of the crankcase; otherwise you will damage the crankshaft and crankcase seal surfaces.*

4. Thread a sheet metal screw into the hole in the seal. Then grab the screw with a pair of pliers (**Figure 19**) and pull the seal out of the crankcase.

> *NOTE*
> *You may be able to remove the seal by only drilling one hole. However, if the seal is tight, you may have to drill another hole, 180° opposite the first hole. Then pull on one screw, then the other to prevent the seal from binding in the case.*

5. Clean the seal bore with electrical contact cleaner.

6. Pack the lip of the new seal with grease and slide it over the crankshaft with its closed side facing out (**Figure 20**).

7. Install the new seal by driving it into place with a large hollow pipe or bearing driver. Install the seal until its outer surface is square with the crankcase and flush with the seal bore (**Figure 17**).

8. Install the stator plate and flywheel (Chapter Nine).

CRANKCASE AND CRANKSHAFT

The crankcase is made in 2 halves (**Figure 21**) of a precision diecast aluminum alloy.

The crankshaft assembly is made up of 2 full-circle flywheels pressed together on a hollow crankpin. The connecting rod big end bearing on the crankpin is a needle bearing assembly. The crankshaft assembly is supported by 2 ball bearings in the crankcase.

Special Tools

To disassemble and reassemble the crankcase assembly you need the following special tools or their equivalents. These tools allow easy disassembly and reassembly of the engine without prying.

   a. Yamaha crankcase separating tool (part No. YU-01135) or equivalent (**Figure 22**). This tool threads into the crankcase and is used to separate the crankcase halves and to press the crankshaft out of the crankcase.

   b. Yamaha crankshaft installing tool (part No. YU-90500) and adapter (part No. YU-90063) (**Figure 23**).

   c. When handling the engine cases, 2 wooden blocks or a fixture made out of wood (**Figure 24**) will assist in engine disassembly and reassembly and will help to prevent damage to the crankshaft and transmission shafts.

Crankcase Disassembly

This procedure describes disassembly of the crankcase halves and removal of the crankshaft, balancer shaft, transmission and internal shift mechanism.

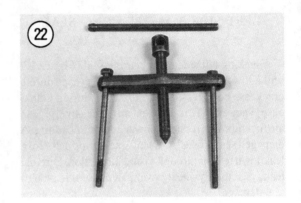

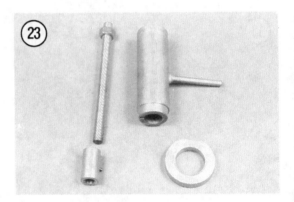

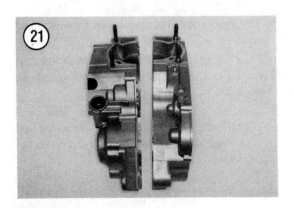

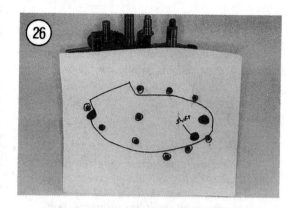

1. Remove all exterior engine assemblies as follows:
   a. Cylinder head, cylinder and piston (Chapter Four).
   b. Clutch (Chapter Six).
   c. Drive sprocket (this chapter).
   d. Primary drive gear and balancer gears (Chapter Six).
   e. Kickstarter (Chapter Six).
   f. External shift mechanism (Chapter Six).
   g. Flywheel and stator plate (Chapter Nine).

2. Place the engine assembly on wooden blocks with the left side facing up (**Figure 25**).

3. Loosen the crankcase screws in a crisscross pattern, 1/4 turn at a time.

4. Before removing the crankcase mounting screws, draw an outline of the crankcase half on a piece of cardboard (**Figure 26**). Then punch holes along the outline for the placement of each mounting screw.

5. Remove the left crankcase mounting screws and place them in the corresponding holes in the cardboard (**Figure 26**).

6. If you intend to reuse the countershaft oil seal, apply grease to a suitable O-ring and install it in the countershaft groove as shown in **Figure 27**.

7. Turn the engine over so the right side faces up. Then remove the crankshaft seal retainer screw and retainer (**Figure 28**).

8. Turn the shift cam and align its ramps with the crankcase as shown in **Figure 29**. Recheck the shift cam during crankcase separation to make sure no contact is made.

9. Mount the crankcase separating tool onto the crankcase and over the crankshaft as shown in **Figure 30**. Apply some grease onto the end of the crankshaft before running the tool's pressure bolt against it.

10. Run the tool's pressure bolt against the end of the crankshaft. Then check to make sure the tool's body is parallel with the crankcase (**Figure 31**). If not, readjust the tool's mounting bolts.

> *CAUTION*
> *If the separating tool is not parallel with the crankcase surface, it will put an uneven stress on the case halves and may damage them.*

> *NOTE*
> *As the right case half is pulled up, the mainshaft and/or countershaft may ride up with its right case bearing, causing the case halves to bind. After every turn of the tool's pressure bolt, tap both shafts with a plastic or rubber mallet to release any binding. This will help the case halves separate more easily.*

11. Hold the engine with one hand and then turn the tool's pressure bolt *clockwise* until the right case half begins to separate. You may hear a small pop when the case halves separate. This is normal, but stop and investigate all the way around the case halve mating surfaces. If everything is normal, continue with Step 12. If there is a problem, release tension from the pressure bolt and make sure all of the screws were removed.

> *CAUTION*
> *Crankcase separation requires only hand pressure on the pressure bolt. Applying excessive force will damage the case halves. If the pressure bolt becomes tight, stop immediately. Make sure all crankcase bolts and external parts are removed. Also make sure the crankcase half if not binding on the transmission shaft.*

12. Continue turning the pressure bolt until the right case half is free, then lift it off the engine. See **Figure 32**.

13. Remove the 2 dowel pins (**Figure 33**).

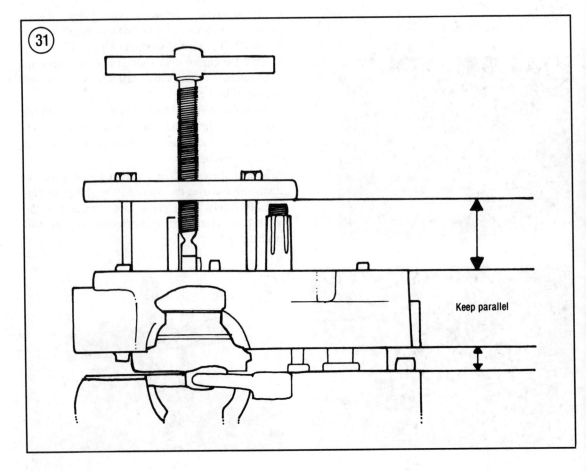

Keep parallel

14. Remove the transmission assembly as follows:

   a. Remove the long shift fork shaft (**Figure 34**).

   b. Remove the short shift fork shaft (**Figure 35**).

   c. Remove the 3 shift forks (A, **Figure 36**).

   d. Remove the shift drum (B, **Figure 36**).

   e. Reposition the left crankcase so both transmission shafts are parallel with the workbench, then tap against the countershaft and remove the mainshaft and countershaft assemblies (**Figure 37**) together from the crankcase half. See **Figure 38**.

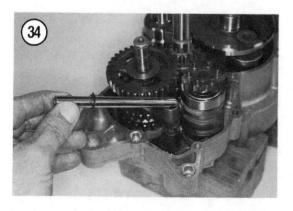

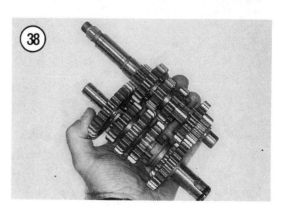

15. Remove the balancer shaft (A, **Figure 39**).

16. Remove the crankshaft (B, **Figure 39**) as follows:

   a. Apply some thick grease onto the end of the crankshaft threads.

   b. Mount the crankcase separating tool onto the left crankcase. Center the pressure bolt with the crankshaft as shown in **Figure 40**. Make sure the tool's body is parallel with the case half. If necessary, back one of the bolts out to level the tool body.

   c. Hold the connecting rod, then turn the pressure bolt clockwise and press the crankshaft out of the crankcase. See **Figure 41**.

17. Clean and inspect the crankcase halves, bearings, crankshaft and balancer shaft as described in this chapter.

18. Service the transmission and internal shift mechanism as described in Chapter Seven.

Crankcase
Cleaning and Inspection

1. Remove the crankcase seals as described under *Crankcase Seal Replacement* in this chapter.

2. Remove all gasket and sealer residue from both crankcase mating surfaces.

3. Clean both crankcase halves (**Figure 42**) and bearings with solvent. Then reclean in hot, soapy water and rinse in clear, cold water.

4. Dry the case halves and bearings with compressed air. When drying the bearings with compressed air, hold the inner bearing races to prevent them from turning. When the bearings are dry, lubricate them with oil.

5. Turn each bearing by hand (**Figure 42**). Each bearing must turn smoothly without catching, bind-

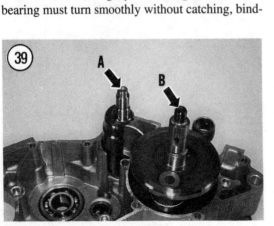

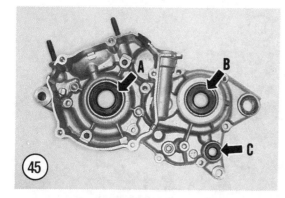

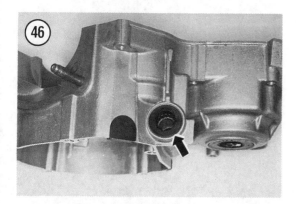

ing or excessive play. If a bearing turns roughly or catches, reclean it. If there is still a problem, replace the bearing(s) as described in this chapter.

6. Carefully inspect the case halves for cracks and fractures (**Figure 43**), especially in the lower areas where they are vulnerable to rock damage.

7. Inspect machined surfaces for burrs, cracks or other damage. Repair minor damage with a fine-cut file or oilstone. A damaged mating surface may require welding and machining.

8. Check the cylinder studs (**Figure 44**) and threaded holes for stripping, cross-threading or deposit buildup. Clean threaded holes with compressed air. If necessary, repair threads with a tap or die. Replace damaged studs as described under *Stud Replacement* in Chapter One.

Crankcase Seal Replacement

Seals are identified as follows:

   a. Left main bearing seal (A, **Figure 45**).
   b. Left countershaft bearing seal (B, **Figure 45**).
   c. Shift shaft seal (C, **Figure 45**).
   d. Clutch release lever seal (**Figure 46**).
   e. Right main bearing seal (**Figure 47**).

1. Before removing the seals, note and record the direction in which the lip of each seal faces for proper assembly. Note the following:

   a. All of the left crankcase seals are installed with their manufacturer's marks facing out (away from crankcase). See **Figure 45** and **Figure 46**.

   b. The right main bearing seal (**Figure 47**) is a double lip seal. The factory seal is marked OUT SIDE (**Figure 48**) on one side and CRANK SIDE on the other side. Install this seal with its OUT-SIDE mark facing out (away from crankshaft).

2. Before removing the old seals, note the depth to which each seal is installed. All of the seals in the left and right crankcases are installed so their outer surface is flush with or slightly below the seal bearing bore. Inspect each seal for unusual wear or damage.

3. Pry out the old seals with a screwdriver, taking care not to damage the case bore. Pad the pry area under the screwdriver (**Figure 49** and **Figure 50**, typical) to prevent damaging the crankcase. See **Figure 51**.

4. Inspect and service the engine case bearings before installing the new seals. Refer to *Crankcase Bearing Replacement* in this section.

5. Compare the new and old seals before installation.

6. Pack grease between the seal lips (**Figure 52**).

7. Using a suitable driver (**Figure 53**), press in the seal until its outer surface is flush with or slightly below the seal bore inside surface.

8. Repeat to install each new seal.

Crankcase Bearing Replacement

The left side crankcase bearings are identified as follows:

    a. Left main bearing (A, **Figure 54**).

    b. Left countershaft bearing (B, **Figure 54**).

    c. Left mainshaft bearing (C, **Figure 54**).

    d. Left balancer shaft bearing (D, **Figure 54**).

    e. Clutch release bearing (**Figure 55**).

The right side crankcase bearings are identified as follows:

    a. Right main bearing (A, **Figure 56**).

    b. Right countershaft bearing (B, **Figure 56**).

    c. Right mainshaft bearing (C, **Figure 56**).

    d. Right balancer shaft bearing (D, **Figure 56**).

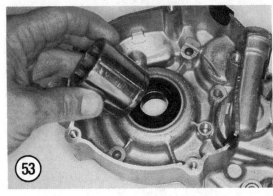

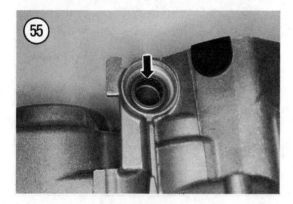

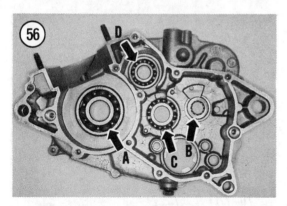

1. All bearings are marked on one side with its respective size code and usually with some type of manufacturer code or name. Before removing the bearings, note and record the direction in which the manufacturer's marks face for proper assembly. Bearings are usually installed with these marks facing out (the marks are visible from the side the bearing is installed from).

2. If a bearing is still on the crankshaft, remove it with a bearing puller.

3. Before replacing the right mainshaft bearing, remove the retainer plate screws and plate (**Figure 57**).

NOTE
*Two methods of replacing the crankcase bearings are described below. Before you begin, read the **Ball Bearing Replacement** section in Chapter One.*

4A. To replace the bearings using heat, perform the following steps:

   a. Before heating the case half, select all of the appropriate bearing drivers for the bearings being removed.

   b. Before heating the case half, place the new bearings in a freezer. Chilling them will slightly reduce their overall diameter while the hot crankcase is slightly larger due to heat expansion. This will make installation much easier.

CAUTION
Before heating the crankcase halves to remove the bearings, wash the cases thoroughly with detergent and water. Rinse and rewash the cases as required to remove all traces of oil and other chemical deposits.

   c. The bearings have a slight interference fit in the case halves. Heat the crankcase to a temperature of about 212° F (100° C) in a shop oven or on a hot plate (**Figure 58**). Heat only one case at a time.

CAUTION
Do not heat the cases with a torch (propane or acetylene)—never bring a flame into contact with the bearing or case. The direct heat will destroy the case hardening of the bearing and will likely warp the case half.

5

d. Remove the case from the shop oven or hot plate—*it is hot*.

e. Support the crankcase on wooden blocks and drive the bearing out from its opposite side. Use a pilot bearing tool to remove bearings installed in a blind hole.

NOTE
Install new bearings so their manufacturer's name and size code faces in the same direction recorded before disassembly. If you did not record this information, install the bearings so their marks are visible from the side the bearing is installed from.

f. While the crankcase half is still hot, install the new bearing(s) into the crankcase. Install the bearing into its bore and drop it into place. If necessary, lightly tap the bearing(s) into the case with a driver placed on the outer bearing race. *Do not* install new bearings by driving on the inner bearing race. Install the bearing(s) until it seats completely.

4B. To replace bearings using a press:

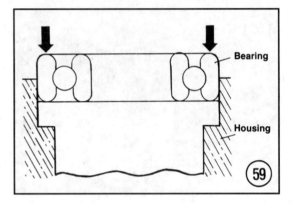

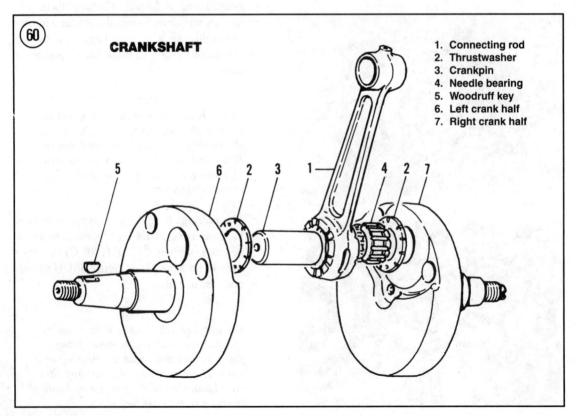

CRANKSHAFT

1. Connecting rod
2. Thrustwasher
3. Crankpin
4. Needle bearing
5. Woodruff key
6. Left crank half
7. Right crank half

a. Support the crankcase on 2 wooden blocks and center the bearing under the press ram.

b. Press the bearing out of the crankcase.

c. Support the crankcase on 2 wooden blocks and center the bearing and bearing bore under the press ram.

d. Place a bearing driver on the outer bearing race (**Figure 59**, typical) and press the bearing into the crankcase until it bottoms.

5. To install and tighten the mainshaft bearing retainer (**Figure 57**), perform the following:

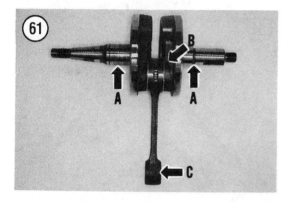

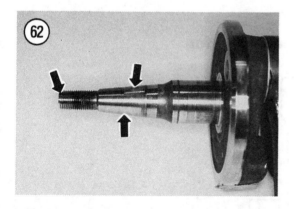

a. Remove all sealer residue from the retainer screw threads and the crankcase threaded holes.

b. Apply ThreeBond threadlock TB1360 (or equivalent) onto the bearing retainer screw threads.

c. Install the mainshaft bearing retainer and screws. Tighten the screws to the torque specification in **Table 2**.

6. Install the seals as described under *Crankcase Seal Replacement* in this chapter.

Crankshaft Inspection

When measuring the crankshaft in this section, compare the actual measurements to the specifications in **Table 1**. Replace the connecting rod assembly if it is out of specification or shows damage as described in this section. To replace the connecting rod assembly, a 20-30 ton press and adapters, V-blocks or crankshaft truing stand and dial indicator are required. If necessary, refer crankshaft overhaul to a dealership or service shop. You can save considerable expense by disassembling the engine and taking the crankshaft in for repair.

When rebuilding a crankshaft, always install a new connecting rod, crankpin, bearing and both thrust washers (**Figure 60**).

1. Clean the crankshaft in solvent, then clean with hot, soapy water and rinse with clear, cold water. Dry with compressed air. Then lubricate the bottom end bearing and crankshaft journals with a light coat of 2-stroke engine oil.

2. Check the crankshaft journals (A, **Figure 61**) for scratches, heat discoloration or other defects.

3. Check the crankshaft seal surfaces (A, **Figure 61**) for grooving, pitting or scratches.

4. Check the crankshaft surfaces (A, **Figure 61**) for chatter marks or uneven wear. Clean minor damage with carborundum cloth.

5. Check threads and k

6.

at the rod's small end, perform the *Piston Pin and Needle Bearing Inspection* procedure in Chapter Four.

9. Measure the connecting rod big end side clearance between the connecting rod and thrust washer with a feeler gauge (**Figure 64**). Replace the connecting rod assembly if the clearance is out of specification.

10. Measure connecting rod small end side play (**Figure 65**) as follows:

   a. Mount the crankshaft on a set of V-blocks.
   b. Turn the crankshaft so the connecting rod is at top dead center (TDC).
   c. Mount a dial indicator so its plunger contacts the connecting rod small end (**Figure 66**).
   d. Slide the connecting rod over so it seats against the lower thrust washer that is on the same side the dial indicator is installed on. Hold the connecting rod in this position.
   e. While holding the lower part of the connecting rod, try to move the upper end by hand. Any movement is small end side play.
   f. Replace the connecting rod if the side play is out of specification.

11. Measure connecting rod big end radial clearance (**Figure 65**) as follows:

   a. Turn the crankshaft so the connecting rod is at TDC.
   b. Move the connecting rod over so it seats against one of the lower thrust washers.
   c. Mount a dial indicator with its plunger contacting the connecting rod big end.
   d. Hold the connecting rod in this position, then try to move it up and down as shown in **Figure 65**. Any movement is big end radial clearance.

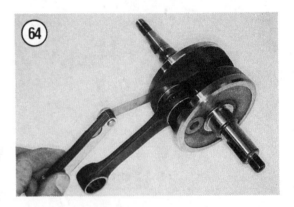

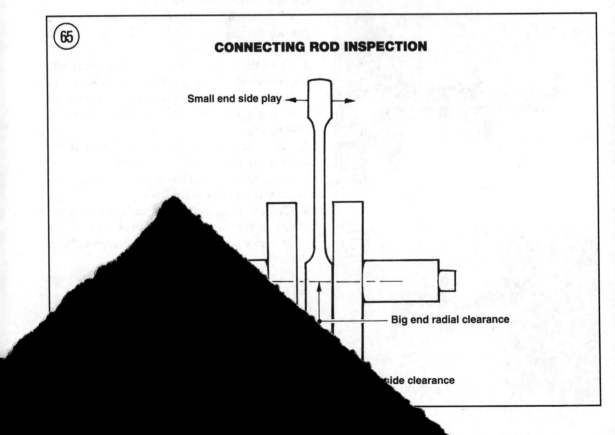

CONNECTING ROD INSPECTION

Small end side play

Big end radial clearance

...ide clearance

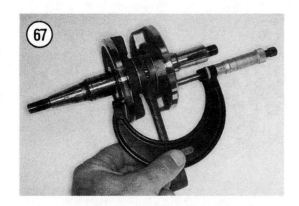

e. Replace the connecting rod if the clearance is out of specification.

12. Measure the crank wheel width every 90° at its machined edge with a micrometer (**Figure 67**) or vernier caliper. Retrue the crankshaft if out of specification.

13. Measure crankshaft runout with a dial indicator and V-blocks as shown in **Figure 68**. Retrue the crankshaft if out of specification.

Balancer Shaft Inspection

1. Clean the balancer shaft (**Figure 69**) in solvent and dry with compressed air.

2. Check the balancer shaft journals (**Figure 69**) for scratches, heat discoloration or other defects.

3. Check the keyway and threads for damage.

Crankshaft Installation

Install the crankshaft in the left case half (**Figure 70**) using the Yamaha crankcase tools described under *Special Tools* in this chapter. The tools are identified as follows:

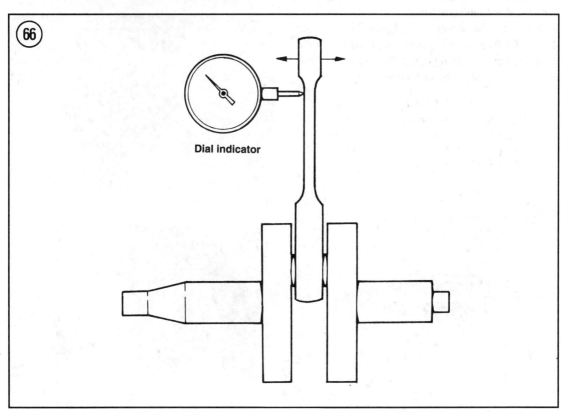

Dial indicator

a. Threaded adapter (A, **Figure 71**).

NOTE
The threaded adapter (part No.
YU-90063) has 12 mm × 1.25 mm
right-hand female threads.

b. Threaded rod and nut (B, **Figure 71**).
c. Pot spacer (C, **Figure 71**).
d. Installing pot (D, **Figure 71**).

1. Clean the crankshaft before installation. Lubricate the big end bearing (B, **Figure 61**) with 2-stroke oil.

2. Install the left main bearing seal as described under *Crankcase Seal Replacement* in this chapter.

3. Lubricate the left crankshaft bearing with 2-stroke engine oil.

4. Carefully install crankshaft's left end (side with taper) into the left side main bearing. Push it in until it stops. See **Figure 72**.

5. Thread the Yamaha threaded adapter (part No. YU-90063) onto the crankshaft until it bottoms, then back out 1/2 turn. See A, **Figure 73**.

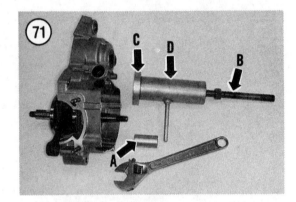

6. Install the threaded rod (B, **Figure 73**) all the way into the adapter.

7. Install the pot spacer (**Figure 74**) over the rod and center it around the crankshaft.

8. Install the installing pot (**Figure 75**) over the threaded rod and engage its slot with the pin in the adapter to lock them together. Then install the nut and thread it against the installing pot.

CAUTION
Hold the connecting rod at TDC or BDC
(Figure 76) when pressing the
crankshaft into its main bearing;
otherwise the rod will contact the side

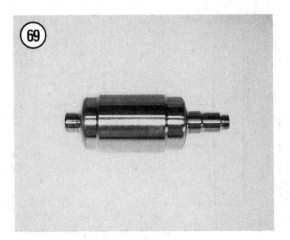

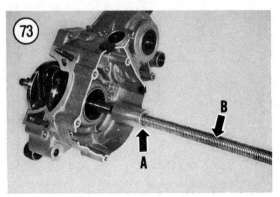

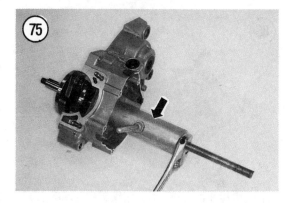

of the crankcase. This will bend the rod and damage the crankcase gasket surface.

9. Hold the installing pot rod, then turn the nut (**Figure 75**) to press the crankshaft into its main bearing. Continue until you feel the crankshaft shoulder bottom against the bearing. See **Figure 77**.

10. Remove the Yamaha tools from the end of the crankshaft, then place the crankcase assembly on wooden blocks (**Figure 78**).

11. Spin the crankshaft by hand, making sure it turns smoothly.

Crankcase Assembly

1. Clean all engine parts before assembly.

2. Pack the crankcase seal lips with grease as described under *Seal Replacement* in this chapter.

3. Install the crankshaft (**Figure 78**) as described under *Crankshaft Installation* in this chapter.

4. Lubricate the crankshaft and right main bearing with 2-stroke engine oil.

5. Place the left side crankcase on wooden blocks (**Figure 78**).

6. Lubricate the transmission and balancer shaft bearings with gear oil.

7. Install the balancer shaft (**Figure 79**) so its keyway faces out (toward the right crankcase).

8. Check the transmission shafts (**Figure 80**) to make sure all the gears, washers and circlips are properly installed. See Chapter Seven.

9. Grease a suitable size O-ring and install it in the countershaft groove (**Figure 81**).

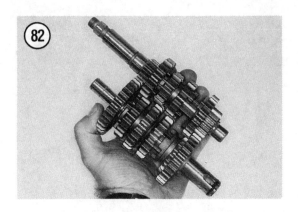

NOTE
The O-ring will help prevent the countershaft splines from damaging the countershaft seal in Step 10.

10. Mesh the mainshaft and countershaft assemblies together (**Figure 82**), then install them into the left crankcase at the same time. See **Figure 83**.
11. Install the dowel pin (**Figure 84**) into each shift fork.

NOTE
Each shift fork is marked with a single identification number (1, 2 or 3) on one

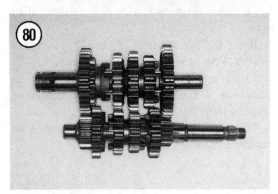

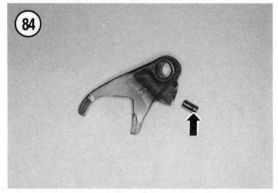

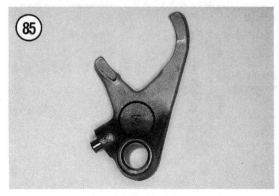

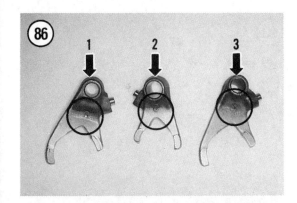

side as shown in **Figure 85**. *These numbers (***Figure 86***) are used to identify the shift forks when installing them in the following steps. The other side of each shift fork is marked with its model code number (2 numbers and 1 letter); disregard these marks during installation.*

NOTE
*Install the shift forks with their identification number (***Figure 86***) facing down (toward left crankcase).*

12. Install the No. 1 shift fork (1, **Figure 86**) into the countershaft sixth gear groove (**Figure 87**).

13. Install the No. 3 shift fork (3, **Figure 86**) into the countershaft fifth gear groove (**Figure 88**).

14. Install the No. 2 shift fork (2, **Figure 86**) into the mainshaft third/fourth gear groove (**Figure 89**).

15. Install the shift drum (**Figure 90**) into the right side case bore. Make sure the shift drum bottoms in the case.

16. Engage the No. 2 shift fork guide pin (**Figure 91**) into the center shift drum groove, then install the

short shift fork shaft (**Figure 92**) through the shift fork and into the left crankcase.

17. Install the long shift fork shaft (**Figure 93**) as follows:

    a. Make sure the circlip (**Figure 93**) is seated completely in the shift fork shaft groove.

    b. Engage the No. 1 shift fork guide pin (A, **Figure 94**) into the left side shift drum groove.

    c. Engage the No. 3 shift fork guide pin (B, **Figure 94**) into the right side shift drum groove.

    d. Install the long shift fork, circlip side facing up, (**Figure 95**) through both shift forks and into the right side crankcase. See **Figure 96**.

> *NOTE*
> *Make sure both shift fork shafts bottom solidly in the left side crankcase before continuing with Step 18.*

18. Spin the transmission shafts and shift through the gears using the shift drum. Make sure you can shift into all 6 speeds.

19. Shift the transmission assembly into NEUTRAL.

20. Support the left crankcase assembly on wooden blocks.

21. Install the 2 dowel pins (**Figure 97**) into the crankcase holes.

> *NOTE*
> *Make sure both crankcase mating surfaces are clean and free of all old sealer residue or oil.*

22. Apply a light coat of a *non-hardening* liquid gasket sealer, such as Yamabond No. 4 or ThreeBond

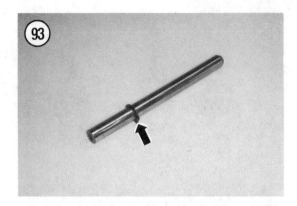

1104, onto the left side crankcase gasket surface (**Figure 98**).

23. When assembling the crankcase halves in Step 24, align the shift cam ramps with the crankcase slots as shown in **Figure 99**. Recheck the shift cam position throughout the crankcase installation procedure to make sure no contact is made.

CAUTION
*Failure to align the shift drum ramps with the crankcase slots (**Figure 99**) will cause crankcase damage.*

24. Align the right crankcase with the crankshaft and transmission shafts, and install it partway over them. Check the shift cam ramps and crankcase slot alignment as the case half is being installed. When the alignment is good, push the case half down until it stops.

25. The case may go all the way down by hand pressure. But, if necessary, tap the case with a soft-faced hammer while making sure the dowel pins engage their mating holes properly. Continue until the right case half seats on the left case half. The gasket surfaces must be flush all the way around the case halves as shown in **Figure 100**. Now make sure the mainshaft, balancer shaft, countershaft, shift drum and crankshaft rotate freely; there must be no binding.

CAUTION
Crankcase halves must fit together without excessive force. If the crankcase halves do not fit together completely, do not pull them together with the crankcase screws. Separate the crankcase halves and investigate the cause of the interference. If the transmission shafts were disassembled, make sure that a gear is not installed backwards. Do not risk damage by trying to force the cases together.

26. Turn the engine so the left side faces up (**Figure 101**), then install all of the crankcase mounting screws (**Figure 102**) finger-tight.

27. Tighten the crankcase mounting screws in 2 stages and in a crisscross pattern to the final torque specification listed in **Table 2**.

28. Rotate the crankshaft and each transmission shaft and check for binding; each shaft must turn freely.

29. Check the shifting as described under *Transmission Shifting Check* in this chapter.

30. Remove the O-ring (**Figure 103**) from the countershaft groove.

31. To install and tighten the crankshaft seal retainer and screw (**Figure 104**), perform the following:

    a. Apply ThreeBond threadlock TB1360 (or equivalent) onto the seal retainer screw threads.

    b. Install the crankshaft seal retainer and screw. Tighten the screw to the torque specification in **Table 2**.

32. Install the engine in the frame as described in this chapter.

33. Install all exterior engine assemblies as follows:

    a. Flywheel and stator plate (Chapter Nine).

    b. Primary drive gear and balancer gears (Chapter Six).

    c. External shift mechanism (Chapter Six).

    d. Kickstarter (Chapter Six).

    e. Drive sprocket (this chapter).

    f. Clutch (Chapter Six).

    g. Piston, cylinder and cylinder head (Chapter Four).

34. After filling the transmission with gear oil and bleeding the oil pump, start the engine and check for leaks. Check the throttle and clutch operation and adjust if necessary.

TRANSMISSION SHIFTING CHECK

The transmission shifting can be checked with the engine mounted in the frame or with it mounted on the workbench. Always check the shifting after reassembling the engine cases.

1. Install the stopper arm assembly (**Figure 105**) as described in Chapter Six.

2. Align the flat ramp on the shift drum with the stopper arm roller as shown in A, **Figure 106**. This shifts the transmission into NEUTRAL. When the transmission is in NEUTRAL, the countershaft and mainshaft will turn freely from each other (that is, when you turn one shaft, the other shaft will not turn).

3. Turn the mainshaft or countershaft while turning the shift drum (B, **Figure 106**) into each gear position. The transmission is in gear when the stopper arm roller seats into one of the shift drum segment ramps. When the transmission is in gear, the coun-

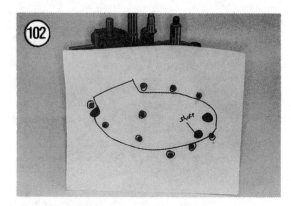

tershaft and mainshaft are engaged and will turn together.

4. If the transmission does not shift properly into each gear, disassemble the engine and check the transmission and the internal shift mechanism.

ENGINE BREAK-IN

The performance and durability of your YFS200 engine depends on a sensible and accurate engine

break-in procedure. If the rings were replaced, a new piston installed, the cylinder replaced, the crankshaft rebuilt or replaced, or new engine bearings installed, the engine must be broken in just as if it were new. If a proper engine break-in procedure is not followed, accelerated engine wear and overheating will result, reducing engine life.

Before starting the break-in procedure, note the following:

a. Make sure the engine oil tank is full and the oil pump bled of all air. See Chapter Three.

b. Make sure the air filter is clean, oiled and properly installed.

c. Make sure the correct heat range spark is installed in the engine.

d. Check the clutch adjustment to make sure the clutch is not slipping or dragging.

e. Perform the break-in procedure on flat ground. To prevent engine overheating, avoid riding in sand, mud or up hills.

f. Do not run the engine with the throttle in the same position for more than a few seconds.

g. Short bursts of full throttle operation (no more than 2-3 seconds at a time) are acceptable. However, rest the engine after each full throttle operation by cruising at a low engine speed for a few minutes. This will allow the engine to rid itself of any excessive heat buildup.

h. Check the spark plug frequently during the break-in procedure. The electrode should be dry and clean and the color of the insulation should be light to medium tan. Refer to Chapter Three for further information on spark plug reading.

i. To control throttle operation at 1/2 and 3/4 throttle positions during break-in, adjust the speed limiter (**Figure 107**) mounted on the throttle housing. If you installed a twist grip throttle on your Blaster, mark the throttle housing and grip with tape and a marking pen (**Figure 108**). Make 4 marks on the housing to represent closed, 1/4, 3/4 and full throttle positions.

j. Keep accurate time records of the break-in procedure.

1. For the first 10 hours, keep the engine speed below 1/2 throttle. Stop and turn the engine off after every hour of continuous riding and allow the engine to cool down for 5 to 10 minutes before continuing.

During this time period, shift the transmission frequently to prevent lugging the engine while also avoiding high engine speed. Do not operate the vehicle for any length of time in any one throttle position.

2. For the next 10 hours, do not ride the vehicle above 3/4 throttle. During this period, shift the transmission frequently to prevent lugging the engine while also avoiding high engine speed.

3. After the first 20 hours of engine operation, the engine break-in is complete.

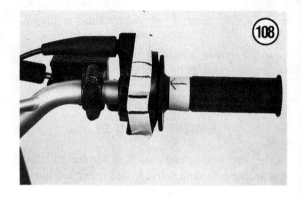

Table 1 CRANKSHAFT SPECIFICATIONS

	New mm (in.)	Service limit mm (in.)
Crankshaft wheel width	57.90 (2.280)	–
Crankshaft runout limit	–	0.03 (0.0012)
Big end side clearance		
1988-2001	0.4-0.7 (0.016-0.028)	–
2002	0.2-0.7 (0.008-0.028)	
Big end radial clearance	0.021-0.035 (0.0008-0.0014)	–
Small end side play	0.8-1.0 (0.031-0.039)	–

Table 2 ENGINE BOTTOM END TIGHTENING TORQUES

	N•m	in.-lb.	ft.-lb.
Autolube pump cover screws	7	62	–
Autolube pump mounting screws	5	44	–
Clutch cover mounting screws	10	88	–
Crankcase mounting screws	8	71	–
Crankshaft oil seal retainer screw	16	–	12
Drive sprocket holder mounting bolts	10	88	–
Engine mount bolts			
Front engine mount	45	–	33
Rear engine mount	33	–	24
Footpeg mounting bolts	55	–	40
Mainshaft bearing retainer screws	10	88	–
Pivot shaft nut	85	–	62

CHAPTER SIX

CLUTCH, KICKSTARTER AND EXTERNAL SHIFT MECHANISM

6

This chapter contains removal, inspection and installation of all components mounted behind the right crankcase cover. These include the clutch, kickstarter, external shift mechanism and the primary drive and balancer gears. Refer to Chapter Ten to service the Autolube injection pump.

Clutch specifications are listed in **Table 1** and **Table 2**. Tightening torques are listed in **Table 3**. **Tables 1-3** are found at the end of this chapter.

RIGHT CRANKCASE COVER

Removal

1. Drain the transmission oil (Chapter Three).
2. Remove the right side footpeg (Chapter Fourteen).
3. Disconnect the oil pump hoses as follows:
    a. Remove the Autolube pump cover screws and cover (**Figure 1**).
    b. Remove the screw and hose clamp (**Figure 2**) from the right crankcase cover.
    c. Disconnect the oil hoses (A and B, **Figure 3**) from the oil pump.
    d. Plug both hoses to prevent oil leakage and hose contamination.

4. Remove the kickstarter pedal mounting nut and remove the kickstarter pedal (**Figure 4**).

NOTE
*Do not remove the 2 oil pump mounting screws (**Figure 5**) when removing the crankcase cover screws in Step 5.*

5. Remove the crankcase cover mounting screws, hose bracket (**Figure 6**) and cover (**Figure 7**).

6. Remove the crankcase cover gasket and both dowel pins (**Figure 8**).

7. Remove all gasket residue from the crankcase cover and crankcase gasket surfaces.

8. If necessary, service the Autolube oil pump as described in Chapter Ten.

9. If necessary, replace the kickstarter shaft seal as described in this section.

Kickstarter Shaft Seal Replacement

If the kickstarter shaft seal (**Figure 9**) is leaking, replace it as follows.

1. Pry the seal out of the cover with a wide-blade screwdriver (**Figure 10**). Pad the screwdriver to prevent it from damaging the cover.

2. Clean the seal bore.

3. Pack the lips of the new seal with grease.

4. Align the new oil seal with the cover so its closed side is facing out. Then install the seal until it bottoms in the seal bore.

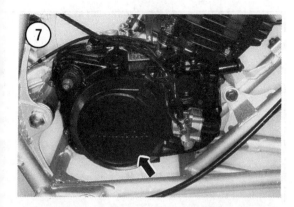

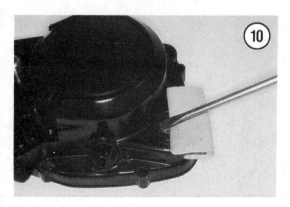

Kickstarter Pedal
Inspection

1. Clean and dry the kickstarter pedal. Remove any rust or corrosion from the kickstarter pedal and shaft splines.
2. Inspect the kickstarter pedal assembly (**Figure 11**) for:
   a. Worn or damaged splines.
   b. Damaged kick arm.
   c. Damaged detent assembly (the kickstarter will not turn and lock when returned to its at-rest position).
   d. Rounded-off or damaged mounting nut.
3. Replace the kickstarter pedal if damaged, or if it will not lock in its at-rest position. Replacement parts for the detent assembly are not available.

Installation

1. If removed, install the oil pump as described in Chapter Ten.
2. Install the dowel pins (**Figure 8**) and a new crankcase cover gasket.

> *NOTE*
> *If the crankcase cover will not fit flush against the engine in Step 3, the oil pump drive gear is not meshing properly with the primary drive gear. If this happens, remove the cover and turn the oil pump drive gear.*

> *CAUTION*
> *Do not force the crankcase cover on or you may damage the oil pump drive gear.*

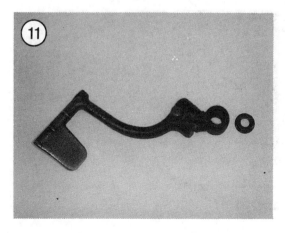

3. Install the crankcase cover (**Figure 7**) and secure it with its mounting screws. Install the oil hose bracket and screw as shown in **Figure 2**. All of the 6 mm screws are the same length (30 mm), except for the front lower screw shown in **Figure 12**. This screw is 35 mm long.

4. Tighten the crankcase cover mounting screws in a crisscross pattern to the torque specification in **Table 3**.

5. Refill the transmission with gear oil (Chapter Three). Check for leaks.

6. Install the kickstarter pedal and its mounting nut. Tighten the mounting nut to the torque specification in **Table 3**.

7. Service the oil pump as follows:
   a. Reconnect the oil hoses (A and B, **Figure 3**) to the oil pump.
   b. Bleed the oil pump as described in Chapter Ten.
   c. Install the Autolube pump cover (**Figure 7**) and tighten its mounting screws to the torque specification in **Table 3**.

8. Install the right footpeg assembly (Chapter Fourteen).

CLUTCH SERVICE

Refer to **Figure 13** when servicing the clutch.

Removal

1. Loosen the clutch cable adjuster (**Figure 14**) at the handlebar.

2. Remove the right crankcase cover as described in this chapter.

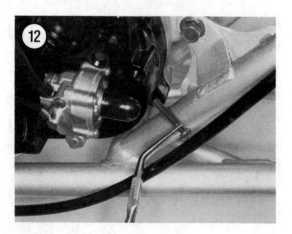

CLUTCH

1. Bolt
2. Clutch spring
3. Pressure plate
4. Locknut
5. Washer
6. Push plate
7. Clutch nut
8. Lockwasher
9. Friction disc (regular size plates)
10. Clutch plate
11. Friction disc (larger inside diameter)
12. Cushion spring
13. Clutch boss
14. Spacer
15. Clutch housing
16. Spacer
17. Spring washer
18. Pushrod No. 1
19. Ball
20. Pushrod No. 2

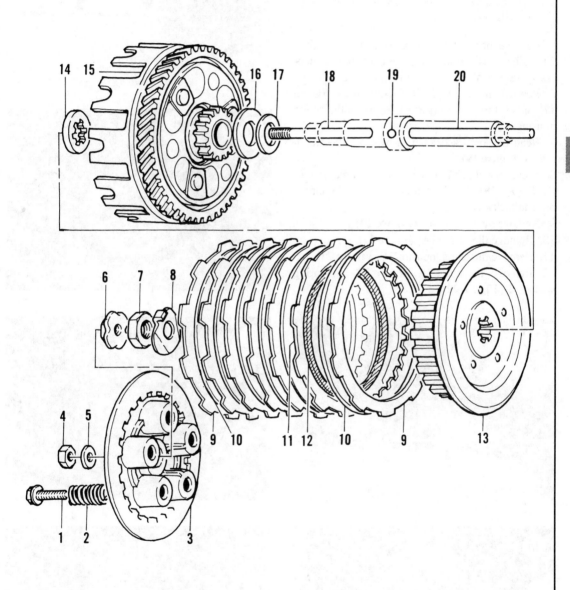

3. Loosen the clutch spring bolts (A, **Figure 15**) in a crisscross pattern. Then remove the bolts, washers and springs.

4. Remove the pressure plate (B, **Figure 15**).

NOTE
*Pushrod No. 1 (A, **Figure 16**) is attached to the pressure plate.*

5. Remove the ball (B, **Figure 16**) and pushrod No. 2 (C, **Figure 16**) from inside the mainshaft. If necessary, remove these 2 parts with a magnet.

6. Remove the clutch plates, friction discs (**Figure 17**) and cushion spring (**Figure 18**) from the clutch housing.

7. Bend the lockwasher tab away from the clutch nut (A, **Figure 19**).

8. Secure the clutch boss with a clutch holding tool (B, **Figure 19**), then loosen and remove the clutch nut and lockwasher.

9. Remove the clutch boss (**Figure 20**).

10. Remove the spacer (A, **Figure 21**).

11. Remove the clutch housing (B, **Figure 21**).

12. Remove the spacer (A, **Figure 22**) and spring washer (B, **Figure 22**).

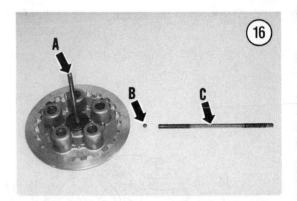

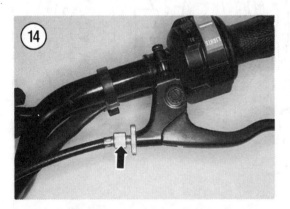

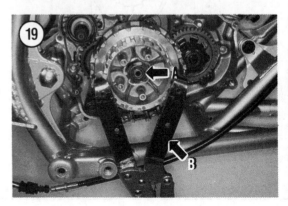

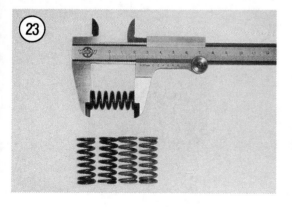

Clutch Inspection

When measuring the clutch components in this section, compare the actual measurements to the specifications in **Table 2**. Replace parts that are damaged or out of specification as described in this section.

1. Clean and dry all parts.

2. Measure the free length of each clutch spring (**Figure 23**) with a vernier caliper. Replace the springs as a set if any one spring is too short.

3. The friction material used on the friction discs (A and B, **Figure 24**) is bonded to an aluminum plate for warp resistance and durability. Measure the thickness of each friction disc with a vernier caliper (**Figure 25**). If 1 friction disc is out of specification, replace all friction discs as a set.

6

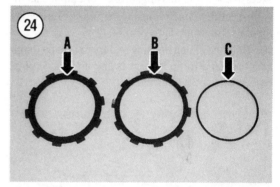

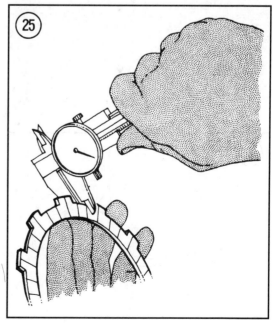

4. Inspect the cushion spring (C, **Figure 24**) for damage.

5. Inspect each clutch plate (**Figure 26**) for excessive wear, bluing (indicating heat damage) or other damage.

6. Place each clutch plate (**Figure 26**) on a flat surface and check for warpage with a feeler gauge (**Figure 27**). If 1 clutch plate is out of specification, replace all clutch plates as a set.

7. The friction disc tabs slide in the clutch housing grooves (**Figure 28**). Inspect the grooves (**Figure 29**) for cracks, galling or steps. These grooves must be smooth; otherwise the friction discs cannot slide and release, causing clutch drag. Repair light damage with a file or oilstone. Replace the clutch housing if damage is severe.

8. Inspect the clutch housing gears (**Figure 30**) for excessively worn, missing, broken or chipped teeth.

9. Inspect the clutch housing bushing (**Figure 31**) for cracks or other damage.

10. Hold the clutch housing and try to turn the large gear back and forth. If there is any noticeable play, replace the clutch housing.

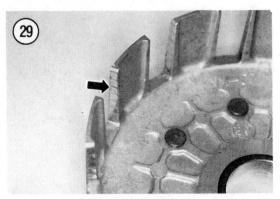

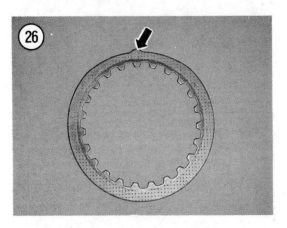

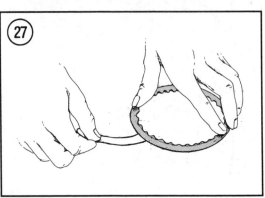

11. The clutch plate inner teeth mesh with the clutch boss splines (**Figure 32**). Check the splines (A, **Figure 33**) for cracks, galling or steps. These grooves must be smooth; otherwise the clutch plates cannot slide and release, causing clutch drag. Repair light damage with a file. Replace the clutch boss if damage is severe.

12. Inspect each clutch boss spring tower (B, **Figure 33**) for cracks or thread damage.

13. Inspect the clutch boss splines (C, **Figure 33**) for excessive wear, galling or other damage.

14. Check the pressure plate (A, **Figure 34**) for warpage, cracks or other damage. Check the spring towers (B, **Figure 34**) for cracks or damage.

15. Inspect the pushrod assembly as follows:

    a. Remove the nut and washer (**Figure 35**), then remove pushrod No. 1 (A, **Figure 36**) and the push plate (B, **Figure 36**).

    b. Check the No. 1 (A, **Figure 36**) and No. 2 (C, **Figure 16**) pushrods for cracks or damaged ends.

    c. Mount each pushrod on a set of V-blocks and measure runout with a dial indicator (**Figure 37**). Replace the pushrod(s) if out of specification.

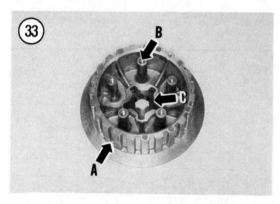

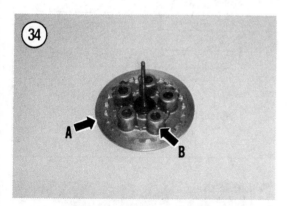

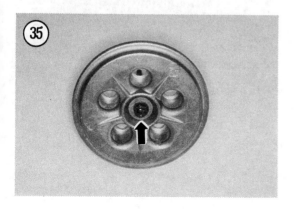

d. Replace the ball (B, **Figure 16**) if damaged.

e. Thread the push plate onto pushrod No. 1, then install the push plate through the pressure plate and secure it with the washer and nut (**Figure 35**).

16. Check the clutch nut, spacers and washers (**Figure 38**) for damage.

Installation

1. Make sure all clutch parts are clean.

2. If you removed the clutch push lever, install it as described in this chapter.

3. Lubricate the following components with transmission oil:

a. Mainshaft outside diameter.

b. Washers.

c. Clutch housing bore.

4. Install the spring washer (A, **Figure 39**) so its convex side is facing toward the mainshaft bearing. See **Figure 40**.

5. Install the flat washer (B, **Figure 39**) and seat it against the spring washer.

6. Install the clutch housing (A, **Figure 41**) and mesh its 2 gears with the primary drive and balancer drive gears.

7. Install the spacer (B, **Figure 41**) with its flat side facing out.

8. Install the clutch boss (**Figure 42**) and seat it against the spacer.

9. Install the lockwasher. Seat the lockwasher tab into the flat notch in the clutch boss (**Figure 43**).

10. Install the clutch nut and tighten finger-tight.

11. Secure the clutch boss with a clutch holding tool (**Figure 44**), then tighten the clutch nut to the torque

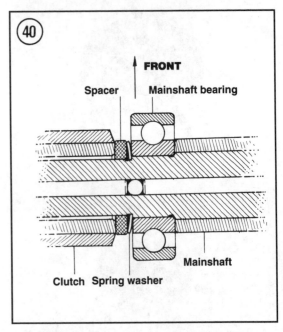

FRONT

Spacer   Mainshaft bearing

Mainshaft

Clutch   Spring washer

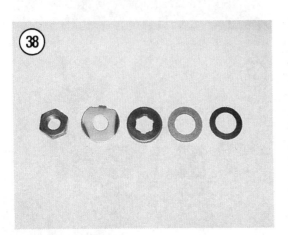

specification in **Table 3**. Remove the clutch holding tool.

12. Bend the lockwasher tab over 1 flat of the clutch nut (**Figure 45**). Make sure the lockwasher tab sits flush against the nut (**Figure 46**).

> *NOTE*
> *The stock clutch uses 2 different size friction plates. There are 5 plates (A, **Figure 47**) of the same size and 1 friction plate with a larger inside diameter (B, **Figure 47**). A cushion spring (C, **Figure 47**) fits inside the large friction disc during clutch assembly. The 5 friction plates of the same size are referred to as regular size plates in the following steps.*

13. Install the clutch plates in the following order:

   a. Lubricate each clutch plate with transmission oil (**Figure 48**).

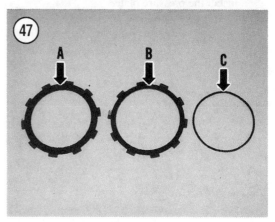

b. Install the first regular size (A, **Figure 47**) friction plate and position its tabs between the clutch housing grooves. See **Figure 49**.

c. Install the first metal clutch plate (**Figure 50**) by sliding it over the clutch boss splines.

d. Install the friction plate with the larger inside diameter (B, **Figure 47**) and position its tabs between the clutch housing grooves (**Figure 51**).

e. Install the cushion spring (C, **Figure 47**) over the clutch boss and position it underneath the friction plate (**Figure 51**).

NOTE
All of the remaining friction plates are the same size as the first friction plate installed. See **Table 1** *for the correct number of clutch plates used in the stock clutch.*

f. Install the remaining friction plates and metal clutch plates. Stagger each metal clutch plate so its plate tab (**Figure 52**) is positioned 60° clockwise from the previously installed clutch plate tab. See **Figure 53**.

g. The last plate installed must be a friction plate (**Figure 54**).

14. Lightly lubricate the steel ball and the push rod ends with grease.

15. Install the pushrod No. 2 (C, **Figure 55**) and steel ball (B, **Figure 55**) into the mainshaft.

16. Install the pressure plate as follows:

a. If removed, install the pushrod No. 1 (A, **Figure 55**), push plate and nut onto the pressure plate.

b. Align the pressure plate mark (A, **Figure 56**) with the clutch boss mark (B, **Figure 56**) and install the pressure plate.

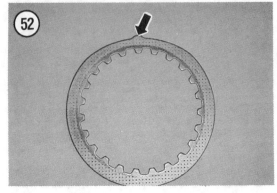

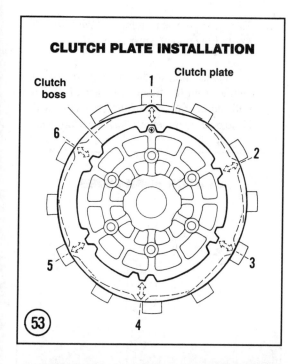

CLUTCH PLATE INSTALLATION

Clutch boss

Clutch plate

1

6

2

5

3

4

53

c. Make sure the pressure plate splines mesh with the clutch boss splines and that the pressure plate seats flush against the last friction plate. See **Figure 57**.

17. Install the clutch springs, bolts and washers (A, **Figure 58**). Tighten the clutch bolts a few turns at a time in a crisscross pattern until they become tight. Then tighten the bolts in a crisscross pattern to 1/2 the torque specification listed in **Table 3**. Go over the sequence a final time, tightening the bolts to the torque specification in **Table 3**.

56

B   A

6

54

57

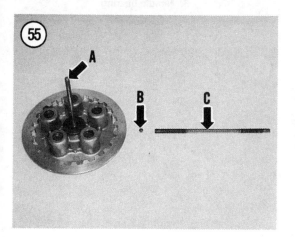

55

A

B   C

58

B

A

18. Reconnect the clutch cable to its handlebar adjuster (**Figure 59**).

19. Adjust the clutch mechanism (B, **Figure 58**) as described under *Clutch Adjustment* in Chapter Three.

20. Install the right crankcase cover as described in this chapter.

21. Recheck the clutch adjustment.

CLUTCH PUSH LEVER

The clutch push lever is installed in the left crankcase (**Figure 60**).

Removal

1. Loosen the clutch cable adjuster at the handlebar (**Figure 59**).

2. Disconnect the clutch cable (**Figure 61**) from the clutch push lever.

3. Remove the clutch push lever (A, **Figure 62**), spring and washer from the crankcase.

Inspection

1. Clean and dry the clutch push lever assembly (**Figure 63**).

2. Inspect the clutch push lever and replace it if excessively worn or damaged.

3. Inspect the flat washer and spring (**Figure 63**) and replace if damaged.

4. Inspect the clutch push lever seal and needle bearing installed in the right crankcase (**Figure 60**). Note the following:

a. To replace the seal, refer to *Crankcase Seal Replacement* in Chapter Five.

b. To replace the needle bearing, remove the engine from the frame (Chapter Five). Then pull the bearing out of the crankcase with a blind bearing remover. Clean the bearing bore,

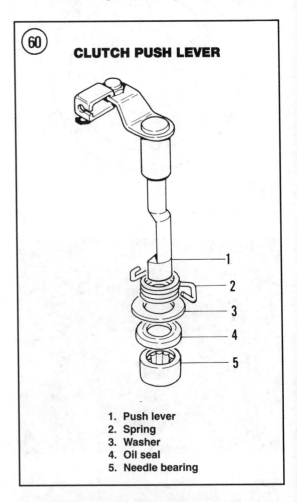

60 **CLUTCH PUSH LEVER**

1. **Push lever**
2. **Spring**
3. **Washer**
4. **Oil seal**
5. **Needle bearing**

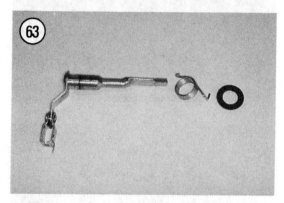

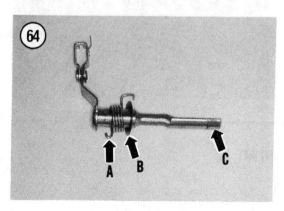

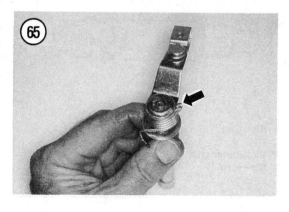

then press the new bearing in until it bottoms in the crankcase bearing bore. Install the bearing with its manufacturer's marks facing out.

Installation

1. Install the spring short end first over the clutch push lever shaft (A, **Figure 64**). Then install the washer (B).

2. Hook the upper end of the spring over the notch in the clutch push lever as shown in **Figure 65**.

3. Apply grease onto the clutch push lever shaft (C, **Figure 64**) where it contacts the pushrod.

4A. Install the clutch push lever shaft through the seal and bearing and into the crankcase. Hook the lower spring end into the notch in the crankcase (B, **Figure 62**).

NOTE
If the clutch push lever fails to go all the way into the crankcase, it is hitting against the clutch pushrod. Perform Step 4B to install the clutch push lever.

4B. Install the clutch push lever as follows:

   a. Remove the right crankcase cover as described in this chapter.

   b. Loosen the clutch adjuster locknut and loosen the adjuster (B, **Figure 58**). This should increase the pushrod free play enough to allow installation of the clutch push lever.

   c. If the clutch push lever still fails to go all the way into the crankcase, remove the clutch pressure plate as described under *Clutch Removal* in this chapter. Install the clutch push lever as described in Step 4A. Then reinstall the pressure plate as described under *Clutch Installation* in this chapter.

5. Reconnect the clutch cable to the clutch push lever (**Figure 61**).

6. Adjust the clutch as described under *Clutch Adjustment* in Chapter Three. Note the following:

   a. If the clutch mechanism adjuster or pressure plate was removed, adjust the clutch mechanism adjuster.

   b. If the clutch push lever was installed without removing the crankcase cover, adjust the clutch at its handlebar adjuster.

   c. If removed, install the right crankcase cover as described in this chapter.

CLUTCH CABLE REPLACEMENT

1. Remove the fuel tank (Chapter Eight).

2. Loosen the clutch cable adjuster locknut and adjuster (**Figure 59**) at the handlebar, then disconnect the clutch cable.

3. Disconnect the clutch cable (**Figure 61**) from the clutch push lever.

> *NOTE*
> *Prior to removing the cable make a drawing of the cable routing through the frame. It is very easy to forget its routing after it has been removed. Replace the cable exactly as it was, avoiding any sharp turns.*

4. Pull the cable out of any retaining clips on the frame.

5. Remove the cable and replace it with a new one.

6. Lubricate the clutch before reconnecting it in the following steps. Refer to Chapter Three.

7. Install by reversing these removal steps. Make sure it is correctly routed with no sharp turns. Adjust the clutch as described under *Clutch Adjustment* in Chapter Three.

KICKSTARTER

Refer to **Figure 66** when servicing the kickstarter.

Removal/Installation

1. Remove the clutch as described in this chapter.

2. Unhook the kick spring from its position in the crankcase (**Figure 67**) and allow the spring to unwind.

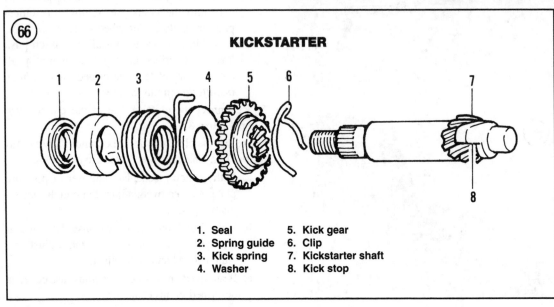

KICKSTARTER

1. Seal
2. Spring guide
3. Kick spring
4. Washer
5. Kick gear
6. Clip
7. Kickstarter shaft
8. Kick stop

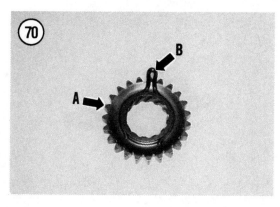

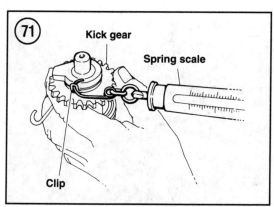

3. Turn the kickstarter assembly (**Figure 68**) *counterclockwise* and pull it out of the crankcase.

4. If necessary, remove the idler gear assembly as described in this chapter.

Disassembly/Inspection

1. Disassemble the kickstarter assembly in the order shown in **Figure 66**.

2. Wash the kickstarter assembly in solvent and dry thoroughly.

3. Check the kickstarter shaft (**Figure 69**) for:
   a. Worn or damaged splines.
   b. Elongation of the kick spring hole.
   c. Scored or cracked operating surfaces.
   d. Damaged threads.
   e. Damaged kick stop.

4. Check the kick gear (A, **Figure 70**) for:
   a. Broken or chipped teeth.
   b. Worn, damaged or rounded splines.

5. Check the kick gear clip (B, **Figure 70**) as follows:
   a. Check the clip for any visible wear or damage.
   b. Check the clip tension by hooking a spring scale onto the clip as shown in **Figure 71**. Hold the kick gear while pulling the spring scale. The spring should not slip or move on the kick gear until the spring scale reads 0.8-1.2 kg (1.8-2.6 lb.). Replace the spring if out of specification.

6. Inspect the kick spring (3, **Figure 66**) and replace it if weak or damaged.

7. Replace the spring guide (2, **Figure 66**) if excessively worn or damaged.

8. Replace the washer (4, **Figure 66**) if bent or damaged.

Assembly

1. Make sure all kickstarter parts (**Figure 72**) are clean.

2. Lubricate all sliding surfaces with transmission oil.

3. If removed, install the kick gear clip (B, **Figure 70**) onto the kick gear. Position the clip so its angled arm faces away from the gear.

4. Slide the kick gear (with clip) onto the kickstarter shaft (A, **Figure 73**) with its clip side facing toward the left side of the shaft.

5. Install the washer (B, **Figure 73**) onto the kick-starter shaft.

6. Install the kick spring with its long arm (A, **Figure 74**) facing toward the left side of the shaft. Then seat the opposite spring arm into the hole in the kickstarter shaft (B, **Figure 74**).

7. Install spring guide with its notch (A, **Figure 75**) facing toward the kick spring. Then insert the notch over the kick spring arm that fits into the shaft (B, **Figure 75**).

Installation

1. If removed, install the idler gear assembly as described in this section.

2. If the kickstarter was disassembled, or if a part slipped off the shaft, check the kickstarter assembly (**Figure 76**) as described under *Kickstarter Reassembly* in this section.

3. Align the kick stop (A, **Figure 68**) and the clip arm (B) with the crankcase. Then install the kickstarter into the crankcase.

    a. Make sure the kick stop seats into the crankcase groove as shown in A, **Figure 77**.

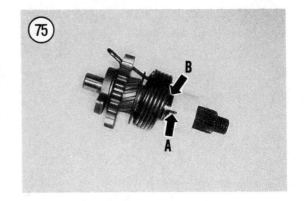

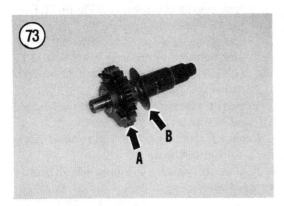

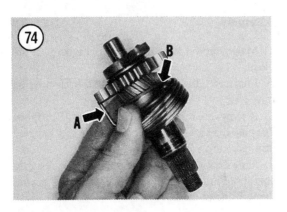

b. Make sure the clip arm seats into the crankcase notch as shown in B, **Figure 77**.

4. Turn the kick spring (**Figure 67**) clockwise and seat it into the hole in the crankcase (**Figure 78**).

5. Temporarily install the kickstarter pedal over the kickstarter shaft. Hold the kickstarter in place and push down on the kickstarter pedal. The kick gear should slide out and engage with the idler gear. Now release the kickstarter pedal and allow the kickstarter shaft to return to its rest position. The kick gear should disengage from the idler gear and slide back toward the engine crankcase. If the kickstarter does not operate as described, remove the kickstarter assembly and check for one or more incorrectly installed parts. Remove the kickstarter pedal.

6. Install the clutch as described in this chapter.

IDLER GEAR

Refer to **Figure 79** when servicing the idler gear assembly.

Removal/Inspection/Installation

1. Remove the circlip, washer, idler gear, washer and circlip (**Figure 80**) from the countershaft.

2. Clean and dry the idler gear assembly (**Figure 80**).

3. Discard the circlips (**Figure 80**).

4. Check the idler gear (**Figure 80**) for:

   a. Broken or chipped teeth.

   b. Scored bore surface.

5. Replace the washers if bent or damaged.

NOTE
The 2 idler gear circlips are identical.
The 2 washers are identical.

6. Install the first circlip (**Figure 81**) with its flat side facing toward the crankcase. Seat the circlip into the countershaft groove completely.

7. Install the first washer (**Figure 82**) with its flat side facing away from the crankcase.

6

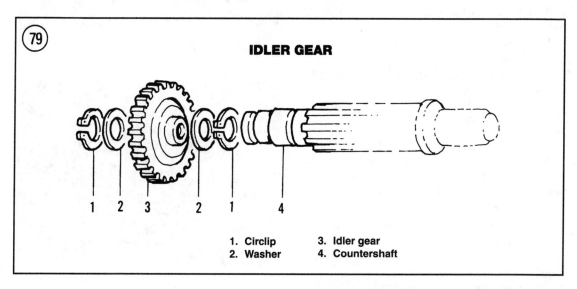

79

IDLER GEAR

1 2 3   2 1   4

1. Circlip   3. Idler gear
2. Washer   4. Countershaft

80

81

8. Install the idler gear with its bevel gear side (**Figure 83**) facing away from the crankcase.

9. Install the second washer (A, **Figure 84**) with its flat side facing toward the crankcase.

10. Install the second circlip (B, **Figure 84**) with its flat side facing away from the crankcase. Seat the circlip into the countershaft groove completely.

11. Spin the idler gear (**Figure 85**) by hand. It must turn freely with no binding or roughness.

12. Install the kickstarter as described in this chapter.

EXTERNAL SHIFT MECHANISM

Refer to **Figure 86** when servicing the external shift mechanism in this section.

Removal

1. Remove the clutch as described in this chapter.

2. Remove the shift pedal pinch bolt and remove shift pedal (**Figure 87**).

3. Pull the shift shaft out of the crankcase and remove it (**Figure 88**).

4. Remove the stopper lever bolt (A, **Figure 89**), stopper lever and spring.

Inspection

Worn or damaged shift linkage components will cause missed shifts and wear to the transmission gears, shift forks and shift drum. Replace questionable parts as necessary.

1. Remove all threadlock residue from the stopper lever bolt and crankcase hole threads.

2. Clean the components in solvent and dry thoroughly.

3. Check the shift shaft (**Figure 90**) for:
   a. Damaged splines.
   b. Corroded, twisted or otherwise damaged shaft.
   c. Weak or damaged return spring (A, **Figure 91**).
   d. Damaged set spring (B, **Figure 91**).

4. Make sure the circlip (C, **Figure 91**) is seated in the shift shaft groove completely.

5. Check the stopper lever (**Figure 92**) assembly for:
   a. Weak or damaged spring.

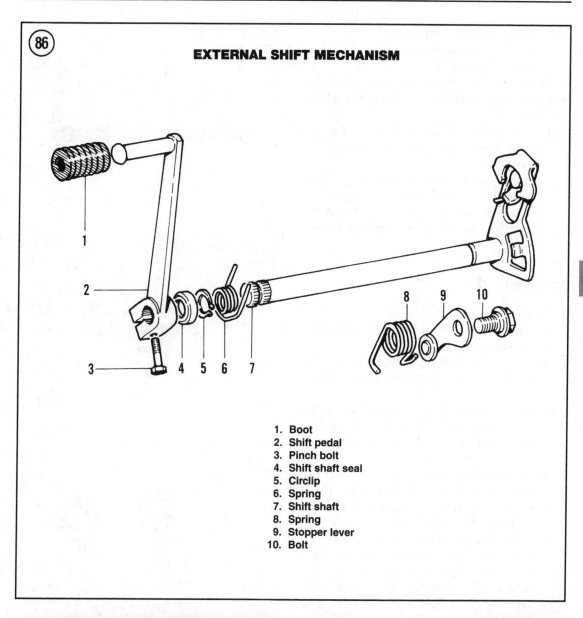

EXTERNAL SHIFT MECHANISM

1. Boot
2. Shift pedal
3. Pinch bolt
4. Shift shaft seal
5. Circlip
6. Spring
7. Shift shaft
8. Spring
9. Stopper lever
10. Bolt

6

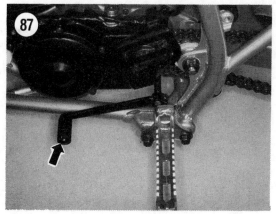

b. Bent or damaged stopper lever.

c. Seized or damaged stopper lever roller.

d. Damaged shoulder bolt.

6. Check the shift shaft seal in the left crankcase for wear or damage. Replace the seal if leaking. Note the following:

    a. Pry the seal out of the crankcase with a screwdriver. Make sure you do not damage the crankcase.

    b. Pack the seal lips with grease, then press the seal into the case closed side facing out by hand or use a small socket and extension. Install the seal so it seats squarely in the case bore.

Installation

1. Install the stopper lever assembly as follows:

    a. Hook the spring over the case bolt hole (**Figure 93**).

    b. Apply a medium strength threadlocking compound onto the stopper lever mounting bolt threads.

    c. Hook the stopper lever (A, **Figure 94**) onto the spring, then install the mounting bolt (B, **Figure 94**) and tighten 4 or 5 turns only. Do not tighten the bolt.

    d. Lift the spring arm (C, **Figure 94**) over the case boss as shown in B, **Figure 89**, while at the same time meshing the stopper lever roller (C, **Figure 89**) with the shift drum ramp.

    e. Tighten the stopper lever mounting bolt (A, **Figure 89**) slowly, making sure the stopper lever rides up and then seats onto the bolt's shoulder. Then tighten the stopper lever mounting bolt to the torque specification in **Table 3**.

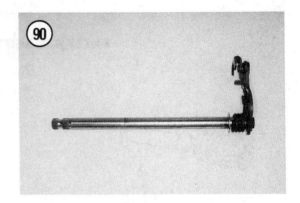

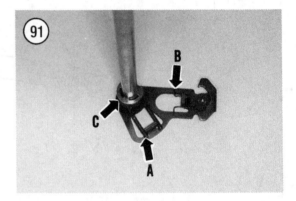

f. Press the stopper lever away from the shift drum and release it. If the stopper lever does not move, or if it moves roughly, the lever is not correctly seated onto the stopper lever mounting bolt shoulder.

2. Lubricate the shift shaft with transmission oil. Lubricate the end of the shaft that will pass through the seal with grease.

3. Install the shift shaft (**Figure 88**) carefully through the crankcase. Center the return spring around the shift fork shaft (A, **Figure 95**) while positioning the shift shaft arm (B, **Figure 95**) around the shift drum.

4. Install the shift pedal and its pinch bolt. Tighten the bolt securely.

5. Check the shifting as described under *Transmission Shifting Check* in Chapter Five.

6. Install the clutch as described in this chapter.

PRIMARY DRIVE GEAR AND BALANCER GEARS

Refer to **Figure 96** when servicing the primary drive gear and balancer gears in this chapter.

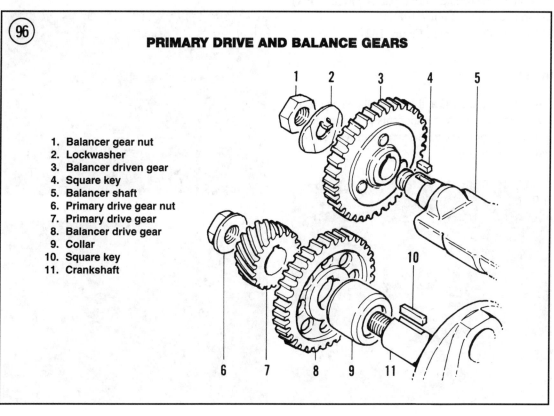

PRIMARY DRIVE AND BALANCE GEARS

1. Balancer gear nut
2. Lockwasher
3. Balancer driven gear
4. Square key
5. Balancer shaft
6. Primary drive gear nut
7. Primary drive gear
8. Balancer drive gear
9. Collar
10. Square key
11. Crankshaft

Removal

1. Remove the clutch as described in this chapter.
2. Remove the flywheel cover (Chapter Nine).

> *NOTE*
> *Have an assistant hold the flywheel with a flywheel holder (**Figure 97**) when loosening the primary drive gear and balancer gear nuts in the following steps.*

> *NOTE*
> *Another way to prevent the crankshaft from turning is to lock the 2 balancer gears together with a separate gear or gear holder.*

3. Pry the lockwasher tab away from the balancer gear nut (A, **Figure 98**).
4. Loosen the balancer gear nut (A, **Figure 98**) and primary drive gear nut (B, **Figure 98**).
5. Remove the balancer driven gear (**Figure 99**) and square key (**Figure 100**).
6. Remove the primary drive gear nut (A, **Figure 101**) and gear (B, **Figure 101**).
7. Remove the balancer drive gear (C, **Figure 101**) and square key (A, **Figure 102**).
8. Remove the collar (B, **Figure 102**).

Inspection

Refer to **Figure 103** and **Figure 104** when cleaning and inspecting the components in this section.
1. Clean the primary drive gear assembly in solvent and dry thoroughly.

2. Check the gears for:

   a. Broken or chipped teeth.

   b. Excessively worn, twisted or otherwise damaged gear splines.

3. Check the collar for pitting, corrosion or other damage.

> *NOTE*
> *A rough or damaged outer collar surface will tear the right crankcase seal and allow oil to be drawn into crankcase. This would richen the air/fuel mixture and cause operating problems.*

4. Inspect the lockwasher and replace it if damaged.

5. Inspect the square keys and replace if damaged.

6. Inspect the balancer shaft and crankshaft keyways for damage.

Installation

1. Lubricate the collar with grease and slide it over the crankshaft, then seat it against the main bearing (B, **Figure 102**).

2. Install the square key (A, **Figure 102**) into the crankshaft keyway.

3. Install the balancer drive gear (A, **Figure 105**) over the key and onto the crankshaft with its timing mark (B, **Figure 105**) facing out.

4. Install the primary drive gear (**Figure 106**) with its shoulder side facing out over the key and onto the crankshaft.

5. Install the primary drive gear nut (A, **Figure 101**) and tighten finger-tight.

6. Install the square key (**Figure 100**) into the balancer shaft keyway.

7. Install the balancer driven gear (**Figure 99**) with its index mark facing out over the key and onto the balancer shaft, while at the same time aligning its index mark with the index mark on the balancer drive gear (**Figure 107**).

8. Install the lockwasher by inserting its tab into the balancer shaft keyway (**Figure 108**). Then install the balancer gear nut (A, **Figure 98**) and tighten finger-tight.

9. Rotate the engine and recheck the balancer gear timing marks (**Figure 107**).

10. Use the same tool to hold the crankshaft, then tighten the balancer gear nut (A, **Figure 98**) and the primary drive gear nut (B, **Figure 98**) to the torque specifications in **Table 3**.

11. Bend the lockwasher tab over the balancer gear nut (A, **Figure 98**).

12 Install the clutch as described in this chapter.

13. Install the flywheel cover (Chapter Nine).

Table 1 CLUTCH SPECIFICATIONS

Clutch type	Wet, multiple-disc
Friction plate quantity	6
Clutch plate quantity	6

Table 2 CLUTCH SERVICE SPECIFICATIONS

	New mm (in.)	Service limit mm (in.)
Friction plate thickness	2.92-3.08 (0.115-0.121)	2.8 (0.110)
Clutch plate thickness	1.05-1.35 (0.041-0.053)	–
Clutch plate warp limit	–	0.05 (0.002)
Clutch spring free length		
1988-2001	32.5 (1.28)	30.0 (1.18)
2002	34.5 (1.36)	
Clutch housing radial clearance	0.015-0.049 (0.0006-0.0019)	–
Push rod bend limit	–	0.15 (0.006)

Table 3 CLUTCH TIGHTENING TORQUES

	N•m	in.-lb.	ft.-lb.
Autolube pump cover	7	62	–
Balancer drive gear nut	55	–	40
Clutch adjuster locknut	7	62	–
Clutch nut	80	–	59
Clutch spring bolts	6	53	–
Crankcase cover mounting screws	10	88	–
Kickstarter nut	65	–	47
Primary drive gear nut	80	–	59
Stopper lever mounting bolt	14	–	10

6

CHAPTER SEVEN

TRANSMISSION AND INTERNAL SHIFT MECHANISM

This chapter describes disassembly and reassembly of the transmission shafts and internal shift mechanism.

Table 1 lists transmission gear ratios for the YFS200 engine. Service specifications are listed in **Table 2**. **Tables 1** and **2** are at the end of this chapter.

TRANSMISSION OPERATION

The transmission has 6 pairs of constantly meshed gears (**Figure 1**) on the mainshaft (A) and countershaft (B). Each pair of meshed gears provides 1 gear ratio. In each pair, 1 of the gears is locked to its shaft and always turns with it. The other gear is not locked to its shaft and can spin freely. Next to each free spinning gear is a third gear which is splined to the same shaft, always turning with it. This third gear can slide from side to side along the shaft splines.

The side of the sliding gear and the free spinning gear have mating *dogs* and *slots*. When the sliding gear moves up against the free spinning gear, the 2 gears are locked together, locking the free spinning gear to its shaft. Since both meshed mainshaft and countershaft gears are now locked to their shafts, power is transmitted at that gear ratio.

Shift Drum and Forks

Each sliding gear has a deep groove machined around it (**Figure 2**). The curved shift fork arm rides in this groove, controlling the side-to-side sliding of the gear, and therefore the selection of different gear ratios. Each shift fork (A, **Figure 3**) slides back and forth on a shaft, and has a pin (B, **Figure 3**) that rides in a groove machined in the shift drum (**Figure 4**). When the shift shaft rotates the shift drum, the zigzag

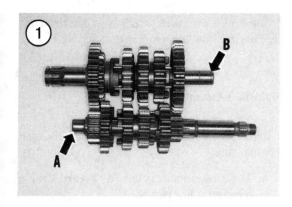

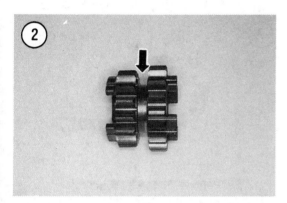

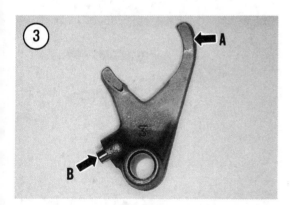

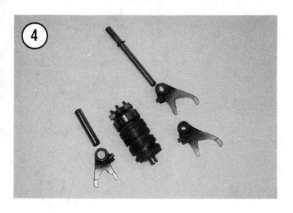

grooves move the shift forks and sliding gears back and forth. The stopper lever roller (**Figure 5**) follows the outer shift drum ramp and helps position the shift drum into each selected gear position.

TRANSMISSION TROUBLESHOOTING

Refer to *Transmission* in Chapter Two.

TRANSMISSION

Removal/Installation

Remove and install the transmission and internal shift mechanism assembly (**Figure 6**) as described in Chapter Five.

Transmission Service Notes

1. When troubleshooting the transmission, inspect each gear, washer and circlip before disassembling the shaft. Spin or slide each gear to check its operation.

7

2. After removing the transmission shafts, place 1 of the shafts into a large can or plastic bucket and clean with solvent. Dry with compressed air or set the shaft on rags to drip dry. Repeat for the opposite shaft.

3. If the gears were intermixed from both shafts (mainshaft and countershaft), use the gear ratio information in **Table 1** and the transmission drawing (found in this chapter under *Transmission Overhaul*) to identify the gears.

4. Store the transmission gears, washers and circlips in a divided container, such as an egg carton (**Figure 7**), to help maintain their correct alignment and position as you remove them from the transmission shafts.

5. Replace all transmission circlips (**Figure 8**) during reassembly. Do not reuse the circlips, as removal may distort them and cause them to fail.

6. Circlips will turn and fold over when removing and installing them on the shafts. To ease service, open the circlip with a pair of circlip pliers, while at the same time holding the back of the circlip with a pair of pliers (**Figure 9**), then remove or install the circlip.

TRANSMISSION OVERHAUL

Mainshaft Disassembly

Refer to **Figure 10**.

1. Disassemble the mainshaft (**Figure 11**) in the following order:

> NOTE
> *The 2 flat washers are different.*

    a. Circlip.
    b. Second gear.
    c. Sixth gear.
    d. Spline washer.
    e. Flat washer.
    f. Circlip.
    g. Third/fourth combination gear.
    h. Circlip.
    i. Flat washer.
    j. Fifth gear.

> NOTE
> *First gear is an integral part of the mainshaft.*

2. Inspect the mainshaft assembly as described under *Transmission Inspection* in this chapter.

Mainshaft Assembly

Before assembling the mainshaft assembly, note the following:

    a. The 3 mainshaft circlips (A, **Figure 12**) are identical (same part No.).

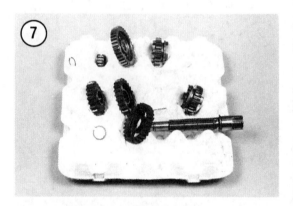

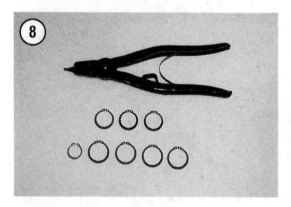

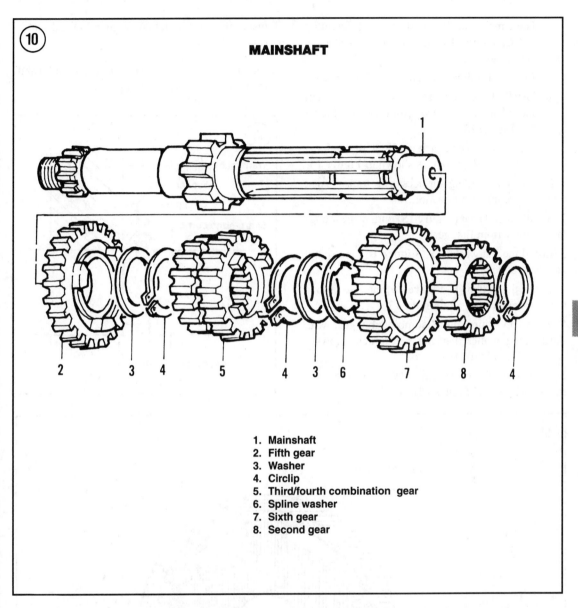

MAINSHAFT

10

1. Mainshaft
2. Fifth gear
3. Washer
4. Circlip
5. Third/fourth combination gear
6. Spline washer
7. Sixth gear
8. Second gear

7

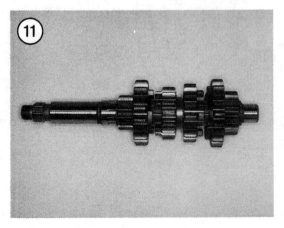

11

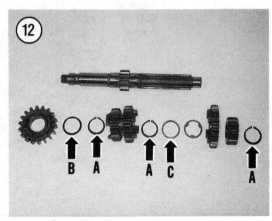

12

b. The 2 mainshaft flat washers are different (B and C, **Figure 12**). Install these washers in their original mounting position.

c. Always install new circlips (A, **Figure 12**).

d. Install the circlips and washers with their sharp edge facing *away* from the thrust load. See **Figure 13**.

e. Align the notch in each circlip with the transmission shaft groove as shown in **Figure 14**.

1. Lubricate all sliding surfaces with transmission oil to ensure initial lubrication.

2. Install second gear (**Figure 15**) with its gear dogs facing away from first gear.

3. Install the flat washer (A, **Figure 16**) and seat it against second gear.

4. Install the circlip (B, **Figure 16**) into the groove next to second gear. See **Figure 17**.

5. Install the third/fourth combination gear with third gear (smaller diameter gear) facing toward second gear (**Figure 18**).

6. Install a circlip (**Figure 19**) into the next mainshaft groove (**Figure 20**).

7. Install the flat washer (A, **Figure 21**) and seat it next to the circlip.

8. Install the spline washer (B, **Figure 21**) and seat it next to the flat washer. See **Figure 22**.

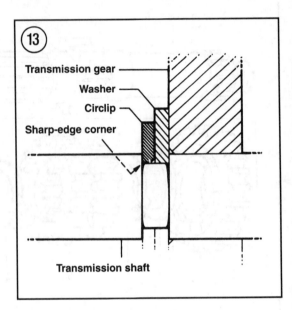

(13)

Transmission gear
Washer
Circlip
Sharp-edge corner

Transmission shaft

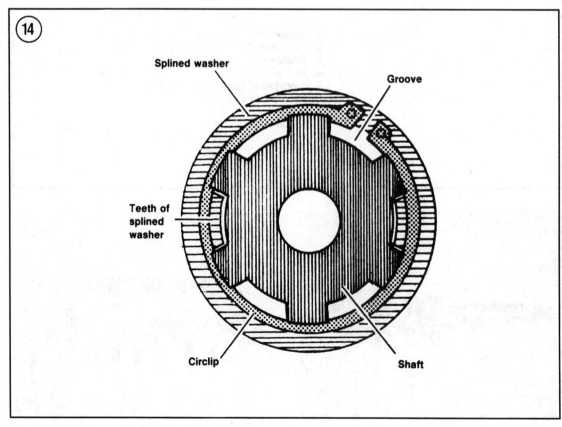

(14)

Splined washer

Groove

Teeth of splined washer

Circlip

Shaft

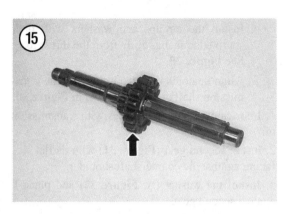

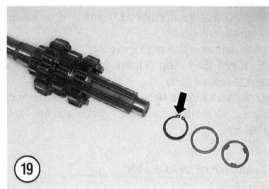

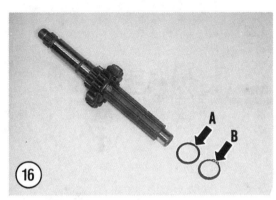

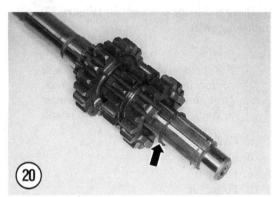

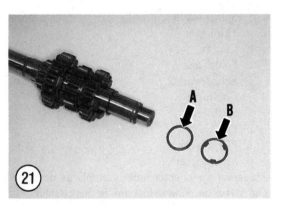

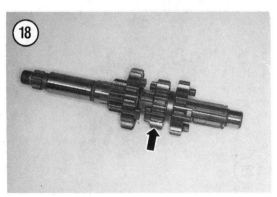

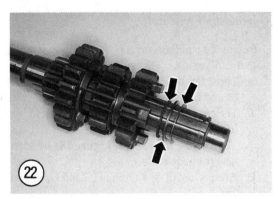

7

9. Install sixth gear (**Figure 23**) with its dogs facing toward fourth gear.

10. Install second gear (**Figure 24**).

11. Install the circlip (**Figure 25**) into the groove next to second gear.

12. Refer to **Figure 10** and **Figure 11** for the correct placement of the mainshaft gears, circlips and washers.

Countershaft Disassembly

Refer to **Figure 26**.

1. Disassemble the countershaft (**Figure 27**) in the following order:

NOTE
The countershaft uses 2 different circlips and 2 different flat washers. Make sure to keep these parts in order when disassembling the countershaft.

  a. Circlip.
  b. Flat washer.
  c. First gear.
  d. Fifth gear.
  e. Circlip.
  f. Spline washer.
  g. Third gear.
  h. Circlip.
  i. Fourth gear.
  j. Spline washer.
  k. Circlip.
  l. Sixth gear.
  m. Circlip.
  n. Flat washer.
  o. Second gear.

2. Inspect the countershaft assembly as described under *Transmission Inspection* in this chapter.

Countershaft Assembly

Before assembling the countershaft assembly, note the following:

  a. The 2 flat countershaft washers are different (A and B, **Figure 28**).
  b. The countershaft uses 2 different size circlips (C and D, **Figure 28**).
  c. The 2 spline washers (E, **Figure 28**) are identical (same part No.).
  d. Always install new circlips (C and D, **Figure 28**).

  e. Install the circlips and washers with their sharp edge facing *away* from the thrust load. See **Figure 29**.
  f. Align he notch in each circlip with the transmission shaft groove as shown in **Figure 30**.

1. Lubricate all sliding surfaces with transmission oil.

2. Install second gear (**Figure 31**) with its flat side facing against the countershaft shoulder.

3. Install the washer (A, **Figure 32**) and place it against second gear.

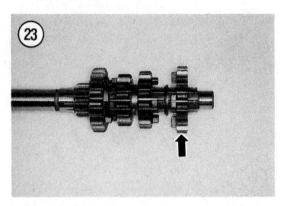

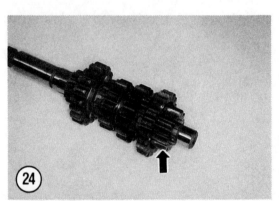

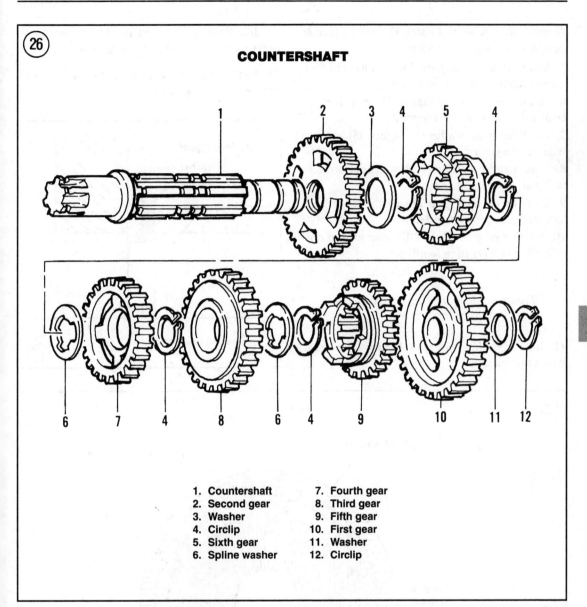

COUNTERSHAFT

1. Countershaft
2. Second gear
3. Washer
4. Circlip
5. Sixth gear
6. Spline washer
7. Fourth gear
8. Third gear
9. Fifth gear
10. First gear
11. Washer
12. Circlip

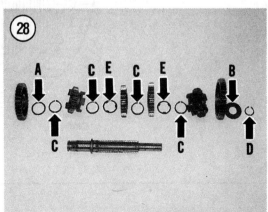

4. Install the circlip (B, **Figure 32**) into the groove next to second gear. See **Figure 33**.

5. Install sixth gear (**Figure 34**) with its shift fork groove facing away from second gear.

6. Install the circlip (A, **Figure 35**) into the next countershaft groove. See **Figure 36**.

7. Install the spline washer (B, **Figure 35**) and seat it next to the circlip.

8. Install fourth gear (**Figure 37**) with its closed side facing away from sixth gear.

9. Install the circlip (**Figure 38**) into the groove next to fourth gear. See **Figure 39**.

10. Install third gear (**Figure 40**) with its gear dog recess facing away from fourth gear.

NOTE
Figure 41 shows the correct fourth (A)
and third (B) gear alignment.

11. Install the spline washer (A, **Figure 42**) and seat it next to third gear.

12. Install the circlip (B, **Figure 42**) into the groove next to the spline washer. See **Figure 43**.

13. Install fifth gear (**Figure 44**) with its shift fork groove facing toward third gear.

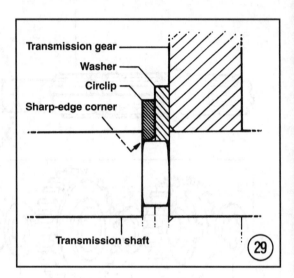

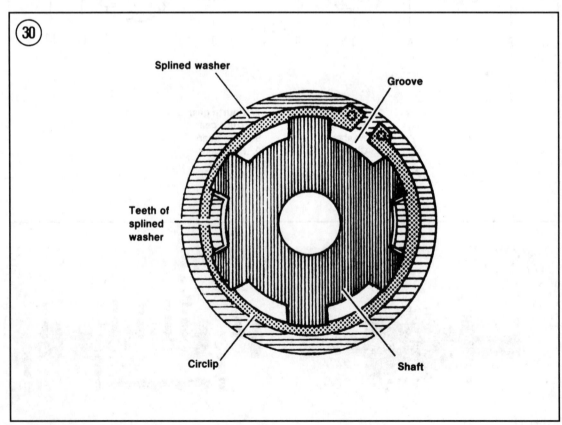

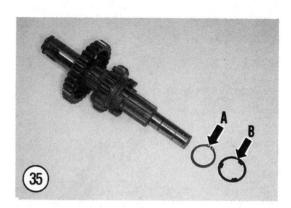

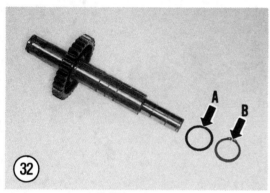

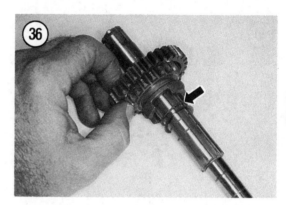

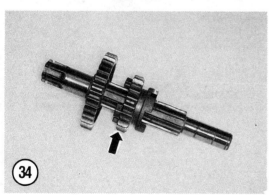

7

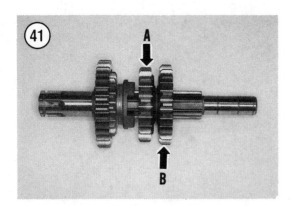

47

48

14. First gear has a bevel cut on one side of the gear (**Figure 45**). Install first gear with its beveled side facing toward fifth gear. See **Figure 46**.

15. Install the flat washer (A, **Figure 47**) and seat it against first gear.

16. Install the circlip (B, **Figure 47**) and seat it against the flat washer. See **Figure 48**.

17. Refer to **Figure 26** and **Figure 27** for the correct placement of the countershaft gears.

TRANSMISSION INSPECTION

Maintain the alignment of the mainshaft (**Figure 49**) and countershaft (**Figure 50**) components when inspecting the individual parts in the following steps.

1. Inspect the mainshaft (**Figure 51**) and countershaft (**Figure 52**) for:

    a. Worn or damages splines.

    b. Missing, broken or chipped mainshaft first gear teeth.

    c. Damaged countershaft shoulder.

    d. Excessively worn or damaged bearing surfaces.

    e. Cracked or rounded circlip grooves.

7

49

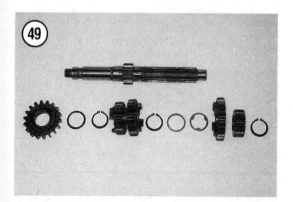

51

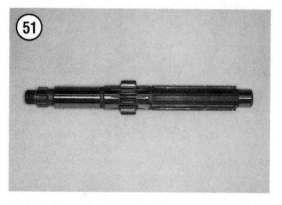

50

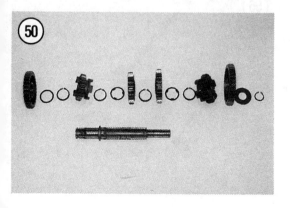

52

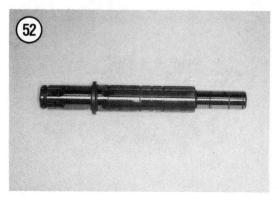

2. Check each gear for:

   a. Missing, broken or chipped teeth.

   b. Worn, damaged, or rounded gear lugs (A, **Figure 53**).

   c. Worn or damaged splines.

   d. Cracked or scored gear bore (B, **Figure 53**).

3. Place each transmission shaft on a set of V-blocks and measure runout with a dial indicator. Replace the shaft if out of specification (**Table 2**).

WARNING
Do not attempt to straighten a bent transmission shaft.

4. Replace each defective gear and its mating gear (**Figure 54**), though it may not show as much wear or damage.

INTERNAL SHIFT MECHANISM

Refer to the **Figure 55** when servicing the internal shift mechanism.

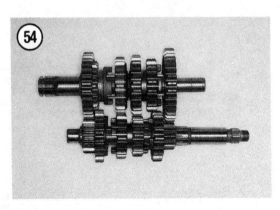

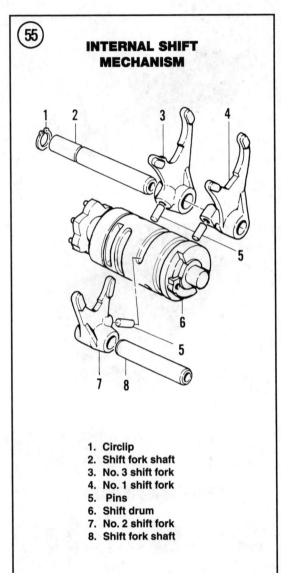

INTERNAL SHIFT MECHANISM

1. Circlip
2. Shift fork shaft
3. No. 3 shift fork
4. No. 1 shift fork
5. Pins
6. Shift drum
7. No. 2 shift fork
8. Shift fork shaft

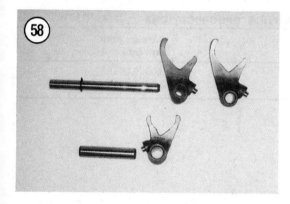

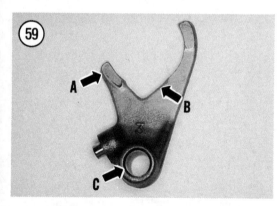

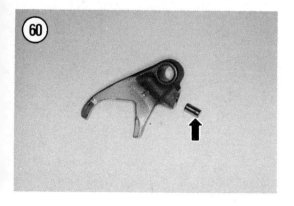

Removal/Installation

Remove and install the transmission and internal shift mechanism (**Figure 56**) as described in Chapter Five.

Shift Drum Inspection

1. Clean and dry the shift drum assembly.
2. Check the shift drum (**Figure 57**) for:
   a. Excessively worn or damaged shift fork pin grooves.
   b. Damaged bearing.
   c. Excessively worn or damaged ramps.
3. Replace the shift drum if necessary.

Shift Fork Inspection

1. Inspect each shift fork (**Figure 58**) for wear or damage. Examine the shift fork contact pads (A, **Figure 59**) where they contact the sliding gear. Both pads must be smooth without excessive wear, bending, cracks, heat discoloration or other damage. As the contact pads wear, their overall thickness is reduced. When excessively worn, look for arc-shaped wear or burn marks on the shift fork between the 2 contact pads (B, **Figure 59**).
2. Check each shift fork pin (**Figure 60**) for scoring or other damage.
3. Check each shift fork shaft for bending or other damage. Roll each shift fork shaft on a piece of plate glass or a surface plate (**Figure 61**). Any clicking or wobbling indicates a bent shaft.
4. Slide each shift fork on its shaft. Each shift fork must slide smoothly without binding. If you notice any binding and the shaft is straight, check the shift fork bore (C, **Figure 59**) for damage.

> *CAUTION*
> *Do not attempt to straighten a bent shift fork shaft.*

7

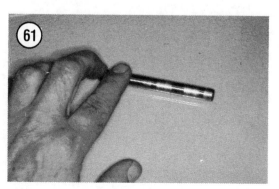

Table 1 TRANSMISSION GENERAL SPECIFICATIONS

Transmission type	Constant mesh 6-speed
Primary reduction system	Helical gear
Primary reduction ratio	71/22 (3.227)
Secondary reduction system	Chain drive
Secondary reduction ratio	40/13 (3.077)
Gear ratios	
1st	34/11 (3.091)
2nd	31/14 (2.214)
3rd	25/15 (1.667)
4th	20/16 (1.250)
5th	19/18 (1.056)
6th	19/21 (0.905)

Table 2 TRANSMISSION SERVICE SPECIFICATIONS

	New mm (in.)	Service limit mm (in.)
Countershaft runout limit	–	0.08 (0.003)
Mainshaft runout limit	–	0.08 (0.003)

FUEL SYSTEM

The fuel system consists of the fuel tank, fuel shutoff valve, carburetor and air filter.

This chapter includes service procedures for all parts of the fuel system. Air filter service is covered in Chapter Three. Reed valve service is covered in Chapter Four.

Table 1 and **Table 2** lists stock carburetor specifications. **Tables 1-4** are at the end of this chapter.

CARBURETOR

Removal

1. Park the vehicle on level ground and set the parking brake.

2. If necessary, remove the seat as described in Chapter Fourteen.

3. Turn the fuel valve off and disconnect the fuel hose from the fuel tank.

4. Loosen the stopper plate screw (A, **Figure 1**), then loosen the carburetor cap (B, **Figure 1**).

5. Disconnect the oil delivery hose (**Figure 2**) from the carburetor as follows:

    a. Slide the metal band off the hose, then disconnect the hose from the carburetor (**Figure 3**).

    b. Plug the hose to prevent oil leakage and contamination.

6. Disconnect the carburetor switch electrical connector (**Figure 4**).

7. Loosen the 2 hose clamp screws (C, **Figure 1**) and remove the carburetor assembly.

8. Remove the carburetor cap and the throttle valve assembly (A, **Figure 5**) from the carburetor.

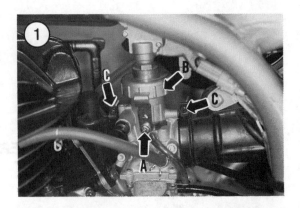

NOTE
If you are not going to remove the jet needle (B, Figure 5), slide a piece of hose over it to protect it from damage.

9. Plug the intake manifold and air box openings to prevent dust and other debris from entering.

Installation

1. Install the throttle valve into the carburetor housing by aligning the groove in the throttle valve with the pin in the carburetor housing.

2. Align the tab on the inner cap with the flat portion machined on the carburetor body (**Figure 6**), then install and tighten the carburetor cap (**Figure 7**).

3. Position the lockplate (A, **Figure 8**) so one of its locking grooves clamps around one of the raised carburetor cap grip flanges. Then tighten the lockplate screw (B, **Figure 8**) securely.

4. Push and release the throttle lever (at the handlebar). The throttle valve must move smoothly without binding.

5. Remove the rags from the hose openings, then install the carburetor and secure it with the 2 hose clamps (C, **Figure 1**).

6. Reconnect the oil delivery hose (**Figure 3**) onto the carburetor hose nozzle, then push the metal band over the hose nozzle to secure the hose.

7. Reconnect the carburetor switch (**Figure 4**) electrical connector.

8. Reconnect the fuel hose onto the fuel tank. Secure the hose with its hose clamp.

9. Check the throttle valve operation once again (see Step 4).

10. Turn the fuel valve on and, check the hose and carburetor for leaks.

Throttle Valve/T.O.R.S. (Throttle Valve Overide Switch) Housing Disassembly

Refer to **Figure 9**.

1. Remove the throttle valve assembly (**Figure 5**) as described under *Carburetor Removal* in this chapter.

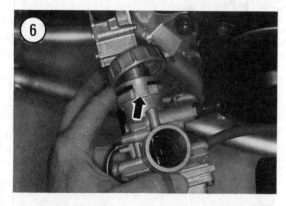

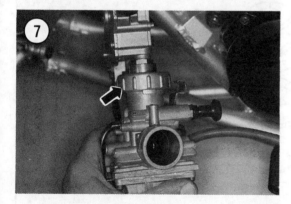

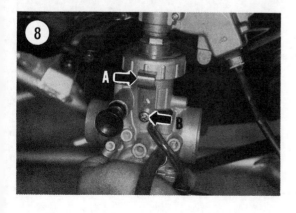

2. Compress the throttle valve spring into the cap and remove the throttle cable lock (**Figure 10**).

3. Push down and then lift out the throttle cable.

4. Remove the throttle valve spring.

5. Remove the 2 screws (**Figure 11**) securing the holder plate to the throttle valve. Then remove the holder plate, washers (**Figure 12**) and jet needle (A, **Figure 13**).

6. To remove the throttle valve cable (A, **Figure 14**), perform the following:

    a. Remove the T.O.R.S. switch housing left side cover screws and cover (**Figure 15**).

    b. Disconnect the throttle valve cable (A, **Figure 16**) from the lever and remove it.

7. To disconnect the throttle cable from the T.O.R.S. housing, perform the following:

    a. Remove the T.O.R.S. switch housing right side cover screws and cover (**Figure 17**).

    b. Pull the cover up and loosen the throttle cable locknut (**Figure 18**).

    c. Disconnect the throttle cable (A, **Figure 19**) from the lever and remove the throttle cable.

NOTE
*The carburetor switch (B, **Figure 19**) is an integral part of the T.O.R.S. switch housing. Do not remove the switch. If the switch is faulty, the T.O.R.S. switch housing assembly must be replaced.*

Throttle Valve/T.O.R.S. Housing Reassembly

Refer to **Figure 9**.

1. To reconnect the throttle cable to the T.O.R.S. housing, perform the following:

    a. Lightly grease the cable pivot on the end of the lever.

    b. Insert the throttle cable into the front side of the T.O.R.S. housing. Then thread the throttle cable adjuster into the housing and tighten the locknut (**Figure 18**).

    c. Reconnect the throttle cable to the lever as shown in A, **Figure 19**.

    d. Make sure the rubber gasket (C, **Figure 19**) is installed into the outer groove in the T.O.R.S. housing. Then install the right side cover (**Figure 17**) and its mounting screws. Tighten the screws securely.

2. To reconnect the throttle valve cable (A, **Figure 16**), perform the following:

8

⑨

THROTTLE VALVE/T.O.R.S. HOUSING

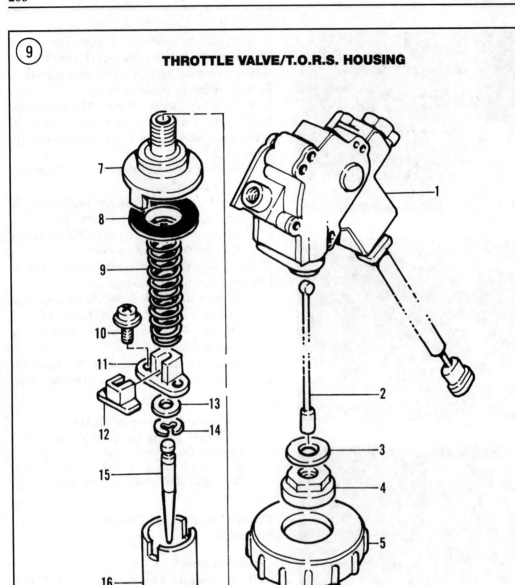

1. Throttle override switch housing (T.O.R.S.)
2. Throttle valve cable
3. Brass washer
4. Nut
5. Outer cap
6. O-ring
7. Inner cap
8. Gasket
9. Spring
10. Screw
11. Holder plate
12. Lock
13. Washer
14. E-clip
15. Jet needle
16. Throttle valve

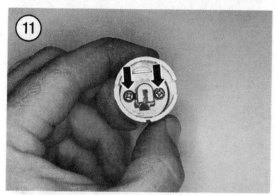

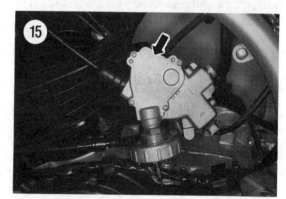

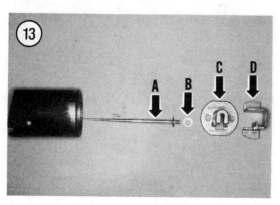

8

a. Lightly grease the cable pivot on the end of the lever.

b. Reconnect the throttle valve lever cable onto the lever as shown in A, **Figure 16**.

c. Make sure the rubber gasket (B, **Figure 16**) is installed into the outer groove in the T.O.R.S. housing. Then install the left side cover (**Figure 15**) and its mounting screws. Tighten the screws securely.

3. Replace the carburetor inner cover gasket (B, **Figure 14**) if damaged. To install the new gasket, or to reinstall a used gasket, apply Gasgacinch sealer to the top gasket surface and mount the gasket to the bottom of the inner cover as shown in B, **Figure 14**.

4. To install the jet needle assembly (**Figure 13**), perform the following:

a. Make sure the E-clip is installed in the correct jet needle clip groove.

b. Install a plastic washer on each side of the E-clip (**Figure 12**).

c. Install the jet needle (A, **Figure 13**) into the center throttle valve hole.

d. Install the holder plate (C, **Figure 13**) and secure it with its 2 mounting screws (**Figure 11**). Tighten the screws securely.

5. Slide the spring over the cable and compress it with your fingers (**Figure 20**).

6. Connect the throttle valve cable to the holder plate groove as shown in **Figure 21**.

7. Install the throttle cable lock so it engages the holder plate groove as shown in **Figure 22**. Then release the spring, making sure that it seats against the throttle cable lock.

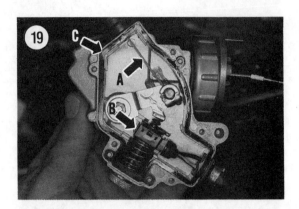

8. Install the throttle valve assembly (**Figure 5**) as described under *Carburetor Installation* in this chapter.

Disassembly

Refer to **Figure 23**.

1. Remove the carburetor as described in this chapter.

2. Disconnect the fuel and overflow hoses (**Figure 24**) from the carburetor.

3. Lightly seat the pilot air screw, counting the number of turns for reassembly reference, and then back the screw out and remove it from the carburetor (A, **Figure 25**).

4. Loosen and remove the choke valve assembly (**Figure 26**).

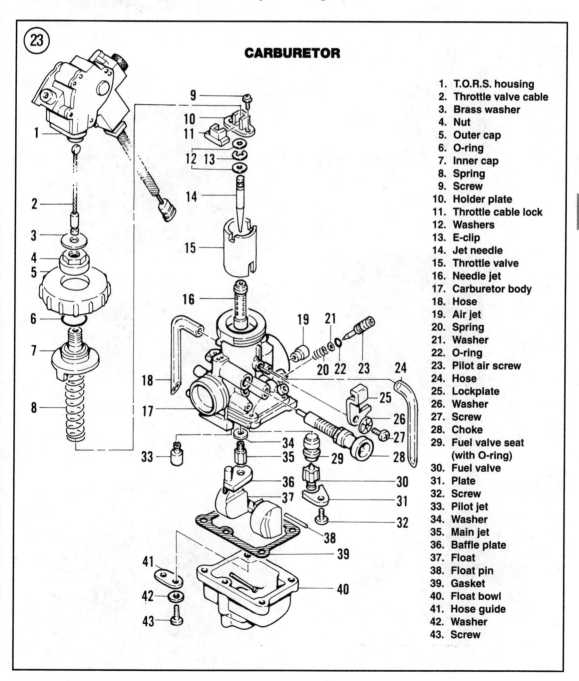

(23)

CARBURETOR

1. T.O.R.S. housing
2. Throttle valve cable
3. Brass washer
4. Nut
5. Outer cap
6. O-ring
7. Inner cap
8. Spring
9. Screw
10. Holder plate
11. Throttle cable lock
12. Washers
13. E-clip
14. Jet needle
15. Throttle valve
16. Needle jet
17. Carburetor body
18. Hose
19. Air jet
20. Spring
21. Washer
22. O-ring
23. Pilot air screw
24. Hose
25. Lockplate
26. Washer
27. Screw
28. Choke
29. Fuel valve seat
    (with O-ring)
30. Fuel valve
31. Plate
32. Screw
33. Pilot jet
34. Washer
35. Main jet
36. Baffle plate
37. Float
38. Float pin
39. Gasket
40. Float bowl
41. Hose guide
42. Washer
43. Screw

8

5. Remove the vent hose (B, **Figure 25**).

6. Remove the float bowl screws, hose guides (A, **Figure 27**) and float bowl (B, **Figure 27**).

7. Lift off and remove the baffle plate (**Figure 28**).

8. Loosen and remove the pilot jet (**Figure 29**).

9. Loosen and remove the main jet (**Figure 30**) and its flat washer (**Figure 31**).

10. Push the needle jet through the top of the carburetor and remove it (**Figure 32**).

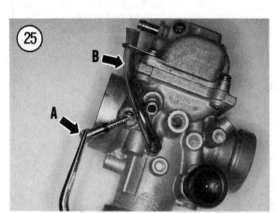

CAUTION
Do not use excessive force when removing the float pin in Step 11 or you may crack or break off one of the pedestal arms, requiring carburetor replacement.

11. Carefully tap the float pin from the pedestal arms with a pin punch (**Figure 33**) and hammer. See **Figure 34**.

12. Remove the float and fuel valve (**Figure 35**) assembly. Lift the fuel valve off the float arm.

13. Remove the screw and plate (**Figure 36**), then remove the fuel valve seat and O-ring assembly (**Figure 37**).

14. Clean and inspect all parts as described in this chapter.

8

Cleaning and Inspection

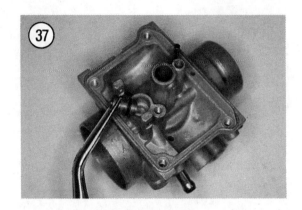

1. Initially clean all parts in a petroleum-based solvent, then clean in hot soapy water. Rinse parts with hot water and blow dry with compressed air.

> *CAUTION*
> ***Do not*** *clean the float or O-rings in carburetor cleaner or other solution that can damage them.*

> *CAUTION*
> ***Do not*** *use wire or drill bits to clean jets as minor gouges in the jet can alter flow rate and change the air/fuel mixture.*

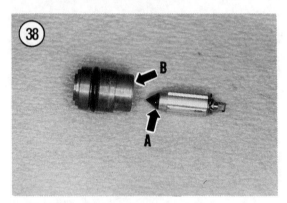

2. Clean all of the vent and overflow tubes with compressed air.

3. Replace the float bowl gasket if leaking or damaged.

4. Inspect the fuel valve assembly as follows:

   a. Check the end of the fuel valve (A, **Figure 38**) for steps, excessive wear or damage. Replace if damaged.

   b. Check the fuel valve seat (B, **Figure 38**) for steps, uneven wear or other damage.

   c. If excessive wear or damage is noted, replace the fuel valve and seat as a complete set.

> *NOTE*
> *A worn or damaged fuel valve and seat assembly will cause flooding, hard starting and a rich fuel mixture.*

5. Inspect the float (**Figure 39**) for deterioration or other visual damage. Check the float by submersing it in a container of water. If the float takes on water, replace it.

6. Inspect the pilot screw assembly (**Figure 40**) for excessive wear or damaged parts. A damaged screw tip will prevent smooth low-speed engine operation. Assemble the pilot screw by installing the O-ring, washer and spring.

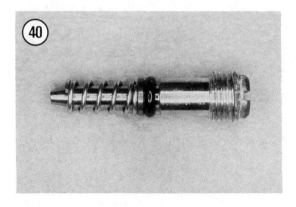

7. Inspect the choke valve assembly (**Figure 41**) for wear or damage. Check the valve tip for deep scratches or other wear patterns. Replace the choke valve if necessary.

8. Make sure all passages and openings in the carburetor body are clear. Clean with compressed air.

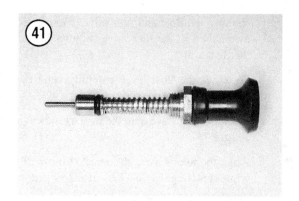

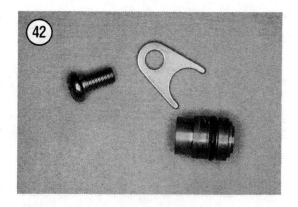

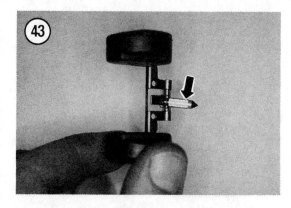

Assembly

Refer to **Figure 23** when assembling the carburetor body.

1. Install the fuel valve seat assembly (**Figure 42**) as follows:

   a. Lightly lubricate the fuel valve seat O-ring with 2-stroke engine oil.

   b. Install the fuel valve seat (**Figure 37**) into the carburetor body. Push it into place until it bottoms out.

   c. Secure the fuel valve seat with the plate and screw (**Figure 36**). Tighten the screw securely.

2. Install the fuel valve and float assembly as follows:

   a. Hook the fuel valve onto the float as shown in **Figure 43**.

   b. Align the fuel valve with its seat (**Figure 35**) while centering the float between the 2 pedestal arms.

   c. Tap the float pin (**Figure 34**) through both pedestal arms. See **Figure 44**.

   d. Measure the float height as described in this chapter.

3. Install the needle jet through the top of the carburetor (**Figure 32**). Align the slot in the side of the needle jet with the pin in the carburetor (**Figure 45**).

4. Install the main jet washer (**Figure 31**) and main jet (**Figure 30**). Tighten the main jet securely.

5. Install the pilot jet (**Figure 29**) and tighten securely.

6. Install the baffle plate as shown in **Figure 28**.

7. Install the float bowl gasket and float bowl (B, **Figure 27**). Install the 2 hose guides (A, **Figure 27**) and the float bowl mounting screws. Tighten the screws securely.

8. Install the choke valve (**Figure 26**) and secure it with its locknut. Operate the choke knob a few times to make sure it moves in and out without binding or roughness.

9. Install the pilot air screw (**Figure 25**) and lightly seat it. Then back the screw out the number of turns recorded during removal, or set it to the number of turns listed in **Table 1** or **Table 2**.

10. Install the vent hoses (B, **Figure 25**).

11. Reconnect the fuel and overflow hoses (**Figure 24**).

12. Install the carburetor as described in this chapter.

FLOAT ADJUSTMENT

The fuel valve and float maintain a constant fuel level in the carburetor float bowl. Because the float level affects the fuel mixture throughout the engine's operating range, this level must be maintained within factory specifications.

Float Height Adjustment

The carburetor must be removed and partially disassembled for this adjustment.

1. Remove the carburetor as described in this chapter.

2. Remove the float bowl screws, hose guides (A, **Figure 27**) and float bowl (B, **Figure 27**).

3. Hold the carburetor so the fuel valve just touches the float arm. At the same time, fully seat the fuel valve into the fuel valve seat. Then measure the float height distance from the carburetor body gasket surface to the top of the float using a ruler (**Figure 46**) or vernier caliper. See **Table 1** and **Table 2** for the correct float height specifications.

4. Adjust the float height as follows:

   a. Lift off and remove the baffle plate (**Figure 28**).

> *CAUTION*
> *Do not use excessive force when removing the float pin in Step 11, or you may crack or break off a pedestal arm, requiring carburetor replacement.*

   b. Carefully tap the float pin from the pedestal arms with a pin punch (**Figure 33**) and hammer. See **Figure 34**.

   c. Remove the float and fuel valve (**Figure 35**) assembly. Lift the fuel valve (**Figure 43**) off the float arm.

   d. To adjust the float level, carefully bend the float arm with a screwdriver (**Figure 47**).

   e. Hook the fuel valve onto the float as shown in **Figure 43**.

   f. Align the fuel valve with its seat (**Figure 35**) while centering the float between the 2 pedestal arms.

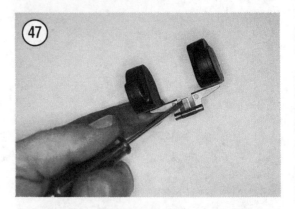

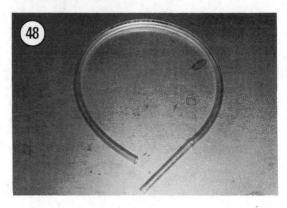

g. Tap the float pin (**Figure 34**) through both pedestal arms. See **Figure 44**.

h. Recheck the float height measurement. Readjust the float if necessary.

i. Install the baffle plate as shown in **Figure 28**.

5. Install the float bowl gasket and float bowl (B, **Figure 27**). Install the 2 hose guides (A, **Figure 27**) and the float bowl mounting screws. Tighten the screws securely.

6. Install the carburetor as described in this chapter.

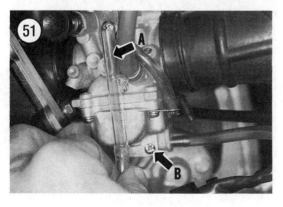

Fuel Level Adjustment

This procedure checks the actual fuel level while the carburetor is mounted on the engine. The Yamaha fuel level gauge (part No. YM-01312-A [**Figure 48**]) or equivalent is required for this procedure.

1. Perform the *Float Height Adjustment* procedure in this section. Reinstall the carburetor onto the vehicle, then continue with Step 2.

2. Park the vehicle on a level surface and set the parking brake.

WARNING
Some fuel may spill from the carburetor when performing this procedure. Because gasoline is an extremely flammable and explosive petroleum, perform this procedure away from all open flames (including pilot lights) and sparks. Do not smoke or allow someone who is smoking in the work area. Always work in a well-ventilated area. Wipe up any spills immediately.

3. Disconnect the overflow hose (**Figure 49**) from the float bowl nozzle and connect the fuel level gauge (**Figure 50**) in its place.

WARNING
Do not run the engine with the vehicle in a closed area as the exhaust gases are poisonous. Make sure there is plenty of ventilation.

4. Hold the fuel level gauge (A, **Figure 51**) vertically next to the carburetor, then loosen the drain screw (B, **Figure 51**).

5. Have an assistant start the engine while you hold the fuel level gauge vertically next to the center of the carburetor housing and float bowl gasket surfaces. Measure the fuel level, starting at the gasket surfaces. The correct fuel level is 0.5-1.5 mm (0.02-0.06 in.) above the carburetor housing gasket surface.

a. If the fuel level is incorrect, remove and disassemble the carburetor and inspect the fuel valve and seat for excessive wear or damage.

b. If the fuel valve and seat are good, check the float height adjustment as described in this chapter.

c. If the fuel level is correct, continue with Step 6.

6. Remove the fuel level gauge and reconnect the overflow hose (**Figure 49**). Secure the hose with its clamp.

7. Wipe up any spilled gasoline.

CARBURETOR REJETTING

Changes in altitude, temperature and humidity can noticeably affect engine performance. This also includes changes that affects the engine's ability to breathe (jetting changes, different exhaust pipes or air filters). To obtain maximum performance from your Yamaha, jetting changes may be necessary. However, before you change the jetting, make sure the engine is in good running condition. For example, if your vehicle is now running poorly under the same weather, altitude and conditions where it once

ran properly, it is unlikely the carburetor jetting is at fault. Attempting to tune the engine by rejetting the carburetor would only complicate matters.

If your vehicle shows evidence of one of the following conditions, rejetting may be necessary:

a. Poor acceleration (too rich).
b. Excessive exhaust smoke (too rich).
c. Fouling spark plugs (too rich).
d. Engine misfires at low-speeds (too rich).
e. Erratic acceleration (too lean).
f. Ping or rattle (too lean).

NOTE
Using old gasoline or gasoline with an insufficient octane rating can also cause engine pinging.

g. Running hot (too lean).

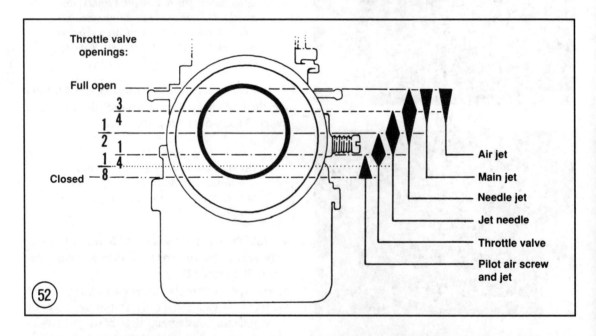

Before checking the carburetor for one of the previously listed operating conditions, consider the following tuning and adjustment variables:

   a. *Carburetor float level*—An incorrect float level will cause the engine to run rich or lean.

   b. *Air filter element*—A dirty air filter element will cause the engine to run rich. Attempting to jet the engine with a dirty air filter element will only complicate engine tuning.

   c. *Ignition timing*—incorrect ignition will degrade engine performance.

   d. *Exhaust flow*—A plugged exhaust pipe silencer, or a heavily carbonized engine top end and exhaust valve system will reduce engine performance.

If the previously mentioned service items are good, the carburetor may require rejetting if any of the following conditions hold true:

   a. A nonstandard air filter element is being used.

   b. A nonstandard exhaust system is being used.

   c. The engine was modified (piston, porting or compression ratio).

   d. The vehicle is operating in a much higher or lower altitude, or in hotter or colder, or wetter or drier climate than in the past.

   e. The vehicle is operating at considerably higher speeds than before and changing to a colder spark plug does not solve the problem.

   f. A previous owner changed the jetting or the jet needle position. See **Table 1** and **Table 2** for the stock carburetor jetting and jet needle clip specifications.

Carburetor Variables

The following carburetor parts may be changed when rejetting the carburetor. **Figure 52** shows the jetting circuits and how they relate to the different throttle valve opening positions.

Pilot jet

The pilot jet (A, **Figure 53**) and pilot air screw (**Figure 54**) setting controls the fuel mixture from 0 to about 1/8 throttle. Note the following:

   a. As the pilot jet numbers increase, the fuel mixture gets richer.

   b. Turning the pilot air screw clockwise enrichens the mixture.

   c. Turning the pilot air screw counterclockwise leans the mixture.

Throttle valve

The throttle valve cutaway (**Figure 55**) affects airflow at small throttle openings. The smaller the cutaway, the richer the fuel mixture. The larger the cutaway, the leaner the fuel mixture. Mikuni throttle valves are identified by their cutaway sizes, where a larger number results in a leaner mixture. The cutaway numbers are in millimeters and are listed from 0.5 to 3.5 mm (0.5 is rich and 3.5 is lean).

Jet needle

The jet needle controls the mixture at medium speeds, from approximately 1/8 to 3/4 throttle. The top of the needle has 5 evenly spaced clip grooves (**Figure 56**). The bottom half of the needle is tapered

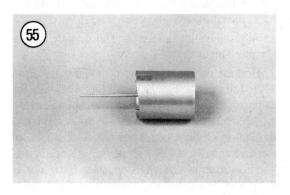

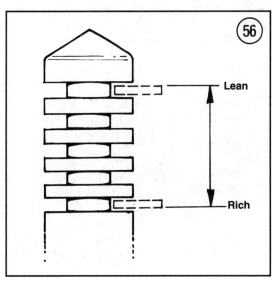

(**Figure 57**); this portion extends into the needle jet. While the jet needle is fixed in position by the clip, fuel cannot flow through the space between the needle jet and jet needle until the throttle valve is raised to approximately 1/8 open. As the throttle valve is opened, the jet needle's tapered portion moves out of the needle jet. The grooves permit adjustment of the mixture ratio. If the clip is raised (thus dropping the needle deeper into the jet), the mixture will be leaner; lowering the clip (raising the needle) will result in a richer mixture.

Needle jet

The needle jet (**Figure 58**) works in conjunction with the jet needle.

On Mikuni carburetors, the letter and number stamped on the side of the needle jet indicates its inside diameter. The mixture gets richer in large steps as the letter size increases (front N through R), and in small steps within the letter range as the number increases (from 0 through 9). Some needle jets have a tab extending 2 to 8 mm into the throttle bore, indicated by /2 through /8 following the letter and number mark. This is called the primary choke, and it causes the mixture to be leaner at low-speeds and richer at high-speeds.

Main jet

The main jet (B, **Figure 53**) controls the mixture from 3/4 to full throttle, and has some effect at lesser throttle openings. Each main jet is stamped with a number. Larger numbers provide a richer mixture and smaller numbers a leaner mixture.

Rejetting

> *CAUTION*
> *A too-lean mixture caused by running a too small main jet can cause serious engine damage in a matter of seconds. When determining proper jetting, always start rich and progress toward a leaner mixture, one step at a time. The engine must be at full operating temperature when checking jetting. Attempting to jet an engine that is not up to temperature can result in an excessively lean mixture when the*

engine reaches full operating temperature.

When jetting the carburetor, perform the procedures in Steps 1-3 to ensure accurate results. Note the following before changing the carburetor jetting:

   a. Referring to **Figure 52**, note the different jetting circuits and how they overlap with each other in relation to the different throttle positions. Then determine the throttle position at which the adjustment should be made. Too often, the main jet is changed when actually the jet needle should be adjusted.

   b. When checking the jetting, run the vehicle on a track or private road where you can safely run at top speed. Keep accurate records as to weather, altitude and track conditions.

   c. Check the jetting in the following order: Pilot air screw, main jet and jet needle.

   d. Refer to the carburetor jetting chart in **Table 3** when jetting the carburetor for cold weather operation.

1. Adjust the pilot air screw and idle as described in Chapter Three.

2. Because the main jet controls the mixture from 3/4 to full throttle, run the vehicle at full throttle for a long distance. Stop the engine with the engine stop switch while the vehicle is running under full throttle. Pull in on the clutch lever and coast to a stop. Remove and examine the spark plug after each test. The insulator must be a light tan color. If the insulator is soot black, the mixture is too rich; install a smaller main jet as described in this chapter. If the insulator is white, or blistered, the mixture is too lean; install a larger main jet.

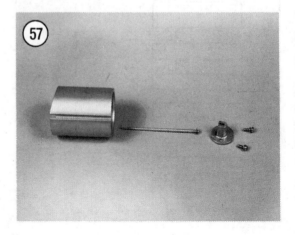

3. Repeat the jetting check in Step 2 at different throttle positions. You may find that the full open throttle position is correct but that the 1/4 to 3/4 operating range is too rich or too lean. Refer to *Carburetor Variables* in this chapter. If changing the jet needle clip position is necessary, refer to *Jet Needle Adjustment* in this chapter.

Main Jet Replacement

> *WARNING*
> *If you are taking spark plug readings, the engine will be HOT! Use caution and have a fire extinguisher and an assistant standing by when performing this procedure.*

> *WARNING*
> *Some fuel will spill from the carburetor when performing this procedure. Because gasoline is extremely flammable perform this procedure away from all open flames and sparks. Do not smoke or allow someone who is smoking in the work area. Always work in a well-ventilated area. Wipe up any spills immediately.*

1. Turn the engine off.
2. Turn the fuel shutoff valve to the OFF position.
3. Loosen the drain screw (B, **Figure 51**) on the float bowl and drain all fuel from the bowl.
4. Remove the float bowl, then remove the main jet (B, **Figure 53**) and install the new jet. Remember, change only one jet size at a time. Reinstall the float bowl.

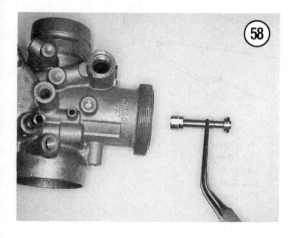

Jet Needle Adjustment

1. Remove the throttle valve and jet needle as described in this chapter.
2. Note the position of the clip. Raising the needle (lowering the clip) will enrich the mixture during mid-throttle opening, while lowering it (raising the clip) will lean the mixture. Refer to **Figure 56**.
3. See **Table 1** or **Table 2** for the standard jet needle clip position.
4. Reverse these steps to install the jet needle.

FUEL TANK

Refer to **Figure 59** when servicing the fuel tank. **Table 4** lists fuel tank capacity.

Removal/Installation

> *WARNING*
> *Some fuel may spill from the carburetor when performing this procedure. Because gasoline is extremely flammable perform this procedure away from all open flames (including pilot lights) and sparks. Do not smoke or allow someone who is smoking in the work area. Always work in a well-ventilated area. Wipe up any spills immediately.*

1. Park the vehicle on level ground and set the parking brake.
2. Remove the seat (Chapter Fourteen).
3. Turn the fuel valve (**Figure 60**) off and disconnect the fuel line from the fuel tank.
4. Pull the fuel fill cap vent tube (**Figure 61**) free from the steering head area.
5. Remove the front cover and fuel tank cover as described in Chapter Fourteen.
6. Remove the fuel tank mounting bolts and remove the fuel tank.
7. Check for loose, missing or damaged fuel tank brackets and rubber dampers. Tighten or replace parts as required.
8. Reverse these steps to install the fuel tank.
9. Secure the fuel hose to the fuel tank with its hose clamp.
10. After reconnecting the hose and turning the fuel valve on, check the hose for leaks.

8

FUEL SHUTOFF VALVE

Refer to **Figure 59** when servicing the fuel shutoff valve.

Removal/Installation

WARNING
Some fuel may spill from the carburetor when performing this procedure. Because gasoline is extremely flammable perform this procedure away from all open flames (including pilot lights) and sparks. Do not smoke or allow someone who is smoking in the work area. Always work in a well-ventilated area. Wipe up any spills immediately.

1. Remove the fuel tank as described in this chapter.

2. Drain the fuel into a gasoline can.

3. Remove the screws and washers and remove the fuel shutoff valve.

4. Remove the handle screw and disassemble the valve. Clean all parts in solvent with a medium soft toothbrush, then dry. Check the small O-ring within the valve and the O-ring gasket; replace if they are

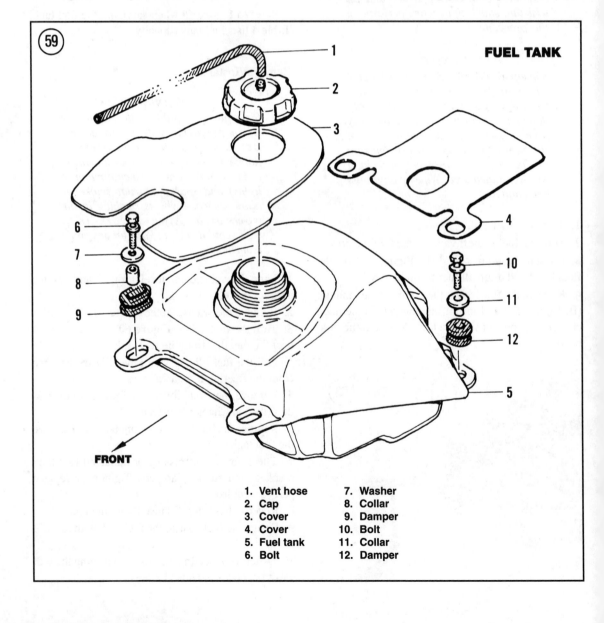

FUEL TANK

FRONT

1. Vent hose	7. Washer
2. Cap	8. Collar
3. Cover	9. Damper
4. Cover	10. Bolt
5. Fuel tank	11. Collar
6. Bolt	12. Damper

starting to deteriorate or get hard. Inspect the wave spring and replace it if weak or damaged.

5. Reassemble the valve and install it on the tank. Do not forget to install the O-ring between the valve and tank.

AIR BOX

The air box is an integral part of the rear fender assembly. To service the intake hose and fittings, refer to **Figure 62**.

THROTTLE CABLE REPLACEMENT

The throttle cable can be replaced without having to disassemble the throttle lever assembly.

1. Park the vehicle on level ground and set the parking brake.
2. Remove the fuel tank as described in this chapter.

3. Disconnect the throttle cable (**Figure 63**) from the throttle valve/T.O.R.S. housing as described under *Throttle Valve/T.O.R.S. Housing Disassembly* in this chapter.
4. Disconnect the throttle cable from the throttle lever as follows:

   a. Remove the throttle cover screws and remove the cover (A, **Figure 64**).
   b. Loosen the throttle cable adjuster locknut (B, **Figure 64**), then turn the adjuster to provide as much cable slack as possible.
   c. Disconnect the throttle cable (**Figure 65**) from the throttle lever arm.

5. Disconnect the throttle cable from any clips holding the cable to the frame.
6. Make a drawing of the cable routing path through the frame, then remove the cable.
7. Lubricate the new throttle cable as described in Chapter Three.
8. Reverse Steps 2-6 to install the new cable, plus the following.
9. Connect the throttle cable to the throttle lever arm first, then connect it to the throttle valve/T.O.R.S. Housing. Installing the throttle cable in this order will allow the cable to be connected to the throttle lever arm without having to remove the throttle lever arm.
10. Apply a light dab of grease onto the upper throttle cable end, then install it to the throttle lever arm (**Figure 65**).
11. Reconnect the lower throttle cable end as described under *Throttle Valve/T.O.R.S. Housing Reassembly* in this chapter.
12. Operate the throttle lever to make sure the cable is installed and routed properly. If operation is rough or if there is any binding, recheck the throttle cable installation and routing path.
13. Adjust the throttle cable as described under *Throttle Cable Adjustment* in Chapter Three.

THROTTLE LEVER ASSEMBLY

Removal

1. Remove the throttle cover screws and remove the cover (A, **Figure 64**).
2. Loosen the throttle cable adjuster (B, **Figure 64**).
3. Hold the throttle lever and remove the nut (A, **Figure 66**) and flat washer (B).

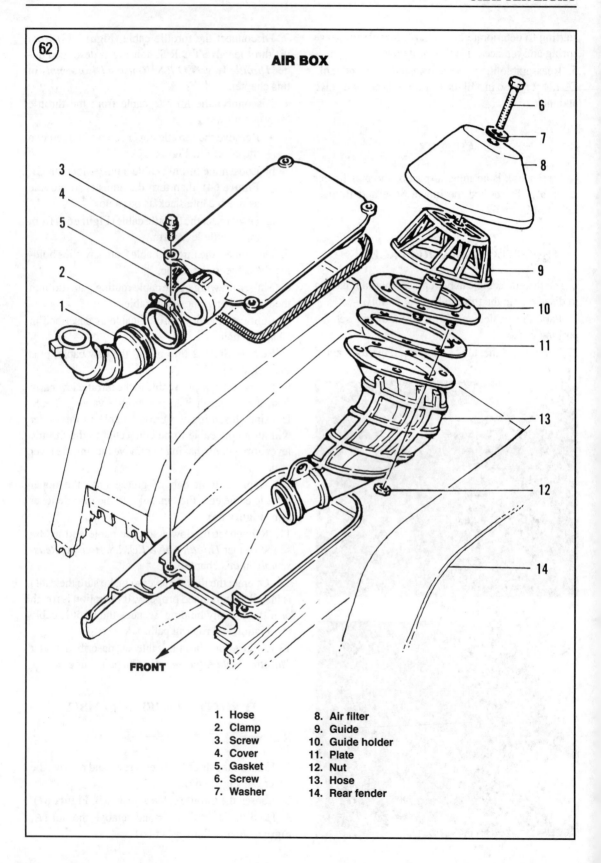

62

AIR BOX

FRONT

1. Hose
2. Clamp
3. Screw
4. Cover
5. Gasket
6. Screw
7. Washer
8. Air filter
9. Guide
10. Guide holder
11. Plate
12. Nut
13. Hose
14. Rear fender

4. Disconnect the upper throttle arm (**Figure 67**) from the throttle cable and remove it from the throttle housing.

5. Remove the collar (**Figure 68**).

6. Disconnect the lower throttle arm (A, **Figure 69**) from the return spring and remove it from the throttle housing.

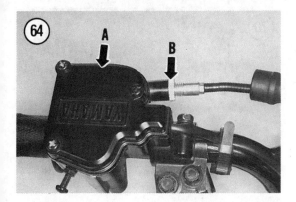

8

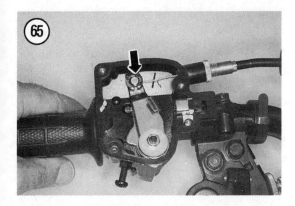

7. Remove the return spring (**Figure 70**).

8. Remove the throttle lever and flat washer (**Figure 71**).

Inspection

1. Clean the inside of the throttle housing if it is contaminated with grease or dirt.

2. Clean and dry all parts (**Figure 72**).

3. Check the condition of the upper (A, **Figure 72**) and lower (B) throttle arms. The round hole in the upper throttle arm and the square hole in the lower throttle arm must not be worn or damaged. Replace if necessary.

4. Replace the return spring (C, **Figure 72**) if it is bent, stretched out of shape, or if its small hook end is cracked or broken off.

5. Replace the nut, washers and collar if worn or damaged.

6. Check the throttle lever shaft, arm and threads (D, **Figure 72**) for excessive wear, cracks or other damage. Replace if necessary.

7. Inspect the throttle lever bushing (**Figure 73**) for excessive wear or damage. If bushing replacement is required, the throttle lever housing will have to be replaced as the bushing is not available separately.

8. Inspect the seal (installed at the bottom of the throttle housing) for excessive wear or damage. Perform the following to replace the seal:

   a. Pry the seal out of the throttle housing with a small screwdriver.

   b. Inspect its mounting bore in the throttle housing for cracks or damage.

   c. Pack the lips of the new seal with grease, then push it into its mounting bore with its closed side facing out.

Installation

1. Lightly lubricate the throttle lever shaft and its washer with a lithium soap base grease.

2. Install the washer onto the throttle lever shaft (**Figure 71**), then install the throttle lever through the bottom of the throttle housing.

3. Install the return spring (**Figure 70**) around the bushing boss inside the throttle housing. The spring's hooked end must be at the top and facing toward the inside of the housing as shown in **Figure 70**.

4. Turn the throttle lever so the thumb part of the lever is in its approximate idle speed position. Then install the lower throttle arm (A, **Figure 69**) by inserting its square hole onto the throttle lever shoulder. At the same time hook the return spring onto the lower throttle arm as shown in B, **Figure 69**. Push and release the throttle lever to make sure the return spring is installed correctly.

5. Install the collar—shoulder side facing up (**Figure 68**)—over the throttle lever shaft and rest it against the lower throttle arm.

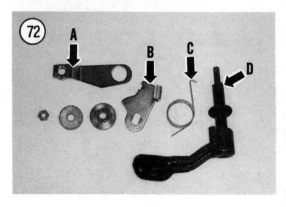

6. Lightly lubricate the throttle cable barrel end with a lithium soap base grease, then connect the cable onto the end of the upper throttle lever (**Figure 67**).

7. Install the upper throttle lever over the throttle lever shaft and secure it with the large flat washer (B, **Figure 66**) and nut (A). Tighten the nut securely.

8. Operate the throttle lever to make sure it is installed correctly. If its operation is rough or if there is any binding, recheck its installation.

9. Install the throttle cover (A, **Figure 64**) and secure it with its mounting screws.

10. Adjust the throttle cable as described under *Throttle Cable Adjustment* in Chapter Three.

8

Table 1 CARBURETOR SPECIFICATIONS (1988-1989)

Type	Mikuni VM26SS
Identification number	2XJ 00
Main jet	220
Pilot jet	32.5
Main air jet	0.7
Jet needle/clip position	5J22/2
Needle jet	P-6
Throttle valve cutaway	2.0
Pilot outlet	0.6
Bypass 1	0.8 × 3.75
Pilot air screw initial setting	1 1/2 turns out
Starter jet	45
Float height	20.0-21.5 mm (0.79-0.85 in.)
Fuel level	0.5-1.5 mm (0.02-0.06 in.)

Table 2 CARBURETOR SPECIFICATIONS (1990-2002)

Type	Mikuni VM26SS
Identification number	2XJ 01
Main jet	230
Pilot jet	32.5
Main air jet	0.7
Jet needle/clip position	5J22/2
Needle jet	P-6
Throttle valve cutaway	2.0
Pilot outlet	0.6
Bypass 1	0.8 × 3.75
Pilot air screw initial setting	1 1/2 turns out
Float height	20.0-21.5 mm (0.79-0.85 in.)
Fuel level	0.5-1.5 mm (0.02-0.06 in.)

Table 3 CARBURETOR JETTING CHART

Temperature	Main jet	Jet Needle Clip Position
Above freezing 32° F (0° C)	220	2nd groove
5° to 41° F (-15° to 5° C)	230	2nd groove
14° to -22° F (-10° to -30° C)	230	3rd groove

Table 4 FUEL TANK CAPACITY

	U.S. gal.	Liters	Imp. gal.
Full	2.38	9.0	1.98
Reserve	0.53	2.0	0.44

CHAPTER NINE

ELECTRICAL SYSTEM

This chapter describes service procedures for the ignition and lighting systems.

General electrical system specifications are found in **Table 1**. **Tables 1-5** are at the end of this chapter.

COMPONENT TESTING

An ohmmeter can be used to test the ignition coil, stator plate coils, switches and wiring.

Resistance Testing

1. Make sure the test leads are connected properly. **Table 2** and **Table 3** lists the wire connections for each test.

2. Make all ohmmeter readings when the engine is cold (ambient temperature of 68° F [20° C]). Readings taken on a hot engine will show increased resistance and may lead you to replace good parts without solving the basic problem.

NOTE
With the exception of certain semiconductors, the resistance of a conductor increases as its temperature increases. In general, the resistance of a conductor increases 10 ohms per each degree of temperature increase. The opposite is true if the temperature drops. To ensure accurate testing, Yamaha performs their tests at a controlled temperature of 68° F (20° C) and base their specifications on tests performed at this temperature.

3. When using an analog ohmmeter and switching between ohmmeter scales, always cross the test leads and zero the needle to ensure a correct reading.

CAPACITOR DISCHARGE IGNITION

All models are equipped with a capacitor discharge ignition (CDI) system. The system consists of the magneto assembly, CDI unit, ignition coil, main ignition switch, engine stop switch, T.O.R.S.

(throttle overide switch) control unit and carburetor switch (**Figure 1**). The magneto assembly consists of the flywheel and stator plate (**Figure 2**). The flywheel is equipped with magnets and is mounted on the crankshaft. The stator plate is mounted onto the engine. The flywheel and magnets revolve around the stator assembly. This solid state system, uses no contact breaker points or other moving parts.

Alternating current from the magneto is rectified and used to charge the capacitor. As the piston approaches the firing position, a pulse from the pulser coil is rectified, shaped, and then used to trigger the silicone controlled rectifier. This in turn allows the

capacitor to discharge quickly into the primary side of the high-voltage ignition coil where it is increased, or stepped up, to a high enough voltage to jump the gap between the spark plug electrodes.

CDI Cautions

Certain measures must be taken to protect the CDI unit when servicing and troubleshooting the ignition system.
1. Keep all connections between the various units clean and tight. Be sure that the wiring connectors are pushed together firmly (**Figure 3**).

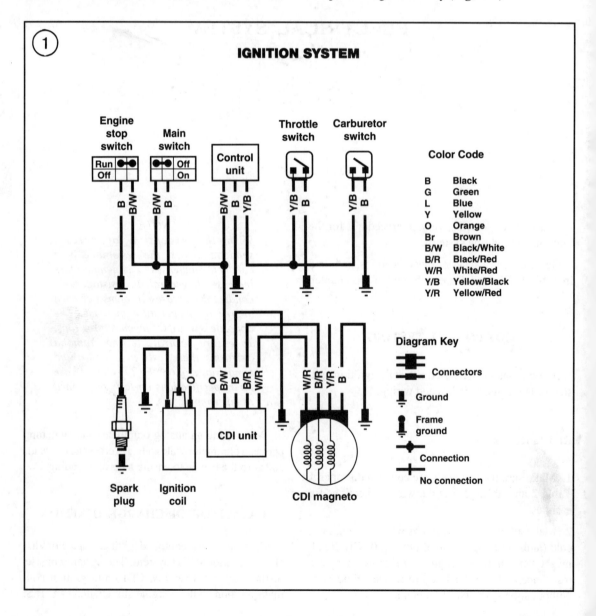

MAGNETO ASSEMBLY

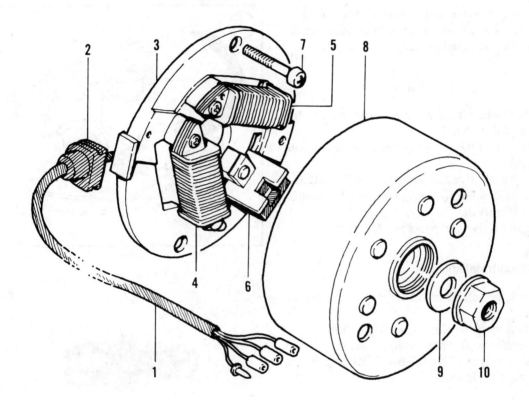

1. Wire harness
2. Grommet
3. Stator plate
4. Lighting coil
5. Charge coil
6. Pulser (pickup) coil
7. Screw
8. Flywheel (rotor)
9. Washer
10. Flywheel nut

2. Never disconnect any of the electrical connections while the engine is running.

3. When cranking the engine with the spark plug removed, make sure the spark plug is installed in its plug cap and grounded against the cylinder head (**Figure 4**), or that the ignition switch is turned off. If not, excessive resistance may damage the CDI unit.

4. The CDI unit is mounted on a rubber vibration isolator or on rubber dampers. Make sure that the CDI unit is mounted correctly.

FLYWHEEL

The flywheel (**Figure 2**) is mounted on the end of the crankshaft (left side).

Use one of the following pullers to remove the flywheel:

    a. Yamaha flywheel puller part No. YU-01235.
    b. Motion Pro flywheel puller part No. 08-026 (**Figure 5**).
    c. K&N flywheel puller part No. 82-0150.

Removal/Installation

1. Park the vehicle on a level surface and set the parking brake.

2. Remove the flywheel cover (**Figure 6**).

3. Secure the flywheel with a holding tool and loosen the flywheel nut (**Figure 7**). Remove the nut and washer (**Figure 8**).

> *CAUTION*
> *Flywheel removal requires a puller that threads into the face of the flywheel. Do not pry or hammer on the flywheel or try to remove it with a different type of*

puller. Damage will result, and you may destroy the flywheel's magnetism or damage the coils mounted on the stator plate.

4. Apply a dab of grease onto the flywheel puller's pressure bolt where it will contact the crankshaft.

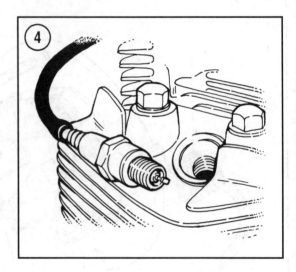

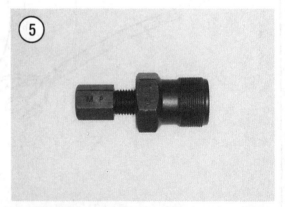

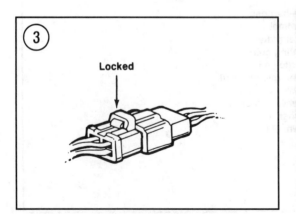

Then thread the flywheel puller (**Figure 9**) into the flywheel. Screw the flywheel puller into the flywheel threads until its stops, then back out 1/2 turn.

CAUTION
Do not apply excessive force to the puller when removing the flywheel. Doing so can cause the puller to strip the threads in the flywheel or damage the end of the crankshaft. If necessary, take the engine to a dealership for flywheel removal.

5. Hold the flywheel puller and turn the flywheel pressure bolt (**Figure 10**) clockwise. When tightening the pressure bolt against the crankshaft, check the puller body to make sure that it is not pulling out of the flywheel. Continue until the flywheel pops free.

6. Remove the flywheel and puller. Do not lose the Woodruff key (**Figure 11**) on the crankshaft.

CAUTION
Inspect the inside of the flywheel (Figure 12) for small bolts, washers or other metal material that may have been

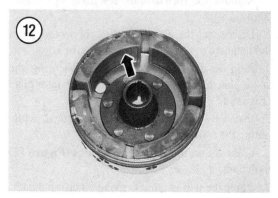

9

picked up by the magnets. These small metal bits can cause damage to the stator plate coils.

7. Install the flywheel by reversing these removal steps, while noting the following.

8. Make sure the Woodruff key (**Figure 11**) is in place on the crankshaft, then align the keyway in the flywheel with the Woodruff key when installing the flywheel.

9. Hold the flywheel with the holding tool, then tighten the flywheel nut (**Figure 11**) to the torque specification in **Table 4**.

10. Tighten the flywheel cover (**Figure 6**) mounting screws to the torque specification in **Table 4**.

Flywheel Inspection

The flywheel is permanently magnetized and cannot be tested except by replacement with a flywheel known to be good. A flywheel can lose magnetism from a sharp blow. If defective, the flywheel must be replaced; it cannot be remagnetized.

1. Check the flywheel (**Figure 13**) carefully for cracks or breaks.

2. Check the flywheel for loose or missing rivets (**Figure 13**).

3. Check the tapered bore of the flywheel and the crankshaft taper for cracks or other abnormal conditions.

Stator Assembly Removal/Installation

Refer to **Figure 2**.

1. Remove the flywheel as described in this chapter.

2. Remove the fuel tank as described in Chapter Eight.

3. Disconnect the electrical wire connectors from the magneto to the CDI unit. See **Figure 1**.

4. Remove the screws (**Figure 14**) securing the stator plate to the engine and remove the stator plate (**Figure 15**).

5. Install by reversing these removal steps, while noting the following.

6. Clean the wiring harness connectors (**Figure 15**) with contact cleaner.

7. Route the wiring harness along its original path.

8. Insert the stator plate wiring harness grommet into the crankcase. If the grommet is damaged, apply RTV sealer onto the grommet before installing it.

Stator Coil Testing

The stator coils (**Figure 16**, typical) can be inspected while mounted on the engine. With the engine off, disconnect the stator plate electrical

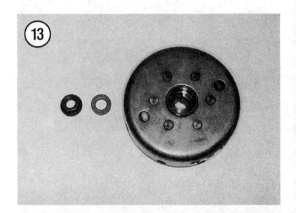

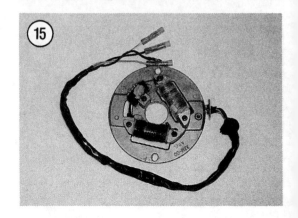

connectors and measure the resistance between the pairs of wire leads listed in **Table 2** or **Table 3**. If the resistance is zero (short circuit) or infinite (open circuit), check the wiring to the coils and the connector pins. If the wiring and its connectors are in good condition, the coil is damaged and must be replaced.

On all models, the stator plate coils can be replaced separately. Identify the stator coils as follows:

   a. Pickup coil (A, **Figure 16**).

   b. Lighting coil (B, **Figure 16**).

   c. Charge coil (C, **Figure 16**).

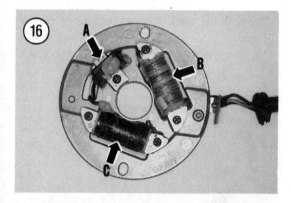

CDI UNIT

The CDI unit (A, **Figure 17**) is mounted underneath the front fender.

Removal/Installation

1. Park the vehicle on a level surface and set the parking brake.

2. Disconnect the CDI electrical connectors.

3. Remove the screw securing the CDI unit to the frame and remove the CDI unit (A, **Figure 17**).

4. Install by reversing these steps.

5. Clean the connectors with electrical contact cleaner.

Testing

Yamaha does not list test procedures or provide test equipment for testing the CDI unit (A, **Figure 17**). Accepted practice is to troubleshoot the ignition system, testing all components, switches, coils and wiring. If a problem in the ignition system is not found, then consider the CDI unit faulty. To troubleshoot the ignition system, refer to Chapter Two.

IGNITION COIL

The ignition coil (**Figure 18**) is mounted on the upper frame rail, underneath the fuel tank.

Removal/Installation

1. Park the vehicle on a level surface and set the parking brake.

2. Remove the fuel tank as described in Chapter Eight.

3. Disconnect the spark plug lead.

4. Disconnect the primary wires from the ignition coil.

5. Remove the screws securing the ignition coil (**Figure 18**) to the frame and remove it.

6. Install by reversing these removal steps. Make sure all electrical connectors are tight and free of corrosion. Make sure the ground wire connection point on the frame is free of rust and corrosion.

9

Testing

When testing the ignition coil in this section, compare the actual resistance readings to the specifications in **Table 2**.

1. Remove the ignition coil as described in this chapter.

2. Inspect the ignition coil body for cracks, carbon tracks or other visible signs of damage. Check the primary and secondary wires for cracks or other damage.

3. Read the information listed under *Component Testing* in this chapter before testing the ignition coil.

4. Measure the coil primary resistance using an ohmmeter set at R × 1 (**Figure 19**). Measure the resistance between the ignition coil (orange) lead and the ground terminal on the ignition coil (**Figure 19**).

5. Measure the secondary resistance as follows:

   a. Remove the spark plug cap (**Figure 20**) from the secondary wire.

   b. Switch the ohmmeter to its R × 1,000 scale.

   c. Measure the resistance between the secondary lead (without spark plug cap) and the ignition coil orange lead (**Figure 19**).

6. Measure the spark plug cap resistance as follows:

   a. Switch the ohmmeter to its R × 1,000 scale.

   b. Measure the resistance as shown in **Figure 21**.

c. Replace the spark plug cap if the resistance reading is out of specification.

> *NOTE*
> *The correct resistance in both the primary and secondary windings is not a guarantee that the ignition coil is working properly; only an operational spark test can tell if the coil is capable of producing an adequate spark from the input voltage. To confirm the coil's condition, take it to your dealership and have a spark test performed.*

7. Reinstall the spark plug cap onto the secondary coil wire.

8. Install the ignition coil as described in this chapter.

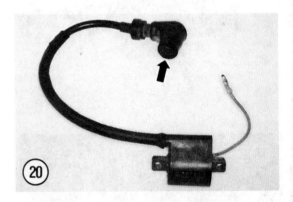

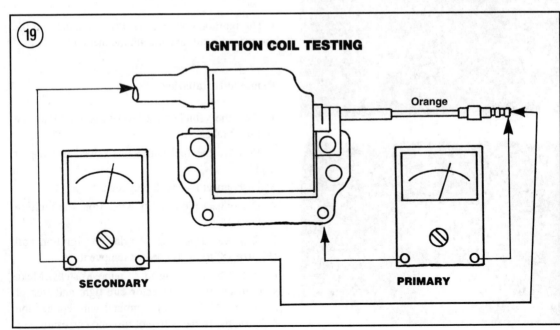

(19)

IGNTION COIL TESTING

Orange

SECONDARY

PRIMARY

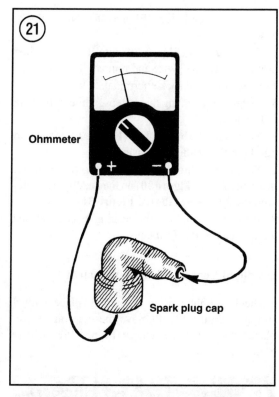

Ohmmeter

Spark plug cap

THROTTLE OVERRIDE SYSTEM
(T.O.R.S.)

On all models a throttle override system is incorporated into the ignition system (**Figure 22**). The T.O.R.S. system consists of a throttle switch, T.O.R.S. control unit and carburetor switch.

The T.O.R.S. system is a safety override system. If the carburetor sticks open (throttle valve will not close) during engine operation, removing your thumb from the throttle lever will cause the T.O.R.S. system to shut off the ignition system.

T.O.R.S. Troubleshooting

Refer to *Ignition System in Chapter Two*.

T.O.R.S. Control Unit
Removal/Installation

The T.O.R.S. control unit is mounted on the upper frame rail (B, **Figure 17**).

9

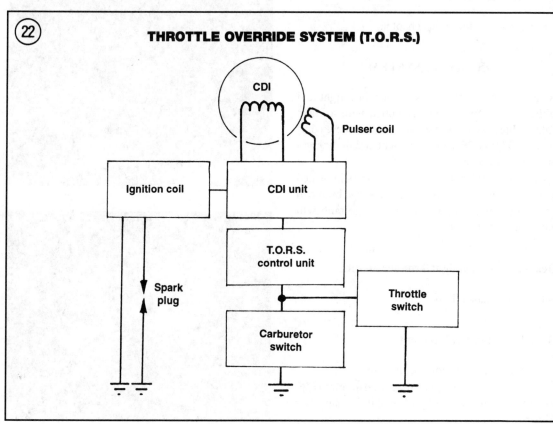

THROTTLE OVERRIDE SYSTEM (T.O.R.S.)

CDI

Pulser coil

Ignition coil

CDI unit

Spark plug

T.O.R.S. control unit

Throttle switch

Carburetor switch

1. Remove the front fender as described in Chapter Fourteen.

2. Disconnect the electrical connector from the T.O.R.S. control unit.

3. Remove the screw securing the T.O.R.S. control unit to the frame and remove the T.O.R.S. control unit (B, **Figure 17**).

4. Install by reversing these removal steps.

T.O.R.S. Carburetor Switch
Removal/Installation

The T.O.R.S. carburetor switch is mounted inside the T.O.R.S. switch housing that is mounted on top of the carburetor (**Figure 23**). The carburetor switch (**Figure 24**) is an integral part of the switch housing. To access or replace the switch housing, refer to the *Throttle Valve/T.O.R.S. Housing* disassembly and reassembly procedures in Chapter Eight. To test the carburetor switch, refer to *Switches* in this chapter.

T.O.R.S. Throttle Switch
Removal/Installation

Refer to *Switches* in this chapter.

LIGHTING SYSTEM

The lighting system consists of a headlight and taillight. 2002 models are equipped with a brake light. **Table 3** lists replacement bulbs for these components. **Figure 25** shows a typical circuit diagram of the lighting system.

Always use the correct wattage bulb as indicated in this section. The use of a larger wattage bulb will give a dim light and a smaller wattage bulb will burn out prematurely.

Headlight and Taillight Troubleshooting

Refer to Chapter Two.

Headlight Bulb Replacement

Refer to **Figure 26** for this procedure.

1. Remove the 2 headlight mounting screws (**Figure 27**) and pull the headlight out of its housing. See **Figure 28**.

2. Turn the bulb holder (**Figure 28**) counterclockwise.

3. Push the bulb (**Figure 29**) into its socket, then turn it counterclockwise and remove it.

4. Clean the bulb socket terminals.

5. Install by reversing these steps, while noting the following.

6. Make sure the bulb holder (**Figure 28**) is secured tightly in the headlight housing.

7. When installing the headlight into the housing, insert the 2 tabs (**Figure 30**) on the headlight rim behind the 2 housing tabs (A, **Figure 31**).

8. If necessary, adjust the headlight as described under *Headlight Adjustment*.

Headlight Lens and Rim Replacement

The headlight lens is secured in place with 4 springs (**Figure 32**). Remove these springs to replace the lens or rim assembly (**Figure 26**). Reverse to install.

Headlight Adjustment

The headlight is equipped with a vertical adjustment only.

Loosen the 2 headlight mounting bolts (**Figure 33**) and adjust the beam by moving the headlight up or down. Tighten the mounting bolts securely.

Taillight Bulb and Lens Replacement

Refer to **Figure 34** for this procedure.

1. Remove the 2 Phillips screws (**Figure 35**) and pull the taillight assembly out of its mounting bracket on the frame.

2. Pry the rubber cover (**Figure 36**) off the back of the lens.

3. Turn the bulb holder counterclockwise and remove the bulb holder and bulb (**Figure 37**).

4. Replace the bulb.

5. Install by reversing these steps, while noting the following.

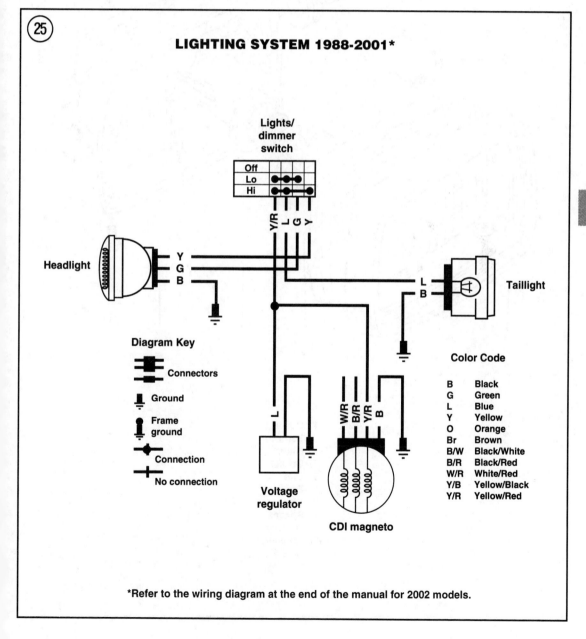

25

LIGHTING SYSTEM 1988-2001*

	Off	Lo	Hi

Lights/dimmer switch

Headlight

Y
G
B

Taillight

L
B

Diagram Key

Connectors

Ground

Frame ground

Connection

No connection

Voltage regulator

CDI magneto

Color Code

B	Black
G	Green
L	Blue
Y	Yellow
O	Orange
Br	Brown
B/W	Black/White
B/R	Black/Red
W/R	White/Red
Y/B	Yellow/Black
Y/R	Yellow/Red

9

***Refer to the wiring diagram at the end of the manual for 2002 models.**

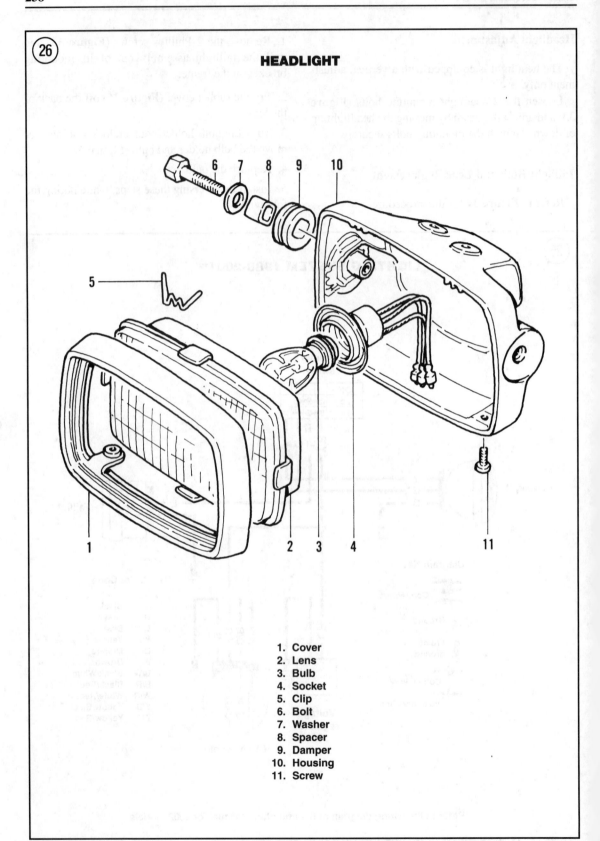

HEADLIGHT

1. Cover
2. Lens
3. Bulb
4. Socket
5. Clip
6. Bolt
7. Washer
8. Spacer
9. Damper
10. Housing
11. Screw

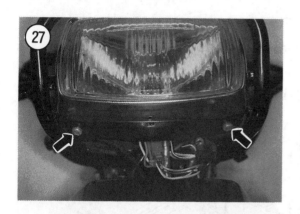

6. Make sure the rubber gasket seal is seated all the way around the lens when assembling the lens and bulb holder (**Figure 36**).

OIL LEVEL INDICATOR SYSTEM

An oil level indicator system, consisting of an indicator bulb (**Figure 38**) and an oil level sensor in the oil tank, allows the rider to monitor the oil level

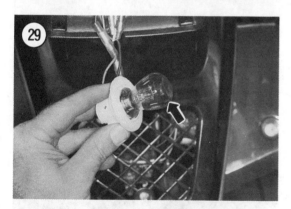

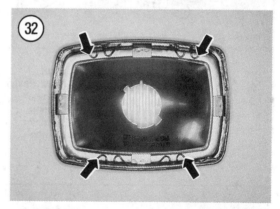

9

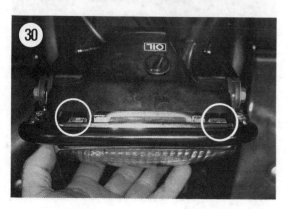

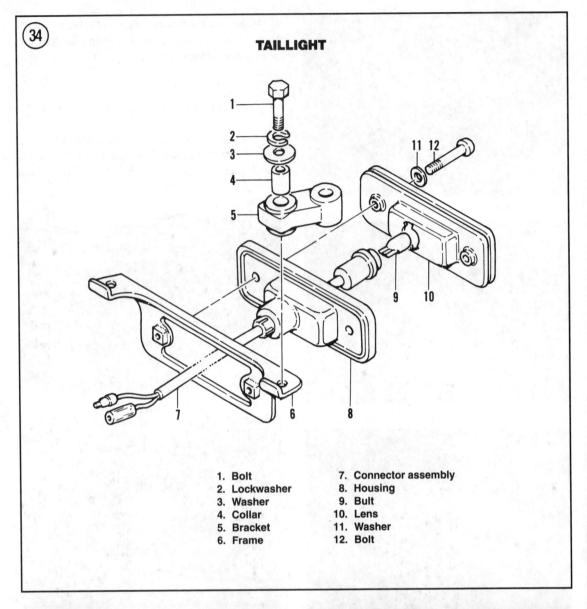

TAILLIGHT

1. Bolt
2. Lockwasher
3. Washer
4. Collar
5. Bracket
6. Frame
7. Connector assembly
8. Housing
9. Bult
10. Lens
11. Washer
12. Bolt

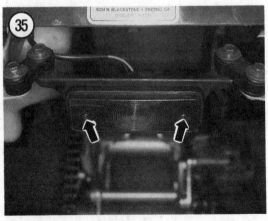

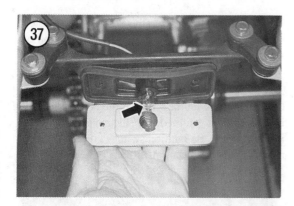

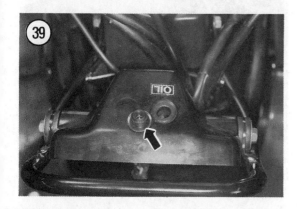

when the engine is running. When the oil level drops to a set level in the tank, the oil level indicator bulb will come on. Always use the correct wattage bulb indicated in **Table 4**.

Troubleshooting

Refer to *Oil Level Indicator System Troubleshooting* in Chapter Two.

Oil Level Indicator
Bulb Replacement

The oil level indicator (**Figure 38**) is mounted in the top of the headlight housing.
1. Remove the headlight as described in this chapter.
2. Remove the indicator plug (**Figure 39**) from the top of the headlight housing.
3. Remove the socket plug (B, **Figure 31**) from the headlight housing.
4. Remove the socket plug from the socket (**Figure 40**) and replace the bulb.
5. Reverse these steps to complete installation.

Oil Level Gauge
Replacement

The oil level gauge is mounted in the oil tank and is secured to the tank with its tight fitting rubber cap (**Figure 41**). To replace the oil level gauge, disconnect its electrical connectors and remove gauge (**Figure 42**). Wipe off the new gauge and install it firmly into the oil tank. Reconnect its electrical connectors.

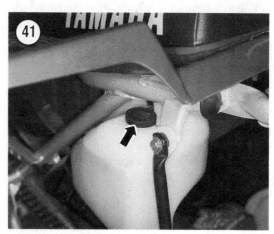

LIGHTING VOLTAGE TESTS

To test the headlight and taillight circuits, perform the troubleshooting procedures in Chapter Two.

VOLTAGE REGULATOR

The voltage regulator (**Figure 43**) is mounted underneath the front fender.

Testing

To test the voltage regulator, test the headlight or taillight circuit as described in Chapter Two.

Removal/Installation

1. Disconnect the voltage regulator electrical connectors.
2. Unbolt and remove the voltage regulator (**Figure 43**).
3. Install by reversing these steps.

SWITCHES

Testing

Switches can be tested for continuity with an ohmmeter (see Chapter One) or a test light at the switch connector.

When testing switches, note the following:

a. After locating a defective circuit, check the connectors to make sure they are clean and properly connected. Check all wires going into a connector housing to make sure each wire is properly positioned and that the wire end or connector pin is not loose.

b. To reconnect the connectors, push them together until they click or snap into place.

Ignition Switch
Testing/Replacement

The ignition switch (A, **Figure 44**) is mounted in front of the handlebar.

1. Locate the main switch electrical connector and disconnect it. The ignition switch connector has 2 wires, black and black/white.

2. Switch an ohmmeter to the R × 1 scale. Connect the ohmmeter leads to the 2 disconnected ignition switch electrical connectors on the switch side.

3. Check continuity with the ignition switch turned OFF, then test with the switch turned ON. When the ignition switch is turned OFF, the meter should read infinity. When the ignition switch is turned ON, the meter should read 0 ohms. Replace the switch if it does not perform as specified.

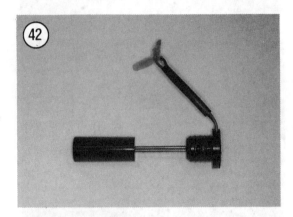

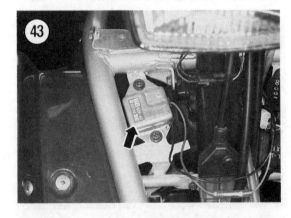

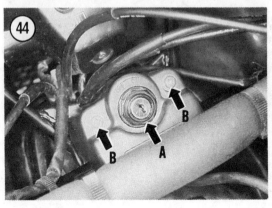

4. To replace the ignition switch:

a. Remove the plastic nut securing the ignition switch to the ignition switch bracket.

b. Remove the 2 screws (B, **Figure 44**) securing the ignition switch bracket to the steering stem, then remove the bracket.

c. Remove the ignition switch (**Figure 45**) from its bracket.

d. Install the switch by reversing the removal procedure. When installing the outer cover, align the outer cover notch with the ignition switch tab (**Figure 44**).

5. Reconnect the ignition switch electrical connectors.

Engine Stop Switch/Dimmer Switch Testing/Replacement

The individual switches mounted in the left handlebar switch housing (**Figure 46**) cannot be

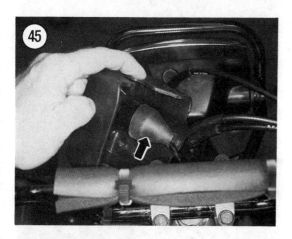

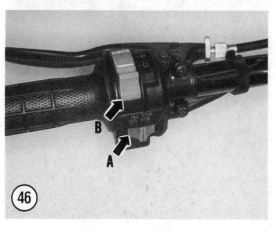

replaced separately. If one switch is damaged, the entire switch assembly must be replaced.

1. Disconnect the engine switch/dimmer switch electrical connectors.

2. To test the engine stop switch (A, **Figure 46**), perform the following:

a. Use an ohmmeter set at R × 1 and connect the 2 ohmmeter leads to the black/white and black wires.

b. Turn the engine stop switch to the RUN position. If the switch is good, the meter will read 0 ohms.

c. Turn the engine stop switch to the OFF position. If the switch is good, the meter will read infinity.

3. To test the dimmer switch (B, **Figure 46**), perform the following:

a. Turn the dimmer switch to the HI position. Use an ohmmeter set at R × 1 and connect the 2 ohmmeter leads first to the yellow and blue wires, then to the blue and the yellow/red wires. If the switch is good, the meter will read 0 ohms.

b. Turn the dimmer switch to the LO position. Use an ohmmeter set at R × 1 and connect the 2 ohmmeter leads first to the yellow/red and blue wires, then to the blue and green wires. If the switch is good, the meter will read 0 ohms.

c. Turn the dimmer switch to the OFF position. Use an ohmmeter set at R × 1 and connect the 2 ohmmeter leads first to the yellow/red and blue wires, then to the blue and green wires. If the switch is good, the meter will read infinity.

4. If the switch fails any of these tests, replace the switch assembly.

5. Remove any cable straps securing the switch wiring harness to the handlebar and frame.

6. Remove the screws securing the switch housing to the handlebar and remove the switch housing.

7. Install by reversing these steps. Start the engine and check the switch in each of its operating positions.

T.O.R.S. Switch Testing/Replacement

The throttle lever switch (**Figure 47**) is mounted in the throttle housing.

1. Check the throttle lever free play adjustment as described in Chapter Three. Adjust if necessary.

9

2. Remove the front fender as described in Chapter Fourteen.

3. Disconnect the throttle lever electrical connector. The connector has 2 wires, black and black/yellow.

4. Use an ohmmeter set at R × 1 and connect the red ohmmeter lead to the black/yellow wire and the black ohmmeter lead to the black wire.

5. Push the throttle lever (**Figure 48**) all the way in. If the switch is good, the meter will read 0 ohms.

6. Release the throttle lever. If the switch is good, the meter will read infinity.

7. If the switch fails this test, replace the switch.

8. To replace the throttle lever switch:

   a. Remove the throttle lever housing cover and gasket.

   b. Remove the screw securing the switch to the throttle lever housing.

   c. Lift the switch out of the housing and remove it (**Figure 49**).

   d. Reverse these steps to install the new switch. Push the grommet on the switch wiring harness into the throttle lever housing.

9. Reconnect the wiring harness connectors.

Carburetor Switch
Testing

The carburetor switch (**Figure 50**) is installed in the T.O.R.S. housing.

1. Check the throttle lever free play adjustment as described in Chapter Three. Adjust if necessary.

2. Remove the fuel tank as described in Chapter Eight.

3. Disconnect the carburetor switch electrical connector (**Figure 51**). The connector has 2 wires, black and black/yellow.

4. Use an ohmmeter set at R × 1 and connect the red ohmmeter lead to the black/yellow wire and the black ohmmeter lead to the black wire.

5. Push the throttle lever (**Figure 45**) all the way in. If the switch is good, the meter will read 0 ohms.

6. Release the throttle lever. If the switch is good, the meter will read infinity.

7. Replace the switch if its continuity is not as specified. To replace the carburetor switch, refer to the *Throttle Valve/T.O.R.S. Housing* disassembly and reassembly procedures in Chapter Eight.

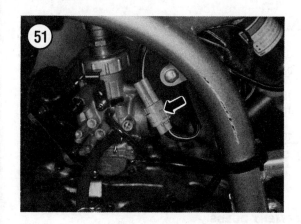

NOTE
*The carburetor switch (**Figure 50**) is an integral part of the T.O.R.S. switch housing. Do not attempt to remove the switch from the housing. If the switch is faulty, the T.O.R.S. switch housing assembly must be replaced as described in Chapter Eight.*

Brake Switches

On models equipped with a rear brake light, refer to the wiring diagram at th end of the manual and test the system as follows:

1. Make sure the bulb is good.
2. Make sure the switches are properly adjusted. If necessary adjust the rear switch as follows:
   a. Hold the main body of the switch.
   b. Turn the adjusting nut counterclockwise to make the light come on sooner.
   c. Turn the adjusting nut clockwise to make the light come on later.
3. If adjustment does not solve the problem, check the switches for continuity with an ohmmeter.
4. Operate the switches from the ON to OFF positions. They should switch from continuity to no continuity. If either switch fails a continuity test, replace that switch.

WIRING DIAGRAMS

Wiring diagrams for all models are located at the end of this book.

Table 1 ELECTRICAL SPECIFICATIONS

Ignition system	Capacitor discharge ignition (CDI)
Charge/lighting system	Flywheel magneto
Magneto	
Model	F2XJ
Manufacturer	Yamaha
CDI unit	
Model	2XJ
Manufacturer	Yamaha
Voltage regulator	
Type	Semi conductor, short circuit type
Model	SH588
Manufacturer	Shindengen

Table 2 IGNITION SYSTEM TEST SPECIFICATIONS[1]

Pulser coil	
Wire test connections	White/red to black
Resistance	72-108 ohms
Charging coil	
Wire test connections	Black/red to black
Resistance	192-288 ohms
Ignition coil	
Minimum spark gap	6 mm (0.24 in.)
Primary coil resistance	
1988-2001	1.44-1.76 ohms
2002	0.18-0.28 ohm
Secondary coil resistance	
1988-2001	5.28-7.92 K ohms
2002	6.32-9.48 K ohms
Spark plug cap resistance	5K ohms

[1]All measurements taken at a temperature of 68° F (20° C).

Table 3 CHARGING SYSTEM TEST SPECIFICATIONS[1]

Charge/lighting coil	
Wire test connections	Yellow/red to black
Resistance	0.16-0.24 ohms
Lighting voltage	
Minimum	12.5 volts @ 3,000 rpm
Maximum	15 volts @ 8,000 rpm
Voltage regulator	
No-load regulated voltage	13.5-14.1 volts

[1]All measurements taken at a temperature of 68° F (20° C).

Table 4 REPLACEMENT BULBS

Type	Bulb wattage × quantity
Headlight	12V, 45W/45W × 1
Taillight	12V, 3.4W × 1
Tail/Brake light	12V, 21W × 1
Oil level indicator light	12V, 3.4W × 1

Table 5 TIGHTENING TORQUES

	N•m	in.-lb.	ft.-lb.
Flywheel cover	10	88	–
Flywheel nut	73	–	53
Shift pedal pinch bolt	14	–	10
Stator plate	8	71	–

OIL INJECTION SYSTEM

All YFS200 engines are equipped with the Yamaha Autolube oil injection system. The Autolube system consists of a gear-driven oil pump, drive shaft and gear, external oil tank and connecting oil hoses.

Oil pump specifications are listed in **Table 1** and **Table 2**. **Table 1** and **Table 2** are at the end of this chapter.

SYSTEM COMPONENTS

Figure 1 shows the Autolube pump assembly for the YFS200 engine. The Autolube pump is mounted on the front of the right crankcase cover with 2 Phillips screws. A separate drive shaft connects the Autolube pump to a nylon pump gear mounted inside the crankcase cover. A solid pin engages the pump gear to the drive shaft where 2 E-clips position the gear axially on the shaft. The pump gear meshes with the primary drive gear. An oil reservoir that supplies oil for the oil injection system is located at the left rear side of the vehicle. An oil supply hose connects the oil tank to the Autolube pump and the oil delivery hose connects the Autolube pump to a nozzle on the carburetor. Gravity supplies a constant supply of oil from the reservoir to the oil pump. When the engine is running, oil is pumped through the oil delivery line to the nozzle in the carburetor. The oil sprays into the carburetor where it then mixes with the air/fuel mixture that passes through the carburetor. The amount of oil that is sprayed into the carburetor is controlled by engine speed.

OIL PUMP BLEEDING

The oil pump must be bled if air enters one of the oil lines or oil pump. If air enters the oil injection system, it blocks the flow of oil to the engine. The

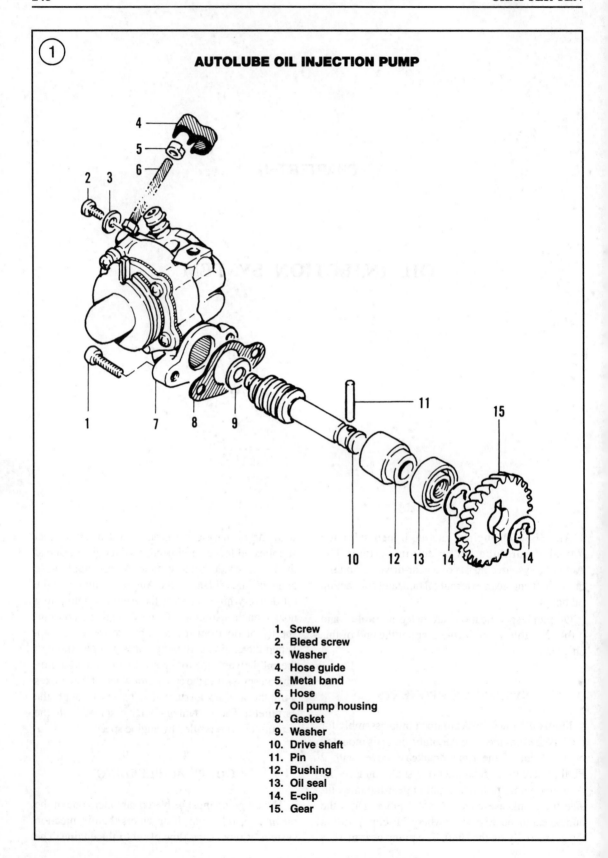

① AUTOLUBE OIL INJECTION PUMP

1. Screw
2. Bleed screw
3. Washer
4. Hose guide
5. Metal band
6. Hose
7. Oil pump housing
8. Gasket
9. Washer
10. Drive shaft
11. Pin
12. Bushing
13. Oil seal
14. E-clip
15. Gear

oil pump must be bled if one of the following conditions have occurred:

a. The oil tank ran empty.

b. If any one of the oil injection hoses were disconnected.

c. The machine was turned on its side.

d. After storing the vehicle for any length of time.

The Autolube oil pump is equipped with a bleed screw installed in the pump body. Removing the screw allows oil to flow from the oil tank through the oil delivery and pump passages, forcing air out of the system.

NOTE
Bleeding the oil pump is a simple procedure that does not take much time and ensures that the engine receives an uninterrupted supply of oil. Bleed the oil pump whenever there is a question of air in the oil lines or oil pump.

1. Remove the Autolube pump cover screws and cover (**Figure 2**).

2. Make sure the oil tank is full of oil. See *Engine Oil* in Chapter Three.

3. Place a drain pan or rag underneath the oil pump.

4. Remove the bleed screw and gasket (**Figure 3**) from the oil pump. Oil should begin to flow from the oil pump (**Figure 4**).

NOTE
*If oil does not flow from the oil pump and there is oil in the oil tank, remove the oil fill cap (**Figure 5**) from the top of the oil tank. If oil now starts to flow from the oil tank, the vent hole in the cap is clogged with dirt or other debris. Clean the vent hole and reinstall the cap. A clogged vent hole will allow a vacuum to build in the tank and prevent oil from flowing from the tank. If oil still does not flow, check for a clogged oil supply hose (from the tank to the oil pump).*

5. If there is air in the system, air bubbles will be mixed in with the oil. Allow the oil to run out of the oil pump until there are no air bubbles in the oil. Then install the bleed screw (**Figure 3**) and its gasket and tighten securely.

6. Fill the oil delivery hose with oil as follows:

10

a. Slide the band clamp down the oil delivery hose, then disconnect the hose from the carburetor nozzle (**Figure 6**).

b. Fill the oil delivery hose with a small syringe (**Figure 7**) that is filled with engine oil.

c. Reconnect the oil delivery hose to the carburetor, then slide the hose over the carburetor nozzle and secure it with its band clamp (**Figure 8**).

7. Install the Autolube pump cover (**Figure 2**) and tighten its mounting screws to the torque specification in **Table 2**.

AUTOLUBE PUMP OUTPUT TEST

Table 1 lists specifications for checking the output of the Autolube oil pump. While the Autolube oil pump is dependable and seldom fails, perform this test when troubleshooting an oil supply problem. The test consists of disconnecting the oil delivery line from the carburetor and running the engine at idle while counting a specified number of pump strokes. The oil that is pumped from the delivery line is measured to determine the oil pump output. Because the oil delivery line is disconnected from the carburetor during this test, engine lubrication must be provided by premixing a small mount of gasoline and oil and adding it to the fuel tank.

1. Park the vehicle on a level surface and set the parking brake.

2. Connect one end of a long piece of fuel hose to the fuel valve on the fuel tank. Insert the other end into a suitable gasoline can. Turn the fuel valve to RES and drain the fuel tank of all fuel. When the fuel tank is empty, remove the fuel hose and reconnect the carburetor fuel hose to the fuel valve.

3. Remove the drain screw from the bottom of the carburetor and drain it also, then reinstall the drain screw.

4. Prepare a 24:1 premix as follows:

a. To make a 24:1 premix, add 2.7 ounces of Yamalube 2-R (or equivalent 2-stroke engine oil) to 1/2 gallon of gasoline.

b. Shake the can thoroughly to mix the oil with the gasoline and pour the premix into the fuel tank.

5. Remove the oil pump cover screws and cover (**Figure 2**).

6. Slide the band clamp down the oil delivery hose, then disconnect the hose from the carburetor nozzle

(**Figure 6**). Insert the open end of the delivery hose into a graduated beaker that can measure a small amount of liquid (0-10 cc).

7. Plug the nozzle on the carburetor to prevent air from being drawn into the engine during this procedure.

8. Remove the rubber cover from the front of the oil pump to expose the piston shaft.

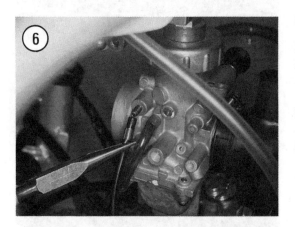

Start counting the oil pump strokes as soon as the engine is started.

9. Have an assistant start the engine and allow it to idle. Count the number of piston strokes up to 200, then turn the engine off and measure the amount of oil discharged into the beaker. The correct oil output

capacity for 200 strokes is 3.47-4.23 cc (0.117-0.143 U.S. oz. [0.122-0.149 Imp. oz.]) of oil.

a. The accuracy of this test depends on your accuracy in counting the pump strokes and measuring the oil output.

b. If the output measurement is correct for 200 strokes, the oil pump is working correctly.

c. If the output quantity differs from the output specification in Step 9, replace the oil pump as described in this chapter.

10. Reinstall the rubber cover onto the front of the oil pump.

11. Drain the premix from the fuel tank and refill the tank with unmixed gasoline.

12. Complete this procedure by bleeding the oil pump as described in this chapter.

AUTOLUBE PUMP

This section describes removal, inspection and installation procedures for the Autolube oil pump assembly. The oil pump is a sealed unit and should not be disassembled. If a problem is suspected with the oil pump, perform the output test as described in this chapter.

Removal

1. Park the vehicle on level ground and set the parking brake.

2. Drain the transmission oil (Chapter Three).

3. Remove the right side footpeg (Chapter Fourteen).

4. Disconnect the oil pump hoses as follows:

a. Remove the Autolube pump cover screws and cover (**Figure 2**).

b. Disconnect the oil supply hose (A, **Figure 9**) and the oil delivery hose (B, **Figure 9**) from the oil pump.

c. Plug both hoses to prevent oil leakage and hose contamination.

5. Remove the right crankcase cover with the Autolube pump (**Figure 10**) attached to the cover as described in Chapter Six.

6. Remove the E-clip (A, **Figure 11**) from the groove in the drive shaft.

7. Slide the oil pump gear (B, **Figure 11**) off of the drive shaft.

8. Remove the pin (**Figure 12**) from the hole in the drive shaft.

9. Remove the second E-clip (**Figure 13**) from the groove in the drive shaft.

10. Remove the 2 screws (A, **Figure 14**) that hold the oil pump to the right crankcase cover and remove the pump assembly (B, **Figure 14**).

11. Remove and discard the oil pump gasket (**Figure 15**).

12. Remove the washer (**Figure 16**) from the end of the drive shaft.

13. Remove the drive shaft (**Figure 17**) from the right crankcase cover.

14. Store the oil pump (**Figure 18**) in a sealed plastic bag until inspection and reassembly.

Inspection

1. Carefully remove any gasket material from the oil pump gasket surface (**Figure 18**). Do not drop any of the gasket residue inside the oil pump.

2. Remove any gasket residue from the gasket surface on the right crankcase cover.

3. Clean all of the parts *except* the oil pump housing in solvent.

4. Visually inspect the oil pump for a leaking seal (**Figure 19**) or other damage. Replace the oil pump if any leakage or damage is noted. The oil pump is a sealed unit and must not be disassembled. Replacement parts for the oil pump housing are not available. If the oil pump is good, store it in a sealed plastic bag until reassembly.

5. Inspect the washer (A, **Figure 20**) for nicks, burrs or damage.

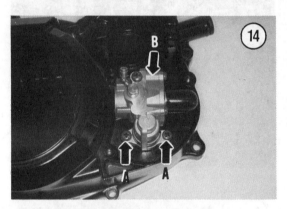

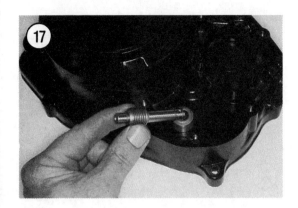

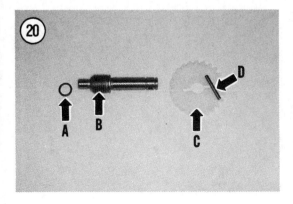

6. Inspect the drive shaft (B, **Figure 20**) for excessive wear, nicks burrs or other damage.

7. Inspect the oil pump gear (C, **Figure 20**) for excessive wear, cracks or other damage.

8. Inspect the drive shaft bushing (**Figure 21**) for excessive wear, damage, or a loose fit in the right crankcase cover. If necessary, replace the bushing as follows:

   a. Remove the drive shaft seal as described in the following procedure.

   b. Support the right crankcase cover and press out the old bushing.

   c. Inspect the mounting bore in the right crankcase cover for cracks or other damage. Replace the right crankcase cover if there is any mounting bore damage.

   d. Press the new bushing (**Figure 21**) into its mounting bore until it bottoms against the cover.

   e. Install a new seal as described in the following procedure.

**Drive Shaft Seal
Inspection/Replacement**

1. Inspect the drive shaft seal (**Figure 22**) for any tearing or oil leaks. Continue with Step 2 to replace the oil seal.

2. Pry the old seal out of the right crankcase cover with a screwdriver and rag as shown in **Figure 23**.

3. Inspect the seal mounting bore (**Figure 24**) for any cracks or other damage. Replace the right crankcase cover if any damage is noted.

10

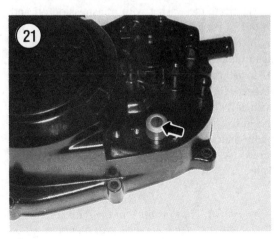

4. Lubricate the lip of the new seal with grease and place it into its mounting bore so its open side (A, **Figure 25**) faces up (toward the inside of the right crankcase cover).

> *NOTE*
> *Step 5 describes how to install the seal with a threaded bolt, nut and 2 flat washers (B, **Figure 25**). The washer placed against the seal must have an outside diameter that is the same size or slightly smaller than the seal's outside diameter.*

5. Install the bolt and one of the washers through the outside of the right crankcase cover and through the seal. Then install the second washer and thread the nut onto the bolt (**Figure 26**). Hold the bolt head with a wrench and tighten the nut (**Figure 26**) to press the seal into the right crankcase cover. Continue to install the seal until it bottoms in its mounting bore (**Figure 22**). If the washer bottoms before the seal, its outside diameter is too large. Use a smaller washer so the oil seal bottoms completely.

6. Remove the nut, washers and bolt from the right crankcase cover.

Installation

1. Lubricate the new seal lip (**Figure 22**) with grease.

2. Remove any burrs or rough spots from the 2 E-clip grooves in the drive shaft (B, **Figure 20**). This will prevent the grooves from damaging the seal when the drive shaft is installed through the seal.

3. Lubricate the drive shaft with transmission oil, then install it into its bushing as shown in **Figure 17**.

4. Lubricate the washer with transmission oil and install it over the end of the drive shaft (**Figure 16**).

5. Install a new gasket (**Figure 15**) and center it against the right crankcase cover.

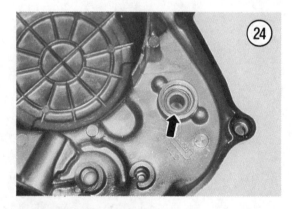

6. Install the oil pump (B, **Figure 14**) by meshing its gear with the drive shaft. Then secure the oil pump with its 2 Phillips screws (A, **Figure 14**). Check that the gasket is positioned correctly between the oil pump and right crankcase cover, then tighten the screws (A, **Figure 14**) to the torque specification in **Table 2**.

> *NOTE*
> *The 2 E-clips installed in the following steps are identical (same part number).*

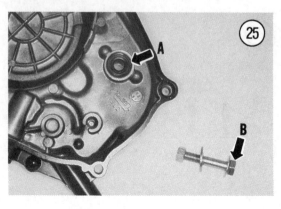

7. Install the first E-clip into the drive shaft groove closest to the seal (**Figure 13**).

8. Install the drive pin through the hole in the drive shaft (**Figure 12**).

9. Install the oil pump gear with its shoulder (**Figure 27**) facing toward the seal. Then align the slots in the drive gear with the pin and install the gear over the shaft (**Figure 28**).

10. Install the second E-clip into the outer drive shaft groove (**Figure 29**).

11. Install the right crankcase cover and Autolube pump (**Figure 10**) as described in Chapter Six.

12. Service the oil pump as follows:

 a. Reconnect the oil supply hose (A, **Figure 9**) and the oil delivery hose (B, **Figure 9**) to the oil pump.

 b. Bleed the oil pump as described in this chapter.

 c. Install the Autolube pump cover (**Figure 2**) and tighten its mounting screws to the torque specification in **Table 2**.

OIL HOSES

Install new oil hoses whenever the old hoses become hard and brittle or damaged. When replacing damaged or worn oil hoses, make sure to install hoses with the correct inside diameter. When reconnecting hoses, secure each hose end with a clamp. Bleed the oil pump after reconnecting one or both oil hoses.

OIL LEVEL INDICATOR

Refer to *Oil Level Indicator System* in Chapter Nine.

OIL TANK

The oil tank that supplies oil for the oil injection system is located at the left rear side of the vehicle (**Figure 30**).

Removal/Installation

1. Park the vehicle on a level surface and set the parking brake.

10

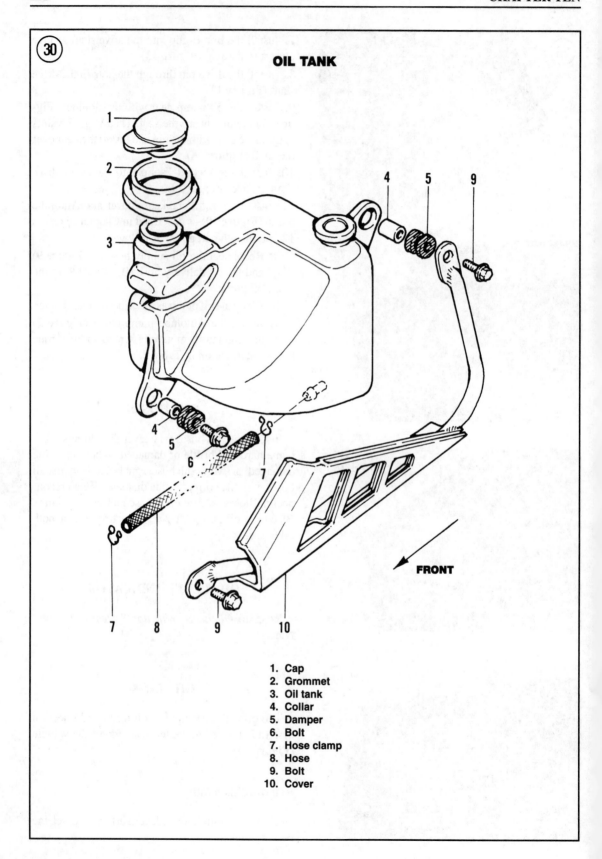

③ OIL TANK

1. Cap
2. Grommet
3. Oil tank
4. Collar
5. Damper
6. Bolt
7. Hose clamp
8. Hose
9. Bolt
10. Cover

2. Disconnect the supply hose from the bottom of the oil tank and drain the oil into a clean container. Then plug the tank and supply hose openings to prevent leakage and contamination.

3. Disconnect the oil level indicator electrical connectors (**Figure 31**).

4. Remove the bolts securing the oil tank to the frame.

5. Remove the oil fill cap (**Figure 32**) from the top of the oil tank, then withdraw the oil tank from the large rubber grommet and remove the oil tank from the frame. Reinstall the oil fill cap onto the oil tank.

6. Install the oil tank by reversing these removal steps, noting the following.

7. Refill the oil tank with the correct type of 2-stroke injection oil (Chapter Three).

8. Bleed the oil pump as described in this chapter.

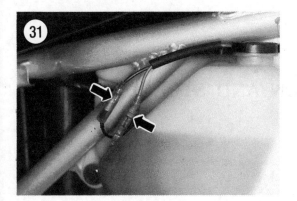

10

Table 1 AUTOLUBE PUMP SPECIFICATIONS

Stroke length	1.95-2.05 mm (0.077-0.081 in.)
Pump output at 200 strokes	3.47-4.23 cc (0.117-0.143 U.S. oz. [0.122-0.149 Imp. oz.])

Table 2 LUBRICATION SYSTEM TIGHTENING TORQUES

	N•m	in.-lb.
Autolube pump cover	7	62
Autolube pump mounting screws	5	44

CHAPTER ELEVEN

FRONT SUSPENSION AND STEERING

This chapter describes repair and maintenance procedures for the front wheels, brake drums, front suspension arms and steering components.

Table 1 lists front suspension and steering specifications. **Table 2** lists tire and wheel specifications. **Tables 1-4** are located at the end of this chapter.

FRONT WHEEL

Removal/Installation

1. Park the vehicle on level ground and set the parking brake.

NOTE
Mark the tires for location and direction before removing them.

2. Loosen the front wheel nuts (**Figure 1**).
3. Support the vehicle with the front wheels off the ground.
4. Remove the wheel nuts and remove the front wheel (**Figure 1**).
5. Clean and dry the wheel nuts.
6. Inspect the wheel nuts and replace them if damaged.
7. Inspect the wheels and replace if damaged. Refer to *Tires and Wheels* in this chapter.
8. Install the wheel.

9. Install the wheel nuts finger-tight, then make sure the wheel sits squarely against the front hub.

10. Repeat for the other wheel.

11. Lower the vehicle so both front wheels are on the ground.

12. Tighten the wheel nuts in a crisscross pattern to the torque specification in **Table 4**.

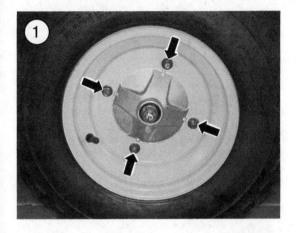

13. Support the vehicle again so both front wheels are off the ground.

14. Rotate the wheels, then apply the front brake. Repeat this step several times to make sure each wheel rotates freely and that each brake is working properly.

FRONT BRAKE DRUM/BEARING ASSEMBLY

The front brake drum/bearing assembly consists of the brake drum/housing assembly, outer seal, 2 ball bearings and a center brake drum spacer. The front brake drum is installed over the brake shoes and is secured to the front axle with a flat washer, axle nut and cotter pin. Four studs pressed into the brake drum are used to secure the wheel to the vehicle.

Refer to **Figure 2** when servicing the front brake drum and bearings. Refer to Chapter Thirteen to service the brake plate and brake shoes.

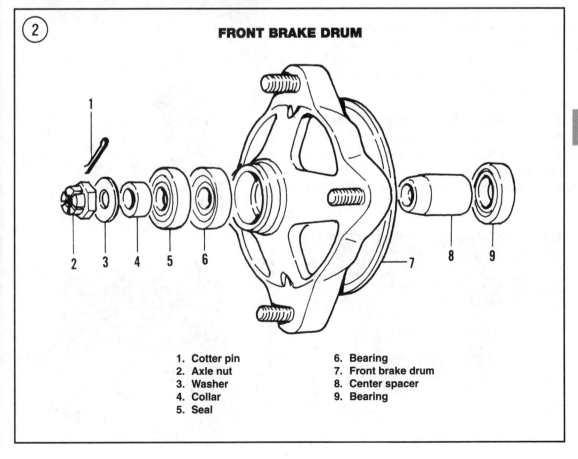

FRONT BRAKE DRUM

1. Cotter pin
2. Axle nut
3. Washer
4. Collar
5. Seal
6. Bearing
7. Front brake drum
8. Center spacer
9. Bearing

WARNING
*When working on the brake drum and brake shoes, **do not** inhale brake dust as it may contain asbestos, which can cause lung injury and cancer. Protect yourself by wearing a disposable face mask and wash your hands thoroughly after completing the work. Wet down (using an aerosol brake cleaner) the brake dust on brake components before working on them. Secure and dispose of all brake dust and cleaning materials properly. **Do not** use compressed air to blow off brake parts. Cover the brake pads and backing plate with a large plastic bag while servicing the brake drum.*

Inspection
(Brake Drum Installed)

Inspect the wheel bearings while they are mounted in the brake drum.

CAUTION
Do not remove the wheel bearings for inspection purposes as they can be damaged during removal. Remove the wheel bearings only if they are to be replaced.

1. Check that the wheel nuts (**Figure 1**) are tightened to the torque specification in **Table 4**.
2. Park the vehicle on level ground and set the parking brake.
3. Raise the front of the vehicle and support it with wooden blocks.

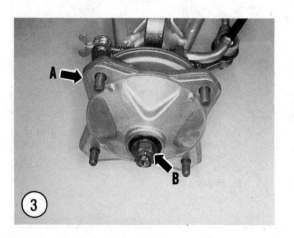

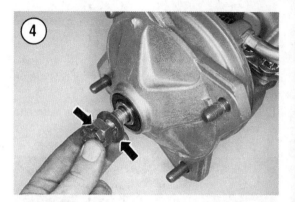

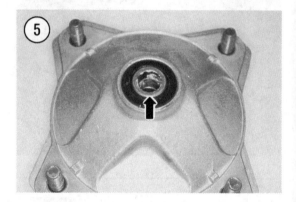

4. Remove the front wheel(s) as described in this chapter.

5. Turn the brake drum (A, **Figure 3**) by hand. The brake drum should turn smoothly, without excessive play or grinding. If the brake drum does not turn smoothly, remove the brake drum and visually check both bearings.

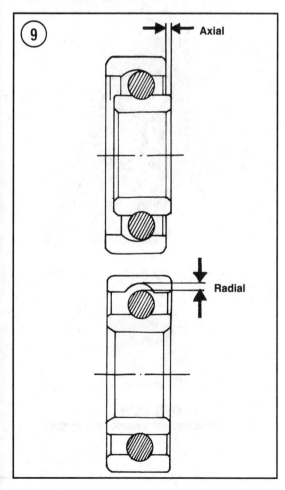

6. Spin the brake drum and apply the front brake. Check for any grinding or scraping noises.

7. Spin the brake drum and apply the front brake hard while watching the backing plate. Look for excessive flexing or cracks at the cam and pivot post positions. If any damage is noted, service the backing plate as described in Chapter Thirteen.

8. Install the front wheel(s) as described in this chapter.

Brake Drum Removal

Refer to **Figure 2** for this procedure.

1. Remove the front wheel as described in this chapter.

2. Remove and discard the axle nut cotter pin (B, **Figure 3**).

3. Remove the axle nut and washer (**Figure 4**) that holds the brake drum onto the front axle.

4. Slide the brake drum (A, **Figure 3**) and its collar off the axle and remove it. If the brake drum is tight, loosen the front brake shoe adjuster, then slide off the drum.

**Inspection
(Brake Drum Removed)**

1. Clean the brake drum surface with an aerosol type brake cleaner. Do not force any cleaner or other solvents into the bearings or outer seal.

2. Remove the collar (**Figure 5**) from the brake drum.

3. Pry the seal out of the brake drum with a screwdriver (**Figure 6**). Support the screwdriver with a rag to prevent damaging the brake drum.

4. Turn each inner bearing race with your fingers. The bearings should turn smoothly, without binding or excessive noise. See **Figure 7** (outer bearing) and **Figure 8** (inner bearing).

5. Inspect each inner bearing race play as shown in **Figure 9**. Check for excessive axial and radial play. If a bearing shows excessive play, replace both bearings at the same time. When replacing the bearings, write down the bearing manufacturer's code numbers (found on the outside of each bearing) to ensure a perfect match.

6. Refer to *Brake Drum Inspection* in Chapter Thirteen to inspect and measure the brake drum inside diameter.

11

7. Inspect the studs (**Figure 10**) on the brake drum assembly. If a stud is damaged, replace it with a press. If a stud is loose in the hub, check the stud hole for cracks or other damage.

Brake Drum Bearing Removal

The brake drum bearings (**Figure 2**) are an interference fit in the brake drum. Force is required to remove the bearings from the brake drum.

This section describes 2 methods of removing the brake drum bearings. The first method (Step 3A) removes the first bearing with a drift and hammer. Because of the close fit between the bearings and brake drum spacer (**Figure 2**), this method can be difficult, as it is easy to damage the spacer when removing the first bearing. Also, because this method removes the first bearing unevenly, the bearing can damage the bearing bore as it is forced out of the hub. This type of damage can cause a loose bearing fit. The second method (Step 3B) requires the use of a wheel bearing remover set that consists of a remover shaft and expandable collets.

Remove the bearings only if they are going to be replaced. Note that the inner and outer bearings are different. The outside bearing (**Figure 7**) is smaller than the inside bearing (**Figure 8**).

1. Remove and clean the brake drum as described in this chapter.

2. Pry the seal out of the brake drum with a screwdriver (**Figure 6**). Support the screwdriver with a rag to prevent damaging the brake drum.

3A. To remove the brake drum bearings without special tools:

   a. Place the brake drum on the workbench.

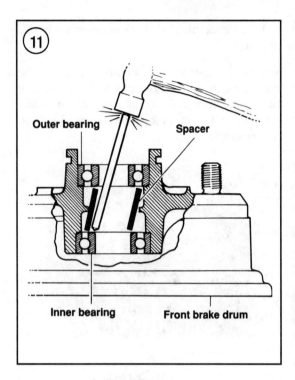

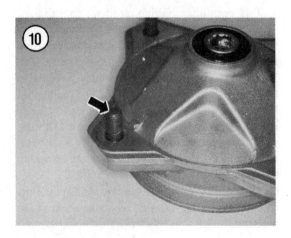

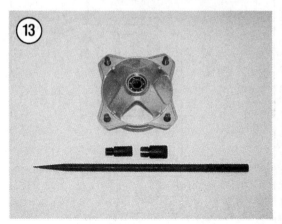

b. Using a long drift, tilt the center spacer away from one side of the bearing as shown in **Figure 11**.

> *NOTE*
> *Try not to damage the spacer's machined surface when removing it. It may be necessary to grind a clearance groove in the drift to enable it to contact the bearing and still clear the spacer.*

c. Tap the bearing out of the brake drum with a hammer, working around the perimeter of the bearing's inner race.

d. Remove the center spacer (**Figure 12**) from the brake drum.

e. Using a suitable bearing driver, drive out the opposite bearing.

> *NOTE*
> *The Kowa Seiki Wheel Bearing Remover set shown in **Figure 13** consists of a remover shaft and expandable collets. These tools are available as a complete set or can be purchased individually through your dealership from K&L Supply Co. in Santa Clara, CA.*

3B. To remove the brake drum bearings with the Kowa Seiki Wheel Bearing Remover set:

a. Select the correct size collet and insert it into the inner bearing (**Figure 14**).

b. From the opposite side of the brake drum, insert the remover shaft (**Figure 15**) into the slot in the backside of the collet. Position the brake drum so the collet is resting against a solid surface (**Figure 16**), then tap the remover shaft to force it into the slot in the collet. Doing so expands the collet so it locks against the bearing's inner race.

c. Reposition the brake drum and drive the remover shaft with a hammer to drive the bearing out of the brake drum (**Figure 17**). Slide the bearing and tool assembly out of the brake drum. Tap the collet to release it from the bearing.

d. Remove the center spacer (**Figure 12**) from the brake drum.

e. Remove the opposite bearing (**Figure 18**) in the same way.

11

CAUTION
Do not reuse the bearings after removal.

4. Clean the brake drum and center spacer in solvent and dry thoroughly.

5. Inspect the brake drum bearing bores for excessive scoring, cracks or other damage. If damage is noted, or if a bearing fits loosely in its bore, replace the brake drum.

6. Replace the center spacer if either end is split or damaged.

Brake Drum Bearing Installation

Install the bearings (**Figure 19**) by pressing them into the brake drum with a suitable bearing driver seated against the outer bearing race. For additional information on bearing installation, refer to *Bearing Replacement* in Chapter One.

1. Blow any dirt or foreign matter out of the brake drum.

2. Two different size bearings are used. Refer to **Figure 20** to identify the new bearings:
   a. Outside bearing, A, **Figure 20**.
   b. Inside bearing, B, **Figure 20**.

3. Pack the bearings with grease.

4. Center the outside bearing in the brake drum bearing bore with its manufacturer's marks facing out (**Figure 21**).

5. Place a suitable bearing driver against the bearing's outer race (**Figure 22**).

CAUTION
Pressing against the inner bearing race will damage the bearing.

6. Press in the bearing until it bottoms in the bearing bore (**Figure 23**).

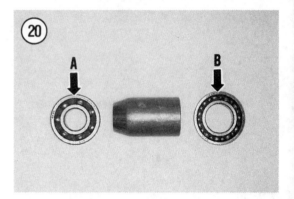

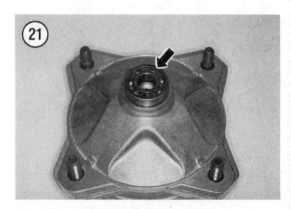

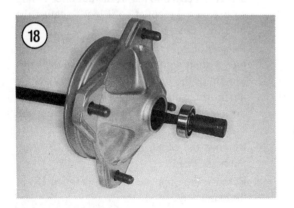

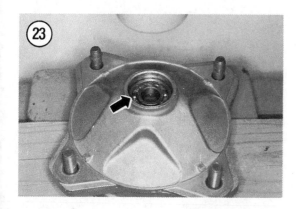

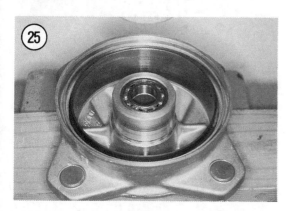

7. Turn the brake drum over and install the center spacer so its tapered end (**Figure 24**) seats against the outside bearing.

8. Center the inner bearing in the brake drum bearing bore with its manufacturer's marks facing out.

9. Place a suitable bearing driver against the bearing's outer race.

10. Press in the bearing until it bottoms in the bearing bore (**Figure 25**).

11. Turn each bearing with your fingers. Make sure they turn smoothly. Then install the brake drum on the front axle and turn it by hand. The brake drum should turn smoothly without binding or excessive play.

12. Install the brake drum as described in this chapter.

Brake Drum Seal Installation

1. Pack the seal lips with grease.

2. Place the seal squarely against the bore opening with its closed side facing out. Select a driver (**Figure 26**) with an outside diameter just slightly smaller than the seal's outside diameter.

3. Press in the seal until its outer surface is flush with the bore surface (**Figure 27**).

4. Lubricate the collar with grease and install it into the seal (**Figure 28**).

Brake Drum Installation

Refer to **Figure 2** for this procedure.

1. Clean the front axle bearing surface, threads and axle nut with solvent or contact cleaner. Blow dry with compressed air.

11

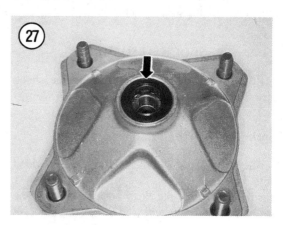

NOTE
If new brake shoes were installed, it may be necessary to loosen the front brake adjuster so the drum can slide over the shoes.

2. If necessary, lubricate the collar with grease and install it into the brake drum seal (**Figure 28**).

3. Carefully slide the brake drum over the axle so the inner bearing race is not damaged by the axle threads. Push the brake drum into position over the brake shoes (**Figure 29**).

4. Install the flat washer and axle nut (**Figure 30**). Tighten the axle nut to the torque specification in **Table 4**. Now check that one of the axle nut grooves aligns with the cotter pin hole in the front axle. If not, tighten the axle nut to align the groove and hole. Do not loosen the axle nut to align the groove and hole.

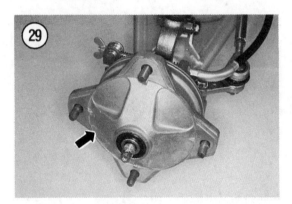

WARNING
Always install a new cotter pin.

5. Insert a new cotter pin through the axle nut groove and axle hole, then bend its arms to lock it in place (**Figure 31**).

6. Install the front wheel as described in this chapter.

7. Adjust the front brake as described in Chapter Three.

FRONT SUSPENSION

Figure 32 shows the front suspension system. The 2 Y-shaped control arms are bolted to mounting brackets welded to the frame. Ball joints connect both control arms to the steering knuckle. The ball joints are an integral part of the control arms and cannot be replaced separately.

Steering is controlled by tie rods connected to the steering shaft and steering knuckle.

SHOCK ABSORBER

Refer to **Figure 32** when servicing the shock absorbers.

Spring Preload Adjustment

The front shock absorber springs are provided with 5 preload positions. See **Figure 33**. The No. 1 position is soft and the No. 5 position is hard. The spring preload can be changed by rotating the cam

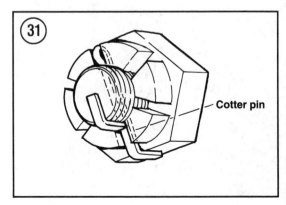

Cotter pin

FRONT SUSPENSION

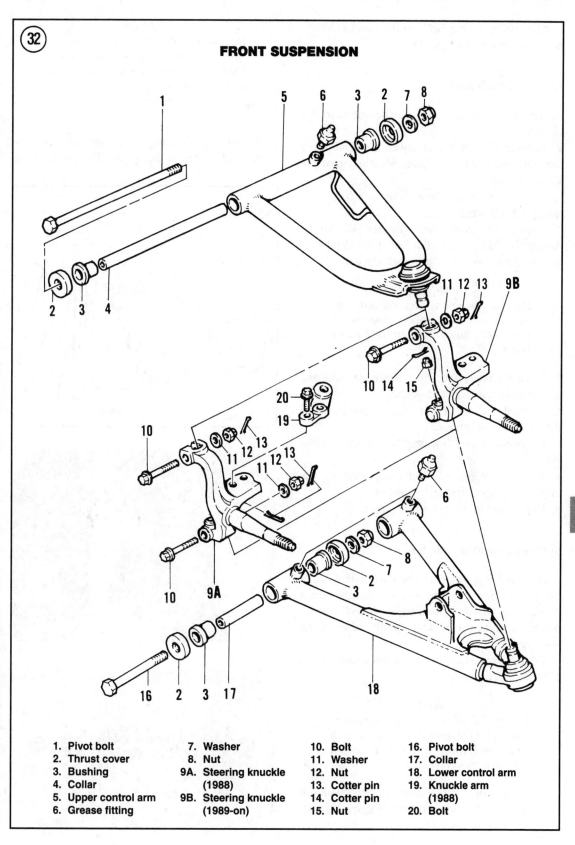

1. Pivot bolt
2. Thrust cover
3. Bushing
4. Collar
5. Upper control arm
6. Grease fitting
7. Washer
8. Nut
9A. Steering knuckle (1988)
9B. Steering knuckle (1989-on)
10. Bolt
11. Washer
12. Nut
13. Cotter pin
14. Cotter pin
15. Nut
16. Pivot bolt
17. Collar
18. Lower control arm
19. Knuckle arm (1988)
20. Bolt

11

at the end of the spring. Set both front shock absorbers to the same preload position.

Removal/Installation

1. Remove the front wheel(s) as described in this chapter.
2. Remove the upper and lower shock absorber mounting nuts and bolts (**Figure 34**) and remove the shock absorber.
3. Install by reversing these removal steps, while noting the following.
4. Inspect the damper unit (**Figure 35**). If the damper is leaking shock fluid or if the damper is dented, replace the shock absorber as a unit.

> ### WARNING
> *Do not attempt to disassemble the damper unit. Disassembly can release gas that is under pressure and cause injury.*

5. Clean the upper and lower mounting bolts and nuts in solvent and dry thoroughly.
6. Lubricate the upper and lower mounting bolts with a waterproof grease.
7. Install both shock mounting bolts from the front side.
8. Tighten the upper and lower shock mounting nuts to the torque specification in **Table 4**.
9. Repeat for the other shock absorber.

Spring Removal/Installation

The shock is spring-controlled and hydraulically damped. The shock damper unit is sealed and cannot be serviced. Service is limited to removal and replacement of the damper unit, spring and mounting bushings.

Table 1 lists spring rate specifications for all 1988-on shock absorbers.

> ### NOTE
> *Yamaha does not list replacement springs for the front shock absorbers. If replacement springs are needed, consult with an aftermarket supplier.*

1. Secure the lower shock mount in a vise with soft jaws, then turn the spring adjuster (**Figure 36**) to its softest position (**Figure 33**).

> ### WARNING
> *Do not remove the spring without a spring compressor. The spring is under considerable pressure and may fly off and cause injury.*

2. Mount a spring compressor onto the shock absorber and compress the spring. Then remove the

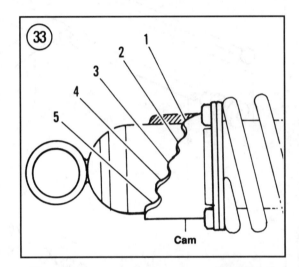

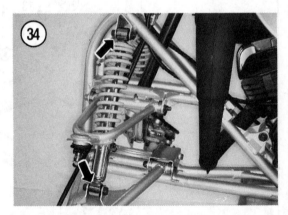

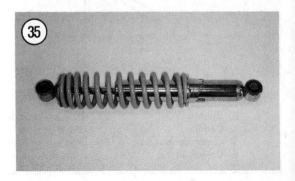

upper spring seat (A, **Figure 37**) and remove the spring.

3. Measure the spring free length (**Figure 38**) and compare it to the stock spring length specification in **Table 1**. Yamaha does not list a service limit for spring free length.

> *NOTE*
> *The damper is a sealed unit and cannot be rebuilt.*

36

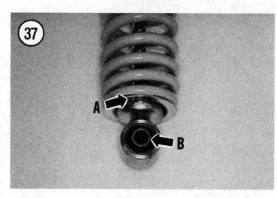

37

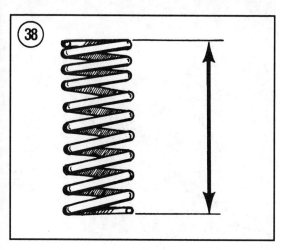

38

4. Check the damper unit. If the damper unit is leaking, dented or if the damper rod is bent, replace the shock absorber as a unit.

5. Check the shock bushings (B, **Figure 37**) for deterioration, excessive wear or other damage. If necessary, replace the bushings as follows:

> *CAUTION*
> *When supporting the shock absorber in a press, do not apply excessive pressure against the damper unit; otherwise you could dent or crush the damper wall.*

  a. Support the damper unit in a press and press out the damaged bushing.

  b. Clean the shock bushing bore to remove any dirt, rust or corrosion.

  c. Press in the new bushing until its outer surface is flush with the bushing bore inside surface as shown in B, **Figure 37**.

6. Assemble the shock by reversing these steps, while noting the following.

7. Install aftermarket springs by referring to their manufacturer's instructions.

8. Make sure the spring seat is properly seated in the spring (A, **Figure 37**).

9. Turn the spring adjuster to adjust the spring preload (**Figure 36**).

> *NOTE*
> *Adjust both shock absorbers to the same spring preload setting.*

STEERING KNUCKLE

Refer to **Figure 32** when servicing the steering knuckle.

Removal

1. Remove the front brake drum(s) as described in this chapter.

2. Remove the front brake backing plate as described in Chapter Thirteen.

3. Remove the front bumper as described in Chapter Fourteen.

> *CAUTION*
> *Do not hammer on any ball joint when trying to remove it. Doing so will damage the ball joint stud and threads. This will require a new ball joint (if available*

11

*separately) or complete replacement of
the tie rod or control arm assembly.*

4. To disconnect the tie rod end from the steering
knuckle:

    a. Remove the cotter pin from the tie rod stud
nut. Discard the cotter pin.

    b. Remove the castellated nut from the stud (**Figure 39**).

> *NOTE*
> *When using a puller to break the tie rod
> and control arm ball joints free, be sure
> not to damage the rubber seal (**Figure
> 40**).*

    c. Install a 2-jaw puller onto the steering knuckle
and center the puller's pressure bolt against the
stud as shown in **Figure 41**.

    d. Operate the puller to apply pressure against
the stud. Then stop and check that the puller is
not leaning to one side or tearing the rubber
seal. When the stud is under pressure, strike
the top of the puller with a hammer to free the
stud from the steering knuckle (**Figure 42**).

5. To disconnect the upper control arm ball joint
from the steering knuckle:

    a. Remove the cotter pin from the upper ball joint
stud mounting bolt. Discard the cotter pin.

    b. Remove the nut, washer and pinch bolt (A,
Figure 43) that holds the ball joint to the
steering knuckle.

    c. Lift the control arm (B, **Figure 43**) and its ball
joint off of the steering knuckle.

6A. On 1988 models, disconnect the lower control
arm ball joint from the steering knuckle as follows:

    a. Remove the cotter pin from the lower ball joint
stud mounting bolt. Discard the cotter pin.

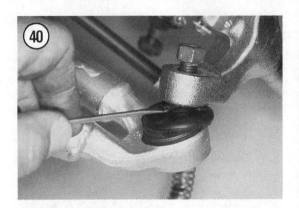

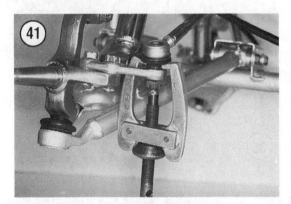

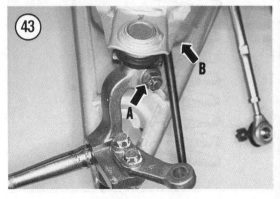

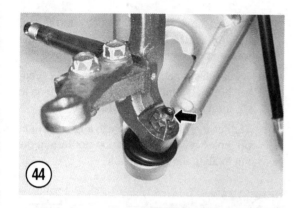

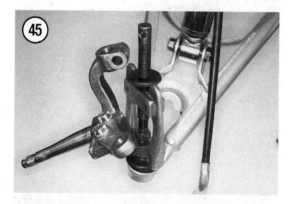

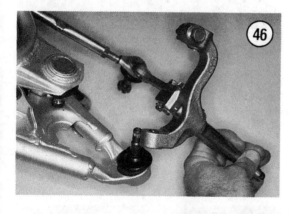

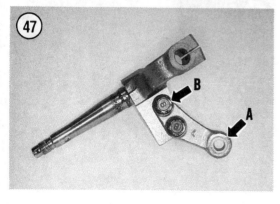

b. Remove the nut, washer and pinch bolt (**Figure 32**) that holds the ball joint to the steering knuckle.

6B. On 1989-on models, disconnect the lower control arm ball joint from the steering knuckle as follows:

a. Remove the cotter pin from the tie rod ball joint stud nut. Discard the cotter pin.

b. Remove the castellated nut from the ball joint stud (**Figure 44**).

NOTE
*When using a puller to break the tie rod and control arm ball joint free, be sure you do not damage the ball joint rubber seal (**Figure 40**).*

c. Install a 2-jaw puller onto the steering knuckle and center the puller's pressure bolt against the ball joint stud as shown in **Figure 45**.

d. Operate the puller to apply pressure against the ball joint stud. Then check that the puller is not leaning to one side or tearing the rubber seal. When the ball joint stud is under pressure, strike the top of the puller with a hammer to free the ball joint from the steering knuckle (**Figure 45**).

7. Remove the puller and steering knuckle (**Figure 46**).

8. To remove the knuckle arm (A, **Figure 47**) from the steering knuckle, remove the cotter pins and mounting bolts (B, **Figure 47**). Discard the cotter pins.

11

Inspection

1. Clean the steering knuckle in solvent and dry with compressed air.

2. Inspect the steering knuckle (**Figure 47**) for bending, thread damage, cracks or other damage.

3. Inspect the axle (**Figure 48**) for wear, corrosion or damage. A hard spill or collision may cause the axle to bend or fracture. If the axle is damaged or worn, replace the steering knuckle.

4. Check the hole (**Figure 49**) at the end of the spindle where the cotter pin fits. Make sure there are no fractures or cracks leading out toward the end of the steering knuckle. If cracks are present, replace the steering knuckle.

5. Check the knuckle arm (A, **Figure 47**) and replace if bent or damaged.

6. Check the pinch bolt(s), washers and nuts for damage. Replace damaged fasteners with the same strength fastener.

Installation

WARNING
All fasteners used in the front suspension and steering must be replaced with parts of the same type. Do not use a replacement part of lesser quality or substitute design, as it may affect the performance of vital components or systems or result in major repair expenses. Torque values indicated in **Table 4** *must be used during installation to ensure proper retention of these parts.*

1. If removed, install the knuckle arm (A, **Figure 47**) onto the steering knuckle as follows:
   a. The knuckle arms are marked with an L (left side) or R (right side). Install the knuckle arm onto its correct side.
   b. Install and tighten the knuckle arm mounting bolts (B, **Figure 47**) to the torque specification in **Table 4**.
   c. Install a new cotter pin through each knuckle arm mounting bolt hole. Bend the cotter pin arms to lock them in place.

2A. On 1988 models, install the lower control arm ball joint onto the steering knuckle as follows:
   a. Install the lower ball joint through the steering knuckle, then install the pinch bolt (**Figure 32**) from the front side.
   b. Hold the pinch bolt in place and lubricate the exposed bolt threads with a lithium based grease, then install the flat washer and nut.

CAUTION
Do not lubricate the pinch bolt before installing it through the steering knuckle. There must be no grease on the part of the bolt that contacts the steering knuckle clamp surfaces.

   c. Tighten the lower control arm ball joint pinch bolt nut to the torque specification in **Table 4**.

2B. On 1989-on models, install the lower control arm ball joint onto the steering knuckle as follows:

a. Position the steering knuckle between the control arms and install the lower control arm ball joint stud through the steering knuckle.
b. Thread the castellated nut onto the lower control arm ball joint (**Figure 44**), then tighten to the torque specification in **Table 4**.
c. Tighten the nut, if necessary, to align the cotter pin hole with the nut slot. Do not loosen the nut to align the slot and hole.

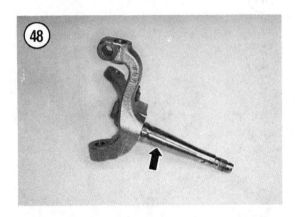

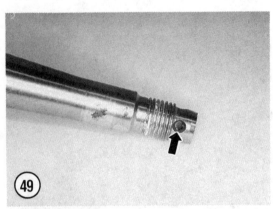

3. Install the upper control arm ball joint onto the steering knuckle as follows:

   a. Install the ball joint through the steering knuckle (**Figure 50**), then install the pinch bolt (**Figure 51**) from the front side.

   b. Lubricate the exposed pinch bolt threads with a lithium based grease, then install the flat washer and nut (**Figure 51**).

> *CAUTION*
> *Do not lubricate the pinch bolt before installing it through the steering knuckle. There must be no grease on the part of the bolt that contacts the steering knuckle clamp surfaces.*

   c. Tighten the upper ball joint pinch bolt nut to the torque specification in **Table 4**.

4. Install the tie rod end stud (**Figure 42**) through the steering knuckle as shown in **Figure 39**. Install the castellated nut and tighten to the torque specifi-

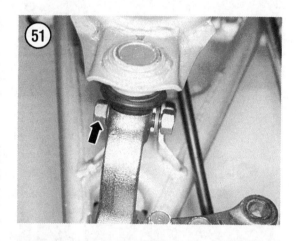

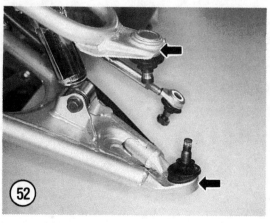

cation in **Table 4**. Tighten the nut, if necessary, to align the cotter pin hole with the nut slot.

5. Install *new* cotter pins through all studs. Open the cotter pin arms to lock them in place. See **Figure 39** and **Figure 44** (1989-on).

6. Install *new* cotter pins through all pinch bolt holes. Open the cotter pin arms to lock them in place. See A, **Figure 43** and **Figure 32** (1988).

7. Turn handlebar from side-to-side and make sure the steering knuckle moves smoothly.

8. Install the front bumper as described in Chapter Fourteen.

9. Install the front brake backing plate as described in Chapter Thirteen.

10. Install the front brake drum as described in this chapter.

CONTROL ARMS

Refer to **Figure 32** when servicing the upper and lower control arms.

Removal

1. Disconnect the control arm(s) from the steering knuckle as described under *Steering Knuckle* in this chapter.

2. Remove the shock absorber as described in this chapter.

3. Before removing the control arms (**Figure 52**), check their movement and side play as follows:

   a. Check the frame arm brackets for any type of damage. If you find a bent or damaged bracket, refer the frame repair to a qualified welding shop. A bent or damaged control arm bracket will affect the movement and position of the control arm(s).

   b. Loosen each control arm mounting bolt and nut, then retighten the nut to the torque specification in **Table 4**.

   c. Move the control arm up and down. The control arm should move smoothly without binding.

   d. Hold the end of the control arm and try to move it from side to side. Check for any noticeable side play.

   e. Replace the control arm inner collar, bushings and thrust covers as a set if there is any binding or noticeable side play.

11

4. Remove the nut, washer, pivot bolt and upper control arm (**Figure 53**).

5. Remove the nut from each pivot bolt that secures the lower control arm to the frame. Then remove the washers and pivot bolts (**Figure 54**).

Control Arm
Cleaning and Inspection

> *NOTE*
> *Do not intermix the pivot bolts, nuts, bushings and thrust covers when disassembling and cleaning the upper and lower control arms in the following steps. Separate the parts so they can be installed in their original mounting position.*

1. Remove the thrust covers and collars from the upper (**Figure 55**) and lower (**Figure 56**) control arms.

> *NOTE*
> *When cleaning the control arms, do not wash the ball joints (**Figure 57**) in solvent. Handle the ball joints carefully to prevent contaminating the grease or damaging the rubber boots.*

2. Clean parts in solvent and dry with compressed air.

3. Inspect both control arms for cracks, fractures and dents. If damage is severe, replace the control arm.

4. Inspect each bushing (A, **Figure 58**) and collar (B) set for severe wear or damage. Replace damaged parts.

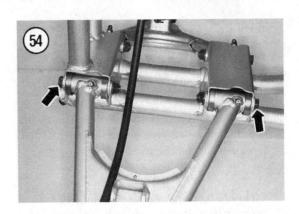

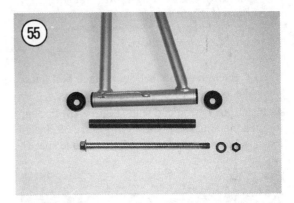

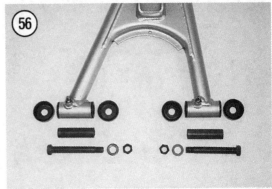

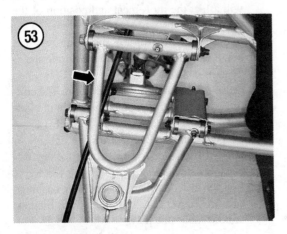

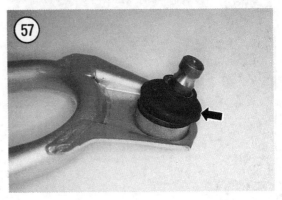

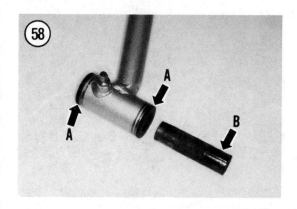

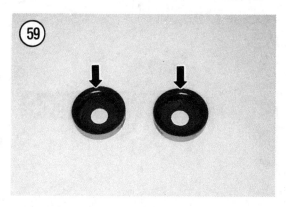

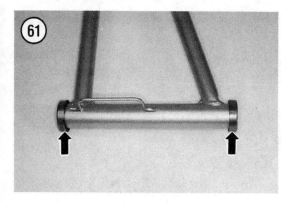

5. To replace the control arm bushings (A, **Figure 58**):

   a. Support the control arm and drive or press out the bushing. Repeat for each bushing.

   b. Clean the control arm bushing bores in solvent and dry thoroughly. Remove all rust and dirt residue.

   c. Support the control arm and press the bushing into place until its shoulder bottoms out.

6. Inspect the rubber seal (**Figure 59**) in each thrust cover. If the rubber seal has hardened or is damaged, replace the thrust cover.

7. Inspect the pivot bolts for bending or other damage. Replace damaged bolts.

> **WARNING**
> *Do not attempt to straighten a bent control arm or pivot bolt. Doing so may dangerously weaken the part and cause it to fail during operation.*

8. Inspect the control arm ball joints (**Figure 57**) as described under *Ball Joint Inspection and Replacement* in this chapter.

Ball Joints
Inspection and Replacement

A single ball joint (**Figure 57**) is permanently mounted on each control arm. Inspect the ball joint rubber boot for tears or other damage. The ball joint is packed with grease. If the rubber boot or ball joint is damaged, replace the control arm assembly as the ball joint cannot be replaced separately.

Installation

1. Apply waterproof grease to each of the following components (**Figure 55** and **Figure 56**):

   a. Collar.

   b. Thrust cover rubber seals.

   c. Pivot bolts.

2. Install the collar (**Figure 60**) and thrust covers (**Figure 61**) onto the upper control arm.

3. Install the 2 collars and 4 thrust covers (**Figure 62**) onto the lower control arm.

4. Position the lower control arm between its mounting brackets and install the pivot bolts, washers and nuts (**Figure 54**). Install both pivot bolts from the outside of the control arm as shown in

11

Figure 54. Tighten both control arm pivot bolt nuts to the torque specification in **Table 4**.

5. Install the front brake cable through the bracket on the bottom side of the upper control arm (**Figure 63**). Then position the upper control arm between its mounting brackets (**Figure 53**) and install the pivot bolt, washer and nut. Install the pivot bolt from the front side. Tighten the control arm pivot bolt nut to the torque specification in **Table 4**.

6. Raise and lower both control arms (**Figure 52**) by hand. The control arms should pivot smoothly without binding or noticeable side play.

7. Remove the shock absorber as described in this chapter.

8. Connect the control arm ball joints to the steering knuckle as described under *Steering Knuckle* in this chapter.

HANDLEBAR

Removal/Installation

1. Remove the front cover (Chapter Fourteen).
2. Remove the fuel tank (Chapter Eight).

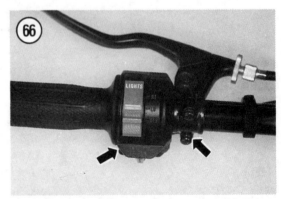

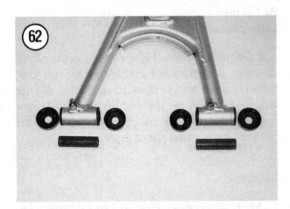

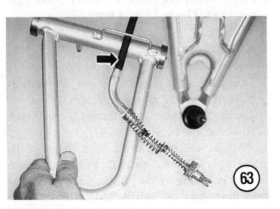

3. Remove the handlebar cover screws (**Figure 64**) and lift the cover off the handlebar.

4. Unhook the cable bands from both sides of the handlebar.

5. Remove the screws and clamps securing the throttle assembly and the front brake lever (**Figure 65**) to the handlebar. Lay both assemblies over the front fender.

6. Remove the screws securing the left-hand switch assembly (**Figure 66**) to the handlebar and set the switch assembly aside.

7. Remove the screws securing the clutch lever assembly (**Figure 66**) to the handlebar and set the lever assembly aside.

8. Remove the handlebar holder bolts, handlebar cover bracket and the handlebar holders (**Figure 67**).

9. Remove the handlebar.

10. Clean the knurled section of the handlebar with a wire brush. Clean the holders of any metal that may have been gouged loose by a slipping handlebar.

11. Inspect the handlebar holders, bolts and handlebar cover bracket for damage (**Figure 68**).

12. Reverse these steps to install the handlebar, while noting the following.

13. Install the handlebar holders with their punch mark facing forward.

14. Tighten the 2 front handlebar holder bolts first, then tighten the 2 rear bolts. Tighten all 4 handlebar holder bolts to the torque specification in **Table 4**. Then check that the front part of each clamp bottoms out against the steering stem as shown in A, **Figure 69**. The gap between the holders and steering stem must be at the rear of each holder assembly as shown in B, **Figure 69**.

15. Install the throttle housing and brake lever (**Figure 65**) as follows:

   a. Install the throttle housing projection into the notch in the front brake lever housing (**Figure 70**).

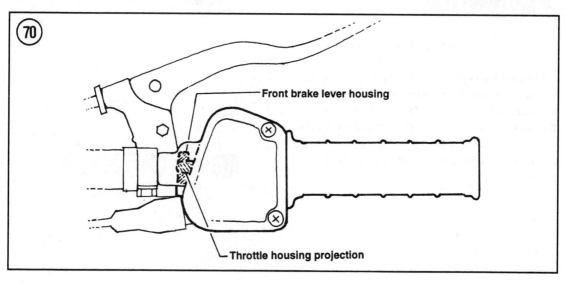

Front brake lever housing

Throttle housing projection

   b. Tighten the throttle housing (A, **Figure 71**) and front brake lever (B) screws to the torque specification in **Table 4**.

16. Check the clutch, brake and throttle cable adjustment as described in Chapter Three.

17. Check each switch and cable operation. Make sure that each cable operates correctly with no binding. Correct any problem at this time.

18. If the throttle moves slowly, binds or pivots roughly, refer to *Throttle Cable Replacement* in Chapter Eight for further information on throttle housing installation.

Handlebar Grip Replacement

1. Slide a thin screwdriver between the grip and handlebar.

2. Spray electrical contact cleaner into the opening under the grip. Then pull the screwdriver out and quickly twist the grip to break its bond against the handlebar. Slide the grip off.

3. Clean the handlebar of all rubber or sealer residue.

4. Install the new grip (**Figure 72**) following its manufacturer's directions. Apply an adhesive, such as ThreeBond Griplock (**Figure 73**), between the grip and handlebar. When applying grip adhesive, follow its manufacturer's directions for drying time.

> *WARNING*
> *Do not ride the vehicle until both grips are tight.*

TIE RODS

   Figure 74 is an exploded view of the steering shaft and tie rod assemblies. The tie rods are comprised of an inner end and outer end. All of the individual parts that make up the tie rod can be replaced separately.

   A 2-jaw puller (**Figure 75**) is required to separate the tie rod ends from the steering knuckle and steering shaft.

Removal

1. Support the vehicle and remove the front wheel(s) as described in this chapter.

> *CAUTION*
> *Do not hammer on any tie rod end to remove it. Doing so will damage the stud and threads.*

2. To disconnect the tie rod end from the steering knuckle:

   a. Remove the cotter pin from the tie rod stud nut. Discard the cotter pin.

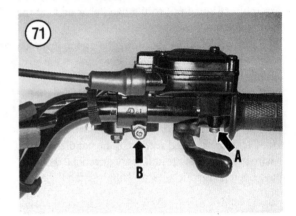

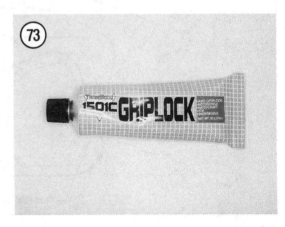

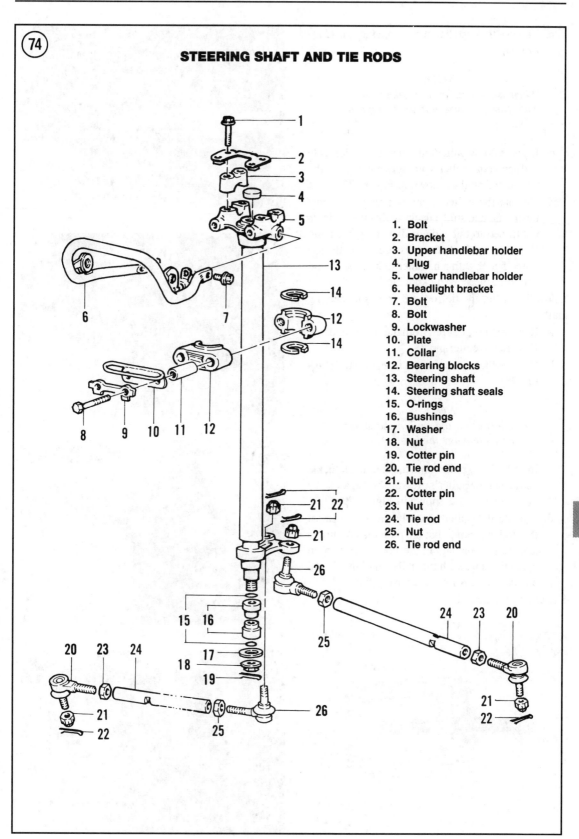

STEERING SHAFT AND TIE RODS

1. Bolt
2. Bracket
3. Upper handlebar holder
4. Plug
5. Lower handlebar holder
6. Headlight bracket
7. Bolt
8. Bolt
9. Lockwasher
10. Plate
11. Collar
12. Bearing blocks
13. Steering shaft
14. Steering shaft seals
15. O-rings
16. Bushings
17. Washer
18. Nut
19. Cotter pin
20. Tie rod end
21. Nut
22. Cotter pin
23. Nut
24. Tie rod
25. Nut
26. Tie rod end

11

b. Remove the castellated nut from the stud (**Figure 76**).

NOTE
When using a puller to break the tie rod ends free, be sure not to damage the boot.

c. Install a 2-jaw puller onto the steering knuckle and center the puller's pressure bolt against the tie rod end stud as shown in **Figure 77**.

d. Operate the puller to apply pressure against the tie rod end stud, checking that the puller is not turned to one side or damaging the boot. When the stud is under pressure, strike the top of the puller with a hammer to free the tie rod end from the steering knuckle.

3. To disconnect the tie rod end from the steering shaft:

a. Remove the cotter pin from the tie rod end nut. Discard the cotter pin.

b. Remove the castellated nut from the stud (**Figure 78**).

NOTE
When installing the puller, make sure you do not damage the boot.

c. Install a 2-jaw puller onto the steering knuckle and center the puller's pressure bolt against the tie rod end stud as shown in **Figure 79**.

d. Operate the puller to apply pressure against the stud, checking that the puller is not turned sideways or damaging the boot. Continue to apply pressure with the puller until the tie rod end pops free from the steering shaft.

4. Remove the tie rod.

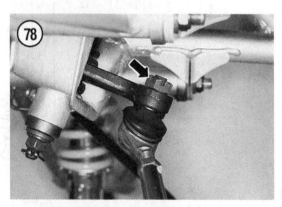

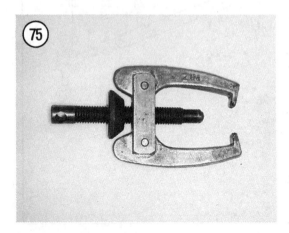

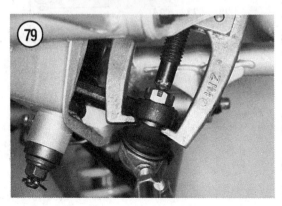

Inspection

> *CAUTION*
> *Do not immerse the tie rod ends into solvent when cleaning the tie rod in these steps. The solvent will contaminate the grease, requiring replacement of the tie rod end.*

1. Inspect the tie rod shaft (A, **Figure 80**) for damage. There should be no creases or bends along the shaft. Check with a straightedge placed against the tie rod shaft.

2. Inspect the rubber boot at each tie rod end (**Figure 81**). The tie rod ends are permanently packed with grease. If the rubber boot is damaged, dirt and moisture can enter the joint and destroy it. If the boot is damaged in any way, disassemble the tie rod and replace the tie rod end(s). Refer to *Tie Rod Disassembly/Reassembly* in this chapter.

3. Pivot the tie rod end stud (**Figure 81**) back and forth by hand. If the tie rod end moves roughly or with excessive play, replace it as described in the following procedure.

Tie Rod
Disassembly/Reassembly

Refer to **Figure 82** when performing this procedure.

1. Hold the tie rod with a wrench across the shaft flat (B, **Figure 80**), then loosen the locknut for the tie rod end being replaced.

> *NOTE*
> *The locknut securing the outside tie rod end (C, **Figure 80**) has left-hand threads. The inside tie rod end locknut (D, **Figure 80**) has right-hand threads.*

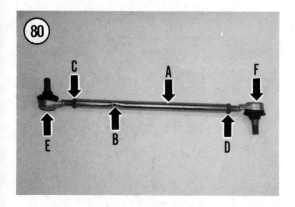

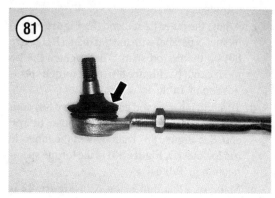

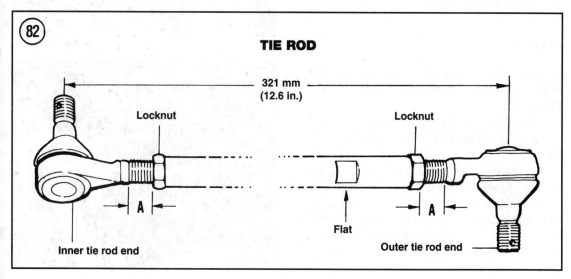

TIE ROD

321 mm (12.6 in.)

Locknut

Locknut

A

A

Flat

Inner tie rod end

Outer tie rod end

2. Unscrew and remove the damaged tie rod end(s).

3. Clean the mating shaft and tie rod end threads with contact cleaner.

4. Identify the new tie rod end with the drawing in **Figure 82**. The outside (E, **Figure 80**) and inside (F, **Figure 80**) tie rod ends are different. Likewise, the left and right tie rod shafts are different.

5. Thread the tie rod end and its locknut into the tie rod shaft.

6. Referring to **Figure 82**, adjust the tie rod length and position the tie rod ends as follows:

   a. Adjust the tie rod ends to obtain the tie rod length measurement shown in **Figure 82**.

NOTE
When adjusting the tie rods in the following steps, note that dimension A in ***Figure 82*** *must be equal for both ends.*

   b. Align both tie rod ends, then continue with substep c.

   c. Adjust the outer tie rod end (E, **Figure 80**) so its stud is parallel with the flat mark (B, **Figure 80**) on the tie rod shaft. Then tighten the tie rod locknut (C, **Figure 80**) to the torque specification in **Table 4**.

   d. Turn the inner tie rod end (F, **Figure 80**) so it is at a 164-166° angle with the outer tie rod end. See **Figure 83**. Then tighten the inner tie rod locknut (D, **Figure 80**) to the torque specification in **Table 4**.

   e. Make sure that dimension A in **Figure 82** is equal for both sides.

Installation

1. Identify the left and right side tie rods by referring to the position of the inner tie rod ends shown in **Figure 83**.

2. Install the tie rod assembly so the flat end of the tie rod shaft (**Figure 84**) is attached to the steering knuckle.

3. Attach the tie rod assembly to the steering shaft (**Figure 78**) and steering knuckle (**Figure 76**).

4. Thread the castellated nut onto each tie rod end stud and tighten to the torque specification in **Table 4**. Tighten the nut(s), if necessary, to align the cotter pin hole with the nut slot. Do not loosen the nut to align the slot and hole.

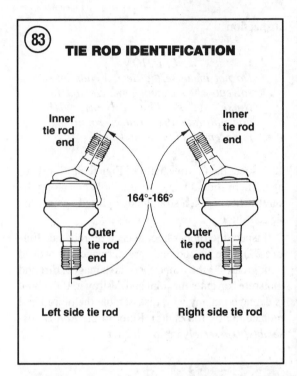

TIE ROD IDENTIFICATION

Inner tie rod end

Inner tie rod end

164°-166°

Outer tie rod end

Outer tie rod end

Left side tie rod   Right side tie rod

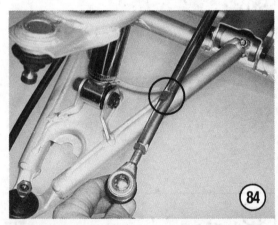

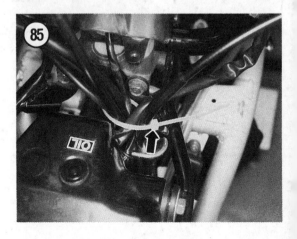

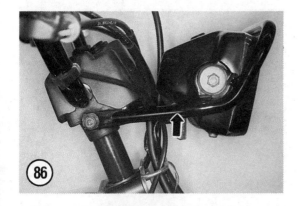

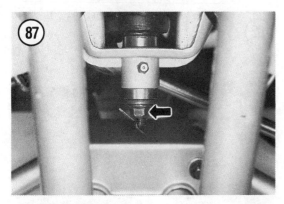

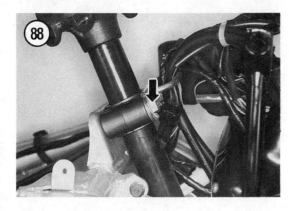

5. Install *new* cotter pins through all tie rod end studs. Bend the cotter pin arms to lock them in place.

6. Install the front wheels as described in this chapter.

7. Check the toe-in and adjust if necessary, as described in Chapter Three.

STEERING SHAFT

Figure 74 is an exploded view of the steering shaft and related components. The steering shaft turns on split bearing blocks at the top and a dual solid bushing assembly at the lower end. Adjustable tie rods connect the steering shaft to the steering knuckles.

Removal

1. Park the vehicle on level ground and set the parking brake.

2. Remove both front wheels as described in this chapter.

3. Remove the seat and front fender as described in Chapter Fourteen.

4. Remove the fuel tank as described in Chapter Eight.

5. Secure the cables and wiring harness with a large plastic tie wrap (**Figure 85**).

6. Remove the handlebar cover screws (**Figure 64**) and lift the cover off the handlebar.

7. Remove the headlight holder bracket bolts and holder (**Figure 86**).

8. Remove the handlebar as described in this chapter.

9. Disconnect both tie rods from the steering shaft as described under *Tie Rods* in this chapter.

10. Remove the cotter pin, steering nut and washer (**Figure 87**) from the bottom of the steering shaft.

11. Make a diagram of the control cables and wiring harness as they pass around the steering shaft for reassembly reference.

12. Pry the lockwasher tabs away from the bolts securing the upper bearing blocks to the frame.

13. Remove the bolts (**Figure 88**) that hold the upper bearing blocks to the frame. Then remove the outer block, collars, split dust seals and inner block assembly.

14. Carefully lift the steering shaft (**Figure 89**) out of the lower frame mount and remove it from the frame.

11

Inspection

1. Clean and dry all parts.
2. Inspect the steering shaft assembly (**Figure 90**). Replace the shaft if bent, twisted or if it shows any other type of damage. Running a damaged shaft will cause rapid bearing wear and place excessive stress on the frame and other steering components. Check for a bent shaft using a set of V-blocks and dial indicator (**Figure 91**).

> *WARNING*
> *Do not straighten a bent steering shaft in an attempt to reuse it. Doing so may weaken the shaft and cause it to fail during operation.*

> *NOTE*
> **Figure 92** *shows a bent steering shaft. The area where the upper bearing block rides (**Figure 92**) is excessively worn.*

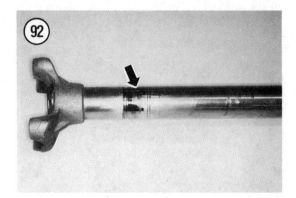

3. Inspect the tie rod attachment holes (**Figure 93**) in the lower section of the steering shaft. Check for hole elongation, cracks or wear. Replace the steering shaft if necessary.
4. Inspect the lower steering shaft bushing surface (**Figure 94**) for scoring, excessive wear or other damage. Check the cotter pin hole for cracks or other damage.
5. Inspect the handlebar mount (**Figure 95**) on the steering shaft for:
   a. Cracked handlebar holder surfaces.
   b. Damaged handlebar threaded holes.
   c. Damaged headlight bracket threaded holes.
6. Inspect the bearing block assembly (**Figure 96**) for:
   a. Excessively worn or damaged dust seals (A, **Figure 96**).

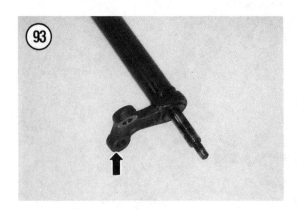

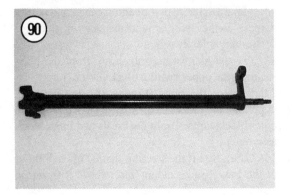

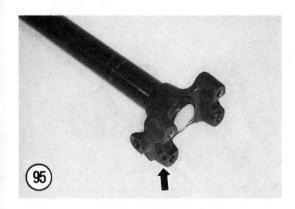

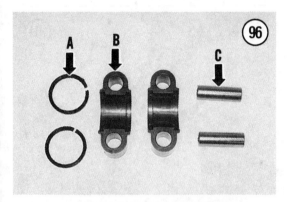

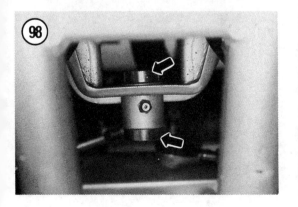

b. Excessively worn or damaged bearing block halves (B, **Figure 96**). Check the dust seal grooves for damage.

c. Corroded or bent collars (C, **Figure 96**). Remove any rust or corrosion with a wire wheel.

7. Clean the lower steering bushings (**Figure 97**) of all old grease.

8. Inspect the O-ring (**Figure 97**) installed in each steering shaft bushing (**Figure 98**). Replace the O-rings if worn or damaged. Lubricate new and used O-rings with grease before installing them.

9. Inspect the bushing surfaces on both the upper and lower bushings. Look for deep wear grooves, cracks or other damage that would allow excessive steering shaft play. If necessary, replace both bushings as a set as described in this section.

10. Inspect the steering shaft bracket on the frame (**Figure 99**) for cracked welds, a bent frame tube or other damage. Refer repair of this type to a welding shop.

Steering Shaft Bushing Replacement

Always replace the upper and lower bushings (**Figure 98**) as a set.

1. Carefully drive the upper and lower bushings out of the frame.

2. Clean the frame area thoroughly. Then check it for cracks or other damage.

NOTE
The upper and lower bushings are identical.

3. Install the upper and lower bushings into the frame. Due to the cramped working area, pull the bushings into place with a threaded rod, large wash-

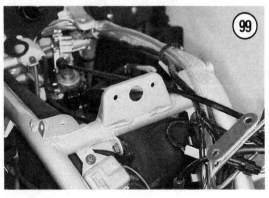

ers and nuts. Install the bushings so their shoulder bottoms against the frame tube.

Installation

1. Lubricate the 2 steering shaft bushing O-rings with grease. Then install an O-ring into each steering bushing groove (**Figure 97**). Make sure the O-rings are correctly seated in the grooves.

2. Lubricate the lower steering shaft bushing surface with grease.

3. Install the steering shaft into the frame with the tie rod brackets toward the back and carefully install its lower end into the lower bushing assembly.

4. Install the washer and steering shaft nut (**Figure 87**). Tighten the nut finger-tight.

5. Assemble and install the upper bearing assembly (**Figure 96**) as follows:

   a. Grease the inner diameter of both bearing block halves.

   b. Grease the dust seals and install them into one of the bearing block halves (**Figure 100**). This bearing block with the dust seals will now be referred to as the inner bearing block.

> *NOTE*
> *The inner and outer bearing block halves are identical.*

   c. Install the inner bearing block and the 2 dust seals between the frame and steering shaft (**Figure 101**).

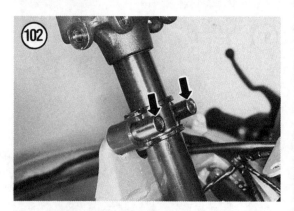

   d. Install the 2 collars (**Figure 102**) and the outer bearing block (**Figure 103**). Be sure the 2 dust seals seat in the grooves in both bearing blocks. Align the bearing blocks with the 2 frame bracket holes.

   e. Install the cable holder, a new lockwasher and the 2 steering shaft bearing block bolts (**Figure 104**).

   f. Tighten the 2 steering shaft bearing block bolts (**Figure 104**) to the torque specification in **Table 4**.

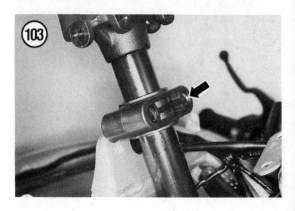

6. Tighten the steering shaft nut (**Figure 87**) to the torque specification in **Table 4**.

7. Turn the steering shaft from side to side. The steering shaft must turn smoothly with no binding or excessive play. If there is a problem, disassemble the bearing block halves and inspect the parts.

8. Bend the lockwasher tabs that secure the bearing block bolts (**Figure 104**) around the bolt heads.

9. Install a new cotter pin through the steering shaft hole (**Figure 87**) and bend its arms over completely.

10. Connect both tie rods to the steering shaft as described under *Tie Rods* in this chapter.

11. Install the handlebar as described in this chapter.

12. Install the headlight holder and tighten its mounting bolts (**Figure 86**) to the torque specification in **Table 4**.

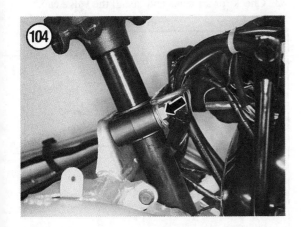

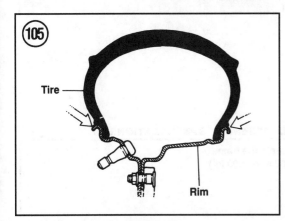

Tire

Rim

13. Install the handlebar cover and its screws (**Figure 64**).

14. Remove the plastic tie wrap previously installed around the control cables and wiring harness.

15. Install the fuel tank as described in Chapter Eight.

16. Install the seat and front fender as described in Chapter Fourteen.

17. Check the toe-in adjustment as described in Chapter Three.

TIRES AND WHEELS

The Blaster is equipped with tubeless, low pressure tires designed specifically for off-road use only. Rapid tire wear will occur if the vehicle is ridden on paved surfaces.

Tire Changing

The front and rear tire rims used on all models are of the 2-piece type and have a very deep built-in ridge (**Figure 105**) to keep the tire bead seated on the rim under severe riding conditions. Unfortunately it also tends to keep the tire on the rim during tire removal as well.

A bead breaker (**Figure 106**) is required for breaking the tire away from the rim.

1. Remove the valve stem cap and core and deflate the tire. Do not reinstall the core at this time.

2. Lubricate the tire bead and rim flanges with liquid dishwashing detergent or any rubber lubricant. Press the tire sidewall/bead down to allow the liquid to run into and around the bead area. Also apply lubricant to the area where the bead breaker arm will contact the tire sidewall.

3. Position the wheel into the tire removal tool (**Figure 106**).

4. Slowly work the tire tool, making sure the tool is up against the inside of the rim, and break the tire bead away from the rim.

5. Using your hands, press down on the tire on either side of the tool and try to break the rest of the bead free from the rim.

6. If the rest of the tire bead cannot be broken loose, raise the tool, rotate the tire/rim assembly and repeat Steps 4 and 5 until the entire bead is broken loose from the rim.

7. Turn the wheel over and repeat to break the opposite side loose.

11

8. Remove the tire rims from the tire.

9. Inspect the rim sealing surface of the rim. If the rim has been severely hit, it will probably cause an air leak. Repair or replace the rim as required.

10. Inspect the tire for cuts, tears, abrasions or any other defects.

11. Clean the rims and tire sealing surfaces.

12. If used, inspect the large O-ring seal (**Figure 107**). If it is starting to harden or deteriorate, replace it.

13. Set the tire into position on the outer rim.

14. Apply a light coat of grease to the large O-ring seal (if used) and place it in the groove in the rim (**Figure 107**).

15. Install the inner rim into the tire and onto the outer rim. Align the bolt holes.

16. Install the wheel onto its hub and install the wheel nuts and washers. Tighten the wheel nuts to the torque specification in **Table 4**.

17. Install the valve stem core.

18. Apply tire mounting lubricate to the tire bead and inflate the tire to the seating pressure specifications listed in **Table 3**.

19. Deflate the tire and let it sit for about one hour.

20. Inflate the tire to the recommended operating air pressure listed in **Table 3**.

21. Check the rim line molded into the tire around the edge of the rim. It must be equally spaced all the way around. If the rim line spacing is not equal, the tire bead is not properly seated. Deflate the tire and unseat the bead completely. Lubricate the bead and reinflate the tire.

22. Check for air leaks and install the valve cap.

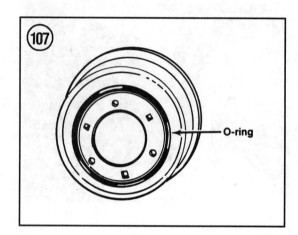

Table 1 FRONT SUSPENSION AND STEERING SPECIFICATIONS

Frame type	Steel tube frame
Front wheel travel	180 mm (7.09 in.)
Steering lock-to-lock angle	
Left	40°
Right	40°
Caster angle	9°
Trail	40 mm (1.57 in.)
Tread (standard)	
Rear	780 mm (30.7 in.)
Front	820 mm (32.3 in.)
Toe-in	0-10 mm (0-0.39 in.)
Front suspension type	Double wishbone
Front shock absorber	Coil spring/oil damper
Shock absorber travel	90 mm (3.54 in.)
Shock absorber spring free length	226.6 mm (8.93 in.)
Shock spring rate	
K1	3.0 kg/mm (168 in.-lb.)
K2	3.5 kg/mm (196 in.-lb.)
Shock stroke	
K1	0-46.7 mm (0-1.84 in.)
K2	46.7-112.2 mm (1.84-4.42 in.)

Table 2 TIRE AND WHEEL SPECIFICATIONS

Tires	
Type	Tubeless
Size	
Front	AT21 × 7-10
Rear	AT21 × 10-8
Type	
Front	Dunlop KT894A/Cheng Shim C873N
Rear	Dunlop KT8995A/Cheng Shim C874N
Rims	
Type	Panel wheel
Material	Steel
Size	
Front	10 × 5.5 AT
Rear	8 × 8.0 AT
Runout limit	2.0 mm (0.08 in.)

Table 3 TIRE INFLATION PRESSURE

	Front kPa (psi)	Rear kPa (psi)
Operating pressure	30 (4.3)	25 (3.6)
Minimum tire pressure	27 (3.8)	22 (3.1)
Maximum tire pressure	33 (4.7)	28 (4.0)
Tire pressure to seat tires on rim	250 (36)	190 (27)

Table 4 FRONT SUSPENSION TIGHTENING TORQUES

	N•m	in.-lb.	ft.-lb.
Control arm pivot bolt nuts	30	–	22
Front axle nut	70	–	51
Front brake lever housing mounting screws	10	88	–
Front shock absorber mounting nuts	45	–	33
Front wheel nuts	45	–	33
Handlebar holder mounting bolts	20	–	14
Headlight holder mounting bracket	15	–	11
Knuckle arm mounting bolts	38	–	27
Lower control arm ball joint pinch bolt nut			
1988	48	–	35
Lower control arm ball joint nut			
1989-on	25	–	18
Steering shaft bearing block bolts	23	–	17
Steering shaft nut	30	–	22
Throttle housing mounting screws	10	88	–
Tie rod nuts at steering knuckle	25	–	18
Tie rod nuts at steering shaft	25	–	18
Tie rod locknut	30	–	22
Upper control arm ball joint pinch bolt nut	48	–	35

11

CHAPTER TWELVE

REAR SUSPENSION

This chapter contains repair and replacement procedures for the rear wheels, rear axle assembly and rear suspension. Service to the rear suspension consists of periodically checking bolt tightness, lubrication of all pivot points, swing arm bushing and bearing replacement and rear shock service.

Rear suspension specifications are listed in **Table 1**. Drive chain size and link numbers are listed in **Table 2**. Tightening torques are listed in **Table 3**. **Tables 1-3** are located at the end of this chapter.

REAR WHEELS

Refer to **Figure 1** when servicing the rear wheels.

Removal/Installation

1. Park the vehicle on level ground and set the parking brake. Block the front wheels so the vehicle cannot roll in either direction.
2. Loosen the rear wheel nuts (**Figure 2**).
3. Lift the vehicle so both rear wheels are off the ground, then support it with jackstands or wooden blocks.
4. Remove the wheel nuts (**Figure 2**) and the rear wheel.
5. Install by reversing these removal steps, noting the following.
6. Install the wheel over the rear hub studs and install the wheel nuts finger-tight. Check that the wheel is sitting flush against the hub.
7. Tighten the rear wheel nuts to the torque specification in **Table 3**.

REAR WHEEL HUBS

Refer to **Figure 1** when servicing the rear wheel hubs in this section.

Removal/Installation

1. Remove the rear wheel as described in this chapter.
2. Remove and discard the axle nut cotter pin.
3. Loosen the nut securing the wheel hub to the rear axle. Then remove the nut and washer (**Figure 3**).
4. Slide the wheel hub (**Figure 3**) off the axle and remove it. If the wheel hub is stuck to the axle, remove it with a puller as shown in **Figure 4**.

CAUTION
The axle hub is designed to be a sliding fit on the axle. However, corrosion on the wheel hub and axle splines (Figure 5) can lock the hub in place. Do not drive the wheel hub off of the axle as the force may damage the wheel hub. Use a puller to remove the hub.

5. Clean the wheel hub and axle splines of all rust and corrosion.
6. Inspect the wheel hub (**Figure 6**). If the wheel hub is bent, damaged or has damaged studs, replace it as an assembly.
7. Check the end of the axle (**Figure 7**) for damaged threads or a cracked cotter pin hole. If damage is noted, replace the rear axle as described in this chapter.
8. Slide the wheel hub (**Figure 3**) onto the axle.
9. Install the washer (**Figure 3**) onto the axle shaft.
10. Thread the rear wheel hub nut (**Figure 3**) onto the axle, then tighten to the torque specification in **Table 3**. Tighten the axle nut, if necessary, to align the cotter pin hole with the slot in the nut. Do not loosen the nut to align the hole and slot.

WARNING
Do not reuse the wheel hub cotter pin.

11. Install a *new* cotter pin through the nut groove and rear axle hole, then bend the cotter pin arms to lock it as shown in **Figure 8**.
12. Install the rear wheel as described in this chapter.

REAR AXLE

Figure 1 shows the rear axle and driven sprocket in relation to the rear axle housing. This section describes complete service to these components. Service to the axle housing and its bearings is described later in this chapter.

The driven sprocket can be removed with the rear axle installed on the vehicle. To remove the driven sprocket without removing the rear axle, refer to *Driven Sprocket* in this chapter.

The brake disc can be removed with the rear axle installed on the vehicle. To remove the brake disc without removing the rear axle, refer to *Brake Disc* in Chapter Thirteen.

When removing and installing the rear axle, a 50 mm wrench will is required to loosen and tighten the axle housing nuts. Use the Yamaha axle nut wrench (part No. YM-37132) [**Figure 9**]) or an equivalent torque adapter wrench that can be used with a torque wrench and breaker bar. Proper tightening of the axle housing nuts is critical to prevent the nuts from backing off and allowing the axle to slide out of the housing.

To avoid starting a procedure that you may be unable to complete, read the following sections through before starting work. Note any tool that you may need and acquire it before starting.

Removal

1. Park the vehicle on level ground and set the parking brake.
2. Support the vehicle and remove both rear wheels as described in this chapter.
3. Remove the rear wheel hubs as described in this chapter.
4. Remove the outer (A, **Figure 10**) and inner (B) axle nuts as follows:
   a. Clean the exposed axle threads with contact cleaner.
   b. Using the Yamaha axle nut wrench and a breaker bar, turn the inner axle nut 1/8 turn *clockwise* (toward the driven sprocket) to break it free (**Figure 11**).
   c. Then turn the outer axle nut *counterclockwise* to loosen it (**Figure 12**).
   d. Both axle nuts (**Figure 13**) should now spin freely on the axle.

12

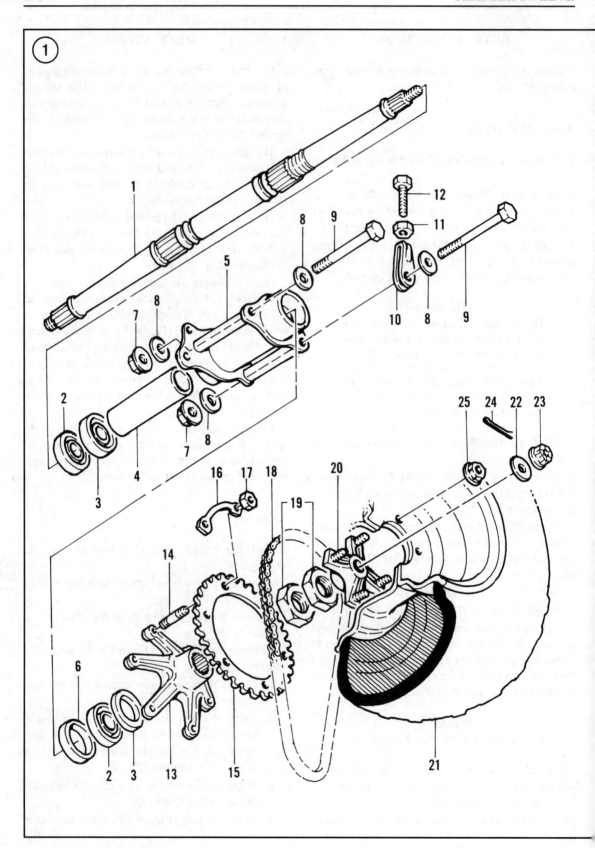

REAR AXLE

1. Rear axle
2. Axle seal
3. Bearing
4. Spacer
5. Rear axle housing
6. Inner collar
7. Nut
8. Washer
9. Bolt
10. Chain adjuster
11. Locknut
12. Chain adjuster bolt
13. Sprocket hub
14. Stud
15. Driven sprocket
16. Lockwasher
17. Nut
18. Drive chain
19. Axle nuts
20. Wheel hub
21. Tire/wheel assembly
22. Washer
23. Axle nut
24. Cotter pin
25. Wheel nut

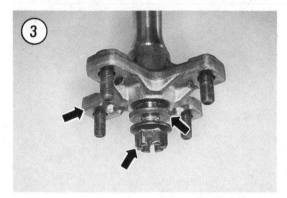

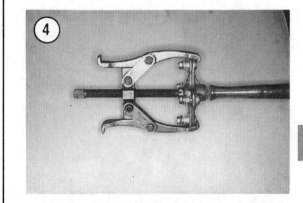

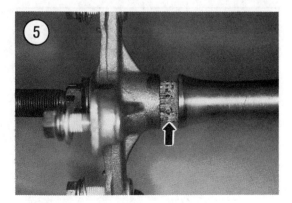

12

5. Remove the bolts that hold the underguard (**Figure 14**) to the rear axle housing. Then free the underguard from the axle housing and remove it.

6. Remove the drive chain as described in this chapter.

7. Remove both axle nuts (**Figure 13**).

NOTE
If you are going to replace the driven sprocket or the sprocket hub, loosen the sprocket nuts before removing the driven sprocket from the rear axle.

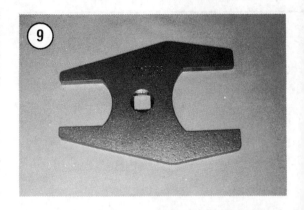

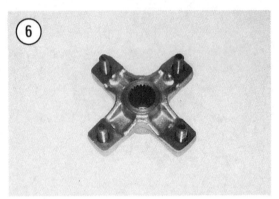

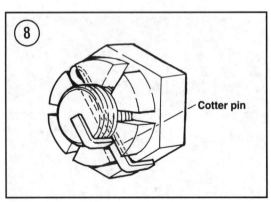

Cotter pin

8. Remove the driven sprocket (**Figure 15**) and its hub from the rear axle.

9. Release the parking brake.

10. Remove the bolts (A, **Figure 16**) that hold the rear brake caliper (B) to the axle housing. Then slide the brake caliper (B, **Figure 16**) off the brake disc and hang it on a piece of stiff wire.

NOTE
Insert a plastic spacer in the caliper between the brake pads. Then, if the brake pedal is inadvertently pressed, the piston will not be forced out of the caliper bore. If this does happen, the caliper must be partially disassembled to reseat the piston.

11. Remove the rear axle (**Figure 17**) as follows:
   a. Make sure the vehicle is secured on its stand.
   b. Slide the left axle hub (A, **Figure 18**) onto the axle.

WARNING
Safety glasses must be worn when driving the axle out of the housing in the following steps.

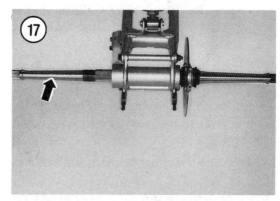

12

CAUTION
When removing the rear axle, never hit directly against the axle as this will damage the axle threads. Use a piece of pipe and hammer as described in the following procedure.

c. Center a piece of pipe against the axle hub as shown in B, **Figure 18**. Drive the pipe with a hammer and remove the axle from the right side. See **Figure 19**.

NOTE
If the axle housing spacer (4, **Figure 1**) seizes onto the rear axle, it will knock out the right side axle housing seal and bearing (**Figure 20**) as it is removed with the axle. If this happens, refer to **Axle Disassembly** in this chapter, to remove the spacer, bearing, seal and brake disc.

d. When the axle is free of the axle housing, remove the left axle hub (A, **Figure 18**) and carefully slide the axle out of the axle housing and remove it. See **Figure 19**.

12. Remove the brake disc as described under *Brake Disc* in Chapter Thirteen.

13. Inspect the axle housing seals (**Figure 21**) and bearings as described under *Axle Housing* in this chapter.

14. Inspect the rear axle as described in this chapter.

Axle Disassembly

If the axle housing spacer, right bearing and right seal (**Figure 20**) comes off with the axle, remove them as follows.

1. Assemble a bearing splitter and puller onto the axle as shown in **Figure 22** and pull the spacer (**Figure 23**) off the axle.

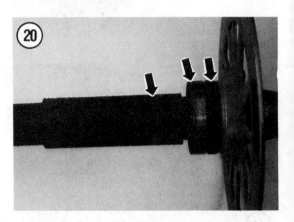

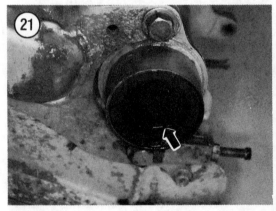

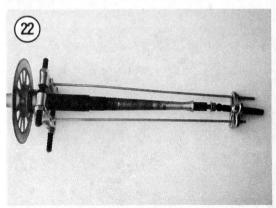

2. Remove the brake disc as described under *Brake Disc Removal/Installation* in Chapter Thirteen.

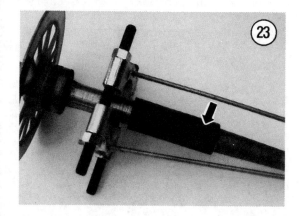

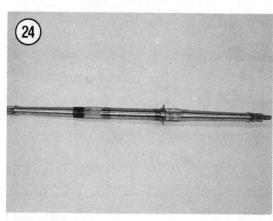

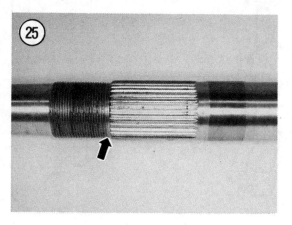

3. Support the axle assembly in a press and press the axle off the right bearing and the right seal.

4. Remove the axle from the press.

Inspection

1. Wash the axle (**Figure 24**) in solvent and dry thoroughly. Handle the axle carefully to prevent scoring the bearing surfaces and splines on the axle.

2. Inspect the axle for signs of fatigue, fractures and other damage. Inspect the splines and threads (**Figure 25**) for wear or damage.

3. Check the hole (**Figure 7**) at each end of the axle where the cotter pin fits. Make sure there are no fractures or cracks leading out toward the end of the axle. If cracks are noted, replace the axle.

4. Check the 2 bearing machined surfaces (A, **Figure 26**) on the axle for scoring, chatter marks or other damage.

5. Inspect the brake disc dust cover (B, **Figure 26**). If the dust cover is bent or damaged, replace it using a press. Install the dust cover so its shoulder faces toward the left side of the axle.

6. Check the axle for straightness using a set of V-blocks and a dial indicator (**Figure 27**) and compare to the runout limit in **Table 1**. Replace the axle if its runout is out of specification.

12

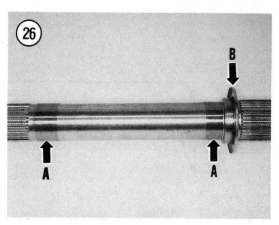

7. Inspect the axle nuts (**Figure 28**) for wear or damage. Replace the axle nuts if the threads are damaged or if the hex portion of the nut is rounded over or damaged.

8. Inspect the driven sprocket hub (**Figure 29**) splines. Replace the hub if the splines are excessively worn or damaged.

Installation

1. Install the brake disc (**Figure 30**) onto the rear axle as described in Chapter Thirteen.

2. Apply a light coat of wheel bearing grease to the lips of both axle housing seals (**Figure 31**).

3. Apply a light coat of grease onto the brake disc dust cover shoulder (**Figure 32**).

4. Working from the right side, slide the rear axle assembly into the axle housing until it stops (**Figure 33**).

5. Install the right side wheel hub onto the end of the axle as shown in **Figure 34**.

> *WARNING*
> *Safety glasses must be worn when driving the axle into the axle housing in the following steps.*

> *CAUTION*
> *When installing the rear axle, never hit the axle or you may damage the axle and threads. Use a piece of pipe and hammer as described in the following step.*

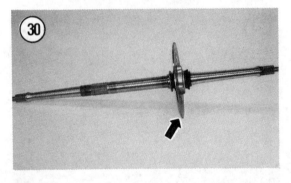

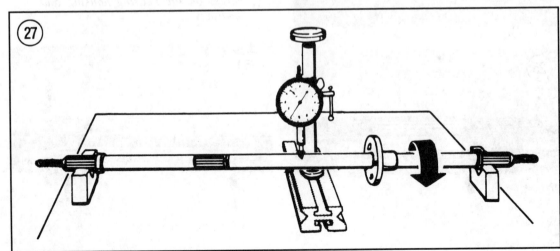

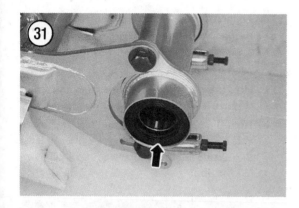

6. Center a piece of pipe against the wheel hub as shown in **Figure 34**. Hammer against the pipe and drive the axle's left side bearing race through the right side bearing. Then stop and slide the axle inward until the right side bearing race contacts the right side bearing. Then hammer against the pipe and drive the left and right side axle bearing surfaces into their respective bearings. Continue until the shoulder on the brake disc hub bottoms against the right side bearing (**Figure 35**).

7. Spin the axle by hand. It should turn smoothly without binding or excessive noise.

8. Apply a light coat of wheel bearing grease onto the driven sprocket hub shoulder (**Figure 29**). Then slide the driven sprocket hub onto the axle splines (**Figure 36**) and push it into the axle housing until it bottoms. See **Figure 37**.

9. Remove the plastic spacer from between the brake pads in the brake caliper.

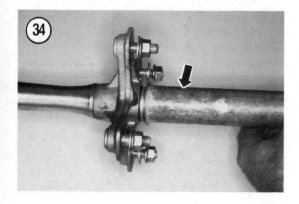

12

10. Slide the brake caliper (A, **Figure 38**) over the brake disc. Then install the 2 bolts (B, **Figure 38**) that hold the brake caliper to the axle housing and tighten to the torque specification in **Table 3**.

NOTE
Apply the rear brake pedal several times to ensure that the brake pads are seated against the brake disc.

11. Install the drive chain as described in this chapter.

12. Set the parking brake.

13. Use the Yamaha rear axle nut wrench (YM-37132) or an equivalent torque adapter and a torque wrench (**Figure 39**) and tighten the rear axle nuts as follows:

NOTE
Because of the rear axle design, the rear axle nuts cannot be tightened with a torque wrench and socket. The Yamaha rear axle nut wrench (YM-37132) or an equivalent torque adapter must be attached to the torque wrench. However, because the rear axle nut wrench (Figure 40) or torque adapter increases the length of the torque wrench, the torque applied will be greater than the torque or dial reading on the torque wrench. When using the Yamaha rear axle nut wrench or a torque adapter to tighten the rear axle nuts, the torque specifications must be recalculated.

   a. Using the tool manufacturer's instructions or the information listed under *Torque Wrench Adapter* in Chapter One, recalculate the following 3 torque specifications: (1) 55 N•m (40 ft.-lb.); (2) 190 N•m (140 ft.lb.); and (3) 240 N•m (170 ft.-lb.).

   b. Apply Loctite 271 (red) to the threads on the rear axle.

NOTE
The inside and outside axle nuts are identical.

   c. Install the inside axle nut (A, **Figure 41**) and tighten hand tight.

   d. Mount the rear axle nut wrench (torque adapter) onto a torque wrench.

   e. Tighten the inside axle nut to 55 N•m (40 ft.-lb.). See **Figure 42**.

   f. Install the outside axle nut (B, **Figure 41**) and hand tighten it against the inside axle nut.

   g. Hold the inside nut and tighten the outside nut (**Figure 43**) to 190 N•m (140 ft.-lb.).

   h. Hold the outside axle nut and turn the inside axle nut (**Figure 42**) *counterclockwise* against the outside nut to a torque reading of 240 N•m (177 ft.-lb.).

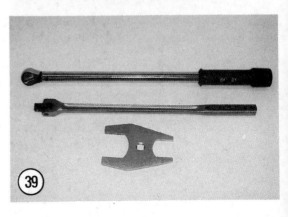

14. Turn the rear axle by hand. It should turn smoothly.

15. Install both wheel hubs as described under *Rear Wheel Hubs* in this chapter.

16. Install the rear wheels as described in this chapter.

17. Adjust the rear drive chain and tighten the rear axle housing nuts and bolts as described under *Drive Chain Adjustment* in Chapter Three.

REAR AXLE HOUSING

The rear axle housing is equipped with 2 ball bearings, 2 seals, inner collar and a center spacer. The bearings are pressed into the rear axle housing and should be installed using a hydraulic press and suitable bearing drivers.

Figure 44 shows the axle housing and related components.

Bearing Preliminary Inspection

Before removing the rear axle housing, check the bearings as follows.

1. Remove the rear wheels and drive chain as described in this chapter. Remove the brake caliper as described in Chapter Thirteen.

2. Turn the rear axle by hand. If the bearings grind or catch and the axle turns roughly, continue with Step 3.

3. Remove the rear axle as described in this chapter.

4. Remove the seals using a wide-blade screwdriver (**Figure 45**). Pad the bottom of the screwdriver to prevent damage to the bearing housing.

5. Wipe off all excessive grease from both bearings.

6. Inspect each bearing (**Figure 46**) for visual damage. Check for overheating, a broken or cracked cage and corrosion. If the seals are damaged, moisture will have entered the axle housing, producing corrosion on the bearing, axle and center spacer.

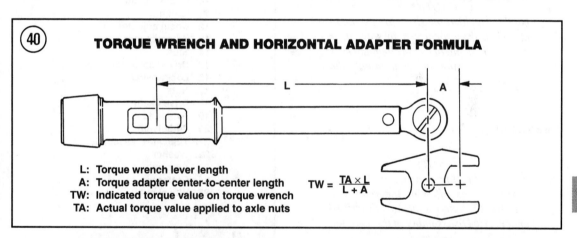

40 **TORQUE WRENCH AND HORIZONTAL ADAPTER FORMULA**

L: Torque wrench lever length
A: Torque adapter center-to-center length
TW: Indicated torque value on torque wrench
TA: Actual torque value applied to axle nuts

$$TW = \frac{TA \times L}{L + A}$$

12

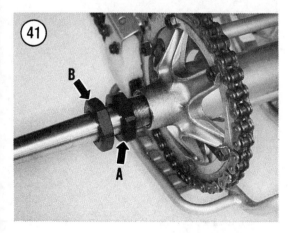

7. Turn each bearing (**Figure 46**) by hand. The bearings should turn smoothly without catching, binding or excessive noise. Some axial play is normal, but radial play should be negligible. See **Figure 47**.

8. Check the bearing fit in the axle housing. If the bearing is a loose fit, the housing bore is damaged and requires replacement.

9. If necessary, replace the bearings or axle housing as described in this chapter.

Removal

1. Remove the rear axle as described in this chapter.

2. Remove the nuts, washers and bolts (A, **Figures 48**) that hold the axle housing to the rear swing arm.

3. Slide the axle housing (B, **Figure 48**) away from the swing arm and remove it and the 2 chain adjusters (C, **Figure 48**).

> *CAUTION*
> *Double shielded bearings are used. Do not wash these bearings in solvent or any other chemical as the chemical may enter the bearing and contaminate the grease.*

Disassembly

> *NOTE*
> *If the right side bearing and center spacer comes off with the rear axle (**Figure 20**), remove them as described under **Axle Disassembly** in this chapter.*

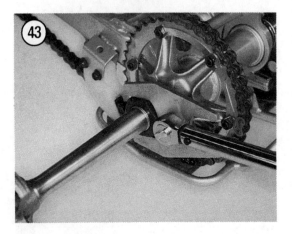

REAR AXLE

1. Rear axle
2. Axle seal
3. Bearing
4. Center spacer
5. Rear axle housing
6. Inner spacer
7. Nut
8. Washer
9. Bolt
10. Chain adjuster
11. Locknut
12. Chain adjuster bolt
13. Sprocket hub
14. Stud
15. Driven sprocket
16. Lockwasher
17. Nuts
18. Drive chain
19. Axle nuts
20. Wheel hub
21. Tire/wheel assembly
22. Washer
23. Axle nut
24. Cotter pin
25. Wheel nut

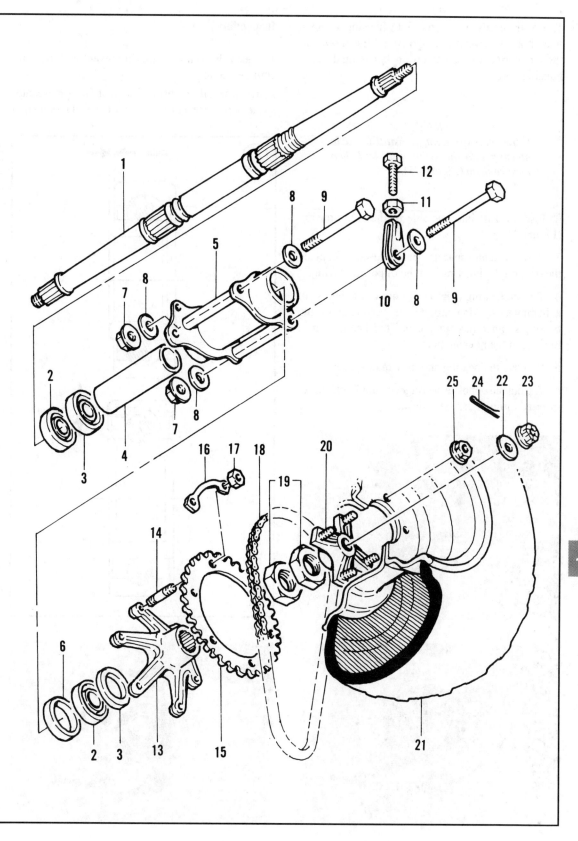

1. Pry the seals out of the axle housing using a wide-blade screwdriver as shown in **Figure 49**. Pad the screwdriver to prevent it from damaging the axle housing bore.

NOTE
If the seals are tight, reinstall the axle housing into the swing arm and then remove them (Figure 45).

2. Insert a drift into one side of the axle housing (**Figure 50**).

3. Push the center spacer over to one side and place the drift on the inner race of the opposite bearing.

4. Tap the bearing (**Figure 50**) out of the hub with a hammer, working around the perimeter of the bearing's inner race to prevent the bearing from binding in the housing bore.

5. Remove the bearing and the center spacer.

6. Tap out the opposite bearing with a suitable driver inserted through the axle housing.

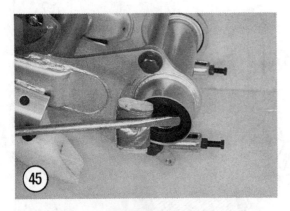

Inspection

1. Clean the axle housing in solvent and dry with compressed air.

2. Remove all corrosion and rust from the center spacer with a steel brush or a wire wheel mounted in

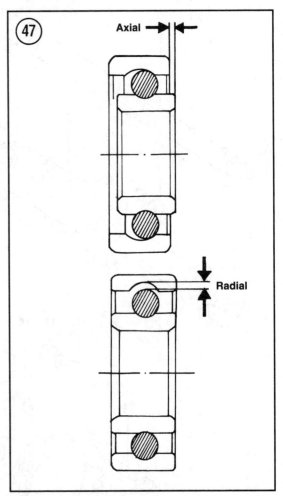

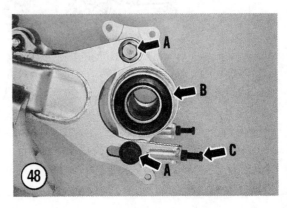

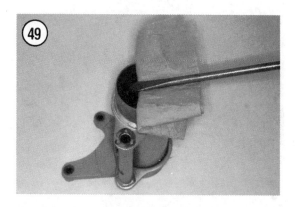

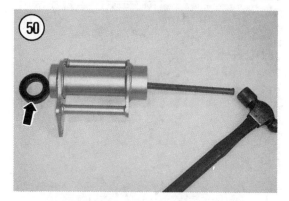

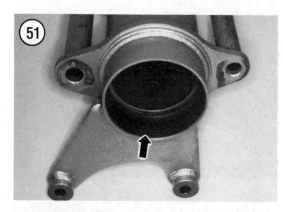

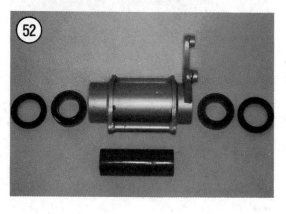

a drill. Then clean the spacer and dry with compressed air.

3. Check the center spacer for cracks, distortion or other damage. Replace if necessary.

4. Check the axle housing bores (**Figure 51**) for cracks or other damage. Remove any burrs or nicks with a file or fine sandpaper.

NOTE
If one or both bearings are loose in their respective housing bore, do not center punch or rough up the area to decrease its bore size. Installing the bearing will flatten these areas, causing the bearing to run loose once again. If the axle housing bearing bores are severely worn or damaged, replace the axle housing.

5. Inspect the axle housing bolts, washers and nuts. Replace any fastener that is worn or damaged.

Reassembly

Single row, deep groove ball bearings (**Figure 52**) are used in the axle housing. Both bearings are double shielded. Prior to installing new bearings and seals, note the following:

   a. Install bearings with their manufacturer's code marks and numbers facing out.

   b. Install bearings by pressing them into the axle housing using a bearing driver (**Figure 53**) that seats against the outer bearing race only.

   c. Install seals with their closed side facing out.

   d. Refer to *Ball Bearing Replacement* in Chapter One for additional information.

12

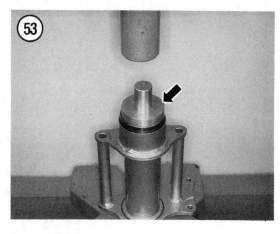

1. Blow any dirt or foreign matter out of the housing and out of the center hub spacer prior to installing the bearings.

2. Press in the first bearing until it bottoms in the axle housing bearing bore (**Figure 54**).

3. Turn the axle housing over and install the center spacer (A, **Figure 55**).

4. Press in the second bearing (B, **Figure 55**) until it bottoms in the axle housing bearing bore or just contacts the center spacer.

5. Remove the axle housing and check that both bearings (**Figure 56**) turn smoothly.

6. Pack the lip of each seal with waterproof bearing grease.

7. Press in the first seal until its outer surface is flush with or slightly below the seal bore inside surface as shown in **Figure 57**.

8. Repeat Step 7 to install the second seal.

Installation

Refer to **Figure 58** when performing this procedure.

1. Install the axle housing (A, **Figure 59**) into the swing arm so the brake caliper mounting bracket (B, **Figure 59**) is on the right side.

2. Install the chain adjusters by positioning them between the swing arm and axle housing with their adjustment marks (**Figure 60**) facing toward the *inside* of the swing arm.

3. Install a washer on each mounting bolt, then install the mounting bolts (C, **Figure 59**) from the left side. Then install the second washer on each bolt and secure it with its mounting nut. Tighten the nut finger-tight.

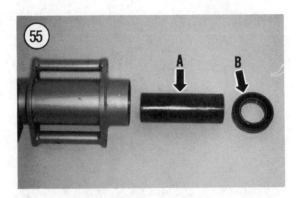

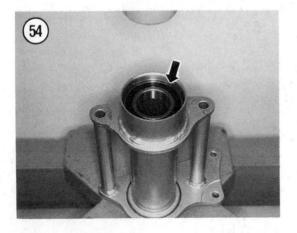

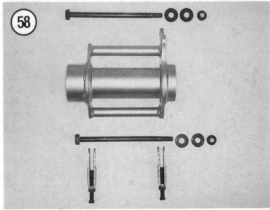

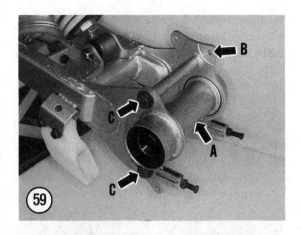

(59)

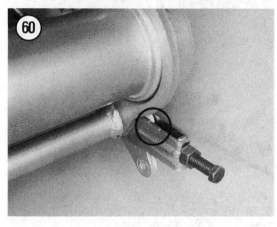

(60)

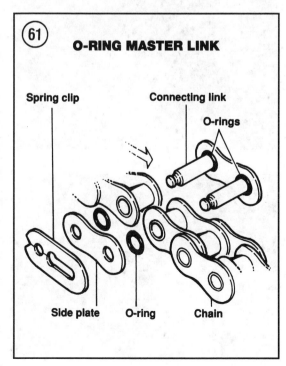

(61)

O-RING MASTER LINK

Spring clip   Connecting link

O-rings

Side plate   O-ring   Chain

4. Install the rear axle as described in this chapter.

5. Install the drive chain as described in this chapter.

6. Adjust the rear drive chain and tighten the rear axle housing nuts and bolts as described under *Drive Chain Adjustment* in Chapter Three.

DRIVE CHAIN

All models are equipped at the factory with a 520 O-ring drive chain. O-ring drive chains are internally lubricated at the time of manufacture. Rubber O-rings located between each side plate seal in the lubricant, while also keeping dirt and moisture out. The master link is equipped with 4 removable O-rings (**Figure 61**).

A press-fit master link is used on all models. On these chains, the side plate (**Figure 61**) is a press-fit on the connecting link. To prevent damage to the chain during service, a chain breaker (A, **Figure 62**) and master link press tool (B, **Figure 62**) is required to remove and install the drive chain.

Table 2 lists drive chain specifications.

Removal/Installation

1. Support the vehicle with both rear wheels off the ground.

2. Turn the rear axle and drive chain until the master link is accessible.

3. Remove the master link spring clip with a pair of pliers (**Figure 63**).

4. Use a chain breaker (**Figure 64**) to separate the side plate from the connecting link. Then remove the side plate (**Figure 65**) and the 2 outside O-rings.

5. Push out the connecting link and remove the 2 inside O-rings (**Figure 61**).

12

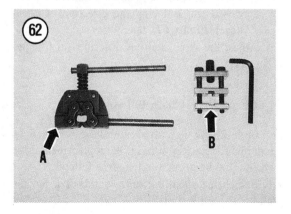

(62)

A   B

6. Pull the drive chain off the drive sprocket and remove it.

7. Install by reversing these removal steps while noting the following.

8. Assemble the drive chain and install the master link as follows:

    a. Install an O-ring on each connecting link pin (**Figure 61**).

    b. Insert the connecting link through the chain to join it together.

    c. Install the remaining 2 O-rings onto the connecting link pins (**Figure 61**).

    d. Push the side plate onto the connecting link as far as it will go. Then press the side plate into position with a press-fit chain tool like the one shown in **Figure 66**.

NOTE
Most commercial press-fit chain tools are designed to press the side plate onto the connecting link to its correct depth. If the side plate is pressed on too far, it will bind the chain where it joins the master link. If the side plate is not pressed on far enough, the spring clip cannot be installed correctly and may come off. Therefore, always press the side plate onto the connecting link so the slide plate is flush with both pin seating grooves in the connecting link.

CAUTION
Attempting to install a press-fit master link without the proper tools may damage the chain and master link. This could cause the chain to break during operation.

    e. Install the spring clip on the master link so its closed end is facing the direction of chain travel (**Figure 67**).

9. Adjust the drive chain as described in Chapter Three.

Cutting A Drive Chain To Length

Table 2 lists the correct number of chain links required for stock gearing. If the replacement drive chain is too long, cut it to length as follows.

1. Stretch the chain out on a workbench. Set the master link aside for now.

2. Refer to **Table 2** for the correct number of links for your chain, then count the links on the new chain. Make a chalk mark on the 2 chain pins where you want to cut it. Count the chain links one more time just to make sure its overall length is correct.

WARNING
A bench grinder or hand-operated high-speed grinding tool is required to cut the chain. When using this equipment, safety glasses must be worn.

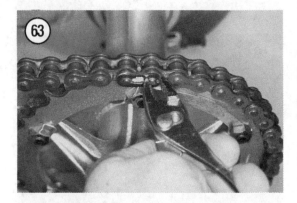

3. Grind the head of 2 pins flush with the face of the side plate, using a suitable grinding tool.

4. Next, use a chain breaker or a punch and hammer and lightly tap the pins out of the side plate. Support the chain carefully when doing this. If the pins are still tight, grind more material from the end of the pins and then try again.

5. Remove the side plate and push out the connecting link.

Drive Chain
Cleaning/Lubrication

CAUTION
The O-rings can be easily damaged by improper cleaning and handling of the drive chain. Do not use a steam cleaner, a high-pressure washer or any solvent that may damage the rubber O-rings.

1. Remove the drive chain as described in this chapter.

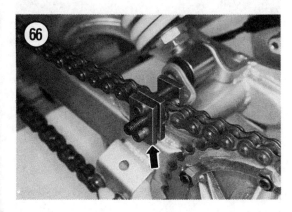

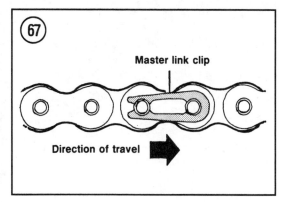

Master link clip

Direction of travel

WARNING
When using kerosene to clean the drive chain, make sure there is plenty of ventilation and always wear appropriate safety equipment.

2. Immerse the chain in a pan with enough kerosene to cover the chain and soak it for about 30 minutes. Periodically move and flex the chain to soften dirt trapped between the links, pins, rollers and O-rings.

CAUTION
In the next step, do not use a stiff wire brush to clean the chain; otherwise, the brush may damage the O-rings, requiring drive chain replacement.

3. Lightly scrub the rollers with a soft brush and rinse away loosened dirt. Do not scrub hard or use a hard brush as the O-rings may be damaged. Rinse the chain a couple of times in kerosene to flush out all dirt and grit from the chain rollers. Hang the chain over a pan and allow the chain to thoroughly dry.

4. After cleaning the chain, examine it carefully for wear or damage. Check the O-rings for damage. Replace the chain if necessary.

5. Externally lubricate the chain with SAE 30-50 motor oil or a good grade of chain lubricant (non-tacky) specifically formulated for O-ring chains, following its manufacturer's instructions.

CAUTION
Do not use a tacky chain lubricant on O-ring chains as it will allow dirt and other abrasive materials to stick to the drive chain, sprockets and chain guides. When the chain is under use, this buildup will grind down and tear the O-rings, causing rapid wear. Remember, an O-ring chain is lubricated during its assembly at the factory. External oiling is required only to prevent chain rust and to keep the O-rings pliable.

DRIVEN SPROCKET

The driven sprocket rides on a hub that is mounted on the rear axle. The driven sprocket can be removed without removing the rear axle from the vehicle. See **Figure 44**.

12

Inspection

Check the sprocket teeth for excessive wear, undercutting or other damage. If the sprocket is damaged, replace both sprockets and chain at the same time. Installing a new chain over worn or damaged sprockets will cause rapid chain wear.

Removal/Installation

1. Park the vehicle on level ground and set the parking brake.
2. Pry the lockwasher tabs away from the driven sprocket nuts (**Figure 68**). Then loosen, but do not remove, each sprocket nut.
3. Remove the left side rear wheel as described in this chapter.
4. Remove the drive chain as described under *Drive Chain* in this chapter.
5. Remove the sprocket nuts, lockwashers and sprocket (**Figure 68**).
6. Install by reversing these steps, while noting the following.
7. Install new lockwashers.
8. One side of the sprocket is stamped with the number of teeth on the sprocket. Install the sprocket with the stamped side facing out.
9. Tighten the sprocket nuts to the torque specification in **Table 3**. Then bend the lockwasher tabs to lock the nuts in position.

TIRE CHANGING AND TIRE REPAIRS

Refer to Chapter Eleven.

SHOCK ABSORBER

All models use a single rear shock absorber and spring unit.

Table 1 lists shock and spring specifications.

Shock Spring Preload Adjustment

The rear shock absorber is equipped with a spring preload adjuster (**Figure 69**) that can be changed to best suit rider weight and riding conditions. The installed spring length (preload) must be maintained

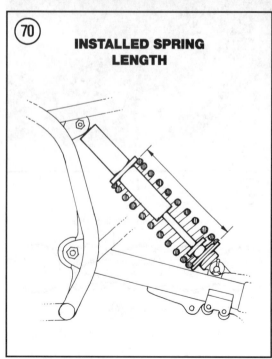

INSTALLED SPRING LENGTH

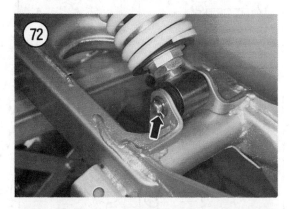

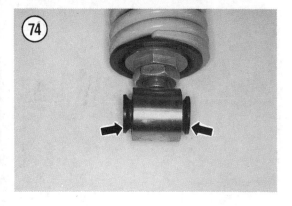

within the minimum and maximum length specifications (**Figure 70**) in **Table 1**.

1. Support the vehicle with both rear wheels off the ground.

2. Clean the threads at the bottom of the shock absorber (**Figure 69**).

3. Measure the existing spring length (**Figure 70**) with a tape measure.

4. To adjust, loosen the locknut (A, **Figure 69**) and turn the adjuster (B, **Figure 69**) in the desired direction, making sure to maintain the spring length within the dimensions listed in **Table 1**. Tightening the adjust nut increases spring preload, while loosening it decreases preload. One complete turn (360°) of the adjuster (B, **Figure 69**) moves the spring 1.5 mm (1/16 in.).

CAUTION
Remember, the spring preload adjustment must be maintained between the minimum and maximum dimensions listed in **Table 1**.

5. After the desired spring preload is achieved, tighten the rear shock absorber spring locknut (A, **Figure 69**) to the torque specification in **Table 3**.

Shock Absorber Removal

Refer to **Figure 71**.

1. Support the vehicle with both rear wheels off the ground. Then support the rear axle housing with wooden blocks so the swing arm does not fall down after disconnecting the lower shock absorber pivot bolt in Step 2.

2. Remove the cotter pin (**Figure 72**), washer and pivot shaft from the lower shock mount at the swing arm.

3. Remove the nut (A, **Figure 73**), washer and pivot bolt that hold the upper end of the shock absorber to the frame and remove the shock absorber.

4. Remove the thrust covers (**Figure 74**) from the lower shock bushing mount.

Shock Inspection

Refer to **Figure 75** for this procedure.

WARNING
The shock absorber damper housing contains nitrogen gas. Do not tamper

12

with or attempt to open the damper housing. Do not place it near an open flame or other extreme heat. Do not dispose of the damper assembly yourself. Take it to a dealership where it can be deactivated and disposed of properly. Read the WARNING label affixed to the damper housing (Figure 76).

1. Clean and dry the shock absorber.

2. Clean the shock pivot shaft, pivot bolt, nut, washers and thrust covers in solvent. Remove any rust or corrosion from the pivot shaft and bolt.

3. Inspect the thrust covers (**Figure 74**) for cracks, deterioration or other damage. Replace if necessary.

4. Inspect the shock absorber (**Figure 76**) for gas and oil leaks.

5. Check the damper rod for bending, rust or other damage.

6. Inspect and service the shock bushings as described in this section.

7. If necessary, remove and inspect the spring as described in this section.

Shock Bushing
Inspection and Replacement

Refer to **Figure 75** for this procedure.

1. Inspect the upper (**Figure 77**) and lower (**Figure 78**) bushings for excessive wear, rust or damage. Inspect the rubber part of each bushing for cracks, tearing or deterioration. The lower bushing is equipped with 2 smaller solid bushings (20, **Figure 75**). Inspect the bushings for damage.

2. To replace the bushings(s):

   a. Note that the upper and lower bushings are different. Install each bushing in its correct position.

   b. The 2 small solid bushings (20, **Figure 75**) can be replaced separately.

   c. Support the shock absorber and press out the bushing.

   d. Clean the shock bushing bore and check it for cracks or other damage.

   e. Support the shock absorber and press in the new bushing. Center the bushing in the shock bushing bore.

   f. Install the 2 solid bushings.

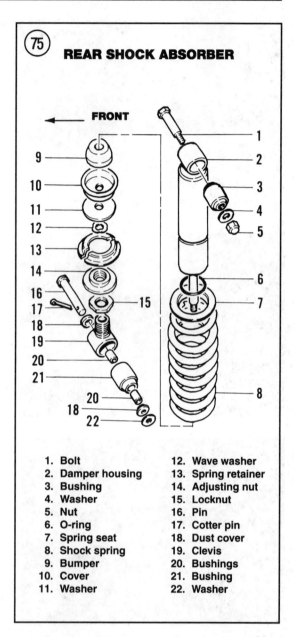

REAR SHOCK ABSORBER

FRONT

1. Bolt	12. Wave washer
2. Damper housing	13. Spring retainer
3. Bushing	14. Adjusting nut
4. Washer	15. Locknut
5. Nut	16. Pin
6. O-ring	17. Cotter pin
7. Spring seat	18. Dust cover
8. Shock spring	19. Clevis
9. Bumper	20. Bushings
10. Cover	21. Bushing
11. Washer	22. Washer

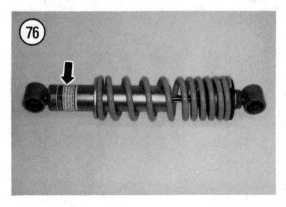

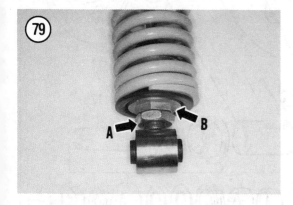

Spring
Removal/Installation

To remove and install the shock spring, perform the following step. This section also describes how to measure the shock spring free length.

1. Remove the shock absorber as described in this chapter.

2. Measure and record the spring preload position as described under *Shock Spring Preload Adjustment* in this chapter.

3. Clean the lower shock threads (**Figure 79**).

4. Secure the shock absorber upper mount in a vise with soft jaws.

5. Loosen the locknut (A, **Figure 79**) and turn it all the way down. Then turn the adjusting nut (B, **Figure 79**) and loosen it all the way to reduce spring preload. There should be no preload on the spring.

6. Secure the spring with a shock spring tool and remove the spring retainer (**Figure 80**) and spring from the shock.

7. Measure the spring's free length with a tape measure (**Figure 81**). Replace the spring if it is appreciably shorter than the free length specification in **Table 1**.

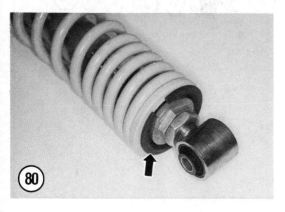

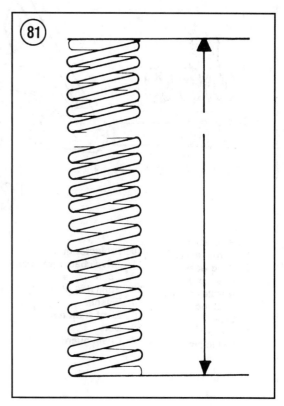

12

8. Install by reversing these steps, while noting the following.

9. Install the spring with its closer wound springs toward the bottom of the shock (**Figure 76**). Then install the spring retainer (**Figure 80**), making sure that is seats flush against the spring.

10. Adjust the spring preload as described under *Shock Preload Adjustment* in this chapter.

Shock Absorber Installation

Refer to **Figure 71** when performing this procedure.

1. Apply a lightweight lithium soap base grease onto the pivot shaft and pivot bolt and to the inside of both bushings.

2. Install the 2 thrust covers (**Figure 74**) onto the lower shock bushing.

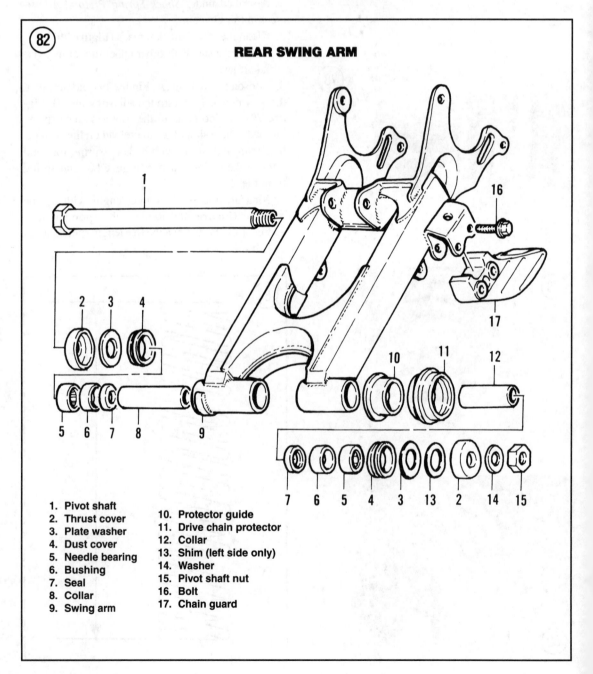

82

REAR SWING ARM

1. Pivot shaft
2. Thrust cover
3. Plate washer
4. Dust cover
5. Needle bearing
6. Bushing
7. Seal
8. Collar
9. Swing arm
10. Protector guide
11. Drive chain protector
12. Collar
13. Shim (left side only)
14. Washer
15. Pivot shaft nut
16. Bolt
17. Chain guard

3. Install the shock absorber between the frame brackets as shown in **Figure 73**. Install the pivot bolt (B, **Figure 73**) from the right side. Then install the flat washer and nut (A, **Figure 73**).

4. Center the shock between the swing arm brackets, then install the pivot shaft (**Figure 72**) from the right side. Install the flat washer and a *new* cotter pin through the pivot shaft hole. Spread the cotter pin arms to lock it in position.

5. Tighten the upper shock absorber pivot bolt nut (A, **Figure 73**) to the torque specification in **Table 3**.

6. Lower the vehicle to the ground.

REAR SWING ARM

Figure 82 is an exploded view of the rear swing arm. A needle bearing and solid bushing is pressed into each side of the swing arm. A collar is installed between each needle bearing and bushing assembly. Dust seals and covers are installed on the outside of each needle bearing and bushing to prevent dirt and moisture from entering and damaging them. Steel

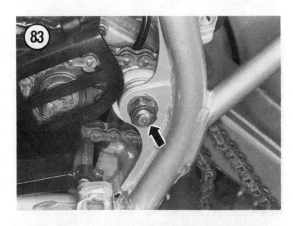

thrust covers are installed on the outside of each seal. A nylon chain protector is installed on the swing arm to prevent chain damage. The pivot shaft is installed through the swing arm from the right side. Plate washers 2.00-2.10 mm (0.079-0.083 in.) thick are installed between the outer thrust covers and dust seals.

Swing Arm Bearing Inspection

Inspect the swing arm needle bearings and bushings periodically for excessive play, roughness or damage.

1. Remove the rear axle housing (with the rear axle assembly installed in the housing) as described in this chapter.

2. Remove the cotter pin (**Figure 72**), washer and pivot shaft from the lower shock mount at the swing arm. Then remove the thrust covers (**Figure 74**) from the lower shock bushing mount.

3. Loosen the swing arm pivot bolt nut (**Figure 83**), then retorque the nut to the specification in **Table 3**.

NOTE
Have an assistant steady the vehicle when performing Step 4.

4. Grasp the rear end of the swing arm and try to move it from side to side in a horizontal arc. There should be no noticeable side play.

5. Grasp the rear of the swing arm once again and pivot it up and down through its full travel. The swing arm should pivot smoothly without binding.

6. If play is evident and the pivot bolt nut is tightened correctly, remove the swing arm and inspect the needle bearings as described in the following sections.

7. Reverse Step 1 and Step 2 if you are not going to remove the swing arm. See **Table 3** for tightening torques.

Swing Arm Removal

1. Support the vehicle with both rear wheels off the ground.

2. Remove the rear axle housing as described in this chapter.

12

3. Remove the cotter pin (**Figure 72**), washer and pivot shaft from the lower shock mount at the swing arm. Then remove the thrust covers (**Figure 74**) from the lower shock bushing mount.

4. Loosen the swing arm pivot shaft nut (**Figure 83**). Then remove the nut and washer.

5. Remove the pivot bolt (**Figure 84**) from the right side. If the pivot bolt is tight, tap it out with a brass or aluminum drift.

6. Pull back on the swing arm and remove it.

7. If you are not going to remove the swing arm thrust cover and bearing assemblies, cover the left- and right-side bearing assemblies with plastic bags.

Swing Arm
Disassembly and Inspection

Store the left and right side bearing assemblies in separate containers so they can be installed in their original locations. Refer to **Figure 82**.

1. Remove the thrust cover, plate washer, dust cover, collar and drive chain protector from the left side of the swing arm (**Figure 85**).

> *NOTE*
> *On some models, there may be a shim placed between the left side thrust cover and plate washer. This shim adjusts the swing arm side play.*

2. Remove the thrust cover, plate washer, dust cover and collar from the right side of the swing arm (**Figure 86**).

3. Pry the 2 inner dust seals out of the swing arm as described under *Swing Arm Dust Seal Replacement* in this section.

4. Wash all parts in solvent and dry thoroughly with compressed air.

5. Check each bushing (**Figure 87**) for excessive wear or damage.

6. Wipe excess grease from the needle bearings. Needle bearing wear is difficult to measure. Turn each bearing (**Figure 88**) with your finger. The bearings should turn smoothly without excessive play. Check the rollers for excessive wear, pitting or rust.

7. Install each collar into its bushing and bearing assembly and turn by hand. Check for roughness, binding or excessive play. If necessary, replace the bearings and bushings as described in this section.

8. Check each collar (**Figure 85** and **Figure 86**) for scoring, cracks or excessive wear. If a collar is ex-

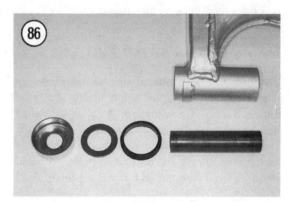

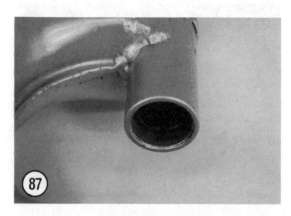

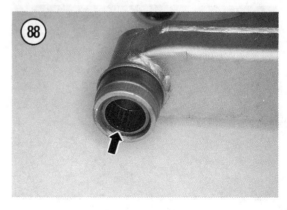

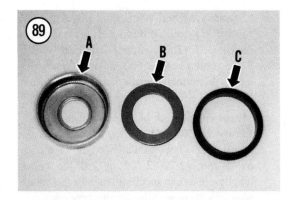

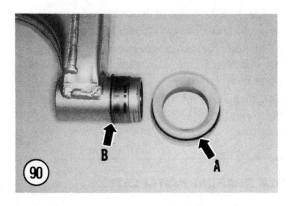

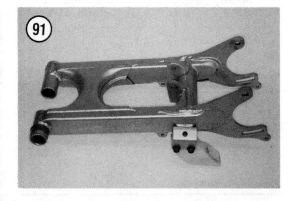

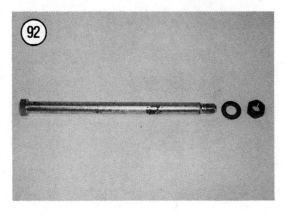

cessively worn, replace the collar and bearings as a set.

9. Check the thrust covers (A, **Figure 89**) and dust covers (C) for excessive wear or damage.

10. Check the plate washers (B, **Figure 89**) for galling, cracks or other damage.

11. Replace the chain protector (A, **Figure 90**) and guide (B) if worn or damaged.

12. Check the swing arm (**Figure 91**) for cracks, bending or other damage. Check the axle housing mounts for damage. Refer repair to a Yamaha dealership or welding shop or replace the swing arm.

13. Check the pivot shaft (**Figure 92**) for cracks or damaged threads. Then roll the pivot shaft on a flat surface with its bolt head laying off the edge of the surface. Replace the pivot shaft if bent or damaged.

> *WARNING*
> *Do not straighten a bent swing arm pivot shaft. Doing so may dangerously weaken the pivot shaft and cause it to fail during use.*

14. If necessary, replace the swing arm needle bearings and bushings as described in this section.

15. Perform the *Swing Arm Side Clearance Check and Adjustment* procedure in this section.

Swing Arm Needle Bearing and Bushing Replacement

Do not remove the swing arm needle bearings and bushings unless replacement is required. Always replace the bushings and bearings as a set.

Refer to **Figure 82** for this procedure.

1. Support the swing arm and press out the old bearings (**Figure 88**) and bushings (**Figure 87**).

2. Clean the bearing bore in solvent and dry thoroughly. Remove any rust or corrosion from the swing arm.

3. Pack the bearings with waterproof bearing grease.

4. Lubricate the outside of each bushing and bearing with grease.

5. To install the needle bearings and bushings:

    a. Install the bearings with their manufacturer's name and size code facing out.

    b. Install the a bearing and bushing into one side of the swing arm to the dimensions listed in **Figure 93**.

12

c. Repeat to install the other bearing and bushing assembly (**Figure 93**).

Swing Arm Side Clearance Check and Adjustment

This procedure describes how to check and adjust the swing arm side clearance. A vernier caliper is required for this procedure.

Refer to **Figure 82** for this procedure.

1. Replace all excessively worn or damaged parts as described in the previous sections.

> *NOTE*
> *Record each measurement obtained in Steps 2-5 as they will be used to determine the swing arm side clearance.*

2. Measure the engine mount boss width (**Figure 94**). Record the measurement as dimension A.

3. Measure the length of each collar.

a. Measure the length of the right side collar (A, **Figure 95**). Record this measurement as dimension B. The standard length is 91.30-91.45 mm (3.594-3.600 in.). If the collar length is less than specified, replace the collar. Measure the new collar for this procedure.

b. Measure the length of the left side collar (B, **Figure 95**). Record this measurement as dimension C. The standard length is 69.30-69.45 mm (2.728-2.734 in.). If the collar length is less than specified, replace the collar. Measure the new collar for this procedure.

4. Measure the width of the swing arm at the pivot bosses (**Figure 96**). Record this as dimension D.

5. Measure the thickness of each plate washer (**Figure 97**). Record the washer thicknesses as dimensions E and F.

6. Calculate swing arm clearance using the following forumla: $(A + B + C) - (D + E + F) =$ side clearance.

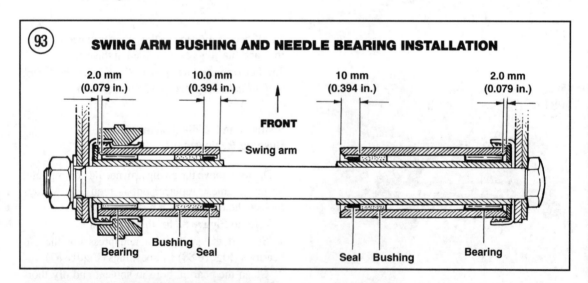

(93) SWING ARM BUSHING AND NEEDLE BEARING INSTALLATION

2.0 mm (0.079 in.)   10.0 mm (0.394 in.)   10 mm (0.394 in.)   2.0 mm (0.079 in.)

FRONT

Swing arm

Bearing   Bushing   Seal   Seal   Bushing   Bearing

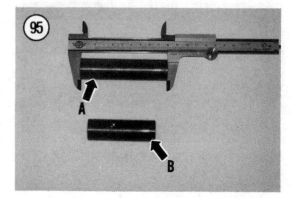

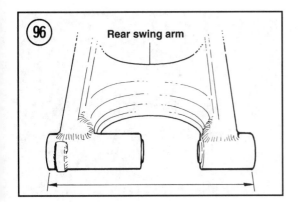

96

Rear swing arm

Example:
A = **59.68 mm (2.350 in.).**
B = **91.35 mm (3.596 in.).**
C = **69.35 mm (2.730 in.).**
D = **215.5 mm (8.484 in.).**
E = **2.00 mm (0.079 in.).**
F = **2.00 mm (0.079 in.).**

Side clearance = (59.68 + 91.35 + 69.35) – (215.5 + 2.00 + 2.00) = 220.38 – 219.5 = 0.88 mm.

7. The correct swing arm side clearance is 0.4-0.7 mm (0.016-0.028 in.).

8. If the side clearance is incorrect, 1 or 2 adjusting shims will be required. Adjusting shims are available in one thickness only: 0.3 mm (0.012 in.).

NOTE
In the above example, the side clearance is out of specification. To bring it within the specification listed in Step 7, add 1 shim (0.88 – 0.3 = 0.58 mm).

9. If a shim is required, install in on the left side between the thrust cover and plate washer (13, **Figure 82**).

Swing Arm Dust Seal Replacement

1. Pry the 2 dust seals (**Figure 98**) out of the swing arm. See **Figure 99**. Save one of the old seals to help install the new seals.

2. Inspect, service and lubricate the swing arm bearings and bushings as described in this chapter.

3. Pack the lip of the new dust seal with grease, then push it into the swing arm bore with its closed side (**Figure 100**) facing out.

97

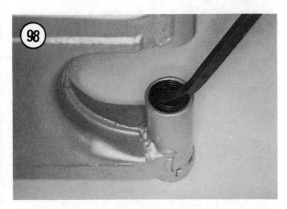

98

99

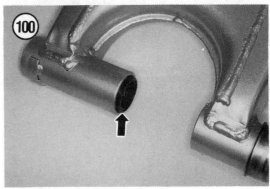

100

12

NOTE
Press the dust seals into the swing arm with a bolt arrangement as shown in Figure 101.

4. Assemble the bolt, 2 washers and nut onto the swing arm (**Figure 102**).

5. Hold the bolt and tighten the nut (**Figure 103**) until the inner washer bottoms out against the swing arm.

6. Remove the nut and the inner washer. Then install 1 of the used dust seals (**Figure 104**) to the bolt and secure it with the inner washer and nut. Hold the bolt and tighten the nut until the seal bottoms against the bushing.

7. Remove the bolt assembly and check that the dust seal (**Figure 105**) is properly seated inside the swing arm bore.

8. Repeat to install the other dust seal.

Swing Arm Assembly

1. Install the dust seals (A, **Figure 106**) as described in this chapter.

2. Lubricate the following parts with bearing grease:
   a. Needle bearings and bushings.
   b. Collars.
   c. Thrust cover (A, **Figure 89**).
   d. Plate washers (B, **Figure 89**).
   e. Dust covers (C, **Figure 89**).
   f. Shim (if used).

3. Assemble the left side thrust cover assembly (B, **Figure 106**) as follows:

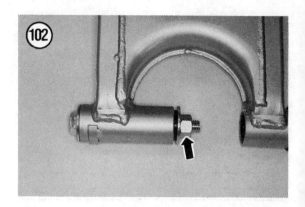
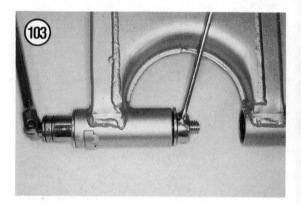
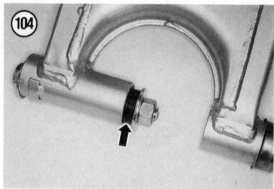
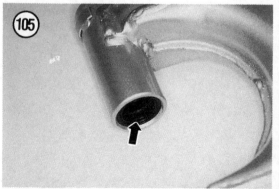

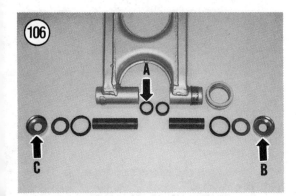

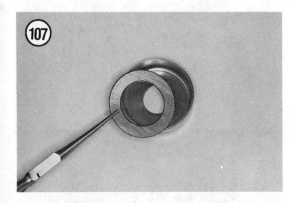

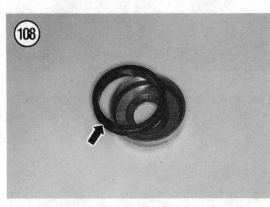

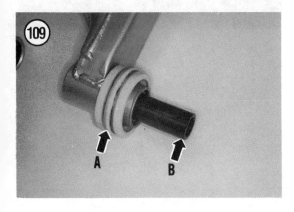

a. If used, install the shim (13, **Figure 82**) into the thrust cover assembly.

NOTE
*The shim (13, **Figure 82**) is only required if the swing arm side clearance is incorrect. If a shim is required, install it in the left side thrust cover.*

b. Install the plate washer (**Figure 107**) into the thrust cover.

c. Install the dust cover (**Figure 108**) into the thrust cover and seat it against the plate washer.

4. Repeat Step 3 to assemble the right side (C, **Figure 106**) thrust cover assembly. Note that the right side does not use a shim.

5. Assemble the swing arm left side (B, **Figure 106**) as follows:

a. If removed, install the guide onto the swing arm as shown in B, **Figure 90**. The shoulder on the guide must face toward the inside.

b. Install the chain protector—tapered bore (A, **Figure 90**) facing inside—onto the swing arm. See A, **Figure 109**.

c. Install the collar (B, **Figure 109**) and center it in the swing arm.

d. Install the thrust cover assembly onto the swing arm (**Figure 110**) and push it firmly into place.

6. Assemble the swing arm right side (C, **Figure 106**) as follows:

a. Install the collar (**Figure 111**) and center it in the swing arm.

12

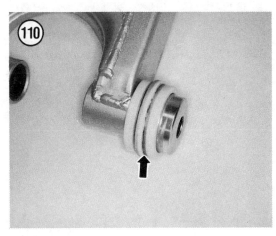

b. Install the thrust cover assembly onto the swing arm (**Figure 112**) and push it firmly into place.

Swing Arm Installation

1. Assemble the swing arm collars and thrust covers (**Figure 113**) as described in the previous section.
2. Lubricate the pivot shaft with waterproof grease.
3. Position the swing arm between the frame and engine, making sure the thrust covers (**Figure 114**) are positioned between the swing arm and frame. Then install the pivot shaft from the right side.
4. Install the swing arm washer and nut (**Figure 115**). Tighten the pivot shaft nut to the torque specification in **Table 3**.
5. Perform the *Swing Arm Bearing Inspection* check as described in this chapter.
6. Install the rear axle housing onto the rear swing arm as described in this chapter.
7. Reconnect the drive chain as described in this chapter.
8. Adjust the drive chain as described in Chapter Three.

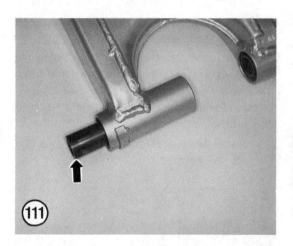

Table 1 REAR SUSPENSION SPECIFICATIONS

Rear suspension type	Swing arm
Rear wheel travel	180 mm (7.09 in.)
Rear shock absorber	Coil spring/gas/oil damper
Shock absorber travel	80 mm (3.15 in.)
Shock absorber spring free length	245 mm (9.65 in.)
Shock spring rate	
K1	5.4 kg/mm (252 in.)
K2	8.0 kg/mm (448 in.-lb.)
Shock stroke	
K1	0-55 mm (0-2.17 in.)
K2	55.0-105 mm (2.17-4.13 in.)
Rear swing arm	
Free play limit	1.0 mm (0.04 in.)
Side clearance	0.4-0.7 mm (0.016-0.027 in.)
Rear axle runout limit	1.5 mm (0.06 in.)
Rear shock absorber spring preload (installed length)	
Standard	230 mm (9.1 in.)
Minimum	222 mm (8.7 in.)
Maximum	234 mm (9.2 in.)

Table 2 DRIVE CHAIN SPECIFICATIONS

Type/manufacturer	520V6/DAIDO
No. of links (for stock gearing)	92
Chain free play	30-40 mm (1.18-1.57 in.)

Table 3 REAR SUSPENSION TIGHTENING TORQUES

	N·m	ft.-lb.
Drive chain adjuster locknuts	16	12
Driven sprocket nuts	24	17
Rear axle hub at swing arm	50	36
Rear axle locknuts	See text	
Rear brake caliper mounting bolts	23	17
Rear shock absorber mounting bolt and nut	25	18
Rear shock absorber spring adjuster locknut	55	40
Rear wheel hub nut	120	88
Rear wheel lug nuts	45	33
Swing arm pivot shaft nut	85	62
Swing arm underguard	23	17

12

BRAKES

All models are equipped with front single leading shoe drum brakes and a rear mechanical brake caliper. This chapter describes service procedures for the front and rear brakes, parking brake and rear brake pedal assembly.

Brake specifications are listed in **Tables 1-3** at the end of this chapter.

FRONT DRUM BRAKE

All models are equipped with a single leading shoe drum brake mounted on each steering knuckle (**Figure 1**). The drum brakes are actuated by a dual cable assembly connected to a hand-operated brake lever mounted on the right side handlebar. Front brake adjustment is covered under *Front Brake Inspection and Adjustment* in Chapter Three.

WARNING
*When working on the brake system, never blow off brake components using compressed air. **Do not** inhale any airborne brake dust as it may contain asbestos, which can cause lung injury and cancer. As an added precaution, wear an approved filtering face mask and thoroughly wash your hands and forearms with warm water and soap after completing any brake work.*

Front Brake Drum
Removal

Front wheel bearings are installed in each brake drum. The brake drums can be removed and installed without removing the bearings. To service the wheel bearings and seal, refer to the *Front Brake Drum/Bearing Assembly* procedures in Chapter Eleven.

1. Remove the front wheel as described in Chapter Eleven.

2. Remove and discard the axle nut cotter pin (A, **Figure 2**).

3. Remove the axle nut and washer (**Figure 3**) that holds the brake drum to the front axle.

4. Slide the brake drum (B, **Figure 2**) and its collar off the axle and remove it. If the brake drum is tight, loosen the front brake shoe adjuster, then slide off the drum.

**Front Brake Drum
Inspection**

NOTE
Cover the 2 brake drum bearings before cleaning the brake drum in Step 1. This will prevent the cleaning solution from contaminating the wheel bearing grease.

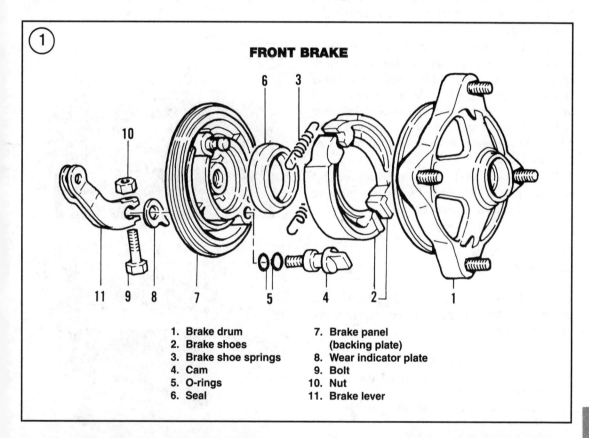

FRONT BRAKE

1. Brake drum
2. Brake shoes
3. Brake shoe springs
4. Cam
5. O-rings
6. Seal
7. Brake panel (backing plate)
8. Wear indicator plate
9. Bolt
10. Nut
11. Brake lever

13

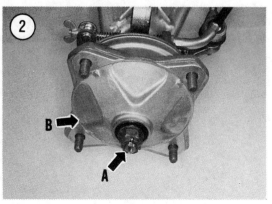

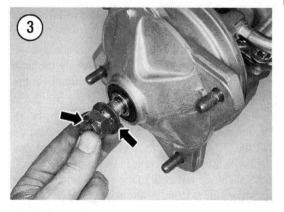

1. Clean the brake drum (**Figure 4**) with hot soapy water. Then allow to dry. Remove any oil or grease from the brake lining surface with a clean rag soaked in lacquer thinner—do not use any solvent that may leave an oil residue.

> *NOTE*
> *Immediately discard the soapy water and wash your hands.*

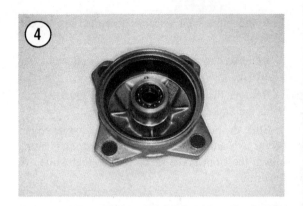

2. Check the brake drum lining surface (**Figure 5**) for cracking, scoring, excessive or uneven wear or other damage.

3. Measure the brake drum inside diameter (lining surface) with a vernier caliper (**Figure 6**) and check against the dimension in **Table 1**. Because the brake drum can wear unevenly, take a minimum of 3 measurements. Replace the brake drum if the inside diameter is out of specification. On original brake drums, the maximum brake drum diameter is cast into each brake drum.

4. To inspect and service the front wheel bearings and seal, refer to the *Front Brake Drum/Bearing Assembly* section in Chapter Eleven.

Front Brake Drum Installation

1. Clean the front axle bearing surface, threads and axle nut with solvent or contact cleaner. Blow dry with compressed air.

> *NOTE*
> *If new brake shoes are installed, it may be necessary to loosen the front brake adjuster so the drum can slide over the shoes.*

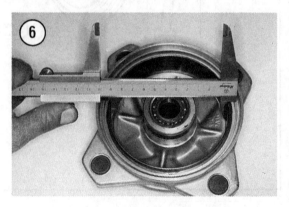

2. Lubricate the collar with grease and install it into the brake drum seal (**Figure 7**).

3. Carefully slide the brake drum over the axle so the inner bearing race is not damaged by the axle threads. Push the brake drum into position over the brake shoes (**Figure 8**).

4. Install the flat washer and axle nut (**Figure 3**). Tighten the front axle nut to the torque specification in **Table 3**. Now check that 1 of the axle nut grooves align with the cotter pin hole in the front axle. If not, tighten the axle nut to align the groove and hole. Do not loosen the axle nut to align the groove and hole.

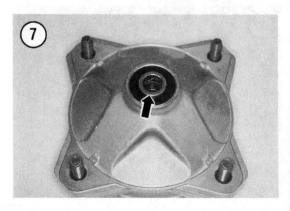

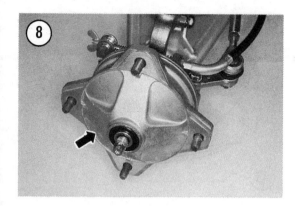

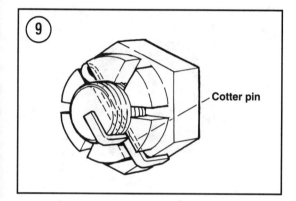

Cotter pin

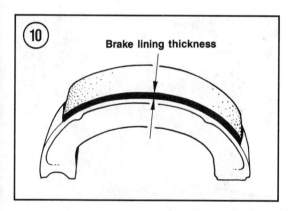

Brake lining thickness

WARNING
Always install a new cotter pin.

5. Insert a new cotter pin through the axle nut groove and axle hole, then bend its arms to lock it in place (**Figure 9**).

6. Install the front wheel as described in Chapter Eleven.

7. Adjust the front brake as described in Chapter Three.

FRONT BRAKE SHOE REPLACEMENT

This section describes replacement procedures for the front brake shoes. To service the brake shoes and brake panel at the same time, refer to *Front Brake Shoes and Brake Panel* in this chapter.

Replace the left and right side brake shoe sets at the same time.

NOTE
If the brake shoes are not replaced in sets, uneven braking or difficult brake adjustment may result.

Refer to **Figure 1** for this procedure.

1. Remove the front brake drum as described in this chapter.

2. Measure the brake shoe lining thickness (**Figure 10**) and check against the specification in **Table 1**. Replace all 4 brake shoes as a set if the lining thickness of any 1 shoe is out of specification.

3. Loosen the front brake cable adjuster at the brake panel (**Figure 11**).

4. If the original brake shoes are going to be reused, mark each shoe (**Figure 12**) with an L (left side) or R (right side) to indicate their original mounting position.

5. Grasp the side of each brake shoe and pull outward against spring tension (**Figure 13**), then pull the shoes off the upper and lower shafts and remove them.

6. Disconnect the brake shoe springs (**Figure 14**) from the brake shoes. Both springs are identical (same part No.).

7. Inspect the springs for stretched areas, hook damage or rust contamination. Measure the springs free length and compare with the specification in **Table 1**.

8. If installing the original brake shoes, assemble them with their marked side (Step 4) facing out.

9. Match the upper and lower brake shoe ends and connect the brake shoes with the 2 springs (**Figure 14**).

10. Lightly grease the pivot pin and brake cam surfaces with a high-temperature wheel bearing grease.

11. Spread the brake shoes open (**Figure 13**) and install them over the brake plate pivot shafts. See **Figure 12**.

12. Make sure both spring hooks are connected fully to the brake shoe holes.

13. Install the front brake drum as described in this chapter.

14. After servicing the opposite front brake assembly, adjust the front brakes as described under *Front Brake Inspection and Adjustment* in Chapter Three.

FRONT BRAKE SHOES AND BRAKE PANEL

The brake panel operates on the steering knuckle. A seal keeps dirt and water from entering the brake drum on the brake panel side. The brake panel can be removed with or without the brake shoes attached. If only the brake shoes require replacement, refer to *Front Brake Shoe Replacement* in this chapter.

Removal

Refer to **Figure 1** for this procedure.

1. Remove the brake drum as described under *Brake Drum Removal* in this chapter.

2. Disconnect the front brake cable from the brake panel as follows:

    a. Remove the brake cable adjusting nut (**Figure 11**) collar and spring.

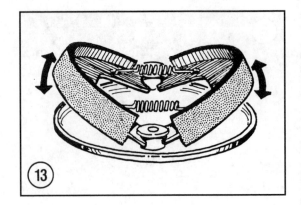

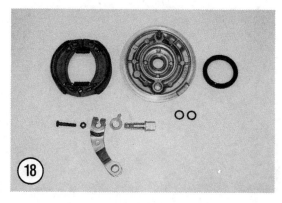

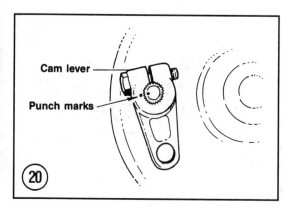

b. Pull the rubber boot (**Figure 15**) off of the brake cable housing.

c. Remove the E-clip (**Figure 16**) securing the brake cable to the brake panel.

d. Remove the brake cable from the brake panel.

3. Slide the brake panel (**Figure 17**) off the steering knuckle and remove it.

Disassembly

Refer to **Figure 18** for this procedure.

1. To remove the brake shoes, perform the following:

   a. If the original brake shoes are going to be reused, mark each shoe (**Figure 19**) with an L (left side) or R (right side) to indicate its original mounting position.

   b. Grasp the side of 1 brake shoe and pull outward against spring tension (**Figure 13**), then pull the shoe off the upper and lower shafts. Remove both brake shoes and springs.

   c. Disconnect the brake shoe springs (**Figure 14**) from the brake shoes. Both springs are identical (same part No.).

2. To remove the brake cam, perform the following:

   a. The brake cam and brake lever should be indexed before separating them. This will speed up installation and alignment. Make an alignment mark on the brake lever that aligns with the punch mark on the brake cam (**Figure 20**).

   b. Remove the nut and bolt (A, **Figure 21**) securing the brake lever to the brake cam.

   c. Remove the brake lever (B, **Figure 21**).

13

Cam lever

Punch marks

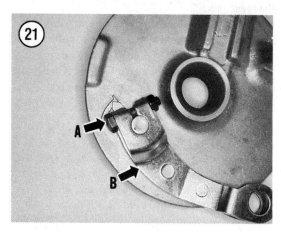

d. Remove the brake wear indicator (**Figure 22**).

e. Remove the 2 O-rings (**Figure 23**) from the brake panel grooves.

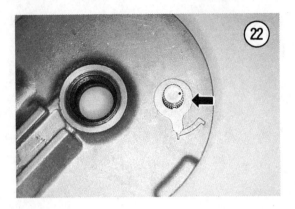

Inspection

Refer to **Figure 18** for this procedure.

1. Clean all parts (except the brake shoes) in solvent and dry with compressed air.

2. Clean the brake shoes with an aerosol type brake cleaner to remove any brake dust. Then lightly sand the brake shoe linings to remove any glaze or chemical residue. If the linings cannot be cleaned thoroughly, replace the brake shoes at both wheels as a set. If the brake linings are in good condition, continue with Step 3.

3. Measure the brake shoe lining thickness (**Figure 24**) and check against the dimension in **Table 1**. Replace the brake shoes at both wheels if the lining thickness of any 1 shoe is out of specification.

4. Check the brake shoe springs as follows:

a. Inspect the brake shoe springs for stretched areas, hook damage or rust.

b. Measure the brake shoe spring free length (**Figure 25**) and compare to the specification in **Table 1**. Replace the springs if there is an appreciable difference between the free length of both springs or if the spring(s) are stretched beyond the specification in **Table 1**.

c. Stretched or damaged brake shoe springs will not pull the brake shoes away from the drum. This will cause excessive brake shoe and brake drum wear. Always replace both springs at the same time.

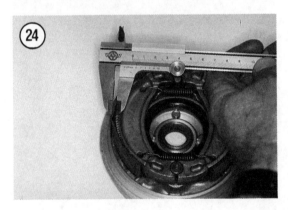

5. Check the brake panel pivot pin (A, **Figure 26**). If the pivot pin is loose, worn or damaged, replace the brake panel.

6. Check the brake cam hole (B, **Figure 26**) in the brake panel for excessive wear, cracks or other damage. A worn or damaged hole will increase cam play and reduce brake performance. Replace the brake panel if any severe wear or damage is noted.

> *WARNING*
> *Do not attempt to repair a loose or damaged pivot pin (A, Figure 26) or repair a damaged brake cam hole (B, Figure 26). If the pivot pin should pull out while the vehicle is under use, brake failure or lockup could occur, causing loss of control.*

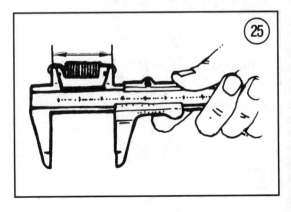

7. Inspect the brake lever and cam assembly (**Figure 27**) for:

  a. Excessively worn or damaged camshaft.

  b. Damaged brake lever.

  c. Damaged brake arm and brake cam grooves.

  d. Damaged mounting bolt and nut.

  e. Damaged brake wear indicator.

8. Check the brake panel for cracks, warpage or other damage. If warpage or damage is present, replace the brake panel.

9. Replace the brake cam O-rings if they are hard or are starting to deteriorate.

10. Inspect the brake panel seal (C, **Figure 26**) for excessive wear, hardening or other damage. If damaged, replace the seal as described in this section.

Brake Panel Seal Replacement

1. Pry the seal out of the brake panel using a wide-blade screwdriver (**Figure 28**). Pad the bottom of the screwdriver to prevent it from damaging the brake panel.

2. Clean and inspect the seal bore. Remove any nicks or burrs and then reclean. Replace the brake panel if the seal bore is cracked or damaged in any way.

3. Pack the seal lips with grease.

4. Place the new seal (A, **Figure 29**) in the bore with its closed side facing away from the brake panel.

5. Using the old seal as a buffer between the new seal and hammer (B, **Figure 29**), tap it at different spots to drive the new seal into the bore. Continue until the seal bottoms in the bore (A, **Figure 30**).

13

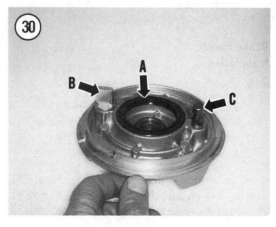

Assembly

1. Perform the following steps to install the brake cam assembly (**Figure 27**):

    a. Lubricate the 2 O-rings with grease and install them into the brake panel grooves (**Figure 23**). Wipe any excess grease off the brake panel.

    b. Lubricate the brake cam shaft with grease and install it through the brake panel (B, **Figure 30**). Then make sure the O-rings were not pushed out of their grooves.

    c. Install the brake wear indicator by aligning its tab with the groove in the cam as shown in **Figure 22**.

    d. Align the brake lever and brake cam index marks (**Figure 20**) and install the brake lever (B, **Figure 21**).

    e. Install the brake lever bolt and nut (A, **Figure 21**) and tighten securely.

    f. Operate the brake lever by hand. The lever should pivot with no binding or roughness.

2. To install the brake shoes, perform the following:

    a. Lubricate the brake cam (B, **Figure 30**) and pivot pin (C, **Figure 30**) with grease.

    b. If installing the original brake shoes, assemble them with their marked side facing out.

    c. Match the upper and lower brake shoe ends and connect the brake shoes with the 2 springs (**Figure 14**).

    d. Spread the brake shoes open (**Figure 13**) and install them over the camshaft and brake pin (**Figure 19**). Center the curved brake shoe ends over the brake pin.

    e. Make sure both springs hook tightly into the brake shoe holes.

    f. Wipe off any excess grease from the camshaft or brake pin.

Brake Panel
Installation

> *NOTE*
> *The brake panels have either an L (left side) or R (right side) identification mark (**Figure 31**). Refer to these marks to identify the brake panels.*

1. Align the slot on the brake panel (A, **Figure 32**) with the boss on the steering knuckle (B, **Figure 32**) and install the brake panel. See **Figure 33**.

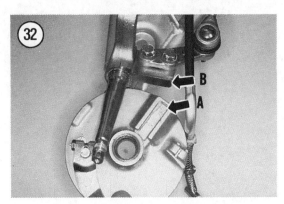

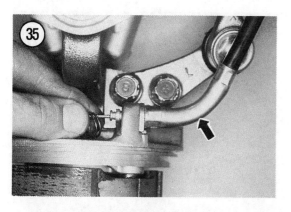

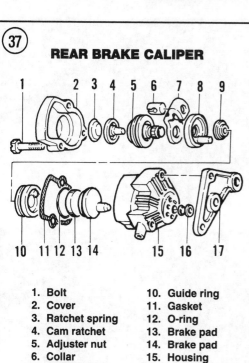

REAR BRAKE CALIPER

1. Bolt	10. Guide ring
2. Cover	11. Gasket
3. Ratchet spring	12. O-ring
4. Cam ratchet	13. Brake pad
5. Adjuster nut	14. Brake pad
6. Collar	15. Housing
7. Cable holder	16. Grommet
8. Adjuster arm	17. Bracket
9. Seal	

2. Connect the brake cable to the brake panel as follows:
   a. Route the brake cable (**Figure 34**) over the top of the tie rod.
   b. Install the brake cable through the boss on the back of the brake panel (**Figure 35**).
   c. Pull the brake cable forward, then install the E-clip into the brake cable groove (**Figure 36**). Make sure the E-clip seats in the groove completely.
   d. Slide the rubber boot over the brake cable and onto the cable housing shoulder (**Figure 15**).
   e. Install the spring, collar and wing nut (**Figure 11**).
3. Install the brake drum as described under *Brake Drum Installation* in this chapter.
4. After both brake panel assemblies are serviced (if required), adjust the front brakes as described under *Front Brake Inspection and Adjustment* in Chapter Three.

REAR BRAKE CALIPER

All models are equipped with a cable operated mechanical rear brake caliper assembly (**Figure 37**). The rear brake caliper is mounted on the rear axle housing and is activated by a brake pedal mounted beside the right side footpeg.

Adjustment procedures for the rear brake and parking brake are covered under *Parking Brake Adjustment* in Chapter Three.

> *WARNING*
> *When working on the brake system, never blow off brake components using compressed air. **Do not** inhale any airborne brake dust as it may contain asbestos, which can cause lung injury and cancer. As an added precaution, wear an approved filtering face mask and thoroughly wash your hands and forearms with warm water and soap after completing any brake work.*

Removal/Installation

If the brake caliper must be disassembled, the brake pads replaced or the rear brake cable disconnected, refer to the rear brake caliper *Disassembly* in this section.

13

1. Shift the transmission into gear and block the front wheels so the vehicle cannot roll in either direction.

2. Release the parking brake at the handlebar.

3. Remove the bolts (A, **Figure 38**) that hold the rear brake caliper to the axle housing.

4. Lift the rear brake caliper (B, **Figure 38**) off of the brake disc and hang it on a piece of stiff wire.

5. Insert a plastic spacer in the caliper between the brake pads. Then, if the brake pedal is inadvertently pressed, the brake pads will not be forced together in the caliper. If this does happen, the caliper must be partially disassembled to reseat the brake pads and adjuster unit.

6. Reverse these steps to install the rear brake caliper. Tighten the rear brake caliper mounting bolts to the torque specification in **Table 3**.

7. Apply the rear brake pedal several times to ensure that the brake pads are seated against the brake disc.

WARNING
Do not ride the vehicle until the rear brake is working correctly.

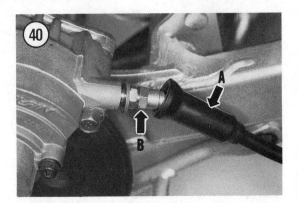

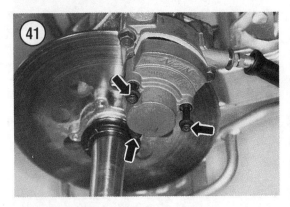

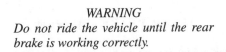

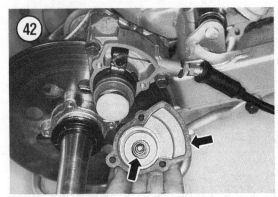

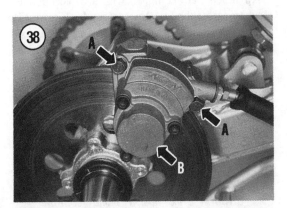

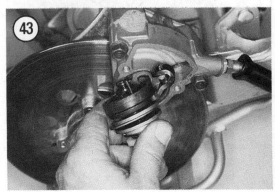

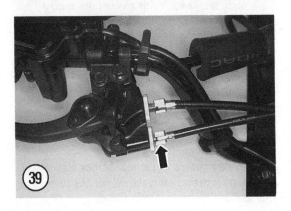

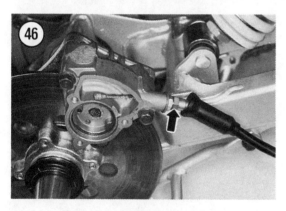

Disassembly

The rear brake caliper must be disassembled to remove the brake pads. Use this procedure for brake pad removal and brake caliper disassembly.

Refer to **Figure 37** for this procedure.

1. Shift the transmission into gear and block the front wheels so the vehicle cannot roll in either direction.

2. Release the parking brake at the handlebar. Then loosen the parking brake adjuster locknut and turn the adjuster (**Figure 39**, typical) *clockwise* to increase brake cable free play.

3. Pull back the brake cable cover (A, **Figure 40**) at the caliper. Then loosen the brake cable adjuster locknut and turn the adjuster (B, **Figure 40**) *clockwise* until it stops.

4. Remove the 3 brake caliper cover mounting bolts (**Figure 41**) and remove the cover and its gasket (**Figure 42**).

5. Remove the adjuster unit (**Figure 43**) from the caliper housing.

6. Remove the collar and disconnect the brake cable (A, **Figure 44**) from the adjuster arm.

7. Remove the guide ring (**Figure 45**) if it did not come out with the adjuster unit.

8. Remove the brake cable (**Figure 46**) from the caliper housing. Do not loose the flat washer (**Figure 47**) on the end cable adjuster.

> *NOTE*
> *If you only need to disconnect the brake cable, stop after Step 8. Otherwise, continue with Step 9 to remove the brake pads or disassemble the brake caliper assembly.*

9. Remove the 2 bolts (**Figure 48**) that hold the brake caliper housing to the rear axle housing, then

13

lift the brake caliper (**Figure 49**) off the brake disc and remove it.

10. Remove the outer (A, **Figure 50**) and inner (B) brake pads as follows:

   a. Using a flat tire iron (**Figure 51**), carefully pry against the outer brake pad to free its O-ring seal in the bore, then remove the outer brake pad as shown in **Figure 52**.

   b. The inner brake pad (B, **Figure 50**) has a guide pin that fits in a hole (**Figure 53**) in the caliper body. Push against this pin and remove the brake pad as shown in **Figure 54**.

Inspection

Refer to **Figure 55** when performing this procedure.

1. Check the cover (A, **Figure 56**) and caliper housing (B) for wear. If either part is cracked or damaged, replace the brake caliper assembly.

2. Inspect the ratchet spring (**Figure 57**) installed in the cover. If the ratchet spring is broken, warped or twisted, replace it.

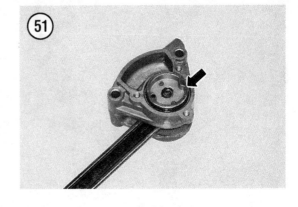

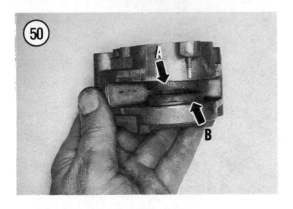

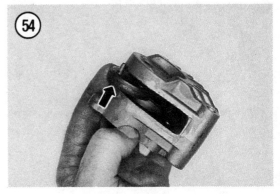

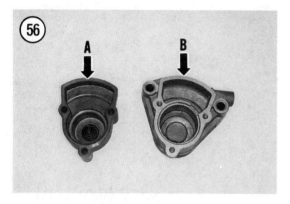

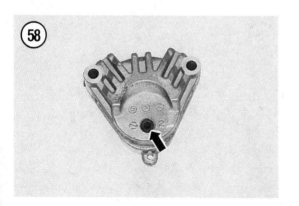

3. Inspect the grommet (**Figure 58**) installed in the caliper body for cracks or other damage and replace if necessary. This grommet helps position and seal the inner brake pad guide pin in its bore. A damaged grommet could cause brake chatter and uneven brake pad wear.

4. Inspect the cam ratchet (**Figure 59**) for stripped teeth, cracks or other damage. Replace if damaged.

NOTE
*Do not disassemble the adjuster unit (**Figure 60**) when inspecting it in Step 5. While the ratchet spring (**Figure 57**) and cam ratchet (**Figure 59**) can be replaced separately, the adjuster unit is sold as a complete assembly.*

5. Inspect the adjuster unit (**Figure 60**). If there are any excessively worn or broken parts, replace the adjuster unit assembly.

NOTE
Steps 6-10 describe inspection of the brake pad assembly.

13

6. Clean the brake pads (**Figure 61**) with an aerosol type brake cleaner to remove any brake dust.

7. Inspect the friction surface on both brake pads (**Figure 61**) for any cracks, scoring, embedded matter or oil or grease contamination. Break the pad glaze with some fine or medium grade sandpaper and clean with brake cleaner. Replace the brake pads if they cannot be cleaned thoroughly.

8. Inspect the guide pin (A, **Figure 62**) on the inner pad for damage.

9. Inspect the O-ring (B, **Figure 62**) on the outer pad for excessive wear, cracks or damage.

10. Measure the thickness of the friction pad material on the inner (**Figure 63**) and outer (**Figure 64**) brake pads and compare to the service limit in **Table 2**. Replace the brake pads as a set if any 1 pad is out of specification.

11. Purchase a factory brake pad repair kit if any part of the brake pad assembly is worn or damaged.

NOTE
The brake pad repair kit consists of parts that cannot be purchased separately: inner and outer brake pads, inner brake pad O-ring and housing gasket. The kit also includes a small tube of silicone grease for lubricating the outer brake pad O-ring and the pin on the inner brake pad during reassembly.

Assembly

NOTE
If you are only connecting the rear brake cable to the rear brake caliper assembly, start with Step 6.

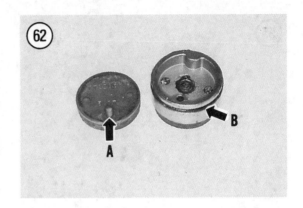

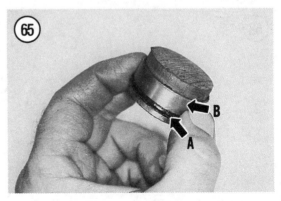

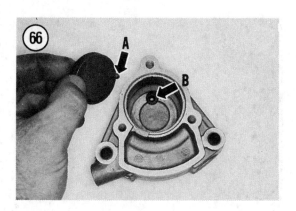

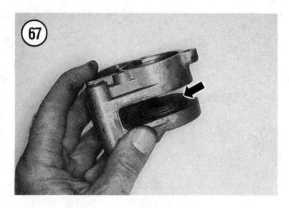

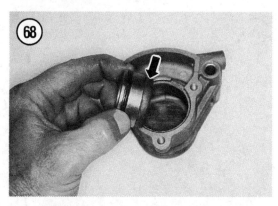

1. Lubricate the inner brake pad guide pin (A, **Figure 62**) and the outer brake pad O-ring (A, **Figure 65**) and pad holder (B) with silicone grease. Do not get any grease on the brake pad friction surfaces. When installing a factory repair kit, use the silicone grease included with the kit; otherwise, use an aftermarket silicone grease.

> *CAUTION*
> *Silicone grease is a special water-resistant, high-temperature grease that can be used to lubricate some brake components. Do not use any other type of lubricant as it may thin out at high temperature and contaminate the friction surface on both brake pads.*

2. Install the inner (A, **Figure 62**) and outer (B) brake pads as follows:

   a. Install the inner brake pad by inserting its guide pin (A, **Figure 66**) into the rubber grommet (B) in the caliper housing. See **Figure 67**.

   b. Install the outer brake pad O-ring side facing out, into the caliper bore (**Figure 68**). Turn the brake pad when installing it to avoid tearing or dislodging the O-ring.

   c. Turn the outer brake pad and align its punch mark with the punch mark on the caliper housing (**Figure 69**).

   d. Install the guide ring (**Figure 70**) by inserting its outer tab into the caliper body notch as shown in **Figure 71**.

3. Install the flat washer (A, **Figure 72**) onto the brake cable adjuster, then thread the adjuster (B, **Figure 72**) into the caliper housing.

4. Install the rear brake caliper over the brake disc. Then install and tighten the rear brake caliper mount-

13

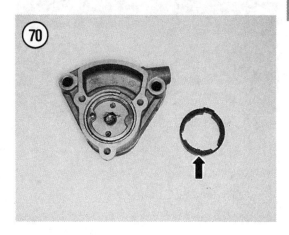

ing bolts (**Figure 73**) to the torque specification in **Table 3**.

5. Reset the adjuster unit bolt (A, **Figure 74**) as follows:

   a. Pull the ratchet (B, **Figure 74**) out approximately 4-5 mm (3/16 in.) so it is not contacting the stopper spring (C, **Figure 74**).

   b. Turn the ratchet (B, **Figure 74**) *counterclockwise* until it stops, then push it back in place so its ratchet teeth contacts the stopper spring (C, **Figure 74**). Doing so resets the adjust bolt (**Figure 75**) for reassembly.

6. Install the adjuster unit as follows:

   a. Insert the rear brake cable through the adjuster unit arm as shown in A, **Figure 76**.

   b. Install the collar into the adjuster unit arm with its large hole side (B, **Figure 76**) facing toward the end of the brake cable.

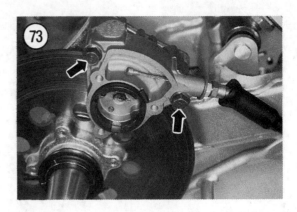

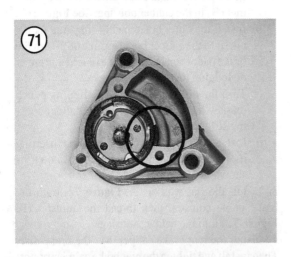

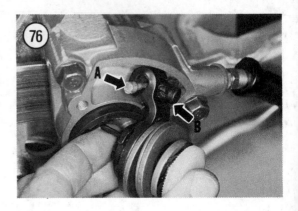

c. Push the brake cable back toward its housing while pushing the collar over the cable end (**Figure 77**).

d. Align the pin (A, **Figure 78**) on the adjuster unit with the hole (B, **Figure 78**) in the guide ring, then install the adjuster unit. See **Figure 79**.

7. Install a new cover gasket (11, **Figure 37**) with its adhesive side facing toward the caliper cover.

8. Install the cover (**Figure 80**) and its mounting bolts. Tighten the rear brake caliper cover mounting bolts to the torque specification in **Table 3**.

9. Perform the *Parking Brake Adjustment* procedure in Chapter Three.

> *WARNING*
> *Do not ride the vehicle until the rear brake is working properly.*

REAR BRAKE DISC

The rear brake disc (**Figure 81**) can be removed with the rear axle mounted on the vehicle. This procedure is shown with the rear axle removed for clarity.

Refer to **Figure 82** when servicing the rear brake disc in this section.

Removal

1. Support the vehicle with the rear wheels off the ground.

2. Remove the right side rear wheel and hub as described in Chapter Twelve.

13

3. Remove the rear brake caliper as described in this chapter.

4. Remove the 2 wire clips from the outer boot (**Figure 83**), then slide the wire clips and outer boot off of the brake disc and axle (**Figure 84**).

5. Remove the 2 wire clips from the inner boot (**Figure 85**), then slide the brake disc off of the inner boot and remove it from the axle (**Figure 86**).

6. Remove the inner boot and both wire clips from the axle.

Inspection

1. Clean the brake disc and hub (**Figure 87**) with an aerosol type brake cleaner. Dry with compressed air.

2. Inspect the brake disc for deep scratches, cracks or other damage.

3. Inspect the brake disc hub (**Figure 88**) for worn or damaged splines. Replace if damaged.

4. To replace the brake disc hub, perform the following:

    a. Slide the brake disc and its hub back onto the rear axle.

    b. Lock the rear axle and remove the 4 bolts (**Figure 88**) securing the brake disc to the brake disc hub.

    c. Remove the brake disc and hub from the axle.

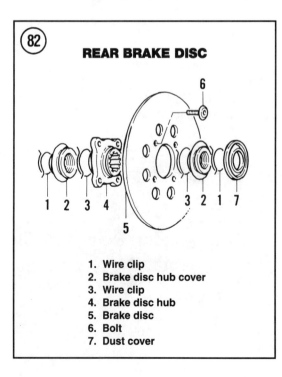

REAR BRAKE DISC

1. Wire clip
2. Brake disc hub cover
3. Wire clip
4. Brake disc hub
5. Brake disc
6. Bolt
7. Dust cover

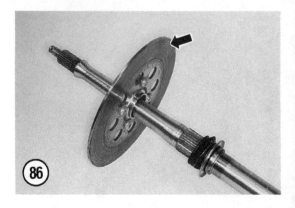

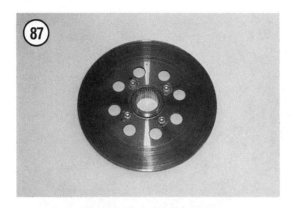

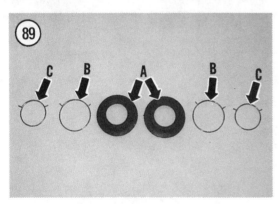

d. Inspect the brake disc mounting bolts and replace if damaged.

e. Before installing a new brake disc, clean it with an aerosol type brake cleaner and then dry with compressed air.

f. Install the brake disc onto its hub and secure it with its 4 mounting bolts.

g. Tighten the brake disc mounting bolts (**Figure 88**) to the torque specification in **Table 4**.

5. Inspect the inner and outer boots (**Figure 89**) for tears or other damage. If one or both boots are damaged, check the brake disc hub and axle splines for corrosion. Replace damaged boots.

6. Replace weak or damaged wire clips (**Figure 89**).

Installation

1. Identify the boots and wire clips as follows:

a. The 2 brake disc boots are identical (A, **Figure 89**). These boots are directional as one end is larger than the other. The larger boot diameter mounts to the brake disc hub shoulder. In the following steps, these boots are referred to as the inner and outer boot.

b. A small and large wire clip assembly is used on each boot assembly. The large wire clips (B, **Figure 89**) mount onto the part of the boot that fits onto the brake disc hub. The small wire clips (C, **Figure 89**) fit onto the part of the boot that fits against the rear axle.

2. Install the boots so their larger opening fits onto the brake disc hub shoulders (**Figure 90**).

3. Secure each boot to the brake disc hub shoulder with a large wire clip. See **Figure 91** (outer boot)

13

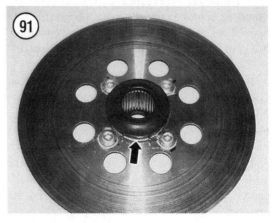

and **Figure 92** (inner boot). Make sure each wire clip seats over the groove machined in the axle.

4. Install a small wire clip (**Figure 92**) over the right side of the axle and seat it next to the dust cover.

5. Install the brake disc over the rear axle with the brake disc mounting bolt side facing toward the dust cover as shown in **Figure 94**.

6. Install the wire clip (**Figure 94**) over the inner boot (**Figure 95**), then slide the end of the inner boot over the groove in the axle and secure it with the wire clip (**Figure 96**).

7. Seat the outer boot (**Figure 97**) over the groove in the axle and secure it with the wire clip (**Figure 98**).

8A. If removed, install the rear axle as described in Chapter Twelve.

8B. If the rear axle is installed in the bearing housing, perform the following:

　a. Install the rear brake caliper as described in this chapter.

　b. Install the right rear hub and wheel as described in Chapter Twelve.

9. Depress the brake pedal to seat the pads against the disc.

> *WARNING*
> *Do not ride the vehicle until the rear brake is working properly.*

FRONT BRAKE CABLE REPLACEMENT

The front brake cable assembly (**Figure 99**) consists of 3 brake cables that can be replaced separately, 1 upper cable and 2 lower cables. All 3 cables are connected to an equalizer housing mounted in front of the steering shaft (**Figure 100**). If the front brakes cannot be adjusted correctly even though the front brake shoes and brake drums are in good condition, one or more of the front brake cables may be excessively worn or damaged.

1. Remove the front cover as described under *Front Cover Removal/Installation* in Chapter Fourteen.

2. Remove both front wheels as described under *Front Wheel Removal/Installation* in Chapter Eleven.

3. Draw a diagram of the upper and lower brake cable routing path from the handlebar to the brake panels. Note any cable guides or clamps on the drawing.

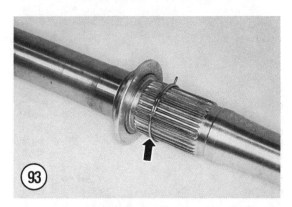

4. Disconnect the lower brake cables from the brake panel as follows:

   a. Remove the brake cable adjusting nut (**Figure 101**), collar and spring.

   b. Pull the rubber boot (**Figure 102**) off of the brake cable housing.

   c. Remove the E-clip (**Figure 103**) securing the brake cable to the brake panel.

   d. Remove the brake cable from the brake panel.

5. Repeat Step 4 for the opposite brake cable.

6. Loosen the upper brake cable locknut and adjuster (**Figure 104**) at the handlebar, then disconnect the brake cable from its lever and perch.

7. Slide the rubber cover off the equalizer housing (**Figure 100**), then remove the screw, washer and cover.

8. Disconnect each cable from the equalizer arm.

9. Remove the upper brake cable.

10. Remove the lower brake cables.

11. Lubricate the new brake cables as described under *Cable Lubrication* in Chapter Three.

12. Reverse Steps 1-10 to install the new brake cables, noting the following.

13. When routing the new cables along the frame and handlebar, follow the cable routing diagram made in Step 3. Install new cables guides or clips where required.

14. Lightly lubricate the cable ends with grease before connecting them to the equalizer cam in the equalizer housing.

15. When installing the lower brake cable E-clips (**Figure 103**), make sure each E-clip seats in its cable groove completely.

16. Adjust the front brake as described under *Front Brake Adjustment* in Chapter Three. Then apply the front brake lever while watching the lower brake cables, first one and then the other. Make sure the cables move smoothly without binding or roughness.

17. Slowly test ride the vehicle, making sure both front brakes work correctly and that they do not grab or lock up a wheel(s).

WARNING
Do not ride the vehicle until the front brakes are working correctly.

REAR/PARKING BRAKE CABLE REPLACEMENT

A one-piece cable assembly is used to control the parking and rear brake assemblies. This cable is connected between the parking brake lever at the left (1988-1989) or right (1990-on) side handlebar and the rear brake caliper. The front part of the cable, attached between the handlebar and brake pedal,

13

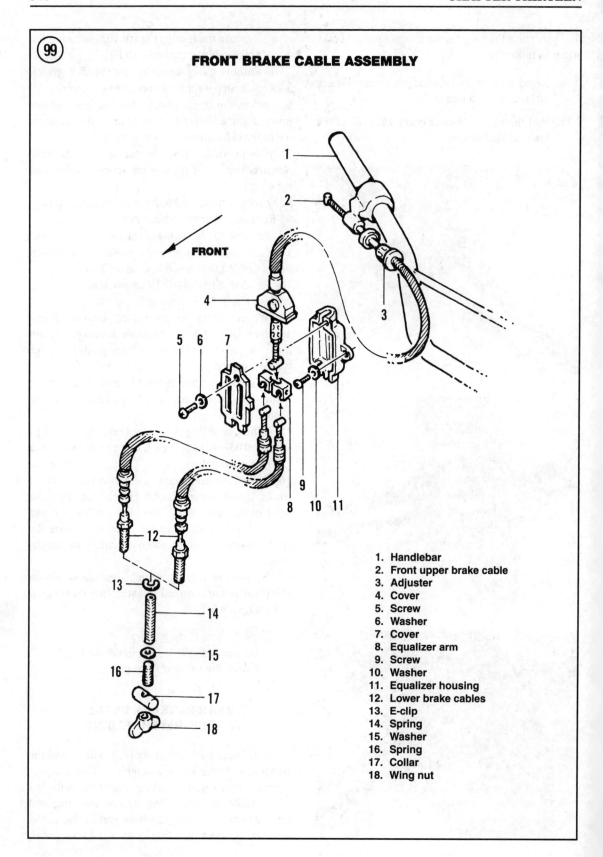

FRONT BRAKE CABLE ASSEMBLY

FRONT

1. Handlebar
2. Front upper brake cable
3. Adjuster
4. Cover
5. Screw
6. Washer
7. Cover
8. Equalizer arm
9. Screw
10. Washer
11. Equalizer housing
12. Lower brake cables
13. E-clip
14. Spring
15. Washer
16. Spring
17. Collar
18. Wing nut

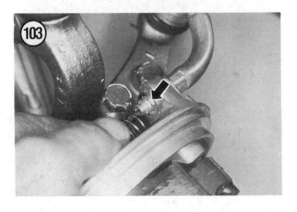

controls the parking brake. The rear part of the cable, attached between the brake pedal and the rear brake caliper, controls the rear brake. A separate metal collar connects the brake cable to the brake pedal assembly.

1. Shift the transmission into gear, then block the front wheels so the vehicle cannot roll in either direction.

2. Draw a diagram of the brake cable routing path from the handlebar to the brake pedal and from the brake pedal to the rear brake caliper. Note any cable guides or clamps on the drawing.

3. Loosen the parking brake cable adjuster locknut and adjuster (**Figure 105**, typical) at the handlebar. Then disconnect the cable from the adjuster.

4. Disconnect the rear brake cable from the rear brake caliper (**Figure 106**). See *Rear Brake Caliper Disassembly* in this chapter.

5. Disconnect the return spring (A, **Figure 107**), then pull the cable (B, **Figure 107**) out of the frame bracket.

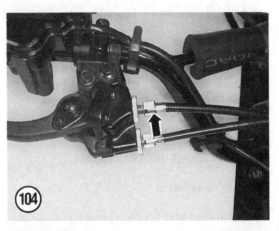

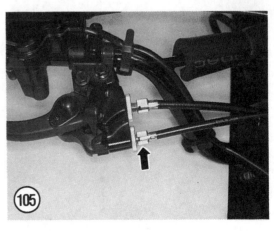

13

NOTE
Figure 108 is shown with the brake
pedal removed for clarity.

6. Slip the brake cable out of the brake pedal and
remove the collar (**Figure 108**).

7. Pass the brake cable through the brake pedal
(**Figure 109**) and frame (**Figure 110**) brackets and
remove it from the vehicle.

8. Lubricate the new brake cable as described under
Cable Lubrication in Chapter Three.

9. Reverse Steps 3-7 to install the new cable, noting
the following.

10. When routing the new cables along the frame
and handlebar, follow your cable routing diagram
made in Step 2. Install new cable guides or clips
where required.

11. Reconnect the brake cable to the rear brake
caliper as described under *Rear Brake Caliper Installation* in this chapter.

12. If the rear brake pedal was removed, install it as
described in this chapter.

13. Perform the *Parking Brake Adjustment* procedure in Chapter Three.

14. Slowly test ride the vehicle and check rear brake
operation.

WARNING
*Do not ride the vehicle until the rear
brake works correctly.*

REAR BRAKE PEDAL

Removal/Installation

Refer to **Figure 111** for this procedure.

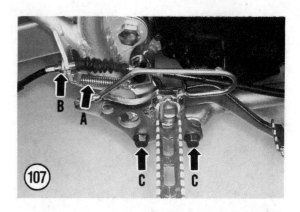

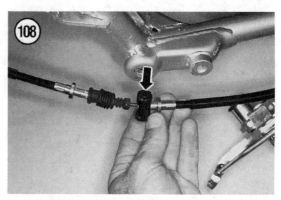

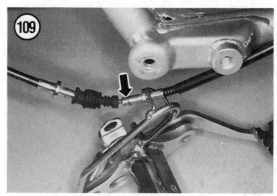

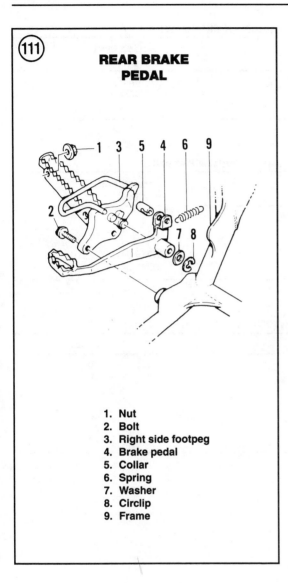

REAR BRAKE PEDAL

1. Nut
2. Bolt
3. Right side footpeg
4. Brake pedal
5. Collar
6. Spring
7. Washer
8. Circlip
9. Frame

1. Shift the transmission into gear, then block the front wheels so the vehicle cannot roll in either direction.

2. Loosen the parking brake cable adjuster locknut and adjuster (**Figure 105**, typical) at the handlebar. Then disconnect the cable from the adjuster.

3. Remove the 2 bolts (C, **Figure 107**) that hold the rear brake pedal and footpeg bracket to the frame.

4. Disconnect the return spring (A, **Figure 107**), then pull the cable (B) out of the frame bracket.

5. Slip the brake cable out of the brake pedal and remove the collar (**Figure 108**).

6. Pass the brake pedal (**Figure 109**) over the brake cable and remove it from the vehicle.

7. Remove the E-clip and washer (**Figure 111**) and remove the brake pedal from its pivot shaft on the footpeg bracket.

8. Reverse these steps to install the brake pedal and footpeg bracket assembly, plus the following.

9. Lubricate the brake pedal pivot shaft with grease, then install the brake pedal, washer and E-clip. Make sure the E-clip seats in the pivot shaft groove completely.

10. Tighten the footpeg mounting bolts (C, **Figure 107**) to the torque specification in **Table 3**.

11. Perform the *Parking Brake Adjustment* procedure in Chapter Three.

12. Slowly test ride the vehicle and check rear brake operation.

> *WARNING*
> *Do not ride the vehicle until the rear brake works correctly.*

13

Tables are on the following page.

Table 1 FRONT BRAKE SERVICE SPECIFICATIONS

	New mm (in.)	Service limit mm (in.)
Brake drum inside diameter	110 (4.33)	111 (4.37)
Brake shoe lining thickness	4.0 (0.16)	2.0 (0.08)
Brake shoe spring free length	50.5 (1.99)	–

Table 2 REAR BRAKE SERVICE SPECIFICATIONS

	New mm (in.)	Service limit mm (in.)
Brake disc outside diameter	220.0 (8.66)	–
Brake disc thickness	3.8 (0.15)	–
Pad thickness		
Inner pad	7.3 (0.29)	1.0 (0.04)
Outer pad	4.8 (0.19)	1.0 (0.04)

Table 3 BRAKE TIGHTENING TORQUES

	N·m	in.-lb.	ft.-lb.
Brake caliper bracket at rear axle housing	28	–	20
Footpeg mounting bolts	55	–	40
Front brake camshaft lever nut	9	78	–
Front axle nut	70	–	51
Rear brake disc mounting bolts	28	–	20
Rear brake caliper cover mounting bolts	13	–	9.4
Rear brake caliper mounting bolts	23	–	17

CHAPTER FOURTEEN

BODY

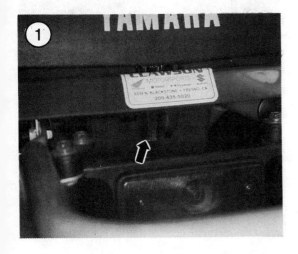

This chapter contains removal and installation procedures for the seat, body panels, fenders and footpegs.

SEAT

Removal/Installation

1. Push the rear seat latch (**Figure 1**), then lift and remove the rear seat.
2. Install the seat sliding its 2 front hooks into the 2 frame channel brackets (**Figure 2**), then push the rear part of the seat down so its rear latch (**Figure 3**) locks into position.

3. Pull up on the front and back of the seat, making sure it is secured in both positions.

WARNING
Do not ride the vehicle with a loose or damaged seat.

FRONT COVER

Removal/Installation

1. Remove the screws securing the front cover (**Figure 4**) to the frame and remove the front cover.
2. Install by reversing these removal steps, noting the following.
3. When installing the front cover, do not pinch any of the electrical wires installed underneath the front cover.

FUEL TANK COVER

Removal/Installation

1. Remove the front cover as described in this chapter.
2. Remove the 2 screws securing the fuel tank cover (**Figure 5**) to the frame.
3. Remove the fuel tank cap and remove the fuel tank cover. Reinstall the fuel tank cap and tighten it securely.
4. Install by reversing these removal steps.

FRONT GUARD

Removal/Installation

1. Remove the 2 front guard screws (**Figure 6**) and remove the front guard.
2. Install by reversing these removal steps.

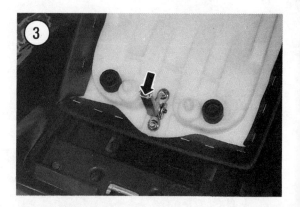

FRONT BUMPER

Removal/Installation

1. Remove the front bumper as described in this chapter.

2. Remove the front bumper mounting bolts and remove the front bumper (**Figure 7**).

3. Install by reversing these removal steps.

FRONT FENDER

The front fender assembly consists of separate left- and right-side fenders and a fender mounting bracket (**Figure 8**).

Removal/Installation

1. Park the vehicle on level ground and set the parking brake.

2. Remove the screws, washers and nuts securing the front fender to the frame (**Figure 9**, typical) and

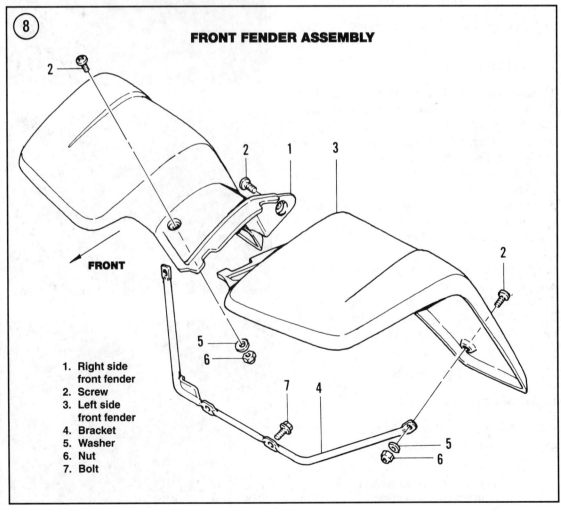

FRONT FENDER ASSEMBLY

FRONT

1. Right side front fender
2. Screw
3. Left side front fender
4. Bracket
5. Washer
6. Nut
7. Bolt

14

to the fender mounting bracket (**Figure 10**). Remove the front fender.

3. Repeat for the other side.

4A. To remove the fender mounting bracket (A, **Figure 11**), remove its mounting bolts and remove it from the frame.

4B. If the fender mounting bracket is to be left on the vehicle, cover both ends of the bracket with a piece of 1/2 in. hose (**Figure 12**). These pieces of hose will prevent the bracket ends from cutting your hands, arms and face when performing other service procedures.

5. Install by reversing these removal steps, noting the following.

6. After installing the fender mounting bracket (A, **Figure 11**), route the parking brake cable through the bracket's cable guide as shown in B, **Figure 11**.

REAR FENDER

Refer to **Figure 13** for this procedure.

Removal/Installation

1. Remove the seat as described in this chapter.

2. Loosen the intake boot hose clamp at the carburetor (**Figure 14**).

3. Remove the nuts, bolts and washers securing the foot guards (**Figure 15**, typical) to the rear fender.

4. Remove the nuts, bolts and washers securing the rear fender to the frame.

5. Remove the oil tank fill cap (**Figure 16**) from the oil tank, then remove the rear fender (**Figure 17**) from the frame. Reinstall the oil tank fill cap into the top of the oil tank.

6. Cover the carburetor opening to prevent dirt from entering the carburetor.

7. Reverse these removal steps, noting the following.

8. Install the intake boot over the carburetor and tighten its hose clamp (**Figure 14**) securely.

FOOTPEGS

Removal/Installation

Refer to **Figure 18** when removing and installing the left and right footpeg assemblies.

Figures 14-18 and Table 1 on the folowing pages.

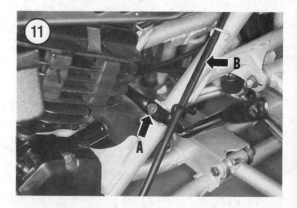

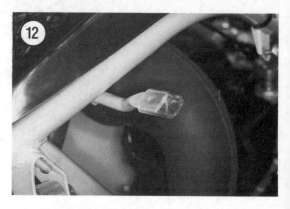

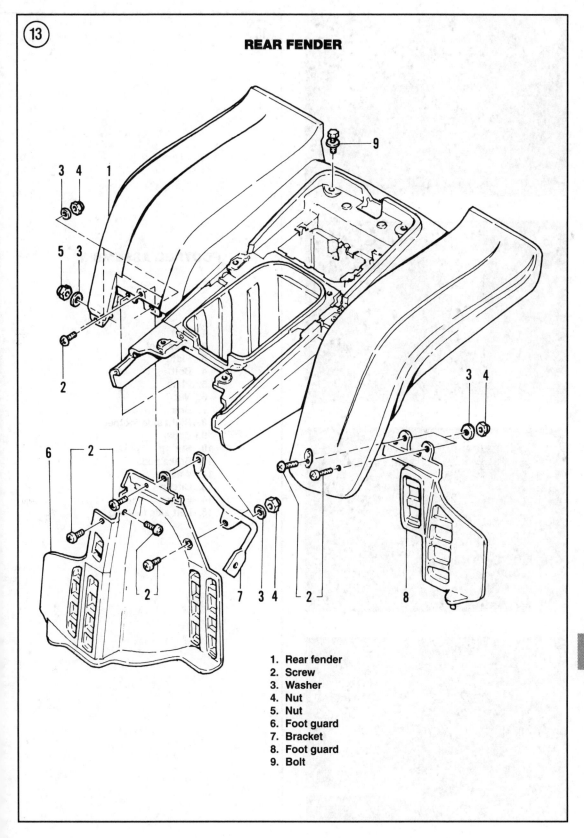

REAR FENDER

1. Rear fender
2. Screw
3. Washer
4. Nut
5. Nut
6. Foot guard
7. Bracket
8. Foot guard
9. Bolt

14

FOOTPEG ASSEMBLY

1. Bolt
2. Grommet
3. Plate
4. Bolt
5. Plate
6. Nut
7. Bolt
8. Right side footpeg
9. Collar
10. Spring
11. Brake pedal
12. Washer
13. Circlip
14. Frame
15. Left side footpeg

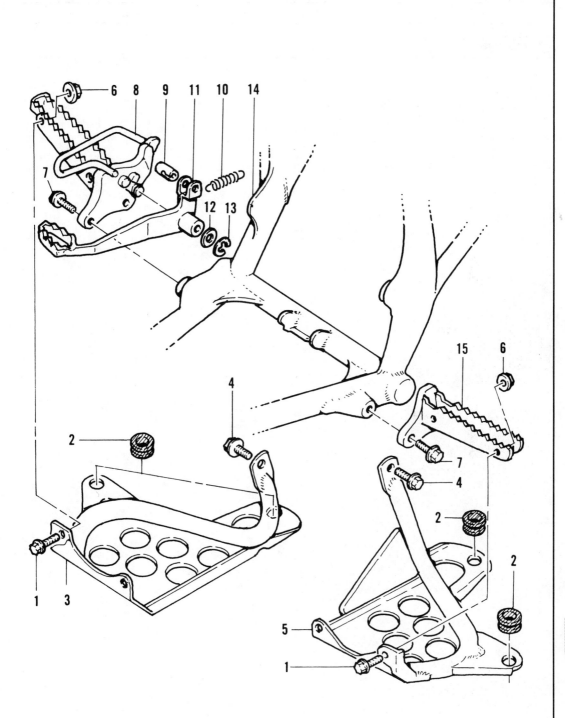

Table 1 BODY TIGHTENING TORQUES

	N·m	ft.-lb.
Footpegs	55	40
Front bumper	26	19

INDEX

15

15

1988-2001 YFS200

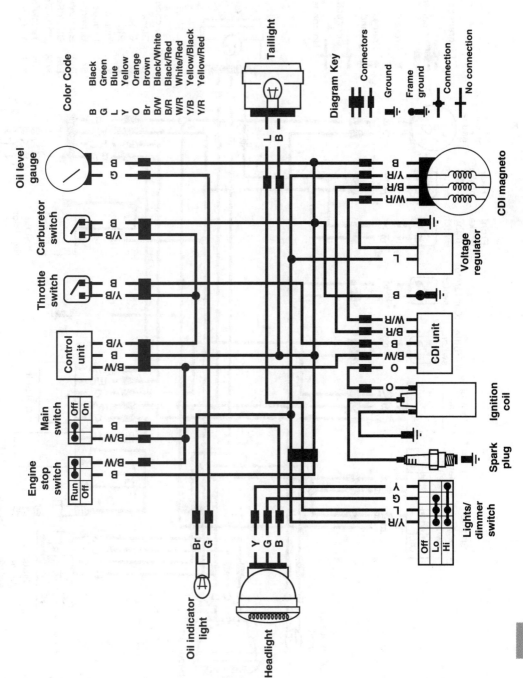

2002 YFS200

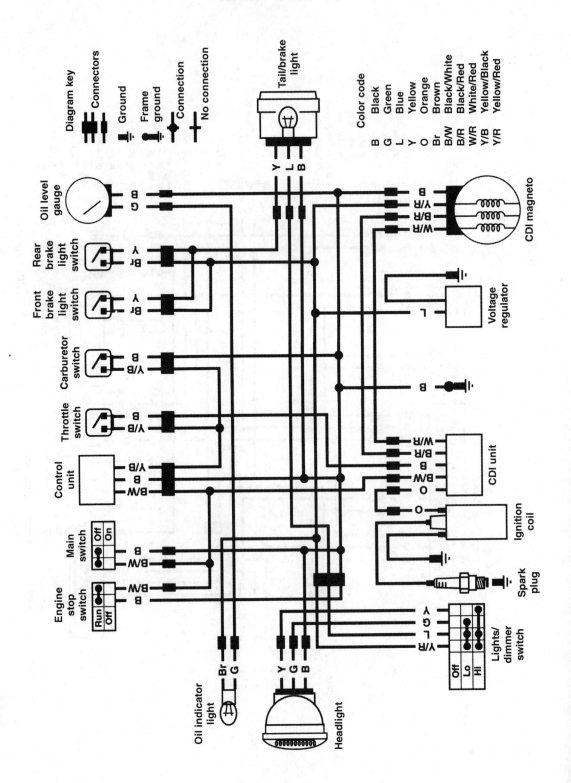

MAINTENANCE LOG

Date	Miles	Type of Service

BMW

M308	500 & 600 CC twins, 55-69
M502	BMW R-Series, 70-94
M500	BMW K-Series, 85-95
M503	R-850 & R-1100, 93-98

HARLEY-DAVIDSON

M419	Sportsters, 59-85
M428	Sportster Evolution, 86-90
M429-3	Sportster Evolution, 91-02
M418	Panheads, 48-65
M-120	Shovelheads,66-84
M421	FX/FL Softail Big-Twin Evolution,84-94
M422	FLT/FXR Big-Twin Evolution, 84-94
M424	Dyna Glide, 91-95
M425	Dyna Glide Twin Cam, 99-01
M430	FLH/FLT 1999-2002

HONDA

ATVs

M316	Odyssey FL250, 77-84
M311	ATC, TRX & Fourtrax 70-125, 70-87
M433	Fourtrax 90 ATV, 93-00
M326	ATC185 & 200, 80-86
M347	ATC200X & Fourtrax 200SX, 86-88
M455	ATC250 & Fourtrax 200/250, 84-87
M342	ATC250R, 81-84
M348	TRX250R/Fourtrax 250R & ATC250R, 85-89
M456	TRX250X 1987-1988, 91-92; TRX300EX 93-96
M446	TRX250 Recon 1997-02
M346-3	TRX300/Fourtrax 300 & TRX300FW/Fourtrax 4x4, 88-00
M459	Fourtrax Foreman 95-98
M454	TRX400EX 1999-02

Singles

M310-13	50-110cc OHC Singles, 65-99
M315	100-350cc OHC, 69-82
M317	Elsinore, 125-250cc, 73-80
M442	CR60-125R Pro-Link, 81-88
M431-2	CR80R, 89-95, CR125R, 89-91
M435	CR80, 96-02
M457-2	CR125R & CR250R, 92-97
M443	CR250R-500R Pro-Link, 81-87
M432	CR250R & CR500R, 88-96
M437	CR250R, 97-01
M312-12	XL/XR75-100, 75-02
M318	XL/XR/TLR 125-200, 79-87
M328-2	XL/XR250, 78-00; XL/XR350R 83-85; XR200R, 84-85; XR250L, 91-96
M320	XR400R, 96-00
M339-6	XL/XR 500-650, 79-02

Twins

M321	125-200cc, 64-77
M322	250-350cc, 64-74
M323	250-360cc Twins, 74-77
M324-4	Rebel 250 & Twinstar, 78-87; Nighthawk 250, 91-97; Rebel 250, 96-97
M334	400-450cc, 78-87
M333	450 & 500cc, 65-76
M335	CX & GL500/650 Twins, 78-83
M344	VT500, 83-88
M313	VT700 & 750, 83-87
M460	VT1100C2 A.C.E. Shadow, 95-97
M440	Shadow 1100cc V-Twin, 85-96

Fours

M332	350-550cc 71-78
M345	CB550 & 650, 83-85
M336	CB650,79-82
M341	CB750 SOHC, 69-78
M337	CB750 DOHC, 79-82
M436	CB750 Nighthawk, 91-93 & 95-99
M325	CB900, 1000 & 1100, 80-83
M439	Hurricane 600, 87-90
M441-2	CBR600, 91-98
M434	CBR900RR Fireblade, 93-98
M329	500cc V-Fours, 84-86
M438	Honda VFR800, 98-00
M349	700-1000 Interceptor, 83-85
M458-2	VFR700F-750F, 86-97
M327	700-1100cc V-Fours, 82-88
M340	GL1000 & 1100, 75-83
M504	GL1200, 84-87

Sixes

M505	GL1500 Gold Wing, 88-92
M506	GL1500 Gold Wing, 93-95
M462	GL1500C Valkyrie, 97-00

KAWASAKI

ATVs

M465	KLF220 Bayou, 88-95
M466-2	KLF300 Bayou, 86-98
M467	KLF400 Bayou, 93-99
M470	KEF300 Lakota, 95-99
M385	KSF250 Mojave, 87-00

Singles

M350-9	Rotary Valve 80-350cc, 66-01
M444	KX60-80, 83-90
M351	KDX200, 83-88
M447	KX125 & KX250, 82-91 KX500, 83-93
M472	KX125, 92-98
M473	KX250, 92-98

Twins

M355	KZ400, KZ/Z440, EN450 & EN500, 74-95
M360	EX500/GPZ500S, 87-93
M356-2	700-750 Vulcan, 85-01
M354	VN800 Vulcan 95-98
M357	VN1500 Vulcan 87-98
M471	VN1500 Vulcan Classic, 96-98

Fours

M449	KZ500/550 & ZX550, 79-85
M450	KZ, Z & ZX750, 80-85
M358	KZ650, 77-83
M359	900-1000cc Fours, 73-80
M451	1000 &1100cc Fours, 81-85
M452-3	ZX500 & 600 Ninja, 85-97
M453-3	Ninja ZX900-1100 84-01
M468	ZX6 Ninja, 90-97
M469	ZX7 Ninja, 91-98
M453	900-1100 Ninia, 84-93

POLARIS

ATVs

M496	Polaris ATV, 85-95
M362	Polaris Magnum ATV, 96-98
M363	Scrambler 500, 4X4 97-00
M365	Sportsman/Xplorer, 96-00

SUZUKI

ATVs

M381	ALT/LT 125 & 185, 83-87
M475	LT230 & LT250, 85-90
M380	LT250R Quad Racer, 85-88
M343	LTF500F Quadrunner, 98-00
M483	Suzuki King Quad/ Quad Runner 250, 87-95

Singles

M371	RM50-400 Twin Shock, 75-81
M369	125-400cc 64-81
M379	RM125-500 Single Shock, 81-88
M476	DR250-350, 90-94
M384	LS650 Savage Single, 86-88
M386	RM80-250, 89-95

Twins

M372	GS400-450 Twins, 77-87
M481-3	VS700-800 Intruder, 85-02
M482	VS1400 Intruder, 87-98
M484-2	GS500E Twins, 89-00

Triple

M368	380-750cc, 72-77

Fours

M373	GS550, 77-86
M364	GS650, 81-83
M370	GS750 Fours, 77-82
M376	GS850-1100 Shaft Drive, 79-84
M378	GS1100 Chain Drive, 80-81
M383-3	Katana 600, 88-96 GSX-R750-1100, 86-87
M331	GSX-R600, 97-01
M478-2	GSX-R750, 88-92 GSX750F Katana, 89-96
M485	GSX-R750, 96-99
M338	GSF600 Bandit, 95-00

YAMAHA

ATVs

M394	YTM/YFM200 & 225, 83-86
M487-3	YFM350 Warrior, 87-02
M486-3	YFZ350 Banshee, 87-02
M488-3	Blaster ATV, 88-01
M489-2	Timberwolf ATV,89-00
M490-2	YFM350 Moto-4 & Big Bear, 87-98
M493	YFM400FW Kodiak, 93-98

Singles

M492-2	PW50 & PW80, BW80 Big Wheel 80, 81-02
M410	80-175 Piston Port, 68-76
M415	250-400cc Piston Port, 68-76
M412	DT & MX 100-400, 77-83
M414	IT125-490, 76-86
M393	YZ50-80 Monoshock, 78-90
M413	YZ100-490 Monoshock, 76-84
M390	YZ125-250, 85-87 YZ490, 85-90
M391	YZ125-250, 88-93 WR250Z, 91-93
M497	YZ125, 94-99
M498	YZ250, 94-98 and WR250Z, 94-97
M491	YZ400F, YZ426F & WR400F, 98-00
M417	XT125-250, 80-84
M480-2	XT/TT 350, 85-96
M405	XT500 & TT500, 76-81
M416	XT/TT 600, 83-89

Twins

M403	650cc, 70-82
M395-9	XV535-1100 Virago, 81-99
M495	XVS650 V-Star, 98-00

Triple

M404	XS750 & 850, 77-81

Fours

M387	XJ550, XJ600 & FJ600, 81-92
M494	XJ600 Seca II, 92-98
M388	YX600 Radian & FZ600, 86-90
M396	FZR600, 89-93
M392	FZ700-750 & Fazer, 85-87
M411	XS1100 Fours, 78-81
M397	FJ1100 & 1200, 84-93

VINTAGE MOTORCYCLES

Clymer® Collection Series

M330	Vintage British Street Bikes, BSA, 500 & 650cc Unit Twins; Norton, 750 & 850cc Commandos; Triumph, 500-750cc Twins
M300	Vintage Dirt Bikes, V. 1 Bultaco, 125-370cc Singles; Montesa, 123-360cc Singles; Ossa, 125-250cc Singles
M301	Vintage Dirt Bikes, V. 2 CZ, 125-400cc Singles; Husqvarna, 125-450cc Singles; Maico, 250-501cc Singles; Hodaka, 90-125cc Singles
M305	Vintage Japanese Street Bikes Honda, 250 & 305cc Twins; Kawasaki, 250-750cc Triples; Kawasaki, 900 & 1000cc Fours